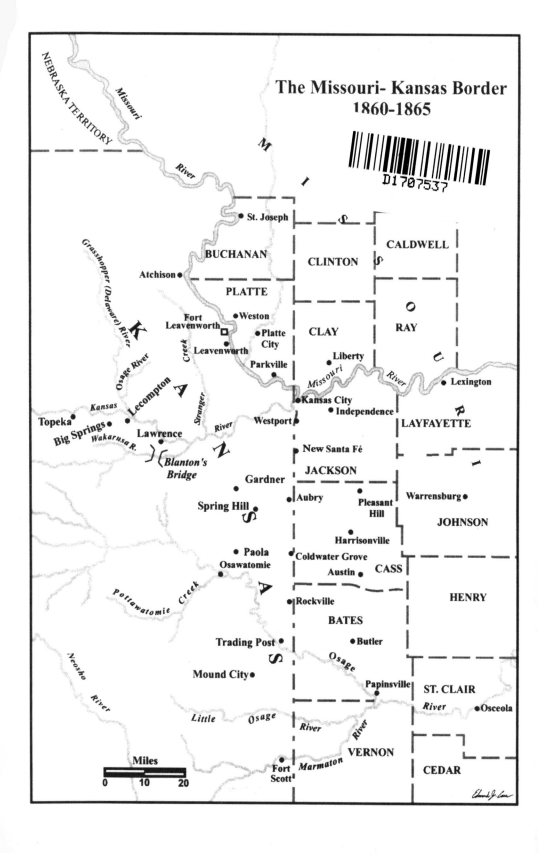

The Missouri- Kansas Border
1860-1865

Civil War
on the
Missouri-Kansas
Border

Civil War
on the
Missouri-Kansas Border

By Donald L. Gilmore

PELICAN PUBLISHING COMPANY
Gretna 2008

Copyright © 2005
By Donald L. Gilmore
All rights reserved

First printing, January 2006
Second printing, December 2008

*The word "Pelican" and the depiction of a pelican are trademarks
of Pelican Publishing Company, Inc., and are registered in the
U.S. Patent and Trademark Office.*

Library of Congress Cataloging-in-Publication Data

Gilmore, Donald L.
  Civil War on the Missouri-Kansas border / by Donald L. Gilmore.
    p. cm.
  ISBN-13: 978-158980-329-9
  Includes bibliographical references and index.
  1. United States—History—Civil War, 1861-1865—Underground move-
ments. 2. Missouri—History—Civil War, 1861-1865. 3. Kansas—
History—Civil War, 1861-1865. 4. Quantrill, William Clarke, 1837-1865. I.
Title.
  E470.45.G55 2005
  973.7'09778—dc22

                                    2005016539

Jacket illustration courtesy State Historical Society of Missouri

Printed in the United States of America
Published by Pelican Publishing Company, Inc.
1000 Burmaster Street, Gretna, Louisiana 70053

To D. M. Giangreco for his unflagging support

Contents

Acknowledgments

I especially wish to thank Dr. Jerry D. Morelock (colonel, U.S. Army, retired), former director, Combat Studies Institute (CSI), U.S. Army Command and General Staff College (CGSC), Fort Leavenworth, Kansas; former executive director, Winston Churchill Memorial and Library, Westminster College, Fulton, Missouri; and currently, managing editor/senior historian, *Armchair General Magazine*, for his help on this project. From 1994 to 1999, Dr. Morelock was the director of CSI, the history department at CGSC. During his tenure, I was the editor of CSI and the CGSC Press. While I was at CSI, Dr. Morelock invited me to conduct four staff rides, two to Lawrence, Kansas, for the history faculty. He also encouraged me for several years to write a book on the subject of the Border War. At one time, we planned on writing the book together. Dr. Morelock has provided me with longstanding inspiration, support, and advice and was kind enough to read and critique my draft manuscript, suggesting a number of insightful and significant changes that drew on his wide knowledge of history and military operations.

Two other stalwarts providing me with valuable, longtime encouragement and underpinning have been Lt. Col. Edwin L. Kennedy Jr. (U.S. Army, retired), and Col. James Speicher (U.S. Army, retired). They also cheerfully agreed to read and critique my draft manuscript and made many useful emendations and suggestions. Lt. Col. Ed Kennedy has been a treasured mentor. The interest of the above three men in the subject and project and their honest appraisals were deeply appreciated.

I wish to give special thanks to the president of Pelican Publishing Company, Dr. Milburn Calhoun, for his *vision, encouragement, and support*. Dr. Calhoun has a well-earned reputation for allowing writers to explore the Southern side of the ongoing disputes over the Civil War, not just the traditional Northern view. I also thank Dennis Giangreco, author of a number of significant historical works and an editor at the *Military Review*, the Army's professional journal at Fort Leavenworth, for his continuous support, advice, and encouragement. Fritz Heinzen also provided me with critical advice, and I much appreciate his kindness.

I also want to express my appreciation to Dr. Jerold E. Brown, my longtime friend and adviser; Ms. Nina Kooij, editor-in-chief, Pelican Publishing Company, for her splendid and conscientious editing; Claiborne Scholl Nappier; Robert C. Stevens; Col. Clay Edwards, director, Combat Studies Institute; Susan Hejka; Dr. James W. Goodrich, executive director, State

Historical Society of Missouri; William Voran Powell; Carol Unnewehr; Tony Swindell; Lt. Col. David Chuber, U.S. Army, retired; Jack Dryden; Dr. Richard Swain, colonel, U.S. Army, retired; Dr. Robin Higham, Professor Emeritus, Kansas State University; Rev. Don Conrad; Dr. S. J. Lewis; Jack Cashill; Edward J. Carr; Dr. Michael D. Pearlman; Dodie Maurer; Barney Klaus; John Seals; Gordon Marsden; Gregory Lalire; Frances Vaughn; Arba E. Gilmore Jr.; Gregg Higginbotham; Christie Stanley (Library and Archives Division, Kansas State Historical Society); Nancy Sherbert (Kansas State Historical Society); Christine Montgomery (The State Historical Society of Missouri); Gary Toms (Reference Librarian Mid-Continent Library, Independence, Missouri); "Kevin," Reference Department, Kansas City Public Library; Patrick Marquis; Bob Clutter; Dr. Paul Perme; Dr. Nancy Cervetti; Dorothy Lane; Lt. Col. Tim Thomas; Dr. Jonas Spatz; Jack and Diane Lindberg; Paul Stuewe; Orlena, Donald A., Melissa, Harvey, and Carole Gilmore; George Cook, Roger Ramirez; Cathy Devlin; Al Dulin; James Hearon; Dixie Wantland; Richard Bussell; Betty Farmer; Allen and Mary Gilmore; Dr. John Michael Moore; Carolyn Conway; Sharon Torres; Robin Kern; Don Carlson; Phil Roberts; Carolyn Simmons; Bev Miramon; Lynn Kamplain; Irvin Ward; John Dreiling; Nancy Mazzia; Don Pile; Ray Evans; Barabara Baechle; Clayton Perry; Dr. David Wineglass; Dr. Mike Yates; and John Ertzgaard. For her critical contributions to this work, I wish to thank especially Ms. Lindsey Reynolds. Her painstaking, meticulous, and insightful editing were brilliant.

Above all, I wish to thank those many tireless and brilliant historians and researchers in Missouri, Kansas, and elsewhere who, for over a century, have plodded through archives, documents, newspapers, and letters to form part of the compendium of valuable information and reflection available to other scholars. They forged the way and set the standard for us all. For any mistakes I may have made, I regretfully but readily accept responsibility.

Introduction

The Civil War and Border War were really two wars, one fought with bullets and guns, the other fought with words and propaganda. The South lost both wars, the propaganda one most thoroughly. And although the shooting war largely ended in 1865, the propaganda war, to some extent, is still being prosecuted today as it was 140 years ago.

It is particularly true in reference to civil wars that "history is written by the winning side." In these bitter contests, when one side finally emerges triumphant from the bloodbath, the defeated—usually demonized during the ferocity of the conflict—are subject to the often-arbitrary laws and prerogatives of the prevailing government. In the case of the American South, once it lost the Civil War, it was an occupied territory susceptible to the administration of martial law for a dozen years. For many more years after that, through formal and informal censorship, many of its historians were silenced, prevented from explaining the conflict from the perspective of the now-discredited losing side. Moreover, the educational system in the post-Civil War United States—the product of the winning side in the conflict—taught the victorious North's version of history to the succeeding generations of Southern youth.

Thus, a sort of "winner's logic" has governed histories of the Civil War. Incidents of the war that might, in a true accounting, prove embarrassing or uncomfortable to the victors were either ignored or envisioned to put the onus on the losers. Likewise, historical personalities took on the aura created by the "righteous" winners or the "demonic" losers. Since the cause itself is "righteous," so goes the logic, the champions of that cause must themselves all be good men and true. But, if as was once asserted, truth is the first casualty of war, the "victors' version" of history is often the last casualty. Today, therefore, it is unusual to meet someone with a truly Southern perspective (in the 1860s sense of the term).

The history you are about to read might be termed "revisionist" by some historians. That is, it is an account that, in a number of respects, revises, reinterprets, or conceives from a somewhat different perspective what is normally accepted about this particular historical period. No "winner's logic" here. Often, the term "revisionist history" is applied pejoratively, as if there were really only one way to explain the "truth," interpret the "facts," or account for events, and any other point of view should be read with suspicion if not outright hostility. But ideally, any history, if it is to withstand scholarly and rigorous scrutiny, should be subjected to careful examination to discover the bias inevitably inherent in the writer's personal and cultural background. This is especially true of civil war histories.

I am a Missourian, my family having lived in the state for over a century. But my ancestors on my father's side came from Binghamton, New York, and the rest from liberal, northern European countries. My Scotch-Irish family on my father's side, since 1700, lived in the small town of Raynham, Massachusetts, only fifteen miles south of Boston, and married into Puritan stock. In short, my heritage is at apparent opposite poles from the stereotypical Southerner. Moreover, four closely related ancestors of mine from Binghamton fought on the Northern side in the Civil War, as did scores of my more distant relatives. This book, therefore, is not a personal vendetta meant to settle the score for some real or imagined wrong inflicted by Northerners on my Southern ancestors between 1861 and 1865. On the contrary, the Civil War Gilmores in my family wore Union blue.

Rather, this book is an attempt to correct the mistaken notions recorded in the histories of the border region. Most of the recent histories of the Border War have had major faults. Some have been little more than adroit compilations of quotations from archives. Many have merely mimicked some earlier interpretation or structure. Nearly all have reflected the traditional interpretation of the events of the Border War. I judge these efforts to be flawed as "true histories." The bias of the authors is most easily recognized in the diction used in the works. The books, both early and more recent, are replete with pejorative references to the Missouri combatants as "Bushwhackers," "Pukes," "Border Ruffians," and "bandits." In some of the earlier works, even the Missouri people who were noncombatants were unfairly referred to as a "drunken rabble" and "de po' white folk," by no less a personage than Sara Robinson, the wife of Kansas's wartime abolitionist governor.

These prejudicial and demeaning terms are not only unfair, but they are also demonstrably not true, as this book will show. Even the premier early historian of the Border Wars, William Elsey Connelley, referred to the Missouri guerrillas as "poor white trash," an allegation he must have known was untrue as he penned the insult. Similarly, the press of the 1860s promoted this distortion by incessantly expressing its outrage over the supposed treatment of antislavery Kansans by trumpeting the propaganda epithet "Bleeding Kansas!" Many writers today uncritically shout the same slogan, as if only Northerners were bleeding. Recent scholarship, in fact, has established that more proslavery Southern men and women died in "Bleeding Kansas" than did antislavery Northerners.

What is often written in Border War histories are egregious examples of substituting value-laden, loaded terms for verifiable facts. Terms like

"Border Ruffian" are imbued with negative affective connotations and were used, essentially, for propaganda purposes a century ago. Today, either deliberately or unknowingly, these loaded terms are too often included in modern histories, their virulence clouding the reader's judgment and perception of events and concealing what actually happened behind a veil of still-existing propaganda.

Border War histories often are filled with distortions as frequently by what they do not mention as by what they do. For instance, anyone familiar with the Border War knows about the Missouri "guerrillas," young men who defied the Federal government by armed rebellion. But how often do readers find the Free Staters in Kansas Territory—who themselves also brazenly exhibited armed, often lethal, defiance of the federal government and its authorities from 1854 to the end of the war—referred to as Kansas "guerrillas" or "revolutionaries"?

Another situation invariably not mentioned or emphasized is the arbitrary nature of the extermination policy the U.S. Army perpetrated against the young guerrillas in Missouri who fought against the Union during the Border War. Universally unconsidered, also, is the effect this extermination policy and its brutal implementation had on the guerrillas' psychological dispositions. The Federal policy of relentlessly hunting down these men and killing them upon capture literally turned many of the guerrillas into savages.

In addition, the extent of the unbridled confiscation or destruction by Kansans and Union troops of Missouri private property from 1858 through 1865 is often either ignored or underemphasized, especially during the prewar years. Normal security disappeared along the border as early as 1858, and a violent, incredible terror and chaos unfolded, lasting until the end of the war (and even beyond the end, in some regards). The culmination of this government-sponsored reign of terror for the inhabitants of the Missouri border counties was the issuance of the infamous General Orders Number 11 of September 1863. Union general Thomas Ewing, Federal commander of the region, ordered the entire population of the border counties deported from the region.

Enforcing the decree were the same notorious "Jayhawkers" and "Red Legs" that had pillaged and murdered their way across this region at the war's beginning. The resulting theft, murder, and devastation earned this part of Missouri the appellation of "The Burnt Region" for years to come. This desperate and destructive act was not only an abject admission by Federal authorities that their military policy for eliminating the guerrilla threat was totally bankrupt, it surely represented a nineteenth-century version of the "ethnic cleansing" of today's headlines. This situation, although little reported in the typical history of the Border War, helped create the extraordinary circumstances that bred the vicious behavior of the guerrillas.

Though at times deserving of such descriptions as "vicious," the characters of the personalities involved in the Border War drama are treated invariably with bias. William Clarke Quantrill, the best known of the guerrilla leaders, in most histories is treated as a "demon," a "devil," a thoroughly depraved man without any human decency. Actually, his historical reality was quite different. He was a typical guerrilla chieftain whose violent actions, seen in the broader context of history and considering the relentlessly ruthless manner in which he and his followers were persecuted, are understandable.

David Rice Atchison, the leader of the so-called Border Ruffians, is described over and over in the traditional histories as if he was the leader of a lawless band of "thugs." In fact, he was a prominent Missouri senator, president pro tem of the United States Senate, and an important, cultured Southern leader who organized an armed band to fight the armed bands of antislavery Kansans who were preying on his constituents.

Bill Anderson, for good reason considered the most notorious, violent, and feared guerrilla captain, is invariably characterized in histories as a crazed psychopath. By the time of his death in October 1864, he likely was that. But little attempt has been made to determine why he and his men—who were as violent as Anderson—became so violent during the war. The story is typically presented as if the guerrillas were devils, and their leader Satan himself.

It seems inevitable that the stereotyping continues even today. For example, a recent book on Quantrill is titled *The Devil Knows How to Ride*. Even Ang Lee's generally excellent and, in many respects, accurate film had its title changed to *Ride With the Devil*, though the book it was adapted from is titled *Woe to Live On*. Historians and filmmakers, it seems, are incapable of referring to William Clarke Quantrill without at least some reference to the Dark Prince. This book is an exception. I do not demonize the losing side. Instead, I discuss the guerrillas as if they were ordinary people, just like you and me, who became part of a violent war and reacted accordingly and understandably.

Much of the confusion in the characterizations and histories can be accounted for. The very data the historians of the Border War use as the substance of their histories are tainted. The writers contemporary with the period—in letters, newspapers, and other media—are themselves biased, politically polarized to the extreme. Their writing is often outrageously one-sided, either ardently abolitionist or fervently proslavery. In their accounts, they lie, distort, and obfuscate, giving their writings illegitimate and spurious spins. In other words, they are *human,* expressing their natural human prejudices.

What I attempt in this book, and what has not been accomplished with any success in other works, is to examine the power structure and the social milieu in Missouri and Kansas that formed the framework for this historical period. In this way, I hope, the historic pieces of this complex puzzle are joined together in a comprehensible way. I treat the Border War in novel, unconventional ways. For instance, Quantrill's guerrillas are not viewed as "bandits" terrorizing the Missouri-Kansas border for plunder, as they have been invariably treated in most previous histories. Rather, they are treated as they were in the historical epoch in which they lived, fought, and died. They are considered as instruments of the armed forces of the Confederate States of America, operating under general Southern directives, orders, and guidance, and often cooperating with the Southern forces in significant operations, frequently losing their lives in the process. They were, it must be emphasized, predominantly young men who were the sons of affluent slave owners—the landed gentry of the border—who were subjected to extraordinary circumstances. This fact is virtually never mentioned in the earlier histories.

These young men, essentially a rural elite, were roused into violent action by the repeated incursions into Missouri of marauding Kansans from 1858 onward and were turned into vengeful-minded guerrillas by the brutal excesses committed by Union militias and Federal troops occupying their land during the war. Early in the war, these guerrillas were "outlawed" by the United States government forces and systematically and successfully exterminated. This relentless attempt to exterminate these young men brutalized them, psychologically transforming some of them into violent individuals who took the scalps of Federal troops as trophies and mutilated the corpses of their fallen enemies.

In this book, the guerrillas are not treated simplistically, unrealistically, or naively. Instead, their transformation from innocents to cold-blooded killers is demonstrated. Other soldiers involved in total wars—wars without quarter—around the world and throughout history have reacted in much the same way. The Missouri guerrillas' behavior may be seen not as an exception but as a phenomenon occurring frequently in similar, extremely violent scenarios. Historically, men and women have often resorted to the behavior exhibited by the Missouri guerrillas of 1861-65: in Spain, France, Russia, Vietnam, the Philippines, and even in Revolutionary War-era America. The Missouri guerrillas were *not*, as most previous histories stereotyped them, natural-born killers who, through the historical accident of the period of their births, came of age in a place and at a time where their inborn malevolence and cruelty was freely set loose on an innocent population. They were ordinary, and in many instances, cultured young men whose violent acts were provoked by other violent acts sanctioned by the Lincoln administration and committed against them and their families.

To understand the guerrillas' reactions against the Federal policy, the U.S. Army's "rules of engagement" in fighting the guerrillas is examined and exposed for the policy of extermination that it became. The Federal

army modeled its actions in accordance with the Lieber code. But how jus-
tifiable or humane was this code with its explicit extermination policy? The
Lieber code was modeled after the practices of Napoleon Bonaparte, hardly the great moral arbiter and exemplar in such matters. For example, were
his practices in Spain during the Napoleonic Wars inhuman and beastly?
Clearly they were. This virtually unaddressed topic needs airing to correct
the historical record.

The extreme Union response was not directed toward unassociated individuals or renegade bands of men but toward members of the Confederate
army. The Missouri guerrillas' role was a specific one: to create chaos
behind Federal lines and to attack the Union army's lines of communications—railroads, river traffic, and horse-, mule-, and ox-drawn convoys.
This they did, and successfully. The expected result of this military activity was to force the Federal army to muster a force twenty or more times
the strength of the guerrilla bands to resist and forestall them. As a result,
and as Southern leaders rightly anticipated, the Federal army was unable to
field as many men against the South in the eastern and southern campaigns. It should also be noted that the guerrillas involved in the Border
War in western Missouri were only a handful of the guerrillas operating
against Federal forces in the state. Guerrilla warfare was rampant throughout Missouri and the other Border States as well.

Nor were the army commanders, Southern and Northern, who fought
along the Missouri-Kansas border operating on their own hooks: major
politicians in Lawrence, Kansas; St. Louis, Missouri; Washington City
(Washington, D.C.); and Richmond, Virginia, influenced their actions. I
examine these ligaments of power and how they interrelated to shape events.

Meanwhile, the activities of a Kansas politician and general, the eccentric and violent senator and major general, James Lane, are spotlighted.
Lane, supported by radical and violent followers and subordinates such as
James Montgomery, Col. Charles Jennison, and Lt. Col. Dan Anthony, as
well as prominent politicians from Lawrence, Kansas, performed some of
the worst depredations and atrocities in Missouri during the war. Yet Lane's
atrocities, every bit as vicious and outrageous as the guerrillas', are largely
unreported or underemphasized in histories. Unconstrained by national
Union politicians or Pres. Abraham Lincoln, Lane's men rampaged in the
southern border counties of Missouri, totally out of control in 1861.
Meanwhile, his subordinates, Jennison and Anthony, created chaos and
performed atrocities in the northern border counties, terrorizing the citizens and destroying any semblance of order and civilization. These raids
by Lane and his subordinates were enthusiastically supported by rank and
file Kansans and repudiated by only a few.

When Regular Army commanders like Maj. Gen. Henry Halleck, commander of the Department of Missouri, complained to Lincoln about

Lane's and Jennison's carnage and brutality in Missouri, the president protected Lane time and again. Lincoln's utmost desire, to keep Missouri in the Union by any and all means, overcame his better-known propensity for mercy and justice. In this, America's most-beloved president exhibited a practical but cynical nature.

The politics of the border were a complex matrix of relationships, and this book attempts to sort and clarify them. The Border War was really a war within a war. And many of the participants of the Border War—Frank Blair, Abraham Lincoln, James Lane, Henry Halleck, Missouri's pro-Southern governor Claiborne Jackson, and Sen. David Rice Atchison—influenced both struggles.

However, politicians were not the only forces behind the war. The Border War was a popular struggle. At first, it was a contest between Missourians and people from the East who were purposely settled in Kansas to overthrow the legal, federally sanctioned proslavery government in Kansas Territory. In reaction, a Missouri army led by David Rice Atchison and U.S. Marshal Israel P. Donalson invaded Kansas and put down this popular rebellion, "sacking" Lawrence in 1856. This became known as the First Sacking of Lawrence and resulted in only one fatality—one of the raiders. Eventually, the flood of Free Staters created an antislavery majority among the citizens of Kansas. They were led by a highly organized, manipulative, and intelligent group of emigrants and their agents from Massachusetts, who finally took over legal control of the state by 1861.

In 1861 at the outset of the Civil War, pro-Southerners in Missouri, led by Claiborne Jackson, Sterling Price, and others, were overthrown by a Federal invasion headed by Union general and abolitionist Nathaniel Lyon, who was backed by the powerful St. Louis politician Frank Blair Jr., and Blair's close friend, President Lincoln. Lyon employed veteran regiments of German immigrants from St. Louis, fresh from the revolutionary battlefields of Europe and under Blair's control. The legally elected governor of Missouri, Claiborne Jackson, and his colleagues were driven from the state, and politicians friendly to the North were installed as governor and legislators without resort to popular approval. Lyon imprisoned the Missouri State Guard in prisoner-of-war camps, enforced martial law in the state, and Missouri (like Maryland before it) became an occupied member of the Union—which likely prevented a generalized revolt by its populace under what became an increasingly harsh occupation.

Many historians have emphasized that the state government that supplanted Jackson, the Gamble administration, favored the sustainment of the Union. What they do not always stress as well is that Gamble's government was a proslavery one, and Missouri in 1861 was an overwhelmingly proslavery state. In fact, slavery remained legal in Missouri under Union control until the Thirteenth Amendment to the U.S. Constitution ended slavery in America in 1865. Another fact not emphasized is that the political sentiment of Missouri from 1861 to 1865 was never static but changed continuously and dynamically, much like opinions during modern political campaigns. Finally, by 1865, once ex-Southerners in the state had been disenfranchised, the sentiment, as expressed by the politicians in power in Missouri, countered that of 1861. In fact, the state became radically Republican and fiercely antislavery.

In keeping with the popular roots of the Border War, from 1858 to 1861, it was the antislavery Kansans of Linn County, along the border of Bates and Vernon Counties in Missouri, who ruthlessly invaded, killed, and pillaged Missourians. At the outbreak of the Civil War in 1861, the invasion was intensified, spearheaded by regiment-sized units of Jayhawkers led by General Lane and his radical subordinates, Colonels Jennison and Montgomery, and Lt. Col. Dan Anthony (brother of the famous suffragette, Susan B. Anthony).

By this time, most of the Southern men of military age in western Missouri were already fighting in the South and East with the Confederate army. Thus, western Missouri was left undefended. In self-defense and to protect their families and personal property in the area, the young men remaining in western Missouri rose up in a popular rebellion in defiance of the occupying Union forces and marauding Jayhawkers. Led at first by Andrew Walker, the son of a prominent slaveholder, the guerrillas soon chose William Clarke Quantrill as their commander. Quantrill, a clever tactician from Ohio with a checkered past, led his guerrillas in aggressive operations in western Missouri that disorganized and panicked the Federals. Frustrated by the guerrillas and unable to devise any conventional military policy that could effectively counter them, desperate Union commanders outlawed them and, in ruthless search and destroy operations, hunted them down like wild animals.

It is an understatement to write that history has not been kind to the memory of Quantrill and his partisans. Historians have usually discussed the guerrillas by employing the same abstract morality a preacher might employ in church on a bright Sunday. But war, especially guerrilla warfare, is beyond the pale of such morality and exists in an environment where violence can become, under the right circumstances, virtually unlimited. Guerrilla war fighting, in a total war where no rules or qualities of mercy apply, falls outside normal morality and can only be understood in the violent context in which it exists. This book tries to understand the Missouri guerrilla war as a phenomenon of total war, like guerrillas involved in such wars in other lands, today and in the past. To understand guerrillas in this sort of environment requires an open-minded perspective, an unconventional outlook.

Fully understanding the actions of the Missouri guerrillas during the fighting involves an analysis of the reasons they entered the war. Because the Border War involved the institution of slavery, serious dialogue regarding the perspective of Southern leaders immediately before and during the Civil War is often given short shrift. Indeed, to even suggest the examination of Confederate views and motivations places one at risk of being branded a racist. Yet how are we to truly understand great historical events without fully examining the perspectives of each side? Those interested in the Civil War and in seeing it in a fair light should be prepared to not only see the war and its complexity from the Northern perspective but also from the Southern perspective. As an intellectual exercise, it is an extremely valuable means of getting at the truth of an issue.

To the South, the war was an attack on their personal property, individual liberty, Constitutional rights, economic system, and way of life. While Northerners initially maintained that the purpose of the Civil War was to uphold the Union, today, the Civil War is referred to most often as the war to end slavery. Southerners, in contrast, maintain that they fought the war in defense of States' Rights. Since the Emancipation Proclamation was not decreed until January 1863, two years after the beginning of the war, and then addressed only the slaves in the rebellious Southern states and not those of the Northern or Border States, the Southern position has to be considered.

Certainly, though, the threat to the accumulated wealth of the slave owners in the South—much of it black chattel slaves—posed by the election of abolitionist-backed Abraham Lincoln was an important part of the problem. Because a considerable amount of the personal property of the Southern elite class existed as slave manpower, bought and paid for within a tragic, but nonetheless longstanding legal system, their fortunes and futures were made precarious by Lincoln and the Radical Republicans. No person wishes to countenance the seizure of his personal property without compensation, no matter what the basis for the seizure, and the Southerners were no exception.

From this perspective, therefore, the North posed an overwhelming threat to most Southerners' customary way of life and manner of existence. Most Southerners were willing to fight and, if need be, die to reject the Northern domination and preserve what they considered to be their freedom. It was a strong motivation, and it created a violent resistance to Federal authority. In the West, when you couple this conviction with the palpable fear for life and property engendered by the brutal acts of Federally uniformed raiders, sanctioned by the same government that sought to end the Southern way of life, the result was a powerful commitment to resistance.

Let these various thoughts remain a backdrop to the following history.

Chapter 1

Uneasy Union: The Roots of the Border War

The war fought on the border of Missouri and Kansas—the Border War, 1854-65—in many respects, marked the beginning of the American Civil War and was one of the preliminary political and military struggles that degenerated into that awful conflict. But the process that created the Border War and the Civil War was of far earlier origin. The roots of these two wars extended to the conventions that drafted the original Articles of Confederation and the Constitution, eighty years before the Civil War erupted. The states that formed the United States were never truly united or compatible from the start. That is why the original document binding the sections of the new country was referred to as "The Articles of Confederation," which better defined the relationship between the various sovereign entities. The United States, despite the implications of its name, was more a confederation or league than a unified country in its early decades. And later, when the South rebelled from the United States and formed its own nation, it referred to itself as a "confederacy," denoting a collection of sovereign powers.

As the United States grew and prospered, the cultural differences already apparent in the various sections of the country when it was formed—the various dialects, social customs, and styles of living—became even more pronounced. Economically, the Northern states by the 1850s had become industrialized and commercialized, while the Southern states maintained a relatively static, agrarian organization based, in large part, on the labor-intensive plantation system. Meanwhile, both regions had developed distinctive elite classes, and the South had produced a number of political geniuses that successfully supported and protected Southern interests. Over time, the incompatibilities of the two sections of the country created a simmering animosity. One of the most profound differences was the institution of slavery, which formerly had existed legally in both the North and South but which increasingly became a Southern phenomenon. The divisions between the two parts of the country became further aggravated in 1820 when the national legislature passed the Compromise of 1820, allowing the entrance of Missouri into the Union as a Slave State but restricting any further slavery to those parts of the United States south of thirty-six degrees thirty minutes in latitude—a solution not pleasing to either section of the country. Northern politicians wanted no slavery; Southern politicians wanted unlimited slavery.

Historian Ronald C. Woolsey wrote, "From the slaveholder's viewpoint, the issue [of slavery] seemed primarily a constitutional question concerning state and federal jurisdiction." The Southern argument was rooted in the belief "that America consisted of a compact of states and each state retained a degree of independence from possible encroachment by the federal government." Thus, an important issue in the 1820 Missouri controversy concerned federal jurisdiction over the domestic affairs of the states. James Barbour, a senator of Virginia at the time, believed that "all powers not expressly delegated are reserved to the states." P. P. Barbour, a Virginia representative, added that the states were "free and independent, and entitled to exercise all the rights of sovereignty, of every description whatever." Georgia senator Freeman Walker asked at the time: "Shall we take from them [the people of Missouri] the right of judging for themselves upon a subject so intimately connected with their welfare?"[1]

But other leaders saw the subject of slavery as more than merely the substance for a rhetorical exercise or debate. They recognized the gathering of the ominous clouds of an impending war between the states. Thomas Jefferson, now advanced in age, hoped that Americans "would not have to wage another Peloponnesian war to settle the ascendancy between them."[2] Georgian Freeman Walker recognized "a storm portending" and feared "the bursting of that storm" because of the Missouri controversy. Sen. Richard Johnson of Kentucky stated that the restriction of slaves in Missouri "may possible ultimate in a civil war."[3] Other Southerners wished "at once a dissolution of the Union."[4] Georgian Thomas Cobb believed the controversy over the Missouri Compromise of 1820 "kindled a fire which all the water of the ocean cannot put out, which seas of blood can only extinguish,"[5] a remark foreshadowing the beliefs of the fanatical John Brown.

The 1820 agreement, however, was to be only the first of a number of compromises over the issue of slavery, and as time elapsed, it was generally understood by Northern and Southern leaders that the slavery issues were increasingly agreed upon only to preserve the Union and that a permanent solution was being postponed. Nonetheless, in a sort of competitive ardor, the two sections of the country continued to further their own selfish designs. At the close of the Mexican War of 1846-48, David Wilmot, after a debate in the House of Representatives over the appropriation of two million dollars to purchase Mexican territory in the Southwest, proposed an amendment to the bill specifying that "neither slavery nor involuntary servitude shall ever exist in any part of said territory." Because many Southern politicians considered the area west of the old Louisiana Purchase still subject to the intentions of the old Missouri Compromise of 1820, the "Wilmot Proviso" caused increased agitation, not only in the South, where Wilmot was seen as trying to change the rules of the game, but also in the North, through the failure of the amendment to be accepted. Nineteenth-century historian A. Theodore Andreas said: "Never before in the history of the country has such popular excitement on any political question prevailed. The North and South alike were stirred to their very depths. The spirit of uncompromising opposition was aroused on both sides." The North began derisively calling the Southern elites the "Slave Power," even though Southern power, economic and numeric, was much less than the North's. This animosity signaled a growing rivalry between the parts of the country and increasingly dangerous implications.

When the Thirty-first Congress convened in December 1849, more divisive issues arose between the North and South, again in relation to changes in national policy as the result of the Mexican War.[6] Exacerbating the situation was California's recently drafted constitution prohibiting slavery. Also on the table was the slavery policy for the new territories of New Mexico and Deseret (Utah). In addition, the Southern states wished Congress to consider a stronger fugitive slave act. Northern congressmen also sought the abolition of the slave trade in the District of Columbia. Henry Clay—the Great Compromiser—in an attempt to resolve these issues and push them through Congress, tied them together in an omnibus bill that specified, "(1) the admission of California as a state into the Union without mention of slavery; (2) the establishment in Utah and New Mexico of territorial governments expressly forbidden to legislate on slavery; and (3) a boundary settlement that granted the southeastern corner of New Mexico to Texas."[7] After the omnibus bill foundered, Stephen A. Douglas, a prominent leader of the Democratic Party from Illinois, pushed the provisions found in the original omnibus bill through the Senate in the form of individual bills.

Many leaders in Congress and the nation believed the passage of these bills, called the Compromise of 1850, had resolved what some people called "these political nightmares which had almost driven the country into a state of national hysteria." Thomas H. O'Connor stated, "In theory, the compromise had appeased the South by admitting its constitutional privilege to let slavery follow the flag. In practice, however, the Yankee [the citizen of the North] reflected, it was not practical for slavery to expand into the western prairies, and so, *de facto*, the freedom of the West was assured." At the time, many people in the North and the South believed that slavery was not viable in the West and required the right soil and climate to thrive.

But Southerners were aware that the Compromise of 1850 gave the North two more senatorial votes—California—that upset the political equilibrium of the nation and represented a great threat to Southern interests. But overriding these considerations, the elite class and its representative congressmen in the Northeast believed the compromise was "indissoluble," and its intentions were to be honored and inviolable in the future. Northern antislavery and Southern proslavery adherents were baffled by Douglas's position because he discussed the matter of slavery "with a coolness exasperating to the extremists on either side."[8]

On January 4, 1854, four short years after the compromise, Douglas, still an influential Illinois senator, proposed a Kansas-Nebraska bill that would organize the new territories of Kansas and Nebraska in accordance with the constitution by which they entered the Union. Thus, the people of the new territories would decide for themselves what system they wished to live under. Douglas called the solution "Popular Sovereignty" and argued for the justice of such a plan, believing that it was democratically inspired. But many in the North believed the bill was a betrayal of the Compromise of 1820 *and* that of 1850 as well. Now, new territories could conceivably enter the Union as slave states from areas earlier prohibited to slavery— that is, north of the thirty-six degrees and thirty minutes stipulated in the Compromise of 1820. Though a duly constituted, legal U.S. Congress passed the Kansas-Nebraska Act, many influential Northeasterners believed its passage was "a demonstration of bad faith" by Southerners and those whom they had manipulated. On February 23, 1854, some three thousand of the "solid" men of Boston, headed by Abbott Lawrence, Robert C. Winthrop, and Samuel Elliot, held a great meeting at Faneuil Hall "to protest the way in which they had been cheated and ridiculed by the machinations of cheap demagogues."[9]

Most wealthy cotton merchants of the Northeast (called "Cotton Whigs") now abandoned all Southern support—even though their livelihoods were dependent on cotton, the principal product of the South. Robert C. Winthrop cried bitterly: "If I could have prescribed a recipe for reinflating Free-Soilism and Abolitionism, which had collapsed all over the country, I should have singled out this precise potion from the whole *materia medica* of political quackery." Amos Lawrence chimed in that all the wealthy merchants and retired gentlemen of State Street were going over to the antislavery side and added, "These constitute pretty much all the 'slave power' in this community, and if they give up the Compromises and say that they have been cheated, we all know that sympathy for the South [in Boston] and their 'institution' must be gone."[10] These New England Whigs "felt themselves consumed by righteous wrath at what they considered to be the selfish designs of unscrupulous politicians who had gambled with national unity for the sake of railroad ties [discussed later] and caucus votes." One of the people that they felt had especially betrayed them was Sen. Stephen Douglas.[11]

Many historians have pointed to the passage of the Kansas-Nebraska Act as a watershed in the eruption of the Border War and Civil War. Certainly the act precipitated the complex interactions that incited violence between Missouri and Kansas. But the underlying reasons why the Kansas-Nebraska Act was enacted at the time it was have remained somewhat shrouded. It was certain that Kansas and Nebraska would become states, but the timing of the act was designed by a number of powerful men in and out of government. Their main interest in seeing that the act was passed related to the building of a transcontinental railroad across the new territory. Had the passage of the act been postponed for several years, perhaps relations between the states might have turned out much differently.

A key individual in the railroad's development was Stephen Douglas. Douglas, the "Little Giant," made his home in Chicago, Illinois, and was a senator from that state as well as a prominent national figure. Kansas historian James C. Malin said, "Douglas identified himself with Chicago by not only making it his residence, but by investing in Chicago real estate, thereby tying his personal fortunes with the rise of that city as the commercial and transportation center of the West." Because of his financial interests in the city, Douglas "conceived the plan of making Chicago the Eastern terminus of the Pacific Railroad." He promoted the organization of the Kansas and Nebraska Territories because they would facilitate the extension of the road for his transcontinental railroad. But first, the two territories would have to become states, thereby ensuring the settlement of the regions.[12] The Indians, of course, would have to be shunted aside and the place made secure by "continuous lines of settlement, with civil, political and religious institutions all under the protection of law."[13]

Meanwhile, Douglas, an adroit politician, hoped to bypass the slavery question. With this in mind, he promoted "Popular Sovereignty," what he thought was a fair resolution to the problem. To the amazement of Douglas, it turned out to be an explosive solution. Douglas's attempt to settle the new territories, which began as a relatively high-minded endeavor allowing the settlers of the territories to decide their own political fates, caused him to be hated. The wrath of the Northeast descended upon the "Little Giant." After the passage of the Kansas-Nebraska Act, Douglas claimed he could ride from Boston to Chicago by the light provided by the burning effigies of him that lined the tracks. His enemies charged that he "first, wantonly destroyed the peace that the Compromise of 1850 had brought; second, that the repeal of the Missouri Compromise of 1820 was a violation of a solemn compact between the sections and a gross breach of faith; and third, that his object was to secure the support of the South and by means of it win for himself the presidency." Nothing Douglas could say seemed to blunt these charges.[14]

Whatever were Douglas's intentions, he had opened a Pandora's box of trouble and strife. Now, the proslavery agitators of the South and the fiery abolitionists of the North would collide on the prairies of Kansas to decide a national issue—whether slavery or "freedom" would triumph in the new territories. As it turned out, Nebraska was not a point of contention. It was generally considered unsuitable for slavery and along the natural emigration route for Northerners.

Kansas was a different matter altogether; in fact, it was the opposite of Nebraska, and along the natural corridor for Southern emigration, principally from Kentucky and Tennessee. The abolitionists would have to reverse that trend if they were to ensure that Kansas became what they called "free." Therefore, the interest, money, and aggressive overtures of influential people in the Northeast were directed at the settlement of Kansas.

But there are those who say this aggressive policy toward Kansas was unnecessary, that Kansas was unsuitable for slavery. Kansas University professor James Malin said, "There was no real danger of Kansas ever becoming a slave state, and the whole Kansas crusade of antislavery-abolitionism was a trumped up affair in which the country was victimized by propaganda, and history has been dominated ever since by that falsehood."[15] At the time, however, all of this was a moot point once the competition for the settlement of Kansas began. Southerners, for their part, were concerned that if they lost both Kansas and Nebraska, then the North would secure four more senatorial votes to add to those they had gained already with the entrance of California into the Union. The South, which had controlled Congress for a number of years, was faced with the reality that national policy might be dictated by Northerners, some of whom, in the Southern view, were abolitionist fanatics. The patience of the Southern elite class, the class threatened by the new abolitionism (after all, it was their capital property in the form of expensive slaves that was at stake), was reaching the breaking point. Meanwhile, the abolitionists of the Northeast began to mobilize their free-soil juggernaut.

In the spring of 1854, in reaction to the passage of the Kansas-Nebraska bill, the Massachusetts Emigrant Aid Company formed. It was soon renamed the New England Emigrant Aid Company (and often known as the New England Emigrant Aid Society). Its principal purpose was to settle the state of Kansas with Free Staters, people sympathetic with the abolitionist cause. Its principal agent, Samuel Clarke Pomeroy wrote to his friend Edward Everett Hale that the company's intention was to ensure "the *right* impetus [was] given to [Kansas's] early Settlement, that the best principles of our resting fathers may be transplanted there! And that thus our untold domain may be saved from the blighting—withering—deadening—damning—influence of American Slavery!!"[16]

The New England Company was conceived by its founders as something of a "combination of philanthropic nature and money-making scheme." The initial plan was to "first, disseminate information and encourage migration to Kansas; second, to assist eastern emigrants by securing reduced railway and steamboat fares and by organizing them into conducted parties; [and] third, to invest all the capital that could be raised in mills, hotels and other local improvements in Kansas in order to attract settlers from all parts of the North."[17] The intention, of course, was to pre-empt any Southern attempt to make Kansas a Slave State.

Eli Thayer and Amos Lawrence became the guiding figures of the New England Company. Thayer believed that the purpose of the company should be to "plant" settlers at points in Kansas "favorably situated to win the territory for freedom."[18] The company was meant to be self-sustaining. In his views toward the company, Thayer expressed a sort of cultural-religious utopianism, saying, "Why is it worse for a company to make money by extending Christianity than by making cotton cloth? . . . The truth is that the highest civilization is the greatest creator of wealth. She is the modern Midas, with power to turn everything into gold. Properly equipped, and with proper direction, she will conquer and supplant any inferior condition of men."[19] (Of course, implicit in this statement is the notion of the Southerner's cultural, economic, and religious inferiority to Northerners.)

Amos Lawrence, the most important philanthropist involved with the New England Company, and also its treasurer, was less euphoric and more honest about the company's financial prospects. He "advised prospective subscribers [to the company] to invest no more than they could afford to lose or were willing to contribute to the cause."[20]

A number of other abolitionists rushed to help the fledgling company obtain money and recruits. Although the company was never able to raise more than $140,000 throughout its entire existence, Eli Thayer and one of the company's propagandists, Edward Everett Hale, made it known to the nation through the press that the company intended to raise $5 million and send twenty thousand settlers to Kansas immediately. This was never a realistic goal and was meant only to encourage settlers to believe that the venture had considerable capital behind it and that the situation in Kansas would be reasonably comfortable. Propagandists surfaced to further trumpet the company's cause: Horace Greeley of the *New York Tribune,* Thurlow Weed at the *Albany Journal,* and William Cullen Bryant of the *New York Evening Post.* Writers Edward Everett Hale (*Kanzas* [sic] *and Nebraska*) and Sara Robinson (*Kansas; Its Interior and Exterior Life*) further promoted the cause in their widely read books. But the New England Company was not the only emigration organization to form. The American Company of New

York would send a party to Burlingame, Kansas, and other groups formed in Pennsylvania, Wisconsin, and Ohio. All were influenced by the propaganda emanating from the New England Company and its adherents.[21]

Amos G. Lawrence, the money and much of the intelligence behind the New England Company. The city of Lawrence, Kansas, was named after him. *The Kansas State Historical Society, Topeka*

Ultimately, the New England Emigrant Aid Company was directly responsible for fewer than 2,000 people coming to Kansas. But the propaganda fostered by the company generated a much larger influx of emigrants from other parts of the country. Those interested in the history of the Border War must ask themselves why the company exercised influence that was, as one historian described it, "so out of proportion to their numbers." The answer seems to be that the company brought to the Kansas situation intelligence, organization, and leadership. In the area of leadership, Charles Robinson, an early agent for the company, became the first governor of "free" Kansas. Samuel Pomeroy, its principal agent, became the mayor of Atchison, one of Kansas's first U.S. senators, and a leader of a bank and prospective railroad. Martin Conroy, another company agent, became the state's first representative. Daniel Reed Anthony (the brother of Susan B. Anthony) would become mayor of Leavenworth, and Dr. John Doy would be an "engineer" and "conductor" of the Kansas underground railroad.

Though clearly the New England Company was rich in leadership, the purposes, ethics, and morality of this leadership should be scrutinized closely. Doy, upon reaching Kansas, almost immediately began to "free" wealthy Missourians of much of their principal capital investments—that owned in the form of expensive slave property. Once the Civil War started, Anthony would lead an invasion into Missouri that destroyed Missouri homes, killed its inhabitants, and illegally released even more slaves. Because it was still legal to own slaves, Doy and Anthony were breaking the law willfully, committing felonies willy-nilly.

Along with its prominent leadership, further enhancing the New England Company's prestige and influence with the new settlers in the state was its record in town founding. Lawrence, Topeka, and Osawatomie became company towns. Company agents Isaac T. Goodnow and Luke P. Finch would settle Manhattan, Kansas, originally called "Town of Boston," and Samuel Pomeroy would help found Topeka.

The New England Company also bought a hotel in Kansas City, the Gillis House, soon to be renamed the American hotel, and built the Eldridge House hotel in Lawrence. The American hotel was operated as a way station for settlers on the way to Kansas; once built, the Eldridge House served as quarters for Kansans in the Lawrence area until they were settled in more permanent abodes and, later, as a fort to defend them.

Continuing to present great leadership, the New England Company also built sawmills at various locations in Kansas, further enhancing settlement and their own prestige and influence. The company built mills at Lawrence, Topeka, Manhattan, Osawatomie, Burlington, Waubansee, Atchison, Balcheller (Milford), and Claflin. When Kansas became a state, the New England Company owned half the privately owned mills in Kansas—some of the largest in the state.

Strengthening its influence in the state, the company bought or started a variety of newspapers: the *Herald of Freedom* in Lawrence, *Die Kansas Zeitung* and *The Freedom's Champion* in Atchison, and the *Chindowan* in Quindaro. When proslavery adherents started the influential *Squatter Sovereign* in Atchison, Kansas, Samuel Pomeroy, using New England Company money, bought the paper and 51 percent of the town lots and turned the entire town, a proslavery bastion, into another Free State colony.

The company also founded or helped start a number of churches, including the Plymouth Congregational church in Lawrence and the Lawrence Episcopalian church and school, which ultimately became the University of Kansas.[22] With such enterprises, the New England Company, despite the fact that a relatively modest number of New Englanders came to reside in Kansas, virtually dominated the state of Kansas from its beginning. This fact exposes the misinformation that proslavery forces from Missouri represented the only "outside influences" threatening the popular sovereignty of the territory.

Along with its influential position in the state, the company controlled the politics of Kansas through key leadership roles. On this front, Amos Lawrence (after whom the town of Lawrence, Kansas, is named), Eli Thayer, and the board of the New England Company proved sagacious in their choice of agents. The leaders of the company appear to have selected their agents for particular roles in the new territory. As their point of personal contact with the rough and tough proslavery men in the territory, the company chose Charles Robinson, a man of prepossessing personality, boldness, bravery, perseverance, and judgment. The business dealings of the company, however, were entrusted to Samuel Pomeroy, a canny businessman and astute politician.

Charles Robinson, a rather handsome, tall, and bald-headed man of thirty-five came to the company with an impressive pedigree. At the age of thirty, on March 19, 1849, he had gone to the California gold fields with fifty-one men from Boston. The men were part of a joint-stock company and were organized like a militia. The company was composed of men from all social strata and walks of life. Twenty-five percent of the men had military backgrounds, and most of the men were armed with "rifles, revolvers, bowie knives, and sabres."[23] The expedition got no farther than Kansas City when a general mutiny broke out. As Robinson described it, "The officers in control were subjects of suspicion, jealousies, innuendoes, reflections, and open charges of incapacity, inefficiency, crookedness, theft, and robbery."[24] Robinson was one of three men chosen to divide the company's supplies when the party split into two groups. Already, Robinson was demonstrating strong leadership qualities.

Robinson later spent twenty-two months in California, some of the time mining, part of the time keeping an eating house (soon destroyed in a disastrous flood). Subsequently, he started a newspaper called the *Miners and Settler's Grant* and involved himself in a heated land controversy. In 1850, he was made president of the Squatter's Association. In this capacity, during a confrontation with land speculators in the area who thought they owned the land, Robinson was shot near his heart. In response, he bashed in his attacker's skull with an iron bar, killing him. Robinson was charged with murder, assault, and conspiracy and placed in a prison ship off the coast of California. While in prison, he was elected to the California legislature! It was this violent, complex experience of Robinson's that signaled to the New England Company leadership the sort of strong, bold, and shrewd man they needed for the difficult settlement of Kansas.[25] Because their undertaking was likely to turn violent, they chose a man whose record indicated he was eminently capable of meeting violence with violence of his own. In an "eye for an eye" confrontation, Robinson had proven he could hold his ground.

Samuel Pomeroy, however, was seen by company officials in an entirely different light. Short and plump, a man with a seemingly benign smile and sanctimonious air, Pomeroy would act as the principal business agent for the company. Pomeroy, often called "Pom the Pious," also had leadership qualities that made him valuable to the company. Pomeroy had been a member of the legislature of Massachusetts and was an adroit businessman and deal maker. In addition, he had been an ardent abolitionist from the 1840s and was implicitly trusted by the company leaders. The company had the utmost confidence in Pomeroy's business sense and seldom challenged his judgment in that regard. In time, validating the company's confidence in him, Pomeroy concluded a number of sound business transactions and distinguished himself by becoming the mayor of Atchison, one of Kansas's first U.S. senators, and the president of the Kansas Valley Bank as well as the Atchison & St. Joseph Railroad.

Demonstrating from the start their confidence in Pomeroy, the company paid him one thousand dollars a year and "ten percent of the net profits of the company's sales, and rents collected." Robinson and Charles Bronscom, another agent, were paid the same salary but given only 2.5 percent of all sales and receipts. Pomeroy was obviously the company's principal agent. But the company needed a strong, violent man like Robinson, with sound judgment and toughness, to control the fighting and infighting in the opening years of territorial settlement. Robinson more than fulfilled their expectations and guided the company and its settlers as they trod the fine line between legitimate political agitation and outright treason. Together, Robinson and Pomeroy, each adding his unique talents to the effort, led the Free Staters in their major confrontation with the proslavery settlers, some of whom had already rushed across the state line into Kansas and staked out prime claims.

Prominent politicians and leaders in Missouri would back these settlers aggressively. [26]

Sen. Samuel Pomeroy, U.S. senator from Kansas and principal financial agent for the New England Company. *The Kansas State Historical Society, Topeka*

Chapter 2

The View from Across the Border: The Missouri Situation

At the end of July 1854, New England Emigrant Aid Company settlers arrived in Kansas at the site of what would become the town of Lawrence. Many Missourians were already settled on the ground. What is more, the claim stakes of other absent Missourians blanketed the area. Most of these Missourians were in Kansas Territory to make a better home for themselves; they had not been planted there artificially for the political purposes of the proslavery movement. Still others were in the territory to pursue the time-honored American practice of land speculation. Behind these relocated Missourians, however, stood the support and concern of powerful Missouri leaders and politicians. The Missourians and their leaders were all too familiar with the propaganda tracts of the New England Company and considered the new arrivals a threat to slave property, both in Missouri and—should the territory become a state—in Kansas. To understand adequately the significance of this clash between Northeasterners and Missourians on the plains of Kansas Territory, knowledge of conditions that existed in Missouri in 1854 and before that time is useful.

After Missouri became a state in 1821, settlers from Tennessee, Kentucky, South Carolina, and Virginia—people of Southern ancestry—inhabited the state. As a consequence, they transplanted to Missouri the "economic and social culture of the upper South." These people settled along the fertile bottomlands of the great Missouri and Mississippi River valleys, where they raised wheat, tobacco, and hemp, as well as cattle, sheep, and hogs. The settlers brought with them their slaves, who helped cultivate and tend their labor-intensive crops. The new Missourians came with considerable money, which they invested in land, seed, livestock, and more bondsmen. Because they lived along or near the Mississippi and Missouri Rivers, they found an immediate access to the markets of St. Louis and New Orleans, for the river was the main highway of commerce in those pre-railroad days.[1]

As the state developed, Missourians became entrepreneurs and started distilleries, flour mills, rope and machinery factories, and soap- and candle-making works. Meanwhile, Missouri farmers tilled the earth and harvested their crops with nearly state-of-the-art implements, much like those used in the more progressive Northern states. By 1860, Missouri produced $9,484,344 in flour meal; $3,236,962 in lumber; $1,800,000 in sugar;

$1,652,709 in tobacco; $1,650,380 in candles; $1,823,914 in pork, sausages, and beef; $1,810,350 in liquor; $1,563,152 in machinery; and $1,232,840 in cordage, or rope.[2] Some of the larger farms and plantations in Missouri were million-dollar enterprises by today's standards. Missouri was simply one of the most productive states in the Union, an affluent area ruled by a sophisticated, relatively educated elite class, a number of whom lived on plantations and in fine antebellum mansions, some of which are still standing.[3]

But while the Missourians were thoroughly imbued with Southern culture, politically, they were anything but homogeneous. Since 1850, a growing division had been developing between the people of the state. The two major parties, the Whigs and the Democrats, opposed each other over several significant issues. Thomas Hart Benton, a large, canny, aggressive Democratic politician, wielded tremendous influence over a network of supporters in the state. During his early years, Benton had been an aggressive duelist and used the *code duello* to dispense with political enemies he could not intimidate otherwise. But once dueling had been relegated to disrepute, he become adept at vanquishing his political enemies in more conventional ways.[4] Benton was one of Missouri's first U.S. senators and a strong Andrew Jackson man. When Jackson won Missouri by a landslide in 1826, it placed Benton on the right side of the Jackson groundswell. For years, Benton acted as the veritable spokesman for the Democratic Party in Missouri.

But by 1840, Benton's influence began to wane. Many Democrats believed that Benton accommodated the Whigs too often and that he was even in an alliance with that party, especially on monetary issues. On the subject of the use of "hard" (gold) or "soft" (paper) money, for instance, Benton was identified as a "hard," a Whig position. Soon, Benton came to be called "Old Bullion," which did little for his political stock in the Democratic Party. In 1841, ignoring Benton's money position, Missouri's Democratic legislature passed a bill favoring paper money.[5] While Benton's money policy remained "hard," his political support was becoming increasingly "soft." Benton, in fact, was finding it harder to lead while at the same time being dragged by his own party.

By the 1840s, Benton had changed his politics to include an antislavery position. At the same time, Missourians, in general, and Democrats, in particular, were becoming stronger advocates of slavery. The resultant political polarity steadily eroded Benton's political base. While in 1836, Benton had railed about antislavery "incendiaries" and "agitators," by 1844, he was proposing that the future state of Texas be divided between the Slave and Free States. This change in sentiment aroused considerable suspicion, even animosity, in many Democrats. Nonetheless, Benton began taking a firm position against the extension of slavery into the new territories.[6] On May 29, 1847, in a speech at Jefferson City, Benton said that a new slavery controversy had arisen. He was not telling his political enemies anything they did not already know. Staunch proslavery men for some time had considered Benton their antagonist.

In 1848, Benton, in line with his new political position, was in the fore-front of a movement to bar the admittance of Oregon into the Union rather than accept it into the Union on the terms of slavery advocates.[7] Shortly thereafter, a meeting of abolitionists in Chicago thanked Benton publicly for his "noble letter in favor of prohibiting slavery in Oregon."[8] Now, Benton was on a certain collision course with the strong proslavery wing of his own Democratic Party. Most Southerners believed that Congress did not have the right to legislate upon slavery in the territories and called those who did "Free-Soilers." By then, Benton was considered a Free-Soiler, and his fellow Missouri senator, Democrat David Rice Atchison, disassociated himself from Benton. The proslavery wing of the Democratic Party in Missouri considered Old Bullion a pariah.

On January 15, 1849, in reaction to Benton's policies and to clarify the position of the proslavery members of the Democratic Party in Missouri, Claiborne F. Jackson, a state legislator from Howard County and a mem-ber of the state's Committee on Federal Relations, introduced in the Missouri Senate a group of resolutions soon referred to as the "Jackson Resolutions." In the resolutions, Jackson specified that (1) Congress had no right to legislate "so as to affect the institution of slavery in the States, in the District of Columbia or in the Territories," (2) that "the right to pro-hibit slavery in any territory belongs exclusively to the public thereof, and can only be exercised by them in forming their constitution for a State gov-ernment, or in their sovereign capacity as an independent State," (3) that if Congress should pass an act in violation of that right, "Missouri will be found in hearty cooperation with the Slave-holding States in such measure as may be deemed necessary for our mutual protection against the encroachment of Northern fanaticism," and (4) "that our Senators in Congress be instructed and our Representatives be requested to act in con-formity to the foregoing resolutions."[9] The last two resolutions stirred up a hornet's nest of controversy. To many, Benton among them, they sound-ed like a veiled threat of a declaration of war.

The Jackson Resolutions polarized Missouri Democrats. Because of Benton's prominence and influence, antislavery Democrats now rallied around him. Many of these Democrats were among the numerous German immigrants from the St. Louis area who generally held antislavery sentiments. Their local leader, a man destined for greater things with the advent of the Civil War, was the fiery Francis P. "Frank" Blair Jr.

In answer to the Jackson Resolutions, Benton, on May 26, 1849, declared of his enemies, "Between them and me, henceforth and forever, a high wall and a deep ditch! And no communications, no compromise, no caucuses with them."[10] In the same address, which Benton called his "Appeal," he attacked Jackson and his resolutions as a mere aping of John C. Calhoun's earlier pronouncements on the same subject on February 19, 1847, and said they "contained the spirit of nullification, disunion, insubordination, and treason."[11] When Calhoun got wind of Benton's remarks, he called him an "abolitionist."[12] Sen. David Rice Atchison, Benton's colleague in the U.S. Senate, went further, stating, "all who could not engage in war against Col. Benton, and in favor of Jackson's resolutions, are rank abolitionists." Benton, in turn, called his opponents "a gang of scamps," which his enemies considered a particularly vulgar, condescending, and insulting epithet.[13] The schism in the Democratic Party of Missouri was complete, and the Jackson Resolutions became a litmus test of political affiliation. For the next few years, the party was split into pro-Bentonite and anti-Bentonite Democrats. This atmosphere allowed the relatively moribund Whig party of Missouri to establish ascendancy in state politics, as the Democrats now nullified themselves. But even the Whigs were split into Southern Whigs, led by George W. Goode, and free-soil Whigs, under James Sidney Rollins. Nonetheless, combined with the anti-Bentonite Democrats, the Whigs controlled legislative votes by a margin of almost two to one over Benton's Democrats.

All of this political maneuvering boded ill for Benton. In 1851, for the first time in his career, he failed to be elected senator. In response, in 1852, he ran for the House of Representatives from Missouri's Fifth District, a strong antislavery district in eastern Missouri that encompassed St. Louis and its German immigrants. He won. But two years later, when he railed against the passage of the Kansas-Nebraska bill, Luther M. Kennet, a Whig-American candidate, defeated him, and Benton's active political career was over.[14] Replacing Benton as the leader of the antislavery wing of the Democratic Party in Missouri was the formidable Frank Blair of St. Louis, who became a nemesis for proslavery Missourians once the Civil War erupted.

Another politician, a proslavery advocate, who was destined to play a central role in the Border War was Sen. David Rice Atchison, Benton's colleague in the Senate and a western Missourian. Atchison, a senator from Missouri from 1843 to 1855, had the best of Southern credentials. A native of Frogtown, Kentucky, he referred to himself as the "big frog in the puddle." In 1821, at the age of fourteen, Atchison entered Transylvania University in Lexington, Kentucky. Among his classmates were five future U.S. senators: Solomon W. Downs, Louisiana; George W. Jones, Iowa; Jesse D. Bright, Indiana; Edward A. Hannegan, Indiana; and Jefferson Davis, Mississippi. Davis, of course, was to become the president of the Confederacy during the Civil War and was a lifelong friend of Atchison.[15]

Receiving his license to practice law in 1839 at St. Louis, Atchison settled at Liberty, Missouri, in Clay County, some fifteen miles north of Westport Landing (later Kansas City, Missouri) and not far from the Missouri River. There, Atchison associated himself with a local lawyer, William T. Wood, and set up a successful law practice. Atchison subsequently organized and captained a militia company called the "Liberty Blues." Soon, he became one of Clay County's representatives in the lower house of the Eighth General Assembly.[16]

In 1835, Atchison was instrumental in drafting a petition to Congress to annex the Platte territory into the state of Missouri. In 1836, Congress passed legislation authorizing the annexation, and Martin Van Buren approved it on March 28, 1837.[17] One of the new counties carved out of the new annexation was named after Atchison. Two decades later, a town and county in Kansas also would be named after Atchison.

At about this time, Alexander Doniphan, a contemporary of Atchison, described him as "a very ripe scholar; of fine literary taste and very familiar with all the English classics," a man with "a clear, bright, logical mind; [who] had studied well, and kept up with his profession by constant reading."[18] This description will be worth remembering when reading histories of the Border War, in which Atchison is cast in the role of a villain who led a "mob" of so-called Border Ruffians into the state of Kansas in 1856.

In 1841, however, Atchison was recommended by Gov. Thomas Reynolds to be the judge of the twelfth judicial circuit, and he took up residence in Platte City, where he would perform his duties (Platte City was in Platte County, just adjacent to Clay County and abutting Kansas Territory). Alexander Doniphan described Atchison during this period as "a man of imposing presence, six feet two inches high [quite tall for the time]. He was the soul of honor, a fine conversationalist and possessed a good memory." Doniphan said, "As a judge, he was quick, expeditious and industrious; seemed to arrive at his conclusions almost intuitively, and his high sense of justice enabled him to decide equitably. I never knew a judge who gave such universal satisfaction." After his tenure as a judge, Atchison served as a United States senator for Missouri from 1843 to 1855.[19]

By the 1850s, Atchison had become an advocate of the states' rights doctrine of Southerner John C. Calhoun. Atchison promoted Calhoun's view that Southerners should have the right to carry their slaves into all territories of the Union. From Atchison's view, and that of other Southerners, it was ridiculous to have property that was not usable, movable, and valuable anywhere in the nation. It was an infringement of their normal rights as citizens, they believed. (In today's terms, although the comparison may sound indelicate, it would be like telling someone who owned a car in Kansas that he could never drive it in Missouri or Oklahoma and moreover should keep it out of those states entirely.) In 1848, Atchison had acted as Calhoun's lieutenant in the effort to derail the Wilmot Proviso. Later, Atchison vigorously supported the Jackson Resolutions and opposed Benton. Although he disagreed with many of the provisions in Henry Clay's Omnibus Bill of 1850, he nonetheless supported it. When Douglas's individual compromise bills were introduced to substitute for the omnibus bill as a compromise solution, Atchison voted for only part of the package.

When the Thirty-third Congress opened in December 1853, Atchison was the dean of Democrats in the Senate. He had held the position of president *pro tempore* of the Senate since 1846 and on one day had acted as president of the United States. In 1854, Atchison was closely involved in Stephen Douglas's efforts to ram through the Kansas-Nebraska bill. Secret, closed-door negotiations between Douglas, a select group of Southern

Today, a statue of David Rice Atchison stands in front of the Daviess County Courthouse in Plattsburg, Missouri. Atchison was considered a "Border Ruffian" to Kansans, but a hero to many Missourians. *Courtesy of Arba E. Gilmore Jr.*

Democratic senators, and Pres. Franklin Pierce made the passage of the bill possible.[20] The bill ensured that "Popular Sovereignty" would decide the fate of the Kansas and Nebraska Territories, whether they would be Free or Slave States. After passage of the bill in 1854, Atchison returned to western Missouri so that he could mobilize Missourians to relocate to Kansas in order to ensure the territory became a Slave State.

***

Before turning to the confrontation between Missouri's proslavery settlers and New England abolitionists at the threshold of what would become the town of Lawrence, Kansas, it would be illuminating to make a short survey of slavery in Missouri at this time and examine the threat to Missouri slave property posed by both the underground railroads already operating on the borders and those new "railroad" lines emanating from Kansas under the leadership of John Doy and John Brown.

As stated earlier, most of the early settlers to Missouri came from the upper Southern states of Kentucky, Tennessee, Virginia, and North Carolina, bringing their slaves with them and buying more after they arrived. But there were also prominent slave owners in Missouri, like Abiel and Nathaniel Leonard, who came from Vermont and other northern locations. Abiel Leonard was a Dartmouth graduate, a successful lawyer, and a landowner with extensive holdings and slaves. Nevertheless, the bulk of settlers and slave owners in Missouri were from the South.

Missouri was known throughout America, even before its statehood, as a rich, fertile land. As early as 1819, the land along the Missouri River in central Missouri cost as much as six dollars per acre, a very high price at the time since public lands sold for as little as two dollars an acre. If inflationary factors are figured into the cost of this land, it was almost as expensive in 1819 as it was as late as 1946, with all the modern improvements effected in the state.

A year after Missouri became a state, over thirteen thousand whites lived in the "Little Dixie" part of the state with their slaves. Little Dixie was the string of counties north of the Missouri River and east of Kansas that extended to within seventy-five miles of St. Louis. It also included the counties immediately north and west of St. Louis along the Mississippi River. Except for the "boot heel" section of southeastern Missouri, the Little Dixie counties held the greatest concentration of slaves in Missouri. By 1860, the Little Dixie counties in central Missouri had slave populations of 25 to 37 percent while the other Little Dixie counties had a population comprised of between 15 and 24 percent slaves.[21]

With the help of this population, Missouri, from the advent of its statehood, had a vibrant economy. Historian R. Douglas Hurt said that a "market economy existed in Little Dixie from the beginning of settlement" and explained:

In 1819 David Manchester worked in the "distilling business" in Howard County, converting surplus corn from nearby farmers into an easily transported, value-added product that could be shipped downriver to an inexhaustible market. Little Dixie's frontier farmers also began producing tobacco and hemp for sale through local commission men during any season of the year, except when the river froze. Merchants, such as Stanley and Ludlow in Franklin, sought wheat and pork, helped create a diversified market for farm products and prevented the development of the one-crop economy characteristic of the cotton south.[22]

By January 1820 James Brock had established a mill in Franklin to process wheat and corn into flour and meal for sale locally and in St. Louis and New Orleans. Little more than a year later, John McDowell opened a wool-carding operation near Columbia, and William Lamme and R. S. Barr offered to purchase a variety of agricultural products at their store in Franklin for a commission of 5 percent of the sale and "legal interest" on the money spent getting those commodities to market. Upon sale, they agreed to pay the farmers in specie, less any amount advanced in goods prior to the sale. Other merchants, such as E. O. Haire, W. O. Short and William Arnold, purchased farm commodities, including corn, with cash or goods when little specie circulated in Little Dixie. In November 1821 Henry V. Bingham and William Lamme opened a tobacco manufactory in Franklin, where local planters could sell their tobacco for "cash or goods." These entrepreneurs urged the merchants of Missouri and Illinois and the contractors who supplied the army on the Missouri and Mississippi rivers to purchase tobacco from them, satisfaction guaranteed.[23]

When hemp production—a labor-intensive crop—was introduced into Missouri, an even greater demand developed for slave labor. Some planters worked over fifty slaves, which is a large-scale enterprise in commercial agriculture. In such operations, however, considerable supervision was imperative to ensure that work tasks were completed, and this was usually done by the plantation owners or the farmers themselves. With the high cost of land, it was virtually a necessity to employ slaves to ensure profitability. But the slaves were not one-crop specialists. Walter Lenoir, a Boone County farmer, used slaves to sow oats, reap wheat, pick beans, cut cabbages, and cultivate potatoes. So expensive were slaves that when there was not sufficient work on the farms and plantations to occupy them, their owners hired them out to neighbors as "stone masons, bricklayers, waiters, woodchoppers, and salt, brick and shingle makers." Thus, Little Dixie slaves were known as "experienced farm hands" and some were skilled artisans.[24]

Nathaniel Leonard considered slaves so efficient that he told his brother Abiel that he wished "to get along this season without a white man, there are none to be had worth having."[25] Though many Little Dixie farmers had slaves, few had more than twenty, thus achieving the generally acknowl-edged status of "planters." In fact, only about 4 percent of Missouri farm-ers could claim this label. From 1830 to 1860, however, the number of planters in the area swelled from 26 to 215.[26] By the time the Civil War broke out, Cynthia B. Smith was the largest slave owner in Little Dixie, with 106 slaves—a moderate holding by Deep South standards. Slave owners in Missouri owned an average of 6.1 to 12 slaves in the Deep South.

Notwithstanding their smaller population in Missouri, the use of slaves was quite profitable in Little Dixie. In 1850, William D. Swinney of Howard County used fifty-nine slaves to produce 4,000 bushels of corn, 400 bushels of oats, and 13,000 pounds of tobacco. Swinney also used slaves to operate a tobacco manufactory that processed 2.7 million pounds of usable tobac-co worth $120,000. Ten years later, Swinney produced $150,000 of usable tobacco at a labor cost of $1,500 per month per male slave and $300 per month for his female slaves and *some white female employees*. As is evident, slav-ery was big business and an economic institution using an efficient labor system. According to historian R. Douglas Hurt, slavery "spurred not spurned the development of a capitalist economy," and Little Dixie farmers "operated on a scale of technological investment and sophistication com-parable to many commercial farmers in the North."[27]

Farmers and planters considered slaves as a capital investment, and for that reason, some, perhaps many, treated them dispassionately. But it was not unusual for slave owners to treat slaves on a more individual basis. Walter Lenoir thought of selling his slaves in May 1835 but decided not to, as he put it, because "they have conducted themselves well, and have left their connections under the expectations of remaining with me, therefore [I] feel disposed to do by them as I would have them do by me if I was in their stead."[28] Another slave owner, Leland Wright of Howard Country spoke with Abiel Leonard about one of his slaves, Flem, who wanted to marry one of Leonard's slaves: "I am much pleased with him. I expect him to remain in my family as long as he lives."[29] It was not uncommon for slave owners to bury their slaves in their own family plots, and in spite of their patronizing and paternal attitude toward their slaves, there was a genuine affection by many slave owners for their slaves, a fact that has been much distorted and misrepresented in histories.

But the omnipresent threat of slaves being sold down the river to the market in New Orleans was held over the slaves, and some were sold to plantation owners and farmers in the South "as a means of encouraging industry or enforcing discipline." However, J. W. Beatty of Mexico, Missouri, said that there was "a general feeling that the sale of Negroes south was not right." Some slave traders became wealthy and respected men in their communities; others made a scant living. Some slave owners looked down on these traders because of their practices.

Others said the condition of slaves in Missouri was abominable. John

Doy was an underground railroad conductor who came into Kansas with the first settlers and later was convicted of stealing slaves and sentenced to the Missouri Penitentiary. While he was in a Weston jail awaiting removal to the state penitentiary, he said this of his experience of slavery:

> During our imprisonment [in Platte City in the 1850s] numbers of slaves were lodged in the jail by different traders, who were making up gangs to take or send to the south. Every slave when brought in, was ordered to strip naked, and was minutely examined for marks, which with the condition of the teeth and other details, were carefully noted by the trader in his memorandum book. Many facts connected with these examinations were too disgusting to mention.

A gang of men from Lawrence, Kansas, subsequently freed Doy from a St. Joseph jail where he had been moved, and since no extradition could be effected, he continued his work of freeing slaves, breaking the law as he proceeded.[30]

Because slavery was lucrative, the price of slaves skyrocketed over time. In the 1820s, adult slaves brought around $350. But within ten years, a young slave was worth as much as $650 in Little Dixie. Some black women in their mid-thirties brought $750. By 1860 slaves in Little Dixie became even more expensive, bringing prices as high as $1,600 to $2,000 for young male slaves and averaging about $1,300 per slave (probably over $25,000 and $20,000 each, respectively, in today's money, adjusted for inflation). In today's economic terms, a Missouri planter might own over $1,000,000 in slave property.[31] Buying slaves was a big investment, and farming with them could be big business. The "stealing" of such expensive property necessarily had a stiff punishment. As historian Harrison A. Trexler said, "Anyone stealing slaves, or convicted of enslaving a Negro whom he knew to be free, was to suffer death." Thus it was not wise to trifle with either free blacks or enslaved ones. But the 1850s price of Missouri slaves became half and then, by 1863, one-third of their earlier value as the threat to slave property increased through Jayhawker army operations, Union Missouri militia operations, and underground railroads.

***

Jeopardizing the ownership of slaves in Missouri were the men and women who operated clandestine slave "stealing" operations along the perimeter of Missouri in St. Louis, Illinois, and Iowa. Their aim was to divest slave owners of their valuable property through the means of illegal underground railroads.

When Missouri was constituted a state in 1821, abolitionists of some strain or another dwelled there and propagated their beliefs. But it is estimated that these people were outnumbered from seven to one to as many as ten to one by proslavery adherents in the state.[32] Even at this early time, though, abolitionists were vocal. One group, at Herculaneum in Jefferson County, met on April 22, 1820, and issued strong antislavery resolutions, denouncing slavery as evil and pronouncing it an unsound economic system.[33] In St. Louis, in the same year, Joseph Charles wrote editorials calling for the restriction of slavery.[34] Even earlier, in 1798, a minister, John Clark, from New Design, Illinois, preached to Baptists in Missouri in reference to antislavery leanings.[35]

In 1832, a renowned abolitionist, Theodore Weld, established a national theological seminary at Lane Seminary in Cincinnati, Ohio. Financial backing for the college came from Arthur Tappan, a wealthy New York abolitionist. Soon, an abolitionist society was established at Lane and a "Band of Seventy" formed to crusade for abolitionism in the West.

One of the students at Lane Seminary was Arthur Benton of St. Louis. Benton was chosen in 1834 to be the manager of Missouri for the American Antislavery Society.[36] At about the same time, the famous (at that time infamous) William Lloyd Garrison was dragged through the streets of staid Boston, a rope around his neck, mobbed for his so-called radical (actually somewhat conservative) views concerning abolitionism. In St. Louis, on October 24, 1835, a vigilance committee was formed from each city ward to root out the names of people preaching abolitionism. Obviously, at this time, abolitionism was largely an unpopular ideology in the North and West as well as in the South, where slavery was considered to be morally sustainable.

In 1835, Dr. David Nelson, a minister recently converted by Theodore Weld to abolitionism, moved to Palmyra, Missouri, where he acted as the representative for the Agency Committee of the American Antislavery Society. At Palmyra, Nelson founded the town's first Presbyterian church and aided in the founding of Marion College, becoming its first president. After hearing of Nelson's agitation for the abolition of slavery, a number of people from the East began emigrating to the town and settling there. Most were sympathetic to the prohibition of slavery, but some believed only in "colonization"—the exporting of American slaves to other countries. Nelson's little island of Eastern abolitionists, however, found itself surrounded by a sea of proslavery farmers who were infuriated at the abolitionists' teachings at the college. Within a year, they ran Nelson out of town and across the Mississippi River into Illinois. Meanwhile, they expunged all mention of abolitionism from the Marion curricula.

Soon after Nelson exited Missouri and entered Illinois, an underground railroad, a secret network of people cooperating to aid fugitive slaves in reaching sanctuaries in Free States or Canada, was organized in Illinois, with Nelson—now a professor at Mission Institute near Quincy, Illinois— a central figure.[37] In addition, at Knoxville College at Galesburg, Illinois, George W. Gale and Jonathan Blanchard supported the underground effort into Missouri. Moses Hunter, a professor at Mission Institute, also supported the cause. Meanwhile, other conductors operated at Sparta, Godfrey, Quincy, and Galesburg, Illinois. In Iowa, a considerable underground railroad network was conducted out of Tabor.

The only underground railroad operating in Missouri at this time was a short one from Lancaster, Missouri, into Iowa. But outside the borders of Missouri, in Iowa and Illinois, a vast network of lines proliferated. The underground railroad in Illinois ran through "Alton, Farmington settlement west of Springfield, Woodrow settlement on Sand Prairie, Deacon Street, Washington, Matamora & vicinity Cross Creek so on to Ottoway. . . ."[38] Some of the evidence concerning the Illinois lines is sketchy because those who operated them were performing felonious acts that they considered best left unchronicled.[39] Nonetheless, a considerable amount of information of a general nature is known about the various lines.

It is recorded that around 1840, the abolitionist group led by Dr. David Nelson was active in aiding the escape of a number of slaves from the Missouri area directly west of Quincy, Illinois. Nelson placed his students from Mission Institute on patrol along the Mississippi River to guide escaped slaves to a "red barn" east of Quincy, where they would be kept before moving them across and out of the state.[40]

In July 1841, three abolitionists, George Thompson, James Burr, and Alonson Work, from Nelson's Mission Institute, went into Marion County, Missouri, to entice slaves to leave their owners. While the three men were waiting to take them into Illinois, the slaves reported the incident to their owners, and the men were arrested and sentenced to twelve years in the Missouri Penitentiary for "Grand Larceny (Abolition)." They served five years of their sentences.[41] On August 21, 1842, a slave belonging to Chauncey Durkee of Monticello, Missouri, was taken into custody in Quincy, Illinois. Aided by abolitionists, he escaped in a buggy driven by an abolitionist doctor, Richard Eells, a prominent Quincy physician. Eells was later found guilty of "harboring and secreting a slave."[42] In the winter of 1843, in response to these abolitionist actions, a party of Marion County men crossed the ice on the Mississippi River and burned Mission Institute.

In 1845, an Illinois statute providing severe penalties for anyone sheltering runaway slaves was enforced, but the traffic continued, though somewhat abated.[43] Soon, it became apparent to Missouri slave owners that if they did not overtake their property in Missouri, then it was virtually impossible to pursue it into Illinois.[44] The underground network seems to have been organized and run by the elite class in the vicinities where it was prevalent, and the political clout wielded by the people responsible for slaves' escape made the pursuit of slaves that much more difficult.

The underground railroad in Iowa ran as efficiently as the one in Illinois. The underground railroad in Iowa entered the state near Tabor, passed through Lewis, Des Moines, Grinnell, Iowa City, West Liberty,

Tipton, De Witt, and Low Moor, crossing over the Mississippi at Clinton, Iowa, to connect with the Illinois route.[45]

In 1848, when nine slaves belonging to Ruell Daggs of Clark County fled into Iowa, they were apprehended in the town of Salem. However, during a trial before Quaker justice Nelson Gibbs to determine their fate, the fugitives were aided in an escape. A Missouri force soon entered Iowa to punish those responsible. Known for their abolitionist sentiments, a large Quaker group from Denmark, Iowa, met them and drove the Missourians out of the state.

Missouri continued its attempts to staunch the flow of escaped slaves. By 1852, the state of Missouri had placed seven people in the penitentiary for enticing slaves from their owners. By 1853, however, eleven slaves left Palmyra for Illinois, likely aided by abolitionists. Thomas Anderson of Marion County claimed that abolitionists had carried off "eight or ten thousand dollars worth [of slaves] at a time," which amounts to around $150,000 in today's currency.[46]

Once the Border War began, Missouri slaves crossed into Iowa through Harrison County and on to stations at Croton, Bloomfield, Lancaster, and Cincinnati, Iowa.[47] When John Brown made an armed raid into Missouri in 1858 to obtain eleven slaves, he used the underground railroad through Iowa to escape with them. Later, Gerrit Smith of Peterboro, New York, wrote to his friend F. B. Sanborn complaining about the "unfavorable topography" of Missouri for such excursions.[48] Smith and Sanborn, members of the "Conspiracy of Six," financed John Brown's violent exploits in Missouri before the Civil War. Some Southerners alleged at Brown's trial that these (then-unknown) men also knowingly financed Brown's treasonous assault at Harpers Ferry. Some claim John Brown escorted as many as sixty-eight slaves to Canada.[49]

As time passed, abolitionists became prominent in St. Louis: B. Gratz Brown; John How; the Blair brothers, Montgomery and Frank; and the Filleys. These men, once the nation was poised on the threshold of civil war, were the men who gave the country its final shove in that violent direction. By 1854, abolitionists in eastern Missouri, Iowa, and Illinois were operating underground railroads that eliminated a substantial part of Missouri's economy.

Meanwhile, the New England Emigrant Aid Company entered the region, sending a steady stream of emigrants to Kansas Territory. Through its propaganda efforts, the Emigrant Aid Company would elicit emigrants to Kansas from Eastern areas where abolitionist sentiment was strong. With these emigrants were men prepared to install their own underground railroads on Missouri's western border. Already surrounded on two sides by active abolitionist states, the threat of abolitionist settlers in Kansas raised the specter that Missouri was becoming a "peninsula of slavery jutting out into a sea of freedom."[50]

Chapter 3

Confrontation in Kansas

Missourians had been eyeing the territory to their west as early as the late 1840s, partly stimulated by their interest in a continental railroad that might pass through that country but also because of the fertile ground found there, especially in the eastern regions. Another interest among the influential class of Missourians was ensuring that the territory became proslavery in orientation, thus securing what would have become a vulnerable border and preventing the depletion of their slave holdings through underground railroads like those in Iowa and Illinois. The people of Missouri, in the spirit of the Compromise of 1850, believed that the settlers themselves should settle the slavery issue and that a settlement should not be imposed on them. But they naturally expected the settlement of Kansas to follow the historical trend and attract migration from the upper South—composed of their cultural brethren—an eventuality that was assumed to be a fait accompli.[1]

To the delight of Missourians, on January 23, 1854, Sen. Stephen Douglas submitted the Kansas-Nebraska bill to Congress. The bill stated, "The questions pertaining to slavery in the territories, and in the new states to be formed therefrom, are to be left to the decision of the people residing therein, through their representatives." Local tribunals would resolve any "questions of personal freedom" or "cases involving title to slaves." Problems relating to fugitive slaves would be "in accordance with the Constitution and the laws of the United States." Of the Missouri representatives in Congress, only Thomas Hart Benton opposed the bill. Senator Atchison, as mentioned earlier, was instrumental in passing the bill through the Senate on May 30, 1854.[2]

Earlier, on March 11, 1854, while the bill was still being debated, abolitionist Eli Thayer arranged a public meeting in Worcester, Massachusetts, and proposed that "free men" fill up Kansas. Thayer proposed the charter for the Massachusetts Emigrant Aid Company (soon, the New England Emigrant Aid Company) and presented it to the Massachusetts legislature. It passed and a capital of five million dollars was authorized the company. The intention of the company was "to plant a free state in Kansas." There had been no equivocation; the gauntlet was tossed to the South and its friends. This unilateral act by a group of New England activists changed the rules of the game profoundly and permanently. Regional settlement patterns that had gradually (and peacefully) evolved to maintain an uneasy status quo between slave states and "free" states were destroyed virtually overnight. The gradual, peaceful evolution had suddenly been turned into an increasingly violent race.

The plan was to transport twenty thousand persons from Massachusetts and forty thousand foreign emigrants to Kansas each year. Thayer was actively involved in the development of the emigrant companies. As agent for the Emigrant Aid Company stock, he was to receive 10 percent of the receipts. Aside from his ideological leanings, his expected remuneration from the scheme made it little wonder that he was a persuasive advocate. Thayer, president of the New England Company, was also president of emigrant aid companies from New York and Connecticut. Other emigrant companies, encouraged by the New England Company, also formed with the same purpose.[3]

At the passage of the Kansas-Nebraska Act, some fourteen hundred whites already peopled Kansas Territory, half of whom were associated with the territory's military establishments. The other residents were associated with the missions and trading posts and mostly served the Native American population. Some of these people had held slaves for over twenty years in the territory.

Settlers, according to the preemption laws assigned to Kansas Territory, were required to build a cabin and reside in that location for a specific period of time in order to gain title to their claims. These laws would become central to many of the disputes over land that soon commenced. Many Missourians had gone to the new territory, where they founded the towns of Leavenworth, Kickapoo, Atchison, and Lecompton, all but the last along the Missouri River. When Missourians learned of the planned "invasion" by the New England Company, they were outraged. They considered Nebraska a territory suitable for Northern emigrants, but they believed Kansas was the appropriate destination for migrating Southerners. The New Englanders' plot incensed and frightened them, convincing even apolitical Missourians that something must be done. On June 27, 1854, in a meeting in Independence, Missourians had naively expressed the notion "that we, the South be permitted peaceably to possess Kansas, while the North, on same privilege, be permitted to possess Nebraska Territory." The organized emigration by the Northerners (Southerners would call it an "artificially forced" emigration), with its "capital stock, lands, mills, hotels, newspapers, towns, and subsidized settlers" astonished them and fell outside their notion of the concept of popular sovereignty.[4]

Upon learning of the New England Company's intentions, the Missourians began forming "protective societies," organizations that would protect Missouri settlers' claims. One such protective association was the Platte County Self-Defense Association, whose constitution was signed by between five hundred to one thousand Missouri members. The association's professed purpose was to protect its members from fraud in the territory and to turn away Northern settlers. The fear was that "if Kansas should become a 'hotbed of Abolitionism,' then Missouri would be surrounded on three sides by free-soil country; in this case, it required no prophet to see what would become of the Missourians' manpower."[5] Based upon their experiences with the active underground railroads in Iowa and Illinois, it was abundantly clear that an "abolitionist" Kansas would eventually seal the fate of legal slavery in Missouri. Soon, secret lodges such as the Sons of the South, Blue Lodges, Social Bands, and Friends of Society supplanted the Platte County association. As many as ten thousand Missourians were enlisted in these lodges. Some Missourians became even more militant about antislavery developments. The *Liberty (Mo.) Platform* exploded, "Shall we allow such cut-throats and murderers as the people of Massachusetts are, to settle in the territory adjoining our own state? No! If popular opinion will not keep them back, we should see what virtue there is in the force of arms." This was what New Englanders in Kansas often referred to as Missouri "bluster," but there was always some steel behind it.[6]

Meanwhile, in June 1854, the trustees of the Massachusetts Emigrant Aid Company—Eli Thayer, Amos A. Lawrence, and J. M. S. Williams— sent for Dr. Charles Robinson, recently returned to the East from the Squatter Rebellion around Sacramento, California. He had been one of the principal leaders of the rebellion and his character had been tempered in the violence and blood of confrontation. Arrangements were made to send Robinson to the territory with an eye to choosing a good settlement site. A young lawyer, Charles H. Branscomb, another company agent, was assigned to meet Robinson at Springfield, Illinois, and accompany him to Kansas.

Robinson left Massachusetts and traveled through Chicago to St. Louis. There, he purchased a steamboat passage to Westport Landing, present-day Kansas City, Missouri. On arriving at Westport Landing, Robinson and Branscomb stayed at the Gillis House hotel, managed by a man named Gaius Jenkins. (The unfortunate Jenkins later became known in Kansas history for being murdered by Gen. James Henry Lane over the use of a contested well). Branscomb subsequently traveled west, up the Kaw River (called the Kansas River today), toward Fort Riley, looking for a settlement site. Robinson, meanwhile, traveled north of Kansas City, on the Missouri River, toward Fort Leavenworth, with the same thought in mind. Soon, Robinson was ordered to return to Boston to escort the second party of settlers to Kansas. The first party of twenty-nine settlers was already on its way and would be met by Branscomb, one

Colonel Blood, and other sympathizers at Kansas City. The first party was composed of such notables as Daniel R. Anthony, Samuel F. Tappan, A. H. Mallory, Dr. Harrington, and others.[7]

On July 31, 1854, the Massachusetts settlers left Westport Landing for Kansas along the Santa Fé Trail. That night, they camped at the Blue Jacket Crossing of the Wakarusa River, less than fifteen miles from Lawrence. The next morning, August 1, the settlers crossed Blanton's Ford and strode to the top of a high, barren hill, soon to be called Mount

Charles Robinson, a tough, shrewd politician and leader of the more moderate Kansans. He would later become governor of Kansas. *The Kansas State Historical Society, Topeka*

Oread (the present site of the University of Kansas, the site of which is named after Eli Thayer's "castle" in Massachusetts).

Six weeks later, the second party of 130 (some sources say 114) settlers, led by Robinson and Samuel Pomeroy, traveled to the same site and found the first party camped in tents. On October 8, a third party arrived with 162 settlers; a fourth, on October 30, with 230; a fifth party, on November 20, with 100; and a sixth and last party for the year, on December 1, 1854, with but 50 settlers. When Robinson arrived at Mount Oread, the first New England party already had staked out claims in the vicinity.

Soon, a deputation of settlers led by Robinson ventured down to the Kaw River. Robinson decided to pitch a tent on the site, claiming it for the New England Company. Of course, settlers from Missouri already had staked out some of the same land, but this carried no great sway at the time, and Robinson simply ignored the earlier claims. Robinson formed a town association, and after mulling over the names Wakarusa, New Boston, and Yankee Town, fixed on the name Lawrence for the village, after Amos A. Lawrence, the company's treasurer and benefactor. Robinson and some two hundred of the settlers who came with him in the second group camped on the Lawrence site and began building rough shelters, euphemistically referred to as "buildings." They were little more than lean-tos, but anything suggesting tenancy was sought. Even later in 1854, the town of Lawrence consisted of "only a few log buildings, some tents, and several sod-walled structures with hay roofs." Robinson discovered such future notables as S. N. "Sam" Wood, A. Wakefield, and the Reverend Mr. Ferrill already settled in the area, and they soon became allies with him against the Missourians, who teemed in the area and crowded the Free State site. Soon, Missourians tried to intimidate Robinson's group into leaving the town site. Robinson's violent experiences in Sacramento amply prepared him for this eventuality.[8]

Robinson complained later that the Missourians "on or before the passage of the [Kansas-Nebraska] bill rushed into the new territory and marked trees, drove stakes in every direction. No claim could be taken by a Free-State man to whom a pro-slavery man could not be found to assert a prior claim." But the crafty Robinson knew from his Sacramento experience the dynamics of such situations. He said, "no higher authority than physical force or bluster" settled most claim disputes. Resorts to the law were usually too onerous or time-consuming to be useful or effective. One Missourian, John Baldwin, however, dogged the new settlers, claiming 160 acres of land, which fell almost entirely within the perimeters claimed by Robinson and the New England Company. Baldwin, to Robinson's anger and irritation, went beyond "bluster" and hired Babcock, Stone, and Freeman to act as his attorneys to uproot the now well-entrenched New Englanders.[9]

Robinson ignored Baldwin and platted the town of Lawrence with a size of 2.5 miles by 1.5 miles. He disregarded the preemption laws, which stated that only 320 acres could be laid out for town use. Robinson circumvented this law by designating assigned settlers to stake claims to the needed extra acreage. This land would be used for the town once the time was ripe. Robinson's town covered some 2,400 acres, seven times the legally allotted acreage. He freely admitted this deception; in his view and that of most of the other emigrants, the land was, as the expression goes, "up for grabs." Soon, a group of tents sprouted, to be followed by grass-thatched huts, and "rude, squat, mud-plastered log-cabins."[10]

Baldwin, undeterred, laid out a rival city named Excelsior. On October 5, 1854, armed men approached the New England tents with the idea of ejecting certain people and goods from a specified tent and land site. Baldwin's sister and some of his men took down the tent and loaded the belongings within into a wagon brought along for that purpose. When the New Englanders got wind of what was happening, they descended on the site in numbers. One of the men, Edwin Bond, arrived with a revolver. Bond told some of the other settlers to put the tent up again and restore the owners' belongings. Meanwhile, he warily eyed Baldwin's men. That night, the Free Staters organized a "Regulatory Band" for the following day's expected confrontation. At 4:00 P.M. the next day, Baldwin's group sent the following message:

> Kansas Territory, October 6th
> Dr. Robinson—Yourself and friends are hereby notified that you will have one-half hour to move your tent which you have on my undisputed claim, and from this date desist from surveying on said claim. If the tent is not moved within one-half hour, we shall take the trouble to move the same. (Signed,)
> JOHN BALDWIN AND FRIENDS.

Robinson, not at all perturbed or unnerved, replied in another message:

> To John Baldwin and Friends.
> If you molest our property, you do it at your peril.
> C. ROBINSON AND FRIENDS.

E. D. Ladd, in a letter dated October 23, 1854, relates the rest of the confrontation:

> Prior to the notice, they had assembled to the number of eighteen mounted and armed [men], at Baldwin's, the aggrieved man's tent, on the claim, and about twenty rods from our camp. Upon the notice being served, our men—those who were at work about and in the vicinity of

the camp—to the number of about thirty, stationed themselves about ten rods from the contested tent, the enemy being about the same distance from it, the three occupying the angles of a right-angled triangle, the tent being at the right angle. Subsequent to the notice, a consultation was held at our position between Dr. Robinson and a delegate from the enemy's post, which ended on our part with the proposition of Dr. Robinson—which proposition he had previously made, both he Baldwin and his legal adviser, or rather speculator, who wished to make a 'heap of money' as the Missourians say, out of him—to submit the question in dispute to the arbitration of disinterested and unbiased men, to the adjudication of the squatter courts now existing here, or of the United States courts, and on the part of the enemy by the assurance that, at the termination of the notice, they should proceed at all hazards to remove the tent, and if they fell in the attempt, our fate would be sealed, our extermination certain, for three thousand, and if necessary thirty thousand men, would immediately be raised in Missouri to sweep us and our enterprise from the face of the earth.[11]

Finally, Robinson ordered his men to fall into formation, during which they did awkward, but apparently impressive, armed, military drills to intimidate the Missourians. In addition, the Kansans outnumbered the Missourians nearly two to one. The Missourians, nonetheless, remained fast for a while. As some of the Free Staters did their drill, one of Robinson's men, John Hutchison, asked Robinson if Baldwin and his men should remove the tent, should he, Hutchinson, "fire to hit them, or would he fire over their heads." Robinson replied that he would be "ashamed to fire at a man and not hit him." About this time, one of Baldwin's men, a spy, left the Free State camp at a run, and soon Baldwin's men dispersed. Robinson believed it was because of what the spy had heard.[12]

The issue between the two parties went unresolved for months. However, in February 1855, while Robinson was conducting the spring party of settlers to Lawrence from the East (they would arrive in Kansas in March of that year), the matter was solved. Robinson said that the "financial agent of the Aid Company," apparently a reference to Pomeroy, settled the dispute with Baldwin over the land. Robinson later added cuttingly, "Why it [the settlement] was made has never appeared." Obviously, Pomeroy felt Baldwin had enough of a legal case to require a compromise to be made—something Robinson seemed incapable of conceiving or, at least, was determined not to admit. Robinson continued to consider Baldwin and his "friends" to be "town jumpers" and "spoilsmen," an assessment apparently not shared by Pomeroy. Robinson was always peeved by Pomeroy's ascendancy in the eyes of the Emigrant Aid Company, and this feeling may have caused him to berate

Pomeroy's performance in this instance. Robinson said that after this misstep by Pomeroy, the concessions made by him to Baldwin brought "virtually to an end stock subscriptions in the company as an investment, and [an] end to all college building in Lawrence. But few shares of stock were afterwards subscribed, and money had to be raised in the contribution plan." All of this seems fashioned to enhance Robinson's image and make Pomeroy appear inadequate. The New England Company, however, failed to fault Pomeroy over this issue and steadfastly supported him. Indeed, Pomeroy had cleared up a nasty situation that might have redounded against the company when the courts finally took up the case.[13]

Robinson, nonetheless, continued to rail against Pomeroy's actions, saying that the concession of the company to Baldwin did not end the protests and counterclaims made against the company until government officials settled the various suits. Why Robinson expected New England Company claims to be more inviolable than other claims in the area remains unclear. And it is not clear whether Missourians, proslavery Missourians, or some of the new settlers in his own camp made these "protests" and "counterclaims." One of the complaints was that "half of the land composing the city site of Lawrence was owned by five men," which crowded others out of land ownership in the town.[14]

On June 29, 1854, the federal government began to assert its political presence in the territorial dissension. Commissions were assigned to the chief officers of Kansas Territory. Pres. Franklin Pierce appointed Andrew H. Reeder of Pennsylvania to be governor of the territory. On July 7, 1854, Reeder, a man of medium stature with sideburns à la Napoleon and deliberate in walk and talk, took the oath of office. It was assumed at his appointment that he would proceed to Kansas and organize the state with the help of the newly commissioned territorial officers. These men included Daniel Woodson, secretary; Madison Brown, chief justice; Rush Elmore, associate justice; Andrew Jackson Issacks, U.S. attorney for the District of Kansas; and Israel B. Donalson, U.S. marshal of the territory. Donalson, a citizen of Illinois, will figure prominently in the history that follows.[15]

The new governor, however, was to enter the Kansas fray in disarray. With the situation in the territory highly volatile at his accession to the governorship, it would have been prudent for him to arrive in the territory quickly. But Reeder took almost three months to arrive. His tardiness, according to Reeder, was prompted by his need to close an extensive law practice covering six counties in Pennsylvania. As it turned out, he did not reach the territory on the steamboat *Polar Star* until October 7, 1854. On October 17, he set out on an extensive tour of the territory to review conditions, determine places where elections might be held, learn names of suitable people to appoint as election officers, and discover persons to take the various censuses. But the censuses were not taken before the election as ordered by the president of the United States. Again, Reeder excused his actions:

> I deemed it best to order an election for a delegate to Congress as early as possible, and to postpone taking of the census till after that election. I was more convinced of the propriety of this course, by the fact that the common law and many of the United States statutes were in force over the Territory, and could well be administered through the courts established by Congress, and the justices and constables whom I was authorized to appoint; and by the additional fact that whilst the citizens of Missouri were vehemently urging an immediate election of the legislature, the citizens of the Territory were generally of the opinion that no immediate necessity for it existed.[16]

One might question which "citizens of the territory" Reeder was polling when he learned that "no immediate necessity" for an election existed. And upon the president's order to conduct a census before the election, on what basis did Reeder decide his legal understanding canceled out the president's? Upon Reeder's later removal from office, Pres. Franklin Pierce described the seriousness of Reeder's slow ascendancy to the governorship:

> The governor of the territory of Kansas, commissioned as before stated on the 29th of June, 1854, did not reach the designated seat of his government until the 7th of October, and even then failed to make the first step in its legal organization, that of ordering the census or enumerations of its inhabitants, until so late a day that the election of the members of the legislative assembly did not take place until the 30th of March, 1855, nor its meeting until the 2nd of July, 1855. So that for a year after the Territory was constituted by the act of Congress . . . it was without a complete government, without any legislative authority, without local law, and, of course, without the ordinary guaranties of peace and public order.[17]

Most of the altercations so far mentioned between the Missourians and the Free Staters occurred before the governor of the territory had arrived. Reeder was on the scene, however, on November 29, 1854, when an election for a territorial delegate to the U.S. Congress was held. Entered in the race were J. W. Whitfield, the proslavery candidate from Tennessee; Robert P. Flenneken, the Democratic candidate; and Judge John A. Wakefield, "a freesoiler up to the hub—hub and all," some said.[18] Whitfield won the election, but blatant voting irregularities occurred; large numbers of proslavery Missourians, fearful of the burgeoning Northern influence, crossed the border into Kansas and "stuffed" the ballot boxes. The Northern press quickly dubbed them "Border Ruffians" and described them as swaggering drunkenly around Kansas with Bowie knives hanging from their waists. The propaganda war had begun.

Contrary to the usual impressions left by historians, these proslavery units were composed mostly of people generally more affluent and prominent than average Missourians; that is, many of them were members of the

Benjamin Stringfellow, one-time Missouri attorney general and mentor to Missourians in the border disputes. *The Kansas State Historical Society, Topeka*

affluent, slave-owning families of Missouri. They were led by the politically active elites of Missouri, men like Claiborne Jackson and Col. Samuel Young of Boone County, and mentored by the likes of Jackson, Sen. David Rice Atchison, and former Missouri attorney general Benjamin F. Stringfellow. The term "Border Ruffians" was a loaded term, is a loaded term, used then and now for propaganda purposes. These maligned men certainly had no monopoly over Kansans when it came to wearing Bowie knives and acting pugnaciously. And, it should be emphasized, in all particulars when determining the truth about Border War history, as historian Theodore Andreas admitted, there became "the manufacture of slavery and anti-slavery versions of every disorder that occurred."

It was Horace Greeley, that master propagandist of the *New York Tribune,* who coined the term "Border Ruffian." Historian Lloyd Lewis said the term was "diabolically clever. When a free soil settler was killed in a fight for a water hole—a not uncommon custom on the plains—Greeley trumpeted the affair as another murder perpetrated by that fiend, Slavery. If the free-soiler killed the other man, Greeley rejoiced that another embattled farmer had shot a Hessian." Lewis noted also that the same ballot-box stuffing had been committed in the new territory of Nebraska, but somehow that was viewed differently by the popular press:

> Iowans had already gone across the line into the new territorial lands of Nebraska to elect officials and representatives who would make sure the new land was friendly to Iowa. They wanted to control railroad legislation—that was their reason for stuffing the ballot-box. In what is known as the Sarpy Election, Iowa invaded Nebraska as Missourians were to invade Kansas in 1855, but there is a difference in propaganda scales as to whether a fraud is committed in behalf of property like railroads or property like human slaves. Nobody back East made much of the Sarpy invasion, but Missouri's invasion was a hot, black scandal indeed.

The *Kansas Free State* at Lawrence admitted that "A great many of them [the so-called Border Ruffians] to our surprise were as fine a looking class of Missourians as we have ever seen. Considering the large crowd, and the fact that there was a good deal of liquor among them, they behaved exceedingly well. This was all owing to their being well disciplined, and under the command of good leaders." The more frequent description of Missourians by the Kansas and Eastern press and Kansas notables of the period, however, is characterized by such phrases as, for example, Governor Robinson's wife's reference to them as "de po' white folk" and "drunken rabble." Such examples demonstrate the arrogance and insolence exhibited by Easterners toward people from Missouri, specifically, and Southerners, in general. The Missourians were in every way at least

equal to Kansans in culture and superior in affluence. The Missouri voting men were also "well equipped with good teams, wagons and plenty of
provisions." Many had white ribbons in their buttonholes to signal their
political affiliation.

In relation to the election, a Congressional committee investigating the
situation concluded:

> Before any election was or could be held in the Territory, a secret polit-
> ical society was formed in the State of Missouri. . . . Its members were
> bound together by secret oaths, and they had pass-words, signs, and
> grips, by which they were known to each other; penalties were imposed
> [for] violating the rules and secrets of the order; . . . and the different
> lodges were connected by an effective organization. It embraced great
> numbers of the citizens of Missouri, and was extended into other slave
> States and into the Territory. Its avowed purpose was to extend slavery
> not only into Kansas, but also into other Territories of the United States
> . . . its plan of organization was to organize and send men to vote at the
> elections in the Territory, to collect money to pay their expenses, and, if
> necessary to protect them in voting. It also proposed to induct pro-slav-
> ery men to emigrate into the Territory to aid and sustain them while
> there, and to elect no one to office but those friendly to their views.[19]

Aside from the invasion of Kansas to stuff the ballot boxes, much of
the other descriptions—"secret organizations," the extension of an ideology to the new territory, and the exhortation of people to emigrate to
the territory so that their views would be sustained—fit the abolitionists'
intentions as well as that of the proslavery adherents.

Robinson correctly identified David Rice Atchison as one of the
sources of influence that caused the incursions across the border, citing an
article from the *Platte Argus*:

> General Atchison said, that his mission here to-day was, if possible, to
> awaken the people of this country to the danger ahead, and to suggest
> the means to avoid it. The people of Kansas in their first election
> would decide the question whether or not the slave-holder was to be
> excluded, and it depended upon a majority of the votes cast at the
> polls. Now, if a set of fanatics and demagogues a thousand miles off
> could advance their money and exert every nerve to abolitionize the
> Territory and exclude the slaveholder when they have not the least
> personal interest in the matter, what is your duty? When you reside
> within one day's journey of the Territory, and when your peace, your
> quiet, and your property depend upon your actions, you can without
> an exertion send five hundred of your young men who will vote in
> favor of your institutions. Should each county in the State of Missouri

only do its duty, the question will be decided quietly and peaceably at the ballot-box. If we are defeated then Missouri and the other Southern States will have shown themselves recreant to their interest and will have deserved their fate.[20]

Exacerbating the situation was the lack of clarity of the act of Congress that determined who might vote. As historian Russell K. Hickman has noted, "The act of Congress appeared to make almost any 'actual resident' a legal voter." Reeder attempted to strengthen the definition to include those "actually dwelling or inhabiting in the Territory, to the exclusion of any other present domicile or home, coupled with the present *bona fide* intention of permanently residing for the same purpose." How many Missourians, or Kansans, for that matter, attended to Reeder's various pronouncements is unknown.[21] In addition, many Missourians saw no difference in their going to polls, voting in Kansas, and returning to Missouri and New Englanders settling for a time in the territory, voting, then going back to New England, a process that happened frequently.

The outcome of the first territorial election was Whitfield, 2,238; Wakefield, 248; and Flenneken, 305. Charles Robinson judged that of the votes perhaps 1,114 were legal, 1,729 illegal. The majority of the Congressional committee investigating the election concluded:

> Under these circumstances, a systematic invasion from an adjoining State, by which large numbers of illegal votes were cast in remote and sparse settlements, for the avowed purpose of extending slavery into the Territory, even though it did not change the result of the election, was a crime of great magnitude. Its immediate effect was further to excite the people of the Northern States, and to exasperate the actual settlers against their neighbors in Missouri.[22]

Charles Robinson also agreed that the voter incursion from Missouri had no influence on the outcome of the election. He said,

> At this time every considerable settlement in the Territory, except Lawrence and vicinity, was pro-slavery, and an invasion was wholly unnecessary, as Whitfield could have been elected without it. Being unnecessary, it was an inexcusable blunder, as it served to expose the game the pro-slavery men proposed to play and increased the agitation and determination of the North.[23]

Once the votes were in declaring Whitfield the winner, Robinson and the New Englanders lodged a protest:

> To his Excellency, A. H. Reeder, Governor of Kansas Territory:

Believing that a large number of the citizens of the State of Missouri voted at the election of the 29th instant for delegate to Congress representing Kansas Territory, we respectfully petition your honor that the entire vote of the district receiving the votes of citizens of Missouri be set aside, or that the entire election by set aside.

SIGNED NUMEROUS CITIZENS.[24]

Despite his misgivings about the election, Reeder took the pragmatic approach and declared Whitfield the winner. Robinson and the Free Staters were disappointed, but not for long; Reeder soon gravitated toward their political camp.

As it turned out, Atchison and his followers in Missouri committed a grave error in crossing the territorial border to upset the ordinary flow of a territorial election. Atchison spoke of young men "voting for their institutions." Others construed what happened during the territorial election in Kansas as an example of simple ballot-box stuffing, an especially benighted practice in that the proslavery forces in Kansas had all the votes they needed at the time, without the Missouri voter invasion. Ultimately, the ballot-box stuffing lent itself to exploitation by the abolitionist press in the East and in Kansas. It also alienated some of Missouri's friends in Congress and gave the moral high ground to the abolitionists, of which they quickly made ample use. And this first of several episodes of Missourians meddling with the territorial vote in Kansas ended by destroying much of Atchison's reputation. Atchison, through his actions and that of his confederates, allowed the abolitionists to gain the moral ascendancy when they deserved it least. Had it not been for the bad press of the Missourians, deserved because of their flagrant interference in the voting in Kansas Territory as well as their institution of "Black Laws" (i.e., repressive slave laws), it might have gone far worse for Robinson and the abolitionists when they became engaged in a rebellion against the United States government in Kansas.

Barely a month after the election for a delegate to Congress, Reeder now initiated the belated census, ordering it effected in January and February 1855. An election for a territorial legislature was to follow on March 30, 1855. Now, the fire-eating presses on both sides of the Missouri-Kansas border began to froth out purple copy. The *Frontier News* of Westport, Missouri, railed:

The real battle, the decisive conflict, has yet to be fought and think you, Southerners, if we lose it that the South can ever again obtain a foothold in the Territory? Vain thought! The code of Lawrence, digested by Messrs. Robinson, Thayer and Company, and enforced by abolition tyrants, will be the code of Kansas; and the chivalric South must bow beneath the yoke. How galling, how degrading to a sense of your manhood! Are you men? Then gird up your loins, be up and doing; remember, that which has been done once [apparently, stuffing the ballot boxes] can be done again.[25]

When the election for a territorial legislature took place, it was a replay on a larger scale of the earlier election for a territorial delegate to Congress. A majority report from the Congressional committee that investigated the election described it thusly:

> By an organized movement, which extended from Andrew Country in the north, to Jasper Country in the south, and as far eastward as Boone and Cole counties, Missouri, companies of men were arranged in irregular parties, and sent into every council district in the Territory and into every representative district but one. The members were so distributed as to control the election in each district. They went to vote, and with the avowed design to make Kansas a slave State. They were generally armed and equipped, carried with them their own provisions and tents, and so marched into the Territory. . . . They brought with them two pieces of artillery, loaded with musket balls. . . . The Missourians sometimes came up to the polls in procession, two by two, and voted. During the day the Missourians drove off the ground some of the citizens—Mr. Stearns, Mr. Bond, and Mr. Willis. They threatened to shoot Mr. Bond, and a crowd rushed after him, threatening him; and as he ran after them some shots were fired at him as he jumped off the bank of the river and made his escape. The citizens of the town went over in a body late in the afternoon, when the polls had become comparatively clear, and voted.[26]

Again, the Free Staters demanded of Governor Reeder that the election be overturned and a day set for a new election. Reeder's reply was a request to Samuel Pomeroy, principal agent for the New England Company, to have "some friends [abolitionists] near when he [Reeder] should declare the result of the election." According to Robinson, some twelve men from Lawrence quickly volunteered for the task, "ready to die with him [Reeder] if necessary while [the governor was] in the discharge of his official duty." To the Free Staters' surprise, Reeder issued certificates of election to a large majority of the proslavery candidates. Only one Free Stater, Martin Conway, was declared a winner. Soon, a proslavery territorial government was installed at Lecompton, about ten miles west of Lawrence.[27]

By midsummer, Reeder was removed from the governorship by President Pierce for improper land speculation. The governor, evidently, had purchased territorial lots in "Leavenworth, Lawrence, Topeka, Pawnee, and many other 'paper' cities" and had bought them "at cheaper rates than possible except in consideration of his official position." He also illegally speculated in Indian lands (called "half-breed lands"). Reeder promptly went over to the Free State cause. The reason for Reeder's certification of proslavery candidates is likely that he felt the proslavery party in Kansas still had the most support at that time.

Meanwhile, due to all of this turmoil, most Southerners had written off Kansas as of any interest to slave owners. Who could trust the safety of his slaves in this turbulent environment? In contrast, fired up by abolitionist propaganda in the Northern press, settlers continued to flock into the area from the East, mostly from the Middle Atlantic states. However, most had not been able to safeguard claims to property because of the turmoil. Already established settlers like young Edward Fitch were not too secure with what little property they held. In a letter to his mother on July 30, 1855, Fitch said, "I have not dared to go to my claim for a week for I have a bitter enemy in a Pro-Slavery man for my next neighbor. I am going out tomorrow but shall not dare to stay at my cabin without a rifle or gun at my bedside." Likely, Fitch's neighbor felt no more at ease than did Fitch.

A proslavery settler, A. J. Houle, described his thoughts along similar lines:

> These are exciting times here. You may form some idea of them when I tell you that I never lie down without taking the precaution to fasten my door, and fix it in such a way that if it is forced open, it can be opened only wide enough for one person to come in at a time. I have my rifle, revolver, and old home-stocked pistol where I can lay my hand on them in an instant, besides a hatchet & axe. I take this precaution to guard against the midnight attacks of the Abolitionists, who never make an attack in open daylight and no Proslavery man knows when he is safe here in the Terr. Some of them go so far as to guard out every night.

During this uneasy time, Charles Robinson and the New England Emigrant Aid Company calculated a new strategy. Robinson said, "But as Congress had uniformly failed to accomplish anything for freedom for a generation, hope in that direction was vain. . . . But if the conflict was to be settled in Kansas, what steps were to be taken? The first was to be repudiation of the fraud. Should this be attempted, a case must be made out satisfactory to the civilized world, or the repudiators would be repudiated."[28]

Robinson appears to be implying that the federal government could not be trusted, so the people within the state of Kansas had to decide the issue. A significant irony exists in this pronouncement. The very people least disposed to consider the justice of those invoking states' rights when it referred to the South—that is, the Free Staters and abolitionists—were now proposing to act out its tenets when the object at hand was the control of Kansas! On the other hand, the Missourians, staunch advocates of states' rights, contesting with the Free Staters, were increasingly placed in the position of relying on the powers of the federal government to support their cause. So both sides in the controversy, through expediency, were acting out unnatural roles.

Chapter 4
Political Convulsion and War

After the territorial election of 1855, Charles Robinson was convinced that the election—though validated by the governor of Kansas Territory and the president of the United States—must somehow be repudiated. This should occur, Robinson believed, because:

> He had seen what law-making could effect in the control of oppressors in California [when he, Robinson, had led the Squatters' Rebellion], and knew very well what might be expected from the Legislature that had just been legalized by the Governor's act, so far as illegality and fraud could be legalized. The Legislature could pass laws, as did the California Legislature, regarding land titles, purposely to deprive one class of citizens of all legal protection.

So one of Robinson's reasons for seeking to deny the authority of the new Kansas Territorial legislature was to ensure the legitimacy of the Free Staters' land titles. Robinson knew, better than most, that the land titles on both sides were shaky and that it was imperative in this situation to control the federal governor, judges, U.S. marshal, justices of the peace, probate judges, sheriffs, and constables. The proslavery men's land titles would have been just as vulnerable to the Free Staters' manipulations had the election gone their way.[1] In line with this reasoning, Robinson et al., for their own protection, saw to it that, thenceforth, an ordinary citizen, acting without formal, legal authority other than vague local sanction, recorded deeds in Lawrence.[2]

To repudiate the legislature, however, would be a stickier problem. Indeed, as Robinson admitted, "scarcely any man north of the Mason-Dixon line would justify the lifting of a finger against Federal authority. It was necessary to draw a line at that point," he said. The line, of course, was between lawful agitation and treason. For that reason, Robinson asked himself if it would "be possible to hold out that length of time [the time until the current legislators had served out their time] while [Free Staters were] branded as repudiators and traitors by the Federal executive and one-half of the people of the country?" Robinson justified his seemingly treasonous thoughts, as he put it, "by a conviction of right and natural justice," an ambiguous concept.[3]

To implement his insurrectionary plans, Robinson understood that he would need to fortify the Free Staters' arsenal of weapons. Therefore, he penned a letter to Eli Thayer at the New England Company asking for one hundred Sharps rifles, state-of-the-art weapons of high accuracy and fast, sustained fire. In effect, these rifles were the "assault weapons" of their day and more technically advanced than anything even the U.S. Army possessed. George W. Deitzler was entrusted to carry the letter to New England. He arrived on a Friday, and within two hours' time, Thayer had given him an order for Sharps carbines, or rifles. By the next Monday, Deitzler had them packed for shipment, marking the boxes "Books" so that the Missourians would not seize the shipment in transit up the Missouri River. This is the origin of the later reference to the carbines as "Beecher's Bibles" (after the famous abolitionist who helped fund them).

When the weapons reached Lawrence and their existence was broadcast, they sent emotional reverberations throughout the Free State and proslavery camps. But this shipment was to be only the first of many such shipments to the Free Staters, and they sent an intimidating message to the proslavery men of Kansas. A howitzer was included in the latest shipment as an exclamation point—sent through the courtesy of propagandists Horace Greeley, Olmstead, and others.[4] Clearly, Robinson intended to use deadly force to impose the Free Staters' will in Kansas Territory, regardless of the deadly consequences.

Robinson complained, however, in his characteristically sarcastic style, that even with the "wholesome influence" imparted by the Sharps carbines, some of the proslavery men around Lawrence were still troublesome. Robinson's solution to the problem, as he put it, was to form a "secret organization" of Free Staters pledged to "stand by each other" to see that "assailants were properly cared for." Another precaution taken by Robinson was the hiring of what he described as "a California bully," "paid for by the month," whose responsibility it was to "take the offensive with his tongue" while acting defensively "with his fists and revolvers." His name was Dave Evans, and he was said by Robinson to have quieted many a proslavery settler asserting himself too noisily. The first man killed in the confrontation between the two forces was in the fall of 1854, when, according to Robinson, "a proslavery man in an insulting manner assaulted a free-state man who shot him dead." The Free Stater successfully pled self-defense. It is unknown whether the decision was a rational one or one imposed by a stacked jury or corrupt judge. After the election for the legislature, Cole McCrea, a Free Stater, killed Malcolm Clark, another proslavery man. McCrea claimed that Clark had earlier assaulted him. McCrea, too, successfully pled self-defense.[5]

But the violence was not all one sided. The antislavery editors of the *Parkville (Mo.) Luminary* were ordered out of town by a mob and warned: "If we find C. S. Parks and W. J. Patterson in this town then [within three weeks] . . . we will throw them in the Missouri River, and if they go to Kansas to reside, we pledge our honor . . . to hang them wherever we can take them." Proslavery men, however, were sometimes guilty of exaggeration or "bluster," as Robinson called it, and this may be a prime example of the ongoing war of words.

Another Free Stater and abolitionist, Pardee Butler, from Atchison, Kansas, a proslavery bastion at that time, ran into trouble in his community on August 16, 1854, when he confronted Robert S. Kelly, editor of the *Squatter Sovereign,* and complained about his editorial policy. Butler was accosted later in the streets of the town by a mob of thirty or forty people led by Kelly and asked to sign a list of resolutions. Rejecting their request, he was given several options, one of which was "to hold his tongue." When he refused, he was placed on a cottonwood raft with a flag hoisted over it stating, "Rev. Mr. Butler agent for the Underground Railroad," warned never to return, and set adrift down the Missouri River. Butler, however, was persistent. He soon returned to Atchison, Kansas, was tarred and feathered (or, some say, tarred and cottoned), and driven out of town, presumably until the abolitionists later took over the town.[6]

Meanwhile, on June 25, 1855, at a meeting of the Lawrence Association, the Free Staters passed the following resolutions specifying their rejection of the proslavery legislature:

> Resolved, That we are in favor of making Kansas a free Territory and as a consequence a free State.
>
> Resolved, That we look upon the conduct of a portion of the people of Missouri in the late Kansas election as a gross outrage upon the elective franchise and our rights as free men, and a violation of the principles of popular sovereignty; and, inasmuch as many of the

The flag fixed on Pardee Butler's raft when he was banished from Atchison, Kansas, and floated down the Missouri River for his abolitionist agitation. *The Kansas State Historical Society, Topeka*

members of the present Legislature are men who owe their election to a combined system of force and fraud, we do not feel bound to obey any law of their enacting.

Resolved, That the legally elected members of the present legislature be requested, as good citizens of Kansas, to resign and repudiate the fraud.

Resolved, That in reply to the threats of war so frequently made in our neighboring State, our answer is we are ready. (On account of Sharp's rifles.)

Resolved, That we urge upon the people of Kansas to throw away all minor issues, and make the freedom of Kansas the only issue.

Obviously, the New Englanders were spoiling for a fight and, armed with their new Sharps rifles, determined to get one.

On the Fourth of July, to demonstrate their new power, the Free Staters held a parade in Lawrence, during which two uniformed companies marched down Massachusetts Avenue with Sharps rifles and were present-ed with a silk banner from the women of Lawrence. The woman who handed the flag to the soldiers said, "Let not threats of tyrants foreign or domestic intimidate you; but move firmly and fearlessly in the path of truth and right principle, and if you should fail to accomplish the object of your mission, you shall at least have the sweet consciousness of having stood steadfastly in a good cause."[7]

At the same celebration, as part of his address to the people of Lawrence, Robinson said: "Is it politic, is it for our moral, intellectual, or pecuniary advancement to submit to the dictation of a foreign power [the federal government and, by implication, Missouri] in regard to our laws and institutions? This is the question that deeply interests us all, and for the consideration of which this day is most appropriate."[8] A few years later, Southerners spoke words in much the same tenor in reference to their Northern brothers but received much less approbation.

Just two days before the above-described celebration, on July 2, 1855, the territorial legislature met at Pawnee, Kansas, just outside the Fort Riley Military Reservation. Governor Reeder, not yet fired by Pres. Franklin Pierce, gave a grand address. Martin Conway, the only successful Free State candidate elected in the election, at a prearranged moment, rose to his feet, strode up to Reeder, and denounced the whole proceeding, charging that the legislature was ordained by a "daring and unscrupulous league in the state of Missouri and other parts of the South." In closing, Conway said, "I am ready to spurn and trample under my feet its [the legislature's] inso-lent enactments whenever they conflict with my rights or inclinations." This performance of calculated righteous indignation, according to Charles Robinson, had been orchestrated and choreographed earlier by himself, George W. Deitzler, Martin Conway, and Kersey Coates. Conway had not originally chosen to protest at all but was convinced to do otherwise by Robinson and his associates in furtherance of their propaganda campaign. Later, on August 16, 1855, Reeder was fired by President Pierce and fell in with his natural soul mates, the Free Staters. Pierce cited Reeder's improper land speculation in Pawnee, other territorial towns, and Indian lands as part of the reason for his removal.[9]

Another purpose of the Free Staters' rabid contentiousness was to create such a volatile, hostile environment in Kansas Territory that few, if any, Southerners would choose to settle there. Those who did so would hazard their fortunes and possibly their lives. A contemporary New Orleans newspaper said, "The people of the slave states are averse to peril the title to their slaves in a Territory where the free-soil element so extensively prevails, and where there is no security of property."[10]

At this point in the struggle, Robinson and the Free Staters decided to create their own contesting Free State legislature to further challenge the legitimately elected one (legitimate, according to the governor of Kansas Territory and the president of the United States). The reasoning behind this Free State move, according to Robinson, was that

> A large minority [of Kansas men] was indifferent to the question of slavery, and had been driven to act with the Free-State men because of the invasion of their own civil and political rights. Under these circumstances, it was deemed expedient to agitate the question of a State constitution. Such a movement would serve to occupy the minds of the people, attract the attention of ambitious politicians, become a rallying point for all opposed to the usurpation and, in case of necessity, when all other means of self-preservation should fail, be used as a *de facto* government, even though not recognized by Congress.[11]

Of course, creating one's own *de facto* government presupposes committing treason. Certainly, in a few short years, such action by the Confederacy would fit Pres. Abraham Lincoln's definition of treason.

Now a new, dynamic character entered the scene: James Henry "Jim" Lane, a former lieutenant governor and state representative from Indiana and a known Democrat (soon to become Republican, however). Lane has been colorfully, but not accurately, described in histories as having a "Mephistophelean leer" and the "sad, dim eyes of a harlot." Actually, Lane was a tall, gaunt, slipshod man with unkempt black hair who generally looked like he had just climbed out of a haystack. He had extraordinary, albeit eccentric, oratorical skills when his audience was naïve, politically polarized, and easily moved by emotional appeals and demagoguery. His speeches were often harangues delivered in a bizarre, rasping, affected voice, punctuated throughout by audible gasps for air and resembling nothing so

James Lane, general, senator, and close friend of Abraham Lincoln. Lane later led a brigade of Jayhawkers that destroyed the town of Osceola, Missouri, in 1861 then burned and pillaged its way north to Kansas City, Missouri. *Courtesy of Patrick Marquis.*

much as a crazed, backwoods preacher gone mad. But even men of his own party fell under his charismatic sway, and their sanction of him must be considered an indictment against their own characters. Lane was a natural leader, so aggressive, persuasive, and persistent that even Lincoln fell under his spell, unable to resist his importunate advances, saying (not complaining) at one point that every morning Lane was at his door knocking and that is why he so often listened to him. One office seeker said, "Lane gets anything of the President that he asks for while others go begging." During the war, it was said that Lincoln signed Lane's applications for appointments without even reading them. Lane was amoral, totally pragmatic, and shifted his political sails to suit the time, place, and his need for money and political support. He was pugnacious, ruthless—both politically and personally—sometimes crooked, and indifferent to human life and suffering. In fact, while living in Lawrence, he murdered his neighbor in a dispute over a shared well. Historian Theodore Andreas describes him as arriving in Kansas "poor in purse, lax in morals," leaving behind a family in Indiana that "he did not love." Whatever his faults, he was the preeminent politician in Kansas and the leader of the Free State party. One Free Stater described him as "one of our things," with all that implies.[12]

When the Free State leaders met to plan a constitutional convention, they sought Lane's support. He agreed to come aboard if they would promise to back him in his quest to become one of the senators under the new constitution. This they agreed to. When the convention was held on August 14, 1855, Lane, ironically (because he was ordinarily the great firebrand and agitator), provided a balancing force for the Free Staters, influencing them to stay more in line with the law. While many of the Free Staters favored repudiating the current legislature at any cost, Lane steadied them by galvanizing support for a resolution to hold a Free State election in the various districts of the territory in order to select delegates to a convention who would form a state constitution. Lane believed that having written a new constitution the Free Staters could apply at the next session of Congress for admittance into the United States as a Free State; thus they would bypass the current proslavery legislature and avoid a direct, martial confrontation with federal power, which Lane apparently feared.

On September 5, 1855, a general convention of Free Staters was held in Big Springs. At the convention, Lane was elected chairman of the committee on platform; Judge G. W. Smith, president of the convention; J. S. Emory, chairman of the committee on the legislature. Ex-governor Reeder was chosen to write a report to submit to the convention. In his report, Reeder subsequently railed against the elected legislature, claiming, "We owe no allegiance or obedience to the tyrannical enactments of this spurious legislature—that their laws have no validity upon the people of Kansas, and that every freeman among us is at full liberty, consistently with all his obligations

as a citizen and a man, to defy and resist them, if he chooses so to do."
Referring to the Free Staters' political enemies as "outlaws," Reeder castigated the Supreme Court justices of the territory and said that the Free Staters
would carry their disputed questions to "a higher tribunal." However, he was
not referring to the Supreme Court by this concept of a "higher law." He
went on to say that the Free Staters would "resist them [the laws of the ter-
ritory] to a bloody issue as soon as we ascertain that peaceable remedies shall
fail, and forcible resistance shall furnish any reasonable prospect of success."
Reeder was preaching to the choir and was subsequently nominated as a delegate to Congress, a position to be decided by an election on the second
Tuesday of October—not the same date fixed for the election of what they
called the "spurious" or "bogus" legislature, as the Free Staters chose to refer
to the legitimate, lawful legislature.

One embarrassing outcome of this meeting was the adoption of "violent anti-Negro principles," as suggested by Lane. These, however, were
disavowed by Robinson and his clique. Reeder's disconcerting remark
about a "bloody issue" raised eyebrows and caused Stephen Douglas to rail
in Congress about the "defiant revolutionists in Kansas" and to complain
that the government was "equal to any emergency . . . except the power to
hang a traitor!" Another convention was held in Topeka on September 19,
1855, during which Jim Lane, again, was elected president.[13]

From October 23 to November 11, another constitutional convention
was held at Topeka with Lane as president. This convention patched
together a constitution, called the "Topeka Constitution," and planned for
an election on January 5, 1856, to sanction the constitution and elect a
quasi legislature. Later, on April 17, 1856, when Lane presented the memorial of the Topeka legislature to Congress requesting that the state of
Kansas be admitted to the Union, Senator Douglas responded by saying,
"I find that the signatures are all in one handwriting. . . . I perceive on
inspection various interlineations and erasures. All things are calculated to
throw doubt on the genuineness of the document." All of which was true,
and Lane ignominiously withdrew the document.[14]

On November 21, 1855, violence in Kansas escalated. During a land
claim dispute near Hickory Point, Franklin N. Coleman, a proslavery man,
killed Charles M. Dow, a Free Stater, and left Dow's body lying in the road
until his friends retrieved it near sunset that day. Coleman subsequently fled
to Shawnee Mission to escape the wrath of local Free Staters and turned
himself over to the new governor, Wilson Shannon. Meanwhile, Sheriff
Samuel J. Jones learned of a Vigilance Committee of one hundred men
convened by Free Staters to "ferret out and bring the murderers [of
Coleman] and their accomplices to condign punishment." One of the
alleged accomplices, Harrison Buckley, a friend of Coleman, was to be
killed for "egging on the murder." Buckley had heard about these threats

to his life and learned that one of the men making them was Jacob Branson, Dow's landlord and friend. Sheriff Jones, upon learning about the threats to Buckley's life, procured a peace warrant to arrest Branson. Meanwhile, Free State vigilantes drove Buckley's and Coleman's families out of their homes and burned the houses to the ground.

In order to arrest Branson without creating too great a stir, on November 26, Jones proceeded to Branson's house in the middle of the night with a posse of twelve to fifteen men and captured him. Meanwhile, a large network of Free Staters, some twenty-two men led by Samuel N. Wood, received word of the arrest, sent out spies, and after rallying at the home of James B. Abbot, intercepted Jones. After a sharp exchange of words, the Free Staters—among them the fiery Wood (called by Free Staters, with good reason, a "fighting man"), Elmore Allen, Joshua Hughes, Samuel F. Tappan, Samuel C. Smith, and James B. Abbot—drew their weapons. Also allegedly among the Free State group were Philip and Miner R. Hupp, Philip Hutchinson, Collins Holloway, Edwin Curless, Lafayette Curless, Isaac Shapett, J. A. Abbott, John Smith, and Paul Jones. One of the Free Staters called out to Branson: "Come over to your friends." Branson replied, "They say they will shoot me if I do." Wood screamed aggressively, "Let them shoot and be damned; we can shoot too!" Branson replied, "I will come [even] if they do shoot," and rode his mule up to the Free Staters. After an exchange of threats and other offensive remarks, the Free Staters moved on with Branson in tow and rushed to the house of Charles Robinson to determine how to repair the damage or create an alibi. According to proslavery accounts, the Free Staters carried formidable Sharps rifles during the encounter; the Free Staters said, however, that they wielded only "squirrel rifles" and "rocks." Although the entire row began as a land dispute, once it got underway, the volatile situation in Kansas made it a political dispute.[15]

After the antislavery force had fled the territorial authorities, the people of Lawrence harbored Branson and the other men who had helped him escape. Young Lawrence resident, Edward Fitch, in a letter, described aiding "Mr. Mears" [sic], a reference to William Meairs, one of Branson's alleged rescuers: "The sheriff harassed him all last winter, and all the fore part of summer, so that he could not get his crops in, but has never been able to catch him yet. . . . I gave him pants & coat, also a dress for his wife, sent by Mrs. Perry, and some clothes for his children, of which he has three, all small." Evidently, the Free Staters' felonious rebellion was a widespread and collaborative affair.[16]

Sheriff Jones, in an attempt to enforce the law, requested aid from the territory's poorly organized and barely effective militia. Hearing of his call and surmising the militia would be of scant help, David Rice Atchison advanced on Lawrence with a large Missouri force. In response, Lawrence men scrambled to create defensive positions and rallied the "Lawrence Legion."[17] The Eldridge House, called the "Free-State Hotel," was turned into a barracks for soldiers and a headquarters for the Free State officers.[18]

Wilson Shannon, former governor of Ohio and a member of Congress from that state, by this time had taken over the governor's reins in the territory. Governor Shannon, after assessing the situation, feared the outbreak of civil war and called on the U.S. First Cavalry Regiment commanded by Col. Edwin Vose Sumner at Fort Leavenworth to support him. As it turned out, despite his appellation "Old Bull," Sumner was either a procrastinator, too wary to mix in the local political upheaval, or one of those officers always inordinately protecting himself against possible censure. Whatever his true motivation, he refused Shannon's request, saying that orders of such a nature must come from Washington. Shannon, consequently, wired Washington

Abolitionists resisting territorial law, as represented by Sheriff Samuel Jones (shown on horseback). The sheriff had arrested Jacob Branson for threatening to kill Franklin Coleman. When Jones attempted to carry his prisoner off to jail, an armed force of abolitionists intercepted him and freed Branson. *The Kansas State Historical Society, Topeka*

that one thousand armed men were assembled at Lawrence, were defying authority, and posed a threat to territorial law and order. Shannon wanted U.S. troops standing by while Jones served legal papers in the town. Meanwhile, to preserve order, Shannon ordered Jones to postpone any attempt to serve his writs till army troops arrived. The governor had refused to use the local militia, commanded by Major General Richardson, believing that it was too politicized and would only exacerbate the situation. President Pierce, as cautious as Sumner, asked that Shannon tender his request for U.S. troops in writing. Hoping to goad Sumner into some kind of action, the anxious Shannon sent the colonel a copy of Pierce's promise to authorize troops upon written request. On the basis of this information, Sumner agreed to advance on Lawrence, then reversed himself, and finally cautiously advanced to the Delaware River, miles from the town, but no farther.

By this time, the forces in Lawrence, approximately 250 men in guard companies, had organized. Charles Robinson was designated commander in chief with the rank of major general; Lane was given the second rank. The belief was that if the more experienced Lane were placed in command at this "critical juncture," it might offer an "unballasted leadership." Lane, despite his elevation in Free State ranks, was justly considered intemperate, to say the least. The "Lawrence Legion" was given the new, euphemistic title, "Committee of Safety," a term an earlier generation of Massachusetts men had called their revolutionary armed groups opposing the British rule of King George III. Meanwhile, Free Staters assembled in Lawrence day and night, traveling on horseback, afoot, and in wagons from Palmyra, Topeka, Osawatomie, Wakarusa, Bloomington, and settlements along Ottawa Creek. Under the direction of Lane, five redoubts, circular earthworks, and other fortifications were built at every approach to the city. Soon, there were over seven hundred men manning the well-sited defenses.[19]

On December 5, believing that the situation in Lawrence was worsening, Shannon raced to the town, quickly determined that it was a powder keg, and sent another desperate message to Sumner, frantically calling for military aid before a deadly fight broke out between the proslavery and Free State partisans. Later that day, by now expectedly, the ever-cautious Sumner again demurred, saying that this was too important a step to take without written presidential authority. Frustrated, anxious, and intimidated, Shannon managed to secure a treaty with the Free Staters on December 10. A day later, Shannon reported to the president that peace had been secured, but he also warned him that it would be advisable in the future to preauthorize military support, as an explosive encounter had only narrowly been averted. Shannon's temerity won little respect from either party. John Brown, the radical abolitionist, who was one of the defenders at Lawrence with his company of nineteen men, referred to Shannon's "weakness" and "frailty" and noted how the Free Staters scoffed at him in derision. Brown said the Free Staters "took advantage of his [Shannon's] cowardice and folly, and by means of that and the free use of whiskey and some trickery succeeded in getting a written arrangement with him, much to their own liking."[20]

The president, too, weighed in on Shannon's request for federal troops. On December 31, 1855, Pierce announced that while there had been disorder in Kansas, it was not sufficient to warrant federal intervention. Less than a month later, however, he seemed to waver. On January 24, 1856, in an address to Congress, he supported the proslavery legislature at Lecompton and denounced the Free State legislature as "revolutionary." He also suggested that Shannon furnish an available "public force of the United States" to assist Sheriff Jones as a posse comitatus. Pierce, then covering himself, added that it might be necessary to use other state militias if necessary or the U.S. Army.[21]

The federal government's disinclination to involve itself in the strife did not improve the decreasing respect for the territorial agents. On April 20, 1856, Sheriff Jones attempted to arrest one of the prime insurrectionists, Samuel N. Wood, the "fighting man," in Lawrence but failed. According to Charles Robinson, Wood first submitted to the arrest, but then, according to Robinson, "bystanders good-naturedly jostled him [Wood] away from Jones." According to historian Andreas, they "pretended that the arrest of Wood was a joke." One doubts that Robinson's phrase "good-naturedly jostled" and Andreas's portrayal of the affair as a "joke" adequately described a situation in which a federal officer had been obstructed from carrying out a legitimate arrest. While the crowd jostled Jones, they also "stole the pistol of the sheriff," again, not a particularly humorous or good-natured act. Later, returning with a five-man posse, Jones was further thwarted. This time, when he attempted to serve a writ on S. F. Tappan, another Branson rescuer, the sheriff was socked in the face by Tappan (Free Staters insisted on the less aggressive term, "slapped"), and his would-be prisoner was spirited away as the crowd jeered at Jones.

Three days later, on April 23, when Jones asked for military support from Sumner, the colonel finally agreed but sent only six men and an officer. Meanwhile, Sumner warned the people in Lawrence that a small military force was coming under the auspices of the president of the United States to make arrests. Of course, this warning alerted most of the people who were to be served writs enough time to get out of town, especially those expected to be on the list, such as Sam Wood. First Lt. James McIntosh finally arrived in Lawrence with ten or eleven men, including Sheriff Jones, who thereupon arrested John Hutchinson, E. D. Lyman, G. F. Warren, J. G. Fuller, F. Hunt, and A. F. Smith, among others; Wood was not one of the arrested, obviously having taken advantage of Sumner's convenient warning.

Sheriff Samuel J. Jones, sheriff of Douglas County (Lawrence's county), who was shot and wounded in the back by abolitionist rebels during the territorial period while attempting to uphold federal law. *The Kansas State Historical Society, Topeka*

Sheriff Jones decided to stay the night in Lawerence and make a further attempt to serve writs the next day. When Jones and six of his men left their tent in the middle of the night to fetch some water, the sheriff was shot at twice, one bullet passing through his trousers. Jones returned to his tent, and a few minutes later, a man feigning drunkenness wandered into the tent, apparently casing the interior. After the man was ushered out, another shot sounded, and a bullet passed through the tent cloth into Jones' back, entering near his backbone and exiting just below his shoulder blade. Although the young man who fired the shot was said to be "unknown" by the Free Staters, he presumably was well known to them and has since been identified as Harley Lenhart, though historian Theodore Andreas maintains the felon was another Free Stater, James N. Filer. Lenhart, the likely assailant, was a young printer and soon-to-be Free State guerrilla, who later stalked the area around Lawrence with a small, violent band, plundering proslavery farmers and burning their homes.

Still not dissuaded from making arrests, on April 24, McIntosh attempted to serve other writs, but all the men on his list, not surprisingly, had fled or were hidden. When Sumner received word of Jones' injury, he vowed to send two squadrons, perhaps the entire regiment, to Lawrence. While Sumner was slow to arouse, once he became alive, "Old Bull" usually exceeded everyone's expectations.[22]

Meanwhile, in May 1856, Chief Justice Lecompte of the U.S. district court told his court: "All who resist these [territorial] laws resist the power and authority of the United States, and are therefore guilty of *high treason*. Now, gentlemen, if you find that any person has resisted these laws, then, you must, under your oath, find bills against them for *high treason*." The district court then indicted a number of antislavery leaders for treason, among them ex-governor Reeder, George W. Deitzler, G. W. Brown, G. W. Smith, Gaius Jenkins, Charles Robinson, James Lane, and Sam N. Wood.[23]

Several of these men managed to delay or escape prosecution. Reeder fled to Kansas City and remained in hiding there for two weeks at Shalor W. Eldridge's American hotel, the New England Company's hotel in that city. Then, he fled to Illinois aboard a steamboat disguised as a woodchopper. Fearing to publicly board the boat *J. M. Converse* at Kansas City during his escape, Reeder entered the steamboat six miles downstream from Kansas City, at Randolph, floating out to the boat in a skiff piloted by Eldridge's sons, Thomas and Edward.[24] Similarly, James Lane would remain elusive and in constant motion for the next year in order to avoid prosecution. At about this time, Charles Robinson maintained, "So far, the record of the Free-State men was without a blot or blemish of any kind, and was universally applauded." Such a statement is an example of the Free Stater's rather overdrawn rhetoric and abuse of the truth of the matter.

The Free Staters' disregard for the law continued. On May 11, 1856, U.S.

Marshal Israel B. Donalson reported that one of his deputies had been resisted while serving legal papers in Lawrence. The deputy and his small posse claimed that a mob in Lawrence "threatened the life of the deputy" and "one or two hundred of the citizens of Lawrence . . . made such hostile demonstrations that the deputy thought he and his small posse would endanger their lives in executing said process." Donalson, in line with President Pierce's orders, requested the help of citizens of the territory. By May 20, proslavery forces ringed Lawrence, the hotbed of territorial trouble. Donalson thereupon entered the town and arrested a number of people then

U.S. Marshal Israel B. Donalson, a native of Illinois, whose name has passed down in history as a "Border Ruffian" but whose only crime was in attempting to uphold federal law in territorial Kansas. *The Kansas State Historical Society, Topeka*

released his posse. The irrepressible Sheriff Jones assumed command of the militia. Before the day was over, in what has been called the "First Sacking of Lawrence," Charles Robinson's house and a few others were burned; the Free-State Hotel was shelled and burned; and two Lawrence newspapers, the *Herald of Freedom* and *Kansas Free State*, were destroyed and part of their type thrown into the Kaw (Kansas) River. Despite the violence to property, only one fatality occurred—one of Donalson's men.

The specific actions of the posse were suggested three weeks earlier, when a grand jury meeting in Lecompton had recommended the destruction of the hotel and printing presses, citing in the records:

> We are satisfied that the building known as the Free-State Hotel in Lawrence has been constructed with a view to military occupation and defense, and regularly parapetted and port-holed for the use of cannon and small arms, and could only be designed as a stronghold for resistance to law, thereby endangering the public safety and encouraging rebellion and sedition to the country; and we respectfully recommend . . . this nuisance may be removed.

The hotel did somewhat resemble a castle, with portholes appearing atop the walls, which rose above the roof of the building. The holes were plugged with stones that could be knocked out quickly in case of defense. Later, when cannon fired at the building, it fully resisted the assault, whereupon, kegs of powder were placed in the building's basement and set afire, promptly gutting the structure. Charles Robinson, although he was not present, claims that David Rice Atchison was "conspicuous among the mob" as the cannon were being placed for the assault.[25]

To quell the ongoing rebellion, Shannon, on May 21, requested four companies of soldiers under the command of Maj. John Sedgwick. A company each was to occupy the towns of Lawrence, Lecompton, and Topeka. Sumner quickly agreed, now having become more proactive. It is clear, by now, that Shannon understood the Free State strategy. In a letter to Secretary of State Marcy, he wrote:

> I am now able to state, upon reliable information, the whole plan of resistance to the territorial laws and their execution, which has been adopted by those who pretend to deny their validity. This plan is well understood and supported by a dangerous, secret, oath-bound organization of men who, it is believed, from the manifestations and threats already made, will be unscrupulous as to the use of means to accomplish their objects. The plan is this: whenever an officer, whether United States marshal, sheriff, or constable, shall attempt to execute a writ or process issued under any territorial law, aided and assisted by

a posse of United States troops, he is to be evaded, but not openly resisted. Should an attempt be made by any officer to execute any writ or process issued under the laws of this Territory, unaided by a posse of United States troops, he is to be resisted by force at all hazards.

Shannon was clearly aware of the effect of this strategy but seemingly unable to resist it. He said,

> It will be obvious to the President that, if every officer of the Government charged with the execution of legal process, issued under, and to enforce the territorial laws, is compelled to call on a military posse of United States troops to aid in executing the law, that the territorial Government will be practically nullified. It will be impossible to collect the taxes assessed for county or territorial purposes if this plan of resistance should be successful.

Robinson, well trained for the business of flaunting federal authority, said that he had "been through the same process in California [as that instituted by Free Staters in Kansas Territory], and knew what " 'thwarting, baffling, and circumventing' [the law] could accomplish."[26]

However, circumventing the law was obviously not the only strategy willingly employed by the Free Staters. On May 24, 1856, in an act of terrorism, John Brown with a small guerrilla force brutally murdered five proslavery settlers near Pottawatomie Creek in what is called the Pottawatomie Massacre. Brown had little, if any, provocation for his actions other than that the men he murdered were on opposite sides in the Kansas struggle and that people of their alleged party had sacked Lawrence. Brown wanted to send a powerful, violent message to the "Slave Power" (about which more will be written later). Even Major Sedgwick, an ardent antislavery adherent, termed Brown's acts "atrocities." For the rest of the summer, the Second U.S. Dragoons stayed in the field, attempting to quell the disorder, which now had become generalized. At this time, as historian Theodore Andreas noted, "The whole area around Lawrence was infested with free-state guerrillas who robbed and plundered the pro-slavery settlers. They even stole two of Governor Shannon's prize horses. A regular guerrilla war had begun." When Capt. T. J. Wood was ordered to Pottawatomie, he met so many armed bands of guerrillas along the way that required dispersing that it took him two days to reach the town, normally a journey of no more than a few hours.[27]

Soon, the guerrillas under John Brown again would clash with proslavery men. On June 1, 1856, a Missouri force led by Henry Clay Pate, a newspaperman with the *St. Louis Republican,* met John Brown in a skirmish called "The Battle of Black Jack." Pate, commanding the Westport

Sharpshooters, had ridden from Franklin in search of Brown, but Brown had been alerted to Pate's intentions by spies and waylaid him near Black Jack, surrounding him and calling for his unconditional surrender. Pate said he was subsequently captured under a flag of truce. He later said seriocomically, "I went to take Old Brown and he took me." It appears the real reason Pate surrendered is that he saw Capt. James B. Abbot's Free Staters approaching to reinforce Brown. Before Pate and his men were injured or killed, Colonel Sumner, who now had taken the field with two army companies, managed to free them and disperse Brown. The fanatic quickly regrouped, however. Sumner did not know about Brown's participation in the murders at Pottawatomie Creek, or he would have arrested him at the time. Around June 5, Sumner ran into a three-hundred-man Missouri force led by Maj. Gen. Asbury M. Coffey, which had entered Kansas to rescue Pate. Once Sumner informed Coffey of Pate's rescue, Coffey replied, "he should not resist the authority of the general government, and that his party would disperse," which it did.[28]

In late June of that year, acting governor Daniel Woodson ordered both Lt. Col. Phillip St. George Cooke and Sumner to move their forces on Topeka in order to stop an illegal Free State convention scheduled to convene there. Before he would stop it, Sumner, in his usual, reticent, self-protective style, demanded a letter from Shannon declaring, in his words, that the convention was insurrectionary. Once he had the letter, Sumner overreacted to the threat by bringing five companies of soldiers to Topeka and training two artillery pieces on the building where the meeting would convene. Then, when he ordered the Free State legislators out of the building, he sent them opposite signals by telling them that his actions were "the most painful duty of my whole life." The Free Staters, by this time having achieved their objective of creating more political agitation and chaos, canceled their meeting. On July 17, the president of the United States had seen enough, and Sumner was given an extended leave (army jargon for being "fired"), and mercifully replaced by Brig. Gen. Persifor Smith. Sumner's judgment from the beginning of the crisis had been tentative, faulty, and bumbling.[29]

Not satisfied with the current level of nonviolent resistance, on August 12 through August 19, in a series of armed actions called the "Wakarusa War," Free State guerrillas led by Lane and others attacked proslavery strongholds at Franklin, Fort Saunders, Georgia Fort, and Fort Titus in the area surrounding Lawrence. These "forts," as described by Free State accounts, were actually little more than fortified blockhouses, arsenals, and places of protection for the proslavery settlers. And while the Free Staters insisted that the forts were occupied by "brigands," they appear to have been used only for defensive purposes and not as locations from which assaults were being launched. As there were no corresponding forts used by Free Staters in the hinterlands outside Lawrence, it seems clear that the proslavery settlers were the ones under siege.

Nineteenth-century historian William Elsey Connelley, a Free State advocate, described the situation under which the proslavery forts were built:

> From that date [the dispersal of the Free State legislature] guerrilla parties spontaneously appeared in Kansas. Guerrilla warfare spread over the Territory. A state of anarchy prevailed. The Free-State men not only armed to protect themselves but to attack the Pro-Slavery settlers and the Law and Order militia. These guerrilla parties became predatory. They preyed upon Pro-Slavery merchants and settlers. Many a Pro-Slavery settler was stripped of all his property, and was sometimes fortunate to escape with his life. The Border-Ruffians soon began to come in from Missouri. Finding that it was impossible for the Pro-Slavery settlers to remain on their claims, they were advised to assemble in forts. Buford's men and the Missouri Ruffians coming in with them garrisoned these. A fort was established on the claim of J. P. Saunders . . . twelve miles from Lawrence. Franklin was fortified. Col. Henry T. Titus turned his residence into a fortification.

On the night of August 12, 1856, in the first of the Wakarusa War's raids, a company of partisans from Lawrence launched an attack on Franklin, firing fusillades at the defenders for several hours and driving out the proslavery defenders by lighting their structure on fire. Then, the Free Staters plundered the place of provisions, ammunition, guns, and a brass six-pounder, "Old Sacramento." A blockhouse called "Fort Saunders" was the next target. Some four hundred to five hundred men led by Jim Lane, Colonel Harvey, Doctor Cutter, Capt. H. J. Shombre, and Colonel Walker in the role of guerrillas drove out eighty men, capturing prisoners, a stockpile of eleven hundred Springfield muskets, powder, lead, large numbers of wagons and horses, and loads of flour, bacon, sugar, and coffee.

Next came Fort Titus, Colonel Titus's home, which, though it was only two miles away from a U.S. Army detachment manned by Major Sedgwick, was still allowed by the army to be seized and plundered by Free Staters of four hundred muskets, pistols, thirteen fine horses, and considerable provisions. The seriously wounded Titus was captured in this latest assault, and it was only through the intercession of Col. Walker that his life was saved. There might have been collusion between Sedgwick and the Free Staters in this instance, but it is more likely that Sedgwick feared engaging the Free Staters with but thirty men in his command.

Popular rebellion among the Free State guerrillas was rampant, and they were learning the fine art of raiding and plundering, which they would so refine in Missouri only a few short years later. As well as seizing proslavery settlements, during the Wakarusa War the Free Staters burned a number of homes in the general area, took numerous prisoners, and in general terrorized the proslavery settlers of the Lawrence area. In short, they were committing the same depredations that their supporters in the Eastern press establishment were claiming that proslavery bands were committing. Then, the Free Staters marched on the territorial capital, Lecompton. Major Sedgwick, commander of the army force in the town, whose men (according to O. G. Richards, one of the Free State participants) "formed in line and watched us all the time" as the Free State guerrillas captured Fort Titus, finally decided to resist. General Smith quickly reinforced Sedgwick to ensure the safety of the territorial capital.[30]

Shannon, frustrated and overwhelmed by events, resigned on August 21, 1856, and was replaced temporarily by Daniel Woodson, the former secretary of Kansas Territory. Like the governors before him, Woodson proved inadequate to the assignment. Nonetheless, he promptly went into action, calling out the militia. Soon, David Rice Atchison was on the scene, where he confronted John Brown at the Battle of Osawatomie, driving him from the field. Meanwhile, Lane, not wishing to get dealt out of high-visibility action and solicitous for any chances to enhance his political position, advanced toward the border with a military force but was cut off by Cooke's federal troops.

On September 1, Lieutenant Colonel Cooke was ordered to level the fortifications at Topeka. He refused, later explaining himself: "I rejoiced that I had stayed the madness of the hour, and prevented, on almost any terms, the fratricidal slaughter of countrymen and fellow citizens."[31] Unfortunately, five years later there were few kindred souls to mimic these words when the Unites States entered into a slaughter of Southerners on a grander scale than could have been envisaged at Topeka.

When John W. Geary, a tall, gallant-appearing man, replaced Woodson as the new governor, he made moves to stabilize the territory, first commanding the militia to disband and all out-of-state irregulars to leave the territory. Then, he ordered all men from eighteen to forty-five to muster into the territorial militia; if there were going to be armed men afoot, he wanted them in allegiance to the governor and legal government. But on September 14, Geary learned that the conflict was not over. A Free Stater, James A. Harvey, the same man with whom Lane had assaulted the Fort Saunders community, now was attacking Hickory Point with over 100 men. Capt. T. J. Wood was sent to the town and promptly captured 101 prisoners, 2 cannons, several wagons, and numerous weapons. Only one fatality was reported, a participant killed by a cannonball. Meanwhile, Harvey had abandoned his troops and fled. About this time, Geary learned that a 2,700-man Missouri force was investing Lawrence and sent Cooke to intercept them. Cooke convinced the force to disband.[32]

Militating against Geary's attempts to demilitarize the struggle in Kansas, the New England Company in early October 1856 sent a company of 200 men and 20 wagons across southern Iowa into Kansas. The men, organized as a military company, carried 145 breech-loading muskets, 85 percussion muskets, 36 Colt revolvers, 10 Sharps rifles, 63 sabers, 115 bayonets, and cartridges and powder. Capt. T. J. Wood and his U.S. Dragoons halted the force upon its entering Kansas and searched it. Then he arrested the men, noting the absence among the party of agricultural implements, household furnishings, or women and children. The men's weapons were confiscated, but they were allowed to continue without them. Several days later, the young men entered Lawrence, armed with weapons they had hidden. They paraded down Massachusetts Avenue in a dress parade with flags waving. The Eastern press, characteristically bombastic and disregarding the truth, called the army's earlier actions against this military force "an outrage," an "atrocity," a "gigantic crime," a "high-handed invasion of the constitutional rights of American citizens." The newspapermen called the young "settlers" led by "General Shalor Eldridge and Adjutant General Samuel Pomeroy" peaceful settlers harassed by "rapacious army officers and double-dealing Democratic politicians." Free Stater Eldridge later admitted that the company was, indeed, a military unit and was to be used for making war in Kansas. But, he added, "Our numbers had been exaggerated, our equipment magnified and our purposes misconstrued." In fact, Eldridge described how an elderly fellow posing as a surveyor met his and Pomeroy's force along the way and offered his service as a spy to "hover around" for the "discovery of any hostile movements" by the U.S. Army. Eldridge said he learned that the old man was John Brown and warned him away. However, O. G. Richardson, one of the young men in Eldridge's company, later said at a "56ers" convention in Lawrence that the men had been furnished with "Sharps rifles and revolvers" and that "General Lane and John Brown . . . seemed to have charge of the whole free-state forces from Iowa City to Topeka." Richardson said that on arrival, he immediately "went into camp . . . drilling and preparing to capture the proslavery men at Fort Saunders."

This force was not the first group of militarized settlers to be sent to Kansas in 1856. Some time earlier, a company of 79 men armed with Sharps rifles and led by C. B. Lines had been enlisted in New Haven, Connecticut, and had left for Kansas. At about the same time, another force, commanded by James A. Harvey, who was involved later in the attacks on Fort Saunders and Hickory Point, was intercepted by Jo Shelby, David Atchison, and Benjamin F. Stringfellow as Harvey's band traveled up the Missouri River. After being disarmed, Harvey moved north into Iowa and along the northern route into Kansas Territory. Earlier yet, on June 28, Gen. Persifer F. Smith received word that James Lane was leading a force of

250 men through southern Iowa into Kansas. Once Lane's command of the force became public knowledge, the abolitionist brain trust, Dr. S. G. Howe and Thaddeus Hyatt, ordered the "transfer of the command of the expedition from an officer of military prestige . . . to one distinguished only as a civilian. Thus [said Eldridge, a member of the force] the movement was divested of its most striking feature that denoted an insurrectionary expedition." Most of these forces were used eventually for precisely that purpose, and because the force was referred to as Lane's "Army of the North," it sent tremors through the proslavery ranks. Actually, the men were little more than a "ragged" and "penniless" rabble recruited by Lane from the streets of Chicago.[33]

Near the end of 1856, a proslavery Southern settler in Kansas, A. J. Houle, expressed his misgiving about the situation:

> I am of the opinion that there will be a great many Northern emigrants sent here next spring, and it would not surprise me at all if we have more fighting. There is something brewing. Only last week a party of desperadoes went to a man's house, dragged him out of bed, and gave him fifty lashes on his bareback, telling him that, if he did not leave in ten days, they would kill him. They have also threatened others in the same way. These men who have been thus treated and threatened are free-state men, but law and order loving men, and the reason they have been treated thus is because they would not join [Jim] Lane's [free-state] band, but served on the jury in trying some of his robbers. This and signs convince me that there is something in the wind, but let it come. We will meet it like men. But the South should not rest on her oars and think all is saved. If she does, she will be sadly mistaken. The Abolitionists are going to work slyly and cunningly, and if our eyes are not wide open, Kansas will be lost at last.[34]

Houle's trepidation seems justified. As historian Samuel Johnson noted:

> The attack on Lawrence, May 21, 1856, together with the agitation of Republican politicians, aroused the whole North. During June Kansas aid committees sprang up in nearly all the free states and in July a National Kansas committee was formed. These new organizations now took up much of the burden, so far borne by the Emigrant Aid Company of arousing moral and political support for the Free-State cause, recruiting settlers, furnishing arms, and relieving the needy. The Aid Company had a share, and an important share, in this larger effort, but it was now only a part of a movement that extended throughout the North.[35]

According to historian Floyd C. Shoemaker, the proslavery legislature of Kansas Territory had passed an "ultra-severe slave code and the appointment of the local officials in Kansas . . . and saw the territorial executive and judicial departments and the Federal administration from President to United States marshal favor their cause. The machinery of the territorial government was absolutely under their control." But this control, as Shoemaker concluded, was "attacked by able, devious, daring and determined free-state leaders, acting legally, extra legally, and illegally, under arms and without arms, enthused and urged on by editors and correspondents, poets and artists, until within three years [by 1858] the Missouri slavery citadel was swept away."[36]

Geary, meanwhile, went the same route as other ephemeral Kansas governors. Before he resigned, he wrote in a message to Washington: "In isolated country places [of Kansas] no man's life is safe. The roads are filled with armed robbers, and murders for mere plunder are of daily occurrence. Almost every farmhouse is deserted, and no traveler has the temerity to venture upon the highway without an escort." Kansas violence, however, slowly began to diminish over most of the territory, and a series of short-term territorial governors, Robert J. Walker, Frederick P. Stanton, James W. Denver, and Samuel Medary, passed through with much less controversy attached to their tenures. Meanwhile, the steady migration of settlers from the East and Northeast brought Kansas closer and closer to becoming a Free State. Ultimately, on January 29, 1861, Kansas would become a Free State because of this incessant migration, but it was the cunning, organization, and aggressive agitation of the Free Staters that ensured their triumph. People from the South and from Missouri who lived in Kansas—and they were a sizable minority, perhaps 30 percent or more—understood who was triumphing and accommodated themselves increasingly to the brash victors.

By the middle of November 1856, an uneasy peace seemed to reign in northeast Kansas. But in southeast Kansas, the fires of insurrection would burn for four more years until the Northern-inspired rebellion was replaced by a Southern one, and the Civil War commenced in earnest.

Chapter 5

Smoldering War: Attacks and Reprisals in Kansas and Missouri

Terrorism, a new dimension of violence, erupted in the Border War with the cold-blooded assassinations by John Brown and his party on Pottawatomie Creek. These were not killings done in the heat of battle; they were execution-style murders in which the victims were roused in the middle of the night, forced from their beds unarmed and unsuspecting, to be shot and hacked to death. A few Free Staters said later that Brown's actions were necessary for they sent a message to and even cowed the so-called Slave Power. The reverse, however, seems to have been the case. Brown's midnight visit broke any remaining trust between the proslavery partisans and the Free Staters, prompted increased violence across the territory, and sent emotional tremors across the entire nation, North and South.

The genesis of the Pottawatomie incident was the emigration of John Brown's sons to Kansas in April 1855. At that time, Owen, Frederick, and Salmon Brown left Meridosa, Illinois, for Kansas Territory, soon to be followed by their brothers Jason and John Jr. on May 7. The Browns settled near Osawatomie, in Franklin County. Shortly thereafter, John Jr. sent a letter to his father, in which he wrote, "Now we want you to get us these arms. *We need them more than we need bread.*" On October 7, 1855, John Brown Sr., called "Old Brown," arrived at his children's settlement. He told the locals that he sought to ply the trade of surveyor in Kansas. In this regard, he carried a surveyor's compass and telescope, which later became props for some of his spying ventures. Soon, Brown had built a home, sometimes referred to as his "fort," on a defendable mound on the Snyder claim, some quarter mile from hostile Missouri.[1]

John Brown Jr. soon became involved in Free State politics and accepted the position of Free State legislator (a member of the quasi, nonlegal legislature). Early in the spring of 1856, Judge Sterling G. Cato of the Territorial Supreme Court, who was responsible for the southeastern Kansas counties, held a term of court at Dutch Henry's Crossing at Henry Sherman's home, where the California Road crossed Pottawatomie Creek. Sherman's home was the largest and finest in that part of the country. John Brown Jr., by then a captain and commander of the Pottawatomie Rifles, a local militia unit of one hundred men, held a meeting in regard to Cato's court. Brown and his men decided that Cato had no right "to try anyone under the Territorial laws." John Brown Jr. and his father, Old Brown, were designated to give Cato fair warning as to the Free Staters' position on the matter.

When the Browns warned Cato, the Supreme Court justice listened to them and then turned away from the two men without a reply. Following the confrontation, John Brown Jr. assembled his men in military formation near the courtroom and made a martial display to accentuate his and his father's verbal warning. Cato promptly issued warrants for the arrest of the two Browns as well as Henry Thompson, Old Brown's son-in-law, and another member of the Free State quasi legislature, H. H. Williams. The arrest warrants were given to James P. Doyle and his two sons, deputy constables, William and Drury, to serve. The Doyles would soon become victims of the Brown family, arguably for the reason of their involvement with the warrants.[2]

On May 21, shortly after the issuance of these warrants, word reached Pottawatomie Creek that proslavery forces were attacking Lawrence. John Brown Jr. rallied the Pottawatomie Rifles and at 4:00 P.M. started for Lawrence along the California Road to provide military support. Old Brown followed with his own small band. At nightfall, the Pottawatomie Rifles stopped for two hours in the darkness. When the moon rose, allowing them to see, they continued on to Ottawa Creek, arriving just before dawn. They stopped to camp, just west of Ottawa Jones' cabin. Before dawn, a messenger arrived telling them that Lawrence had been "destroyed." The group, after discussing the matter, decided to proceed to Lawrence anyway. But after riding north for some way, the men changed their minds and decided to turn around and return to Ottawa Creek. When they arrived there, Salmon Brown, Old Brown's son, said his father told the other men "that they [he and his small band] were going back to Pottawatomie to break up Cato's court, and get away with some of his vile emissaries before they could get away with us—I mean to steal a march on the slave hounds." Then, Salmon Brown said, his father wrote down the names of some men. Salmon said, "They were the [same] men killed [later] and some others."[3]

Around noon on May 22, John Brown, the elder, formed his company, which was composed of Owen, Frederick, Salmon, and Oliver Brown as well as Henry Thompson, James Townsley, and Theodore Weiner. Old Brown asked Townsley if he would carry the men back to Pottawatomie in his wagon, and Townsley agreed. Weiner would ride alongside the wagon on his pony. Old Brown also told James Hanway of his intentions and asked him to go along. Hanway refused and warned Brown to use "caution." Brown, angered at Hanway's reply, said that the word caution "meant nothing but cowardice." Ominously, before they left camp, the men sharpened

John Brown, the fiery abolitionist perpetrator of the Pottawatomie massacre and leader of repeated raids into Missouri to free slaves. Brown was eventually executed for a treasonous raid on the U.S. Arsenal at Harpers Ferry. *The Kansas State Historical Society, Topeka*

their swords on a grindstone installed in one of the tents. A young boy, Baine Fuller, turned the grindstone for the men, and the blades sent out a spray of bright sparks as they were sharpened to a keen edge. After their preparations, Brown's men set out from Ottawa Creek and stopped to pitch camp about one mile from Dutch Henry's Crossing.[4]

The next day, the elder John Brown asked Townsley to identify for him all the proslavery people that lived along Pottawatomie Creek so that they could "sweep the creek as [they] came down of all the proslavery men living on it." Clearly, Brown meant to kill them all, and Townsley well understood his intent. Townsley supposedly refused and told Brown that he wanted to take his team home, but Brown refused to let him. The band now waited until dark to make their next move. Salmon Brown said they waited for darkness because his father feared they would not be able "to take the doomed men in daylight." At 10:00 P.M., Brown's men headed in a northeasterly direction, striking Mosquito Creek, just upstream from the home of the Doyle family.

The band reached Doyle's cabin around 11:00 P.M. John Brown, three of his sons, and Thompson went to the door of the cabin and knocked. Meanwhile, Weiner, Townsley, and Frederick Brown stood at a distance. Townsley later related that when a large dog attacked the men, Frederick Brown "struck the dog a blow with his short two-edged sword, after which [Townsley] dealt him a blow with [his own] sabre, and [they] heard no more of him." When James Doyle refused to come out, one of the men threw a burning ball of some material in the house. The astonished Doyle soon appeared at the door. Doyle's wife, Mrs. Mahala Doyle, said the men claimed they were with "the Northern Army" and demanded that Doyle "must surrender." Finally Doyle and his two sons, William and Drury, exited the house and were marched down the road toward the crossing. There, Old Brown shot Doyle in the forehead, killing him instantly. According to Townsley, "Brown's two youngest sons immediately fell upon the younger Doyles with their short two-edged swords," hacking them to death. One of the Doyle boys was "stricken down in [an] instant," but the other one "attempted to escape, and was pursued a short distance by his assailant and cut down."[5]

The party then followed Mosquito Creek downstream to the house of Allen Wilkinson, a member of the legal Kansas Territorial legislature, postmaster for Pottawatomie, and sometime member of the territory's judicial branch. Wilkinson's wife suspected the approach of the assailants when the family's dogs "raged and barked furiously." Then, she saw one of the men walk by her window and knock on the door.

"Who's that?" her husband cried.

"I want you to tell me the way to Dutch Henry's," came the blunt answer.

When Wilkinson told them, the man outside shouted, "Come out and show us." When Wilkinson opened the door, he met a number of armed men who captured him. Mrs. Wilkinson, fearing for her husband's life, begged John Brown not to take him. She told Brown that she was deathly sick with the measles—which was true—and that she needed her husband to care for her. Her words were wasted on Brown.

"You have neighbors," Brown said.

Mrs. Wilkinson replied, "So I have, but they are not here, and I cannot go for them."

"It matters not," Brown answered her brusquely. Mrs. Mahala Doyle then asked Brown what he was going to do with Wilkinson.

"Take him a prisoner to the camp," Brown lied to her.

Wilkinson asked for time to put on his shoes, but he was refused. Apparently, he had no need for shoes any longer. Finally, Wilkinson was marched out of the house, two men in front of him, two behind, and marched down the road. He was slain by one of the younger Browns and his body dragged to the side of the road and heaped in the brush.[6]

The John Brown party now crossed Pottawatomie Creek and advanced toward the home of Henry Sherman, known as "Dutch Henry" because of his German ancestry. Sherman's home, as noted earlier, was the finest in the area. All of the men attacked by the Browns were social elites in their neighborhood, while the Browns were quite poor, nearly destitute. Brown's band arrived at Sherman's home at approximately 2:00 A.M. and found Dutch Henry gone. Disappointed, they went to the nearby home of James Harris, knocked loudly at his door, and shouted again that they were "the Northern Army." The noise startled Harris and his wife and child, who were asleep in bed. When Harris opened the front door, three men faced him, two of whom he recognized—Owen Brown and his father John Brown. The assailants entered the large house and made prisoners of Harris and three guests who were staying with him at the time: "Dutch" William Sherman, the brother of "Dutch" Henry Sherman; John S. Whiteman; and a man believed to be Jerome H. Glanville.

Brown and his men ransacked the house, stealing ammunition, two rifles, a bowie knife, and a horse and saddle. Then, Brown took Harris's guests outside, one at a time, and interrogated them, asking them questions about their political affiliations. Wrong answers proved fatal. Harris, Whiteman, and Glanville provided the correct answers, for after a few minutes, they were allowed to return to the house. The last man questioned was William Sherman, whom the raiders kept. A few minutes after Brown and his men had left, Harris said he "heard a cap burst" outside the house. The next morning Harris found Sherman lying in the middle of Pottawatomie Creek, his skull "split open in two places and some of his brains . . . washed out by the water. A large hole was cut in his breast and his left hand was cut off except a little piece of skin on one side." Townsley, a member of Brown's band, said that Brown's youngest sons did the butchery. (Historian

William E. Connelley says that Thompson and Weiner killed Sherman.) John Brown had told Townsley before the men reached the Pottawatomie that he wished to "strike terror into the hearts of the Pro-Slavery party." He had succeeded royally.[7]

Afterward, John Brown insisted that Townsley pilot him through the Pottawatomie community to point out the cabins of other proslavery settlers so that he might kill them as well. Townsley, a veteran military man from the Seminole Indian War, refused, saying, "I am willing to go into Lecompton and attack the leaders, or fight the enemy in open field anywhere, but I [do] not want to engage in killing these men."

Later, Jason and John Brown Jr., who were not involved directly in the killings, were arrested and indicted for murder, as well as Townsley. The Brown boys eventually were released; Townsley was never brought to trial. Meanwhile, Harris fled the area, and Mrs. Wilkinson left for Tennessee, fearful for the lives of herself and her children. Both she and Harris believed that, as material witnesses, their lives were in danger. Glanville, one of Harris's guests, was killed several months later, and some scholars are convinced that Brown either killed him or had him slain.[8]

Many early writers commenting on the Pottawatomie killings attempted to justify the murders by saying that John Brown, recognizing the necessity for fending off the aggressive proslavery men in southeast Kansas, displayed his prescience in sending his violent "message." Charles Robinson, who became the first Republican governor of Kansas and who had as many difficulties with the proslavery men as anyone—in fact, was imprisoned for treason around the time of the attacks—disagreed entirely with this sort of interpretation. Robinson cited for support historian Theodore Andreas's view that this sort of "aggressive warfare" was "not in accordance with the plans or purposes of the leaders of the Free-State movement . . . [and] was in direct opposition to their counsel."[9]

Robinson rejected the spurious defenses offered by John Brown and his followers by asserting,

> It appears that John Brown was not hunting for criminals who had insulted his family, driven off his stock, killed his son or anyone else, but simply for pro-slavery men, innocent or guilty, it mattered not which. It has been seen that Brown could tell the Massachusetts Legislature [later] only that the pro-slavery men had used "threats" of driving off Free-State men. He didn't pretend that anyone had been driven off or molested in any manner. When it is known that such threats were as plenty as blue-berries in June, on both sides, all over the territory, and were regarded as of no more importance than the idle wind, this indictment will hardly justify midnight assassination of all pro-slavery men, whether making threats or not.

Robinson went on to say that John Brown claimed "the Doyles, Wilkinsons, and Shermans were furnishing places of rendezvous and active aid to armed men who had sworn to kill us and others." Robinson, again, was skeptical: "Here are more threats. Had all men been killed in Kansas who indulged in such threats, there would have been none left to bury the dead."[10]

Robinson claimed that no serious enmity existed between the proslavery and Free Staters living along Pottawatomie Creek *before* the Browns' atrocities. Robinson said, in fact, that a meeting was held several days after the murders in which men from both parties unanimously denounced the heinous acts, resolving:

> Whereas, an outrage of the darkest hue and foulest nature has been committed in our midst by some midnight assassins unknown, who have taken five of our citizens at the hour of midnight from their homes and families, and murdered and mangled them in an awful manner; to prevent a repetition of these deed[s], we deem it necessary to adopt some measures for our mutual protection and to aid and assist in bringing these desperadoes to justice."[11]

According to Robinson, no Free State men had been killed south of Douglas County up to this time, and "its [the murders] equal in atrocity must be sought for in the dark ages."[12]

Robinson believed that the only earlier violence committed in the Pottawatomie area had been in April 1856, when a party of Free Staters attacked the house of Rev. Martin White and stole his horses after exchanging gunfire with him for some time. White thereupon moved to Bates County in Missouri. What Robinson was inferring was that, if there had been violent behavior near the Pottawatomie, its source had not been members of the proslavery party. Robinson felt that Brown's unjustified terror attacks were stirring up a hornet's nest in the area.

Brown's atrocities ignited trouble throughout Kansas Territory. In Lecompton, where Robinson was being held at the time for treason, a mob assembled, seeking to hang him. Marshal Donalson, however, came to Robinson's aid, circulating the fact in the proslavery camps that the "treason prisoners" were Masons and Odd Fellows, fraternal "brothers" to many of the proslavery people. When Donalson ultimately discharged his posse, he told Robinson that in case of trouble, he intended to arm the prisoners and fight with them. And to show good faith, he stayed in the same room with the prisoners. Later, when Robinson was taken to Leavenworth and similar attempts were made to lynch him, the commander of the proslavery Kickapoo Rangers, Capt. William Martin, warned the mob that "when a prisoner was placed in his charge by the United States government, he would protect that prisoner while his life should last." Honor among some of these men, Robinson included, was a vibrant reality, despite the many difficulties.[13]

To calm the unrest and attempt to determine the perpetrators, Governor Geary visited the Pottawatomie area after the massacre. On October 21, 1856, he stopped at Dutch Henry's Crossing to take the testimony of people involved in the massacre. Finally, on October 24, he traveled to Fort Scott, but he was overtaken there by news that the home of Judge Briscoe Davis, whom he had just visited the day before, had been attacked by Free Staters. Geary immediately directed army troops to capture the marauders, but the soldiers came back empty handed. The governor, in frustration at this "impudent outrage," offered a two hundred dollar reward for their capture. The leader of the attackers was later discovered to be Capt. James H. Holmes, one of John Brown's "military men."[14]

After the Pottawatomie atrocities, John Brown continued his involvement in Free State activities, and even after warrants were made out for his arrest, he was harbored by many important people in Kansas and in the North, many of them historically famous personalities. Meanwhile, in Brown's wake, lawlessness erupted in southeast Kansas, which continued until the Civil War broke out.

In the autumn of 1856, George Washington Clarke, the Indian agent in Kansas Territory, advanced into Linn County, Kansas, from Missouri with more than one hundred proslavery men and trampled crops, seized horses and cattle, burned several houses, and drove some of the settlers out of the county. After this foray, a number of Linn County settlers organized under the leadership of James Montgomery, a former Campbellite preacher and schoolteacher. Montgomery had been raised in Ashtabula County, Ohio, then took up residence in Kentucky and Missouri, where he taught school for seventeen years. He finally settled in Kansas Territory in 1854. He was an abolitionist of the most extreme ilk.

After Clarke's raid into Linn County, Montgomery crossed into Missouri and posed as a schoolteacher. Within a couple of weeks, he had the names of twenty to twenty-five men who had participated in Clarke's raid. Montgomery then returned to Kansas, rallied his men, and now, as "Colonel" Montgomery, rode back into Missouri and captured many of Clarke's men, intimidated them, and threatened them with further violence if they refused to allow the Free Staters earlier driven out of Linn County to return. But this was only the beginning of Montgomery's plans. Under his guidance, a number of Free State spies were planted in Missouri's secret lodges and other lodges operating in Fort Scott, Kansas. From this time on, Montgomery knew the Missourians' plans and thwarted most of them before they could be acted upon.[15]

In May 1858, Montgomery conceived more ambitious plans for the

Missourians, instituting an infamous policy that came to be called "Jayhawking." The term Jayhawking is said to have originated with the activities of a marauder named Pat Devlin who, when he rode into Linn County one day loaded down with plunder from Missouri, was asked where he obtained it. He said he "Jayhawked" it. When asked what that meant, he explained that in Ireland, his homeland, there was a bird that "worries its prey before it devours it." He claimed that's what he was doing. Others believed Jayhawking was just "a fancy name for horse stealing."[16]

Col. James Montgomery, a nemesis for Missourians before the war. He continued his carnage after the Civil War began as a Union army officer. *The Kansas State Historical Society, Topeka*

Historian Hildegarde Herklotz defines the term more precisely, referring to it as "a species of land privateering or political freebooting. The Jayhawkers banded together and galloped over the country, appropriating horses, cattle, farming implements, guns, and, in short, whatever came in their way. They claimed that they never robbed or hung anyone who entertained the same political organization as themselves."[17] Jayhawkers, in fact, were often indiscriminate robbers and murderers, especially in Missouri after the outset of the Civil War.

In his role as a Jayhawker, Montgomery was considered the leader of a group of Free Staters who believed that it was their duty to help slaves escape from their masters. In the process, however, the Jayhawkers often divested the slave owner in Kansas and Missouri of as much property as they could carry home on their horses and in wagons, thereby enriching themselves. Jayhawking, when unrestrained, was a form of total war, a no-holds-barred, no-rules-applied attempt to destroy one's enemies, physically and economically. The pressures resultant from this onslaught became almost unbearable to slave owners. Because much of the wealthy slave owners' capital was in the form of slave property, Montgomery and his followers were attacking their financial holdings and the solvency and integrity of the agrarian businesses they were conducting, which like all businesses existed in a delicate balance. By May 1858, Montgomery began an aggressive campaign against the Missourians by leading large groups of armed Linn County raiders into Missouri to rob and murder.

In late May, S. G. Allen of Harrisonville, Missouri, visited Gov. Robert M. Stewart and requested that the state of Missouri provide weapons for the western Missourians so that they could defend themselves against the Kansan invaders and their depredations. When Allen returned home, a company was forming in Harrisonville, another a few miles south of Harrisonville, and a third one in Bates County. But the Missourians still lacked effective weapons for defense.

On May 31, Adj. Gen. G. A. Parsons, was ordered by Governor Stewart to western Missouri to "make such investigation as you may deem necessary with regard to the causes of difficulty and the probability of their recurrences." This was a reference to Montgomery and his Jayhawkers. On June 5, 1858, a farmer near West Point, Missouri, Joseph Clymer, was appointed by the "alarmed" local citizens to address another petition to Governor Stewart asking for immediate military aid. Clymer told the governor that around May 1, James Montgomery's Free Staters, after "robbing their houses of everything valuable, stealing their horse etc.," had driven out large numbers of "good and peaceable" proslavery farmers from Linn County into western Missouri.

Clymer said that Montgomery always used bands sufficient in size to accomplish his objectives: "If they went to rob or drive [a man] from his home they took five or ten men, if [a] neighborhood they took 20, if a town 75 to 100." Clymer said that Montgomery had threatened that once he drove all proslavery farmers out of Linn County, he would do the same to the people in the West Point and Butler, Missouri, areas. According to Clymer, Montgomery and his men had recently waylaid a Dr. Rockwell from western Missouri while he visited a patient in Linn County and robbed him of three hundred dollars, his pistols, horse, buggy, and watch.

On May 14, Clymer said Montgomery had ridden into Missouri with his Jayhawkers and robbed Rev. George W. Geyer of two horses, Dr. A. P. Brown of a saddle, and made similar raids on other farmers in the area. On May 20, Clymer said, a large group of Kansans under Montgomery, estimated to be around four hundred men, had approached West Point, reconnoitered the town, then sent one hundred men armed with Sharps rifles galloping into town at full speed. Then, they slowed down and rode their horses down the main street in "military style." Although there were only thirty citizens in town at the time, Clymer said they had been prepared to resist. After "drinking and eating what they wanted," however, Montgomery and his men rode two miles south to the home of Jack Clark, where they robbed him of his money and everything else of value, "even his and his wife's wearing apparel." Clark's furniture was also wantonly destroyed. The mayhem generated by the Kansans created extreme fear and alarm in the local people. Clymer testified that "some of our oldest, best neighborhoods have become nearly or entirely depopulated, their farms, their stock and in many instances their household furniture and clothing have been left at the mercy of these outlaws."[18]

Soon, Montgomery and some twenty-five men rode into Missouri again, spied some local citizens milling around, and chased them into the timber. Clymer said that Montgomery and his men had openly threatened to sack Butler, Papinsville, and West Point. This, according to Clymer, had forced the citizens of these areas "to go armed about our daily avocations" and in continual fear. Eleven citizens of Bates County endorsed Clymer's letter to the governor, giving it added weight.

Finally, Governor Stewart ordered General Parsons to the threatened counties to review the situation and organize the local men for defense. Parsons was ordered not to let anyone cross over into Kansas; Stewart wanted to keep a lid on the violence. On June 5, General Parsons went to Harrisonville and organized the Cass County guards. Cass County, directly north of Bates and Vernon Counties, also was considered under siege. Within the next week, Parsons had organized a total of four guard companies, two of which were called the Pleasant Hill Rangers, another one the Austin "Blews" or Blues (Austin was a small community just south of Harrisonville).[19]

While gathering these guards, Parson had occasion to view the effects of the Jayhawkers and reported to the governor that "a large strip of country within our state is almost entirely depopulated, our citizens driven from their homes, and in many instances property taken, and they are threatened with death should they return. Many of these men we saw in and about Butler and Harrisonville." Parsons warned Stewart that the local units he was organizing would be insufficient to meet the challenge. The local farmers were so involved in farming and located in such widely separated locations that when Montgomery crossed the line into Missouri, it would take the men too long to respond to be effective. According to Parsons, "depredations" in these areas had been "going on to a greater or lesser degree for 4 years."[20]

On June 4, 1858, General Parsons also reported to Stewart that displaced Linn County farmers, proslavery men now living in western Missouri, were arming themselves in preparation for a reprisal raid on Montgomery's Linn County Free Staters. Seventy-five of the well-armed farmers had come into Harrisonville that night (where Parsons was staying), and they were rumored to have one hundred to two hundred men in their force. Parsons relayed to the governor that reliable informants had told him that these men were under the leadership of Charles A. Hamilton (or Hamelton), a wealthy former Georgian. In early spring, Montgomery had ejected Hamilton and his men from their homes near Fort Scott in Linn County. Montgomery had ridden into Trading Post, seized several barrels of "sod-corn whiskey," and dumped them into "the highway." At the same time, he had left a warning for proslavery men to "quit the territory." Knowing Montgomery and his men to be well armed and numerous, Hamilton and the other proslavery men left for Missouri. A meeting was scheduled later between Hamilton and Montgomery's Linn County men to discuss a treaty, but Parsons was told that so much bad blood existed between the two parties that trouble, not conciliation, was expected at the meeting.

Prior to their arrival at Harrisonville, the proslavery men had sought to redress their ejection from their homes. On May 19, 1858, Hamilton, after holding a meeting with the banished Kansans near Papinsville (near modern Rich Hill, Missouri), passed into Kansas with thirty-two men some mile and one-half south of Trading Post, where he struck the "military road." When he arrived at the town, he unfolded a list containing the names of wanted men and sent out squads to arrest them. Hamilton went with a squad to arrest the local blacksmith, Charles Snyder (or Snider). During the attempted arrest, the blacksmith fiercely defended himself and mortally wounded one of the attackers named Bell. Hamilton was enraged by the shooting of Bell, and when he got back to where his men had corralled their prisoners, he had the Free Staters marched single file to a ravine leading to the Marais des Cygnes River, faced eastward, and shot. Four men

were killed outright in the volley, six were wounded, and one man left acci-
dentally unhurt by pretending to be dead. The national press called the
event the "Marais des Cygnes Massacre." In Massachusetts, John Greenleaf
Whittier, abolitionist poet, was inspired by this tragedy to write: "On the
lintels of Kansas/That blood shall not dry." Montgomery, whose own
depredations had precipitated the retaliation, responded by launching a pillaging foray on frontier stores near Lecompton, far to the northeast in
Kansas.[21]

On August 7, 1858, Governor Stewart wrote to Governor Denver of
Kansas Territory informing him that Missouri was arming its border as
protection against Linn County, Kansas, marauders. On August 18, Denver
answered Stewart, politely reassuring him that he had restored peace in that
county with U.S. troops and afterward replaced them with a volunteer
Kansas militia commanded by A. I. Weaver. What neither Denver nor
Stewart had yet learned was that Montgomery's plan was to always disperse
when U.S. soldiers or militias besieged the county. He would simply reor-
ganize his men when the armed pressure was removed. Denver's actions,
therefore, had no impact on the situation whatsoever. Meanwhile, in
Missouri, the exiled Linn County proslavery men continued to make raids
back into Linn County. Whether the goods they were stealing had formerly been their own or were the property of Linn County farmers has never
been determined.

However, a representative of Missouri governor Stewart, J. G. Snyder,
division inspector for the Sixth Military District of the Missouri militia,
complained to the governor that some of these Linn County "proslavery
refugees," Morrow, Bean, Turk, and W. B. Young, had killed a Linn County
man named Pope who had tried to retrieve one of his "stolen" horses. The
horse was found later in Young's barn. As a result, Snyder recommended
that an independent company from St. Louis be sent to the area. It appears,
however, that few regular Missouri farmers, if any, were participating in the
marauding across the state/territorial line as most of the marauders were
ex-Linn County farmers.

At about this time, a U.S. marshal and his deputies attempted to arrest
some of Montgomery's men in Linn County and were apprehended by the
Kansas guerrilla and robbed of their weapons. Later, Montgomery and his
men "arrested" most of the officers of the court at Fort Scott, killing
Deputy Marshal John Little, a federal officer, and looting the town's stores.
This was insurrection against the federal government, a trait exhibited
more than once by members of this group. One of the men in
Montgomery's party was John Kagi, later killed at Harpers Ferry in John
Brown's treasonous raid. Another of the participants, A. H. Tannar, admit-
ted years later "that it was a very serious crime [at Fort Scott] against Uncle
Sam, and to-day would probably be punished relentlessly." But, he said,

Kansans were later "in the hands of our friends [Lincoln and the Republicans] . . . , and no one was ever tried for the offense."[22]

Governor Stewart, concerned about the volatile situation, opened up communications with Pres. James Buchanan, asking him to send federal troops to the area. Secretary John B. Floyd delivered Buchanan's terse answer: the United States did not have any troops to spare.[23]

By late summer 1858, John Brown, who had been harbored by an extensive network of abolitionists in the West and East, returned to southeast Kansas. This was bad news for western Missourians; Brown wasted no time in stirring up trouble. Within months, he rode into Missouri and committed the unpardonable crime (in Missourians' eyes) of stealing eleven slaves from Vernon County, Missouri and conducted them back to Kansas and thence along the underground railroad to Canada. Brown probably chose Vernon County farms to raid rather than Bates County ones because Vernon County was less populated, and he could enter the area and impose his will over the settlers with little difficulty. The raid on Vernon County would also be more dramatic; he could virtually eliminate the entire slave population of the county. Judging from the results of his activities and his often cold-blooded killings, it appears always to have been Brown's intention to commit such violent, flagrant, and outrageous acts that they would galvanize and precipitate the North and South into war. And this raid was no exception. Today, we call such tactics—behaviors that have a goal that transcends the immediate acts of extreme violence— terrorism. After the Pottawatomie massacre, any mention of Brown's actions created great fear on both sides of the Missouri-Kansas border.

In this latest venture, a slave, Jim Daniels, helped John Brown by informing him on Sunday, December 19, 1858, that the slaves on his farm in Vernon County were to be removed to Lafayette and Jackson Counties. The immediate reason for their being moved was to prevent their being freed by Linn County abolitionists. Free State historians claim, however, that the slaves were to be auctioned off in Texas—"sold South"—a serious, adverse occurrence for slaves. (This is an example of the contradictory data with which historians must contend in writing about this period.)

On December 20, John Brown formed his men into two parties to perform the raid. Brown led one of the parties, some twelve to fifteen men. His squad rode to the house of Harvey G. Hicklin, who lived on the north bank of the Little Osage River, on Duncan's Creek. Brown's men pounded on Hicklin's door and demanded his surrender. Hicklin, who was the son-in-law of a deceased man named Lawrence, had been holding Lawrence's slaves until they could be sold to settle his estate. After the raid, Hicklin told N. R. Marchbanks, the local justice of the peace, that Brown had stolen five blacks (two men, one woman, and two children), a yoke of oxen, two horses, one wagon, a shotgun, and various other items.[24] Brown then went to the home of John La Rue, less than a mile away, and freed five slaves, stole La Rue's bed clothing and other apparel, and took six horses. Then he kidnapped La Rue and his boarder, Dr. A. Ervin, taking them as hostages to ensure that he and his marauders made good their escape from the state.[25]

John Brown's other party, led by a man called "Stevens," was composed of nine men. Stevens was really John H. Kagi of the later treasonous Harpers Ferry attack. Kagi and his men rode to the home of David Cruise and attempted to take his female slave. The sixty-year-old Cruise attempted to make a fight of it, but his weapon misfired, and he was shot and killed by the marauders. Kagi and his men stole two yoke of oxen, a wagon full of provisions, clothing, eleven head of mules, and two horses from the dead Cruise. As an afterthought, Kagi stopped at the nearby home of Hugh Martin and stole another mule. Then, Kagi and his men returned to Bain's Fort to rejoin the exultant Brown. Afterward, Brown wrote a long, specious alibi justifying his crime. He titled it "John Brown's Parallels" and in it he claimed that his activities were different than similar episodes involving proslavery people. It was the old "two wrongs make a right" argument. The cynical Brown could not understand why "proslavery conservative Free-State dough faced men & administration tools are filled with holy horror."[26]

Following in the wake of John Brown's latest raid, on December 30, Capt. Eli Snyder rode into Missouri with another band and besieged the home of Jeremiah Jackson, a wealthy farmer from Bates County, who lived just two miles inside the Missouri line. Jackson and his son and son-in-law put up a good fight. Finally, to drive Jackson out, Snyder's men torched the farmer's house. After returning gunfire a while longer, Jackson and his family were forced to retreat, allowing Snyder to rob the estate of goods valued at six thousand dollars, a very large amount of money in those days, perhaps one hundred thousand dollars in today's money. After stealing these goods, Snyder set fire to the rest of Jackson's buildings.[27]

Upon the renewed raids by Brown and his supporters as well as the continued refusal of the federal government to provide troops to protect western Missouri, Governor Stewart, who had replaced Governor Denver after only seven months in office, sought to organize militias in the border counties of Vernon, Bates, Cass, Jackson, Lafayette, Johnson, Henry, and St. Clair. He failed, however, to get legislative support for the initiative. Finally, however, Stewart obtained thirty thousand dollars from nonappropriated money in the state treasury to establish a military force for the Missouri border. Gov. Samuel Medary of Kansas Territory meanwhile placed southeast Kansas under martial law and ordered four companies of dragoons into the area to maintain order. The result, as in the past, was the same: the marauders simply disbanded temporarily.[28]

As if the situation could not get any worse, on January 25, 1859, an abolitionist, John Doy, his son Charles, and a "Mr. Clough," from Lawrence, Kansas, proceeded from that town with thirteen escaped slaves along the underground railroad toward Iowa. According to Doy, the plan was to travel with the blacks as far as Holton, Kansas, then place them on the underground railroad that passed through northeast Kansas Territory into southern Iowa and obliquely northward to Canada. Tabor, Iowa, mentioned earlier, was a station along that route. But in this case, a proslavery posse from Lawrence, getting wind of Doy's plot through spies, accosted him some twelve miles from town, captured the convoy, tied up the escaped slaves, and took the entire party to Weston in Platte County. When the posse and its captives crossed the Missouri River at the Rialto Ferry, they were met by a throng of men congregated around a bonfire on the Missouri side of the river. Apparently, Missouri had its own efficient network of spies. From Weston, Doy was taken to Platte City, and thence to jail in St. Joseph, Missouri. On June 21, 1859, despite an expensive defense by two lawyers paid for by his admirers, Doy was sentenced to five years in the Missouri Penitentiary. Before he could be placed in prison, however, a

John Doy (seated), an aggressive abolitionist who made raids to free slaves and guided them north along the underground railroad. He is surrounded here by men from Lawrence, Kansas, who freed him from a western Missouri jail after he had been convicted of "slave stealing" and sentenced to five years in the Missouri Penitentiary. A few years later, during Quantrill's raid on Lawrence, many of these same men were described in the Eastern press as the "unarmed, helpless people" of Lawrence. *The Kansas State Historical Society, Topeka*

group of men from Lawrence, Kansas, led by Capt. James B. Abbot, broke into the jail; threatened to kill the jailer, W. Brown, if he resisted; and took Doy back with them to Lawrence. This is the same James B. Abbot who was one of the ringleaders involved in the rescue of Branson that preceded the Wakarusa War. It is also worth noting that a number of the same men who broke Doy out of jail were later, in 1859, enlisted to break John Brown out of a jail in Charleston, Virginia, where he awaited execution for treason against the United States government for attacking the U.S. Arsenal at Harpers Ferry and killing a number of civilians and soldiers.[29]

In an address by abolitionist O. E. Morse of Mound City, Kansas, on December 1, 1903, to the Kansas State Historical Society, Morse revealed a number of interesting bits of information about the Harpers Ferry conspiracy:

> Early in October, 1859, Richard J. Hinton came to Kansas, visited James Hanway at Dutch Henry's Crossing (now Lane), and induced Hanway to go with him to Linn county. Arriving at Moneka, they sent for Capt. James Montgomery and Augustus Wattles, both of whom immediately responded, and a conference was held in a room immediately over the post-office, at the Moneka hotel, then kept by Dr. George E. Dennison. This consultation resulted in the planning for the rescue of Brown. Hinton advocated an attempt by force, which necessitated the transporting of a considerable body of men to Virginia. Wattles did not approve of this believing it impracticable, and thinking that chances of success were only possible with a carefully selected few, and the exercise of the keenest tact and highest courage.[30]

Some of the men often referred to in various histories as the "Conspiracy of Six" or "Committee of Six" (wealthy New England financiers of high prominence in the United States involved in financing some of Brown's ventures, possibly even Harpers Ferry) were among the conspirators in this plot. Of these men, one was Thomas Wentworth Higginson while another was F. B. Sanborn. Among the Doy rescuers also chosen to participate in Brown's rescue, according to Morse, who provided as evidence a great deal of documentation, were "Joseph Gardner, Silas S. Soule, Joshua A. Pike, and S. J. Willis." In addition, "James Montgomery, Augustus Wattles, H. D. Seaman and Henry Carpenter came from Linn County, Benjamin Rice from Bourbon County, and Benjamin Seaman, a brother of H. D. Seaman, went from his home in Iowa."[31] Other men offering their aid, physically or in funds to finance the expedition, were J. C. Vaughn; J. W. Le Barnes; Edward Russell; John E. Stewart; W. W. Thayer, the publisher; James Redpath, the journalist; Dr. David Thayer; George Henry Hoyt, future Red Leg and sidekick of Charles Rainsford Jennison, one of the principal leaders of the Kansas Jayhawkers; S. J. Willis; Daniel

R. Anthony, Jennison's future military subordinate; Brachett, the sculptor; and Richard J. Hinton, among others.

The conspirators were carried east by the Hannibal & St. Joseph railroad through the intercession of "Elwood [Kansas] friends, and the additional amount necessary was put up by Major Tuttle, then agent of the [rail]road at St. Joseph . . . who was thoroughly in sympathy with the free-state movement in Kansas, as was Colonel Hayward, then general superintendent with the road." Incidentally, the Hannibal railroad at this time was "financially managed" by "John Murray Forbes and a New England consortium." Forbes knew Brown.[32]

According to Morse:

> The Montgomery party proceeded direct to Harrisburg without further incident of historical importance, where they were joined by the Lawrence party, by Wattles, Ben. Seaman, from Iowa, and R. J. Hinton. While there is no evidence at hand to show that Frederick Douglass joined the party at Harrisburg, it is pretty clear that he was in consultation with the leaders in their progress towards Charlestown [Virginia, where Brown's prison was located].

Soule then met with John Brown in prison and "secured an audience" with him. Soule discovered, Morse said, that "*John Brown refused to be rescued.*" His most credible reason for wishing not to be rescued was that "death on the gallows was a fulfillment of his mission, the rounding out of his effort: the act that would make effective all his work for the freedom of the slaves. In his simple and terse way he said: 'I am worth more to die than to live.' "[33]

Apparently, the men from Lawrence who traveled east to break Brown out of prison were of the rough and ready sort. Abolitionist Joshua A. Pike, their collaborator in the rescue of Doy and Brown, upon meeting some of them later in Lawrence, said: "town full of niggers and abolitionists; a tough set; saw three of the Doctor Doy rescue party, and they were toughs; would not like to meet them after night." Of course, if these men were to break John Brown out of the Charlestown, Virginia, prison, considering the formidable defenses set up by Southerners, they would have had to have been very tough, indeed. This entire episode has to be one of the most bizarre on record, a scandalous incident in U.S. history, though it is seldom mentioned as such, if it is mentioned at all. While the Harpers Ferry raid and the conspiracy to break Brown out of jail were occurring, the conspirators who had financed Brown's small army, wealthy New England financiers and members of the Conspiracy of Six, including Gerrit Smith, Theodore Parker, Dr. Samuel Gridley Howe, Thomas Wentworth Higginson, and F. B. Sanborn had became highly agitated. Howe fled to Canada, Parker to Rome, and Sanborn had fought off federal marshals with the help of a Concord mob.

Journalist and historian Richard O. Boyer described the antics of John

Brown's multitude of conspirators, who had solicited money for their escapades widely, as "the most public conspiracy in the history of the United States." Bronson Alcott said of Brown: "Our best people listen to his words—Emerson, Thoreau, Judge Hoar, my wife—and some of them contribute something in aid of his plans without asking particulars."[34]

Even with Brown's arrest and imprisonment, conditions on the border in Bates and Vernon Counties did not improve in 1860. One of the reasons was that in 1858, a new dark star in the Free State firmament had risen to prominence—Charles Rainsford Jennison. Raised in New York, Jennison, known as "Doc," had received medical training in Wisconsin, moved to Minnesota, and thence to Mound City, Kansas, in 1854. He became an almost instant leader in the area. When a dispute arose concerning whether Mound City or Paris should be the county seat, Jennison led his "boys" over to Paris, trained a howitzer on the courthouse, took the county records, and settled the matter forever. As violent and willful as Montgomery was, the Free Staters soon realized in Jennison someone even more aggressive and radical, and withal audacious. They liked these traits. Perhaps Jennison meant more money for them, more stolen corn for their cribs. Jennison claimed to be the creator of what he termed "self-sustaining" warfare. The concept meant, in ordinary terms, that war would be waged in the old-fashioned way, financed by plunder. This met with no disagreement among the young lads around Mound City. In practical terms, Jennison promoted the goal of pillaging to the utmost and destroying what was not worth carrying away. His men soon went by the sobriquet "Jennison's Jayhawkers," and they earned the title. Jennison was a tiny man, even for his times, but he had resourcefulness, audacity, can-do energy, and a very tall fur hat that he habitually wore to make up for his quite short height.[35]

Jennison was bolstered by the election of Abraham Lincoln, which produced a euphoric state in the people of southeast Kansas. Now, Montgomery and Jennison had three hundred well-armed and provisioned men with adequate ammunition for any venture they wished to pursue and little to restrain them. On November 11, 1860, under Jennison's direction, the Linn County men formed a posse and arrested all the proslavery farmers around Trading Post, whom they claimed their spies learned were conspirators and members of the "Dark Lantern Order." The posse also seized James Russell Hindes (or Hinds), a Missourian who was in Kansas Territory visiting his mother. They lynched him. They said he had been lynched because he had carried a fugitive slave back to his master, Lewis Reece, and therefore must forfeit his life. Montgomery endorsed the hanging, saying that it conformed to Exodus 21:16, that if a man "stealeth a man and selleth him, or if he be found in his hand, he shall surely be put to death." Hindes, he said, was to be "hung by the neck until he [was] dead! Dead!! Dead!!!" The rest of the proslavery settlers were also tried "by

Vigilance Court order" and required to leave the territory within seven days, which they did, taking with them only the property they could carry.[36]

Samuel Scott, once a sheriff in Vernon County, was seized by Jennison's vigilantes and murdered on November 18, also for reclaiming runaway slaves. Other citizens in Bourbon and Linn Counties, "S. D. Moore, Messrs Smith and Bishop," were murdered about the same time. No one knows why. Judge Joseph Williams, presiding judge of the United States district

Col. Charles Rainsford Jennison, leader of the Jayhawkers, the Seventh Kansas Volunteer Cavalry, who committed some of the worst atrocities and depredations in Missouri. *The Kansas State Historical Society, Topeka, Kansas*

court and the other United States judicial officers in Fort Scott became so frightened by Jennison's and Montgomery's threats against their lives that they abandoned the court and fled to Missouri on November 19. Judge Scott warned Governor Stewart of Missouri of Jennison and Montgomery's avowed plan to invade Missouri and to start a crusade there against slaveholders. However, lawlessness reigned in southeast Kansas.

The Free Staters' quarrel with the legal authorities may have arisen as a result of land sales that were to take place on December 3, 1860. The suspicion exists that many of Jennison's and Montgomery's men were so impoverished that they were about to lose their property, which would provide a pecuniary motive in throwing out the local judiciary, especially at a time when they likely had little tenure left with Lincoln ascending to office. This same poverty among Jennison's men would also explain the marauders' preoccupation with raiding the affluent, established farmers of Bates and Vernon Counties in Missouri. Kansans during this period, despite Sara Robinson's remarks about the "drunken rabble" and "de po' white folk" of Missouri, were often dreadfully poor. The destitute condition of Kansans and the wealth of Missourians may go a long way in explaining the wholesale raiding of Missouri farms by Jennison, Montgomery, and Lane et al. at the outset of the Civil War and afterward. As historian Albert Castel said, "From the beginning Kansas had been the constant recipient of aid, both organized and private, from the East," which was necessary to sustain them. In contrast, many Missourians were quite prosperous, making them prime targets.[37]

On November 20, 1860, Adjutant General Snyder informed Governor Stewart of Missouri by telegram that Montgomery had invaded Missouri again. Stewart decided that the unorganized militias of western Missouri were no match for Montgomery and his 300 well-armed marauders. State troops from Jefferson City and St. Louis, commanded by Brig. Gen. D. M. Frost, must be sent. Called the "Southwest Expedition," Frost's Missouri Volunteer Militia would consist of 630 men and carry a strong artillery presence to impress what Frost termed "the outlaw Montgomery and his band." Frost learned by November 28, 1860, that Montgomery was at Fort Scott "in possession of the town [and] holding a Court by his own authority condemning persons whom he has arrested to be hung and otherwise punished." Frost believed, from information provided him by informants, that Montgomery had only around 100 armed men. General Parsons sent a message to Governor Stewart on December 2 claiming that Montgomery, in public speeches, had openly proclaimed that "he intends first to drive out all his enemies from the Territory, and when that is done he intends to enter Missouri at different points and make a clean sweep of that. It is believed here that Montgomery will give Genl Harney [the commander of U.S. troops] a fight if he only has the 150 to 200 regulars that was at Fort

Leavenworth." On December 3, Harney arrived at Fort Scott with 200 U.S. Dragoons, and soon Montgomery's followers held a meeting at Fort Scott vocally opposing Harney's presence. They complained about "the War Department's action in sending troops to the Kansas Territory to exterminate those whom they [Jennison's and Montgomery's men] regarded as 'trusty neighbors, good citizens, and honest men.' " The marauders, oddly enough, were referring to themselves.[38]

Frost concentrated his men along the Marais des Cygnes River, one and one-half miles from the territorial line and about twelve miles from "Montgomery's headquarters." At this point, the Missourians apparently knew little about Jennison and his part in the struggle. Frost discovered that

> Orderly, industrious, and peaceable citizens [of Bates and Vernon Counties] have been warned to leave: or that they would be robbed and hung—many have deserted their homes, taking with them their moveable property, abandoning their farms which can not now be sold, thus presenting the singular anomaly of a rich and fertile country sparsely settled, being rapidly depopulated. . . . Many along our route have failed to treat us with ordinary civility for fear of incurring the displeasure of these Kansas outlaws and marauders.

These remarks infer that Jennison's and Montgomery's spy network was still alive and functioning in the area. In late November, acting governor of Kansas, George M. Beebe, visited the Fort Scott area and later wrote the following to Pres. James Buchanan:

> Upon reaching the neighborhood of the rendezvous of this band [Montgomery and Jennison's] I found the country in the utmost excitement; families were flying, panic-stricken, from their homes, and men were hiding in the woods to elude the vengeance of Montgomery and his desperadoes. From Linn county alone some 500 citizens have fled. The offenders are amply provided with provisions, and arms of the latest and most deadly character; all of which, there is no doubt, were furnished from eastern states.

Beebe appended his remarks by saying, "On their professions [Jennison's and Montgomery's] no reliance can be placed. Nothing short of the death of the ringleaders of the band will give quiet to the country."[39]

By December 8, 1860, General Frost had discovered that Montgomery and Jennison had dispersed their men, their usual tactic, providing no target for the Missouri State Militia or the federal troops now converging on Linn County. The Jayhawkers were fighting like Indians: concentrating when it was possible to overpower their enemies, dispersing when superior forces confronted them. With no reason for his continued presence,

Frost told the governor that he was returning east after only twenty days of service but that he intended to establish a special force of three companies of cavalry (two hundred men) and a battery of artillery at Ball's Mill in Vernon County, which would continue to patrol the state line. In the meantime, as historian Herklotz maintained, "Masters and their slaves left the western borders of Bates and Vernon counties for the interior, and slavery was practically abolished there for a time."[40]

When he succeeded Governor Stewart in 1861, Gov. Claiborne Jackson continued to maintain forces along the Missouri border. Early that year, in a petition, 506 citizens of Bates and Vernon Counties warned Jackson to keep troops on the border to prevent Jennison and Montgomery from committing more robberies and murders in Missouri. If the troops were moved, the Missourians believed, the Kansans would immediately invade the state again.

Once the Civil War broke out in Missouri months later, all of these fears would become a nightmarish reality. The same violent men, Montgomery and Jennison, who had been terrorizing Missourians along the south-central Missouri border for years, now would be made major commanders in the Union army and allowed to function under the lax and permissive control of Gen. Jim Lane while they carried out his violent directives. Now, the southeast Kansas "outlaws" would be operating under the full auspices of the United States government. With virtually no restraints on their conduct, the Kansans would desolate and terrorize the entire Missouri border from south of St. Joseph to Springfield, committing wholesale robbery, arson, murder, and mayhem. But first, the Union army would have to overthrow Missouri's elected governor, Claiborne Jackson, gain control of Missouri's state government, and occupy the state with troops.[41]

Chapter 6

Conflicting Loyalties: The Civil War in Missouri

The result of Missouri's votes in the national and state elections in 1860 charted the state's course during the Civil War. Some 165,618 votes were cast in the national election in Missouri, divided among four candidates: Stephen A. Douglas, Democratic Party; John C. Bell, Constitutional Unionist Party; John C. Breckinridge, Southern faction, Democratic Party; and Abraham Lincoln, Republican Party. Of these men, Breckinridge and Lincoln, popularly perceived to be the secessionist and abolitionist candidates, were the weakest candidates at the polls, receiving only 18.8 and 10 percent of the votes respectively. Douglas and Bell, on the other hand, received 35.5 and 35.4 percent. Since Breckinridge and Lincoln were considered the "radical" candidates, the vote was considered a conservative one, with Missourians expressing their wish both to stay in the Union and to retain slavery.[1]

In line with this conservatism, when Robert M. Stewart, Missouri's proslavery governor, relinquished the governorship to Claiborne Jackson in 1860, he argued for peace and stability, saying, "Missouri to surrender her prosperity in exchange for the mad chimera of secession to be followed by revolution, battle and blood? Never!"[2]

Lincoln, despite his poor Missouri showing, won the national election that year by a plurality of votes, winning on a platform for the suppression (not abolition) of slavery. While Lincoln was considered a "conservative" Republican, within his party were some of the most strident and extreme abolitionists. This caused Missourians to distrust the Republican Party, in general, and Lincoln, specifically. In Missouri, Lincoln carried only St. Louis and Gasconade Counties—and those because of the German vote, which he carried overwhelmingly. Even with the German vote, however, Lincoln won in St. Louis County by only a plurality of 40 percent. In fifteen other Missouri counties, Lincoln received no votes, in eight counties but one vote.[3]

Since Missouri was predominantly a proslavery state, it might be natural to assume that John Breckinridge, considered the proslavery candidate and the favorite of secessionists, would have polled decisively in the counties where the slave owners resided. Instead, Breckinridge did poorly in those

105

counties, and the Constitutional Unionist and Democratic Parties dominated the areas. In fact, Bell, the Constitutional Unionist candidate, captured much of the old-line Whig votes in those counties, while Claiborne Jackson's Democratic "Central Clique" garnered most of the rest. Some of the counties where the slave population was most dense had been predominantly Whig since 1844. But since 1856, the party had been in decline.[4]

By 1860, the Whig Party had become defunct. Its ideology, however, remained potent and was articulated by the influential *Missouri Republican* newspaper in St. Louis. The old Whig political philosophy was still sustained, moreover, in Audrain, Boone, Saline, and Lafayette Counties, areas where large slave populations and many of the wealthiest slave owners resided. Callaway, New Madrid, Saline, and Green Counties also had many residents who shared the old Whig philosophy. Most of the above counties, called "Little Dixie," were situated along the Missouri and Mississippi Rivers. When the Whig Party dissolved, many ex-Whigs became affiliated with the Unionist Party. In 1849, when Claiborne Jackson's "Resolutions" (a proslavery litmus test with potentially secessionist undertones) were voted into effect, of the twenty-seven "no" votes it received, twenty-three had been Whig ones.[5] Prominent slave owners of the Whig persuasion, as a whole, were conservative, traditional aristocrats, dispassionate businessmen, and political realists. They were never at the heart of the secessionist movement in Missouri. In 1854, the Whigs united with pro-Benton politicians to stymie the dominant Democrats, but this coalition dissolved when the Whigs divided into states' rights Whigs under George W. Goode and William P. Darnes and free-soil Whigs under James S. Rollins. This effectively ended the Whig's existence as an organized political force in Missouri. But their ideology remained a powerful influence.

Most slave owners, as historian Sceva Bright Laughlin maintained, "were . . . convinced that the secession of the state, whether successful or not, meant the extinction of slavery."[6] When war broke out, it was believed, Missouri, because of its position to the North, would be overrun. Judge William A. Hall, in an address in Huntsville on December 24, 1860, typified this belief, saying, "Our feelings, our sympathies, would strongly incline us to go with the extreme Southern States if separation takes place. But passion and feeling are temporary; interest is paramount."[7]

By 1860, therefore, members of the Douglas and John Breckinridge factions of the "Democracy" (the Democratic Party) were the dominant popular political group in Missouri. At the Missouri Democratic convention held on April 9, 1860, however, the Douglas Democrats, who were, in many respects, identical with the old Benton forces,[8] were shunted aside in the party's policy-making arena. Only one Douglas man, for example, gained a position on the party's powerful resolutions and platform committee. A strong proslavery platform was the result. As part of their platform, the dominant Breckinridge Democrats affirmed that Congress had no right to abolish slavery or refuse its inclusion into the territories and maintained that the fugitive slave laws should be honored. They also affirmed that John Brown's raid at Harpers Ferry and his incursion into Missouri had been "a genuine demonstration of the intent and purpose of the Republican Party."[9]

The Democrats at the 1860 state Democratic convention nominated Claiborne F. Jackson for governor, Thomas Caute Reynolds (a radical proslavery man) for lieutenant governor, and Benjamin F. Massey for secretary of state. At the end of the convention, one of the delegates, N. C. Claiborne, implored the Democrats of Missouri to "stand firm against the hydra-headed amalgamation of Abolitionism, Douglasism, and Black Republicanism now confronting us intent on abrogating the Constitution and establishing an oligarchy upon the ruins of our Democratic institutions."[10] The Douglas Democrats in attendance naturally received these remarks sullenly. The convention had been rancorous, with anti-Douglas and pro-Douglas factions expressing intense animosity toward one another at times.

Once the national Democratic convention was conducted later in the year, the Missouri Democrats divided their allegiance into Douglas and John Breckinridge factions, forming two tickets. (State elections in Missouri at this time were held in August and national elections in November.) For reasons of expediency, Jackson and Reynolds, both strong Southern men leaning strongly toward secession, were installed on the Douglas national ticket, apparently to ensure their elections.[11] They appeared to believe, and rightly, that Breckinridge lacked national appeal, was not well supported in the state, and therefore should not be allowed to drag other politicians, specifically themselves, to political defeat. The Democratic secretary of state candidate, Benjamin Massey, commented in bewilderment at this development, saying, "Isn't that a stunner?"[12] But even secessionist senator James S. Green, who had formed the state ticket for Breckinridge, finally abandoned Breckinridge's sinking political ship and joined the Douglas Democrats.

When Douglas campaigned in Missouri in 1860, he warned Missourians that "the Democratic party was the only one capable of saving the Union."[13] Many Missourians agreed with Douglas and voted for him for that reason. They believed that if one of the radical candidates, Lincoln or John Breckinridge, should win the presidency, it would mean war. Reflecting the general conservatism of Missourians, Breckinridge ran a poor third in the state election and won in only a number of poorly populated southern Missouri counties.

On August 6, 1860, the Democrats, many leaning toward secession, swept into political office in Missouri. With the election of Lincoln in

November, Claiborne Jackson and many of his Democratic colleagues began agitating for secession. Jackson's earlier desertion of John Breckinridge and some of his other political waffling now caused the Southern leadership to regard him with suspicion.[14] While Jackson's machinations were only ordinary, manipulative political tactics, his reputation as a political "compromiser" still caused Southerners great concern. The strait-laced Jefferson Davis worried about Jackson's sincerity and integrity.[15]

One characteristic of the 1860 election for Missouri legislators would have far reaching significance. While Jackson was elected as part of the Douglas Democratic ticket, the legislature was composed of fourteen hold-over John Breckinridge senators, one Republican senator, and six Douglas and five Constitutional Unionist senators. The reason for the disproportionately large number of Breckinridge senators in the legislature was that the "extreme southern wing of the party had been in control of the state government for four years."[16] The result of this situation was that men more easily swayed toward secession held dominant positions in the current state legislature. Another problem developing in Missouri was the increasing radicalism of some of the old Benton Democrats, many of whom were now being led in St. Louis by Frank Blair Jr., B. Gratz Brown, Edward Bates, and others. They had allied themselves with the militant Germans in that area and had become staunch Republicans. They would give the dominant Democrats in Missouri, led by Claiborne Jackson, the fight of their lives. The Republican's political voice was the old Benton newspaper in St. Louis, the *Missouri Democrat*. Missouri Republicans also had a strong ally in the White House: Abraham Lincoln. Frank Blair Jr., the leader of the St. Louis Republicans, was a close friend of Lincoln, and Frank's brother, Montgomery Blair, had been installed as Lincoln's postmaster general.

On January 3, 1861, Jackson, in his inaugural address, claimed that the Northern states were abandoning the Union and said, "The South are not the aggressors. They only ask to be let alone. . . . We hear it suggested, in some quarters, that the Union is to be maintained by the sword. . . . The project of maintaining the Federal Government by force may lead to consolidation or despotism, but not to Union. . . . [That] stands upon the basis of *justice and equality,* and its existence cannot be prolonged by coercion." Jackson then asked that a state convention be convened in Missouri to canvass public sentiment concerning the crisis and that it "consider the then existing relations between the Government of the United States . . . and [the] people of the State of Missouri; and to adopt such measures for vindicating the sovereignty of the State and the protection of its institutions, as shall appear to them to be demanded." Jackson hoped that the convention would sanction secession and approve the arming of the state.[17]

When the state legislature convened on February 10, it passed a bill, as

Jackson had suggested it should, ordering the election of delegates to a state convention to be held on February 18, 1861. Some 104 delegates were elected to the convention and met in Jefferson City on February 28. As it turned out, not a single member was an avowed secessionist. Of the 140,000 votes cast, the conditional and unconditional Unionist delegates polled nearly 110,000 votes, or almost 8 out of every 10 votes. Sterling Price, a hero of the Mexican War and a popular former governor of Missouri, was chosen president of the convention. At this time, Price was the leader of the Constitutional Unionist Party and known as a conditional Union man (one who favored remaining in the Union under specified conditions). Later, however, he would become the commander of the Missouri State Guard under the Confederacy.[18]

When the convention assembled, it expressed its dissatisfaction with Northern attempts to coerce the South and predicted that these actions would lead to civil war. In its resolutions, however, the convention was adamant "that at present, there was no adequate cause to impel Missouri to dissolve her connection with the Federal Union." This sentiment was not what Governor Jackson and Lieutenant Governor Reynolds had expected. They had hoped for a clear-cut mandate for secession.

But according to James O. Broadhead, an old-line Whig, there still was considerable sentiment in favor of the South in Missouri, and, according to him, "at least two-thirds of the votes of the State outside St. Louis held that if the North . . . should make war upon any Southern State, Missouri would take up arms in its defense."[19] George G. Vest, moreover, made a motion at the convention pledging "the people of Missouri to rally to the side of their Southern brethren and to resist the invader at all hazard to the last extremity." The motion carried by an eighty-four to seventy-four margin. The narrow margin of victory, however, demonstrated that Missourians still were wavering on the issue.[20] Another member of the convention cautioned his fellows, saying, "Owing to their geographical situation [Missouri was surrounded on three sides by free states], secession and adhesion to the Confederacy would mean annihilation."[21] Governor Jackson and his advisers, nonetheless, still remained confident that it was only a matter of time until the people of Missouri were ready for secession.

When the convention was reconvened in St. Louis on March 4, it decided by a vote of sixty-three to fifty-three to listen to L. J. Glenn, commissioner of Georgia, who wished to explain the South's situation and persuade Missourians that they should secede from the Union. Glenn's reception was cordial but only lukewarm. Jackson also failed to gain support at the convention for organizing and arming Missouri's militias. The convention, subject to future recall, adjourned on March 22.

Despite Jackson's failure to mobilize public support for secession, he had been for some time preparing Missouri to secede from the Union.

Jackson rightly concluded that if Missouri were to secede from the United States and become part of the Confederacy, it was imperative for the state to seize the St. Louis Arsenal and its "sixty thousand muskets, 90,000 pounds of powder, 1.5 million ball cartridges, 40 field pieces, as well as all the machinery to manufacture arms and ammunition."[22] In January, Jackson sent Gen. Daniel M. Frost, a West Point graduate and commander of the state militia, to St. Louis to secure control of the arms at the U. S. Arsenal should Missouri decide to secede. In a letter dated January 24, 1861, Frost reported to Jackson that "he had been assured by [Maj. William H.] Bell, then in command of the arsenal, that whenever the time came Missouri would have '*a right to claim it* [the arsenal] *as being upon her soil.*' " Frost said, moreover, that Bell promised he "would not attempt any defense [of the arsenal] against the proper state authorities." Shortly thereafter, however, Maj. Peter V. Hagner, an officer not amenable to Frost and Jackson's plan, replaced Bell.[23] To further advance his scheme to obtain control of the arsenal, Jackson now ramrodded through the legislature a new police law that gave him the right to appoint the St. Louis Board of Police Commissioners, the same men who selected the St. Louis police chief. Since St. Louis's newly elected mayor was favorable to secession, Jackson was gaining control of the town, with the exception of the arsenal and the soldiers in it—a big exception.

Opposing Jackson in his designs was Frank Blair Jr., a U.S. congressman, relative and protégé of Thomas Hart Benton, and the favorite son of Frank Blair Sr., one of the founders of the Republican Party and a former friend and adviser of Andrew Jackson. Related closely to a number of prominent men, including Benton, Confederate general Jo Shelby, and B. Gratz Brown, Frank Jr. was clearly a formidable political adversary. He had become the leader of a powerful clan, and it was said, "When the Blairs went in for a fight, they went in for a funeral." In his earlier days, the fiery Blair had been dismissed from Yale, North Carolina, and Princeton Universities, the last school withholding his degree because he had shot someone in a tavern brawl. Later, in St. Louis, thwarted in an attempt to duel with a local luminary, Lorenzo Pickering, Blair engaged him in a spontaneous, informal duel on Chestnut Street in downtown St. Louis, thrashing Pickering with his umbrella, the only instrument of war available to him. Later, Blair shot it out with Pickering and another man, Thomas Prefontaine, who were allegedly trying to assassinate him.[24]

Blair was also noted for his views toward slavery. His stand on the emancipation of blacks seems somewhat unorthodox today: Blair supported emancipation because, he said, blacks "threatened the free white laborers' economic opportunities." For that reason, Blair favored the "colonization of freed blacks in Central America."[25]

Because the Republicans were a tiny minority in Missouri and disliked by

many, when Blair gave speeches, he often was met with catcalls, and sometimes rocks "hit the wall over his head" or "eggs splatter[ed]" on the platform around him. None of this disturbed Blair, who when he was told that
his "speaking might result in personal injury" seemed "especially eager to
talk."[26] At one point, hecklers and rowdies had plagued Blair's Republican
rallies. The congressman's solution to the problem was to organize what he
called his "Wide Awakes," a mostly German American paramilitary group.
Blair armed these men with long, lead-weighted poles atop which lighted
lamps were attached. At political meetings, he stationed the Wide Awakes so
that when anyone made a disturbance, the German guards beat them with
their poles or splashed them with hot camphene from their lamps.
Thereafter, the Republican meetings were largely free of interruptions.[27]

With such a recognition of the political environment, Blair immediately
understood the importance of the arsenal in St. Louis and knew that it held
more arms and munitions than those "in all of the other slave States." Blair
had told Lincoln that if the "Southern rights administration of Missouri
gained control of the arsenal and its contents the State would be carried into
the Confederacy and with Missouri the other border States would be lost."
Lincoln agreed with Blair and months later told O. H. Browning, in a letter
of September 22, 1861, that if Kentucky and Missouri were lost, Maryland
would follow, "and the job on our hands is too large for us. We would as
well consent to separation at once, including the surrender of the capital."[28]

When Blair learned through his spies about Jackson's renewed interest
in the U.S. Arsenal, he was convinced that the governor was organizing an
attempt to seize it. Blair also knew about the organization in St. Louis of a
secessionist paramilitary group called the "Minute Men," organized by
Basil W. Duke and Colton Greene and headquartered in the Berthold
Mansion at Fifth and Pine Streets. Blair believed that Jackson intended to
use the Minute Men to capture the arsenal and its weapons for the state
militia.[29] In response, Blair reorganized his Wide Awakes, increased their
number, and formed them into what he called the "Home Guards." Blair
drilled these German Americans in the seclusion of the local breweries and
warehouses. Meanwhile, he had his brother, Montgomery, who was now
Lincoln's postmaster general, obtain muskets from Washington to arm the
men. Blair hoped to muster his men into service soon.[30]

To aid him further in his efforts to protect the arsenal, Blair, through his
connections with Lincoln, had Capt. Nathaniel Lyon, a radical abolitionist,
and eighty of his men transferred from Fort Scott, Kansas Territory, to St.
Louis on January 31, 1861. On March 11, Blair wrote Secretary of War
Simon Cameron: "Our friends in St. Louis desire that Captain Lyon may
have the command of the troops at the Saint Louis Arsenal, and be
charged with its defense." On May 13, Lyon was placed in complete control of the arsenal, replacing Hagner, who outranked Lyon but was not as

thoroughly trusted. This move by Blair would even more seriously compli-
cate Jackson's takeover of the arsenal.[31]

Earlier, on April 14, 1861, word was received that Fort Sumter in South
Carolina had fallen to the state militia. Civil war had begun. In response,
the next day Abraham Lincoln made a national call for 75,000 "volunteers,"
hoping to halt the rebellion in its tracks. Missouri's quota would be 3,121
men, and the War Department sent an urgent message to Jackson requesting them. The livid Jackson replied, "Sir:—Your requisition is illegal,
unconstitutional and revolutionary; in its object inhuman & diabolical. Not
one man will Missouri furnish to carry on any such unholy crusade against
her Southern sisters." Jackson then called a special session of the General
Assembly to meet on May 2 to order "measures, . . . for the more perfect
organization, and equipment of the militia of this State, and to raise the
money, . . . as may be required to place the State in a proper attitude of
defence," a measure referred to as the "military bill."

On April 17, Jackson sent two emissaries, Capts. Colton Greene and
Basil W. Duke, the commanders of the St. Louis Minute Men, to Pres.
Jefferson Davis to obtain mortars and siege artillery to take the U.S.
Arsenal at St. Louis. Jackson had now committed himself; in fact, he was
collaborating in treason. Jefferson Davis, on April 23, replied to Jackson
that he was sending "two 12-pounder howitzers and two 32-pounder guns,
with the proper ammunition for each." Davis added, "I concur with you as
to the importance of capturing the arsenal and securing its supplies, rendered doubly important by the means taken to obstruct your commerce
and render you unarmed victims to a hostile invasion." The weapons being
sent by Davis to Missouri were taken just weeks earlier by armed force
from the U.S. Arsenal at Baton Rouge, Louisiana. They arrived in St. Louis
on May 8.[32]

Though Jackson lacked the legal right to call out the militias under his
direct control, it was within his authority to order the militias to establish
training camps in their respective districts, and he did so. At the same time,
Jackson commanded Gen. Daniel Frost to organize a camp on the western
edge of St. Louis, soon to be christened "Camp Jackson." Frost organized
the camp, composed of 891 men, at Lindell's Grove on May 6, 1861. By
this time, it was all too obvious to Blair and his associates what Jackson was
planning.[33]

Days later, when Frost's aide-de-camp, Lt. William D. Wood, asked Lyon
for permission to train his pioneers on the heights overlooking the arsenal,
Lyon and Blair's suspicions were confirmed. Lyon, who was as combative
as Blair, hotly refused the request, considering it a transparent attempt by
Frost to emplace artillery in a position threatening the arsenal.

On the same day that Jackson had refused to comply with Lincoln's call
for volunteers, Blair arrived in St. Louis with an order on the arsenal for

five thousand muskets. At about the same time, a telegram arrived from Washington authorizing Blair to "muster into service four regiments." Blair accomplished this in two weeks by enrolling his Home Guards, the former Wide Awakes.[34]

Jackson, still held back by the reluctance of Missourians to secede from the Union, wrote David Walker of the Arkansas convention (secession conventions were being held all over the South). He wrote, "I have been, from the beginning, in favor of prompt action on the part of the southern states, but a majority of the people of Missouri, up to the present time have differed with me. . . . [M]y present impression is—judging from the indications hourly occurring—that Mo [Missouri] will be ready for secession in less than thirty days; and will secede."[35]

Unfortunately for Jackson, he would not be given the luxury of thirty days. Lyon had learned of Jackson's Southern shipment of mortars and artillery. When the arms arrived aboard the steamer *J. C. Swan* on May 8, one of Lyon's spies among the boat's Unionist crew reported the fact to Lyon, telling him that the arms were in boxes marked "Tamora [marble], care of Greely & Gale, Saint Louis."[36]

Armed with this information, Lyon began planning the conquest of Camp Jackson. By this time, he and Blair had assembled some sixty-five hundred armed and drilled troops at the arsenal, a force sufficiently large to overwhelm the unwitting Frost—if he received no reinforcements. Lyon's relatively large force had been obtained by mustering Blair's Home Guards into active service and by augmenting the force on April 20 with some two or three regiments sent by Illinois governor Richard Yates, at Lyon's request. Blair's St. Louis troops, the "Schwarzer Jägercorps," or "Black Rifles," were the local Unionists' response to Lincoln's request for seventy-five thousand volunteers. Colonels Frank Blair, Henry Boernstein (Heinrich Börnstein), Francis "Franz" Sigel, and Nicolas Schüttner, all Germans except for Blair, would command the various German American regiments.

Colonel Boernstein, in his memoir, described the fervor with which the Germans took to their new military roles. "What a happy, cheerful mood reigned among these volunteers! At all points of the great park surrounding the United States Arsenal, there was ceaseless drilling, and when this labor was done at the end of day, all nooks and crannies sounded with German war songs and soldiers' choirs, Lutzow's 'Wilde Jagd' and the 'Schwerlief.' " Many of these men had performed earlier military training in Germany and Austria during the Revolution of 1848. They were now learning the American system.[37]

Reinforcing Lyon's decision to raise these forces, on April 20, 1861, secessionists in Clay and Jackson Counties seized the U.S. Arsenal at Liberty, Missouri, and carried away fifteen hundred arms and four brass cannon. This event further raised Lyon's apprehension. He now feared that the artillery from Liberty might be used against him in St. Louis, causing him to press ahead rapidly with his plans. Boernstein, who visited the St. Louis Arsenal about this time, said that its entrance "was strictly controlled as a fortress under siege."[38]

While relatively low-ranking Captain Lyon was devising his plans, he was still the subordinate of Maj. Gen. William S. Harney, commander of the Department of the West, whom Blair was fast at work deposing. The conservative Harney's presence in St. Louis complicated Blair and Lyon's conspiracy. Finally, on April 21, using his influence with his brother, Montgomery, and Gov. A. G. Curtin of Pennsylvania, Blair had Harney's command taken from him by Lincoln. Harney seemed oblivious to Blair's machinations until he was suddenly fired by an order carried in Blair's pocket. Harney, who had continually sent messages to Washington asking for guidance, seemed like one of those commanders more interested in absolving himself from blame than in asserting himself through action.[39]

Lyon and his men continued to take action to prevent the secessionists from successfully controlling the arsenal. Boernstein reported that on April 25 he and some of his men went to the St. Louis river front to guard the midnight shipment of some "twenty-one thousand rifles, eight cannon, [and] the necessary sidearms, carts, and corresponding munitions." The arms were being sent by steamboat from the arsenal to Alton, Illinois, to be carried farther east for their protection. Boernstein and some of his men accompanied the steamer, which was "crammed full of weapons" for its secret flight across the Mississippi. The ship was so heavy, the crew had to shift the cargo to dislodge the steamboat from the mud as it pushed away from the river's banks. The boilers of the ship, Boernstein said, were heated minimally in order to prevent a large plume of smoke rising to alert the Missouri authorities.

Lyon's plans against the Missourians culminated with an attack of Camp Jackson. In a council of war on May 9, Lyon conferred with members of the Committee of Public Safety, a Unionist group in St. Louis, to determine the legality of his prospective move on Camp Jackson. The committee's lawyers told him that the camp was legal and flew the American flag. They told Lyon, moreover, that the only way he could enter the camp was with a writ of replevin to be served by a U.S. marshal. Lyon supposedly huffed that he hadn't time for "Mr. Blackstone." The march on Camp Jackson would be difficult, Lyon knew, because his men would have to march through the center of St. Louis to get at Frost's camp. Lyon's plan was to form his sixty-five hundred men in four columns, march them along four different routes, and converge on Camp Jackson quickly, simultaneously, and in overwhelming strength.

A tale crops up in many histories at this point about Lyon's alleged spying expedition to Camp Jackson while dressed up like an old woman.

According to the yarn, proposed to be true, Lyon, wearing a "black bombazine dress" borrowed from Frank Blair's blind mother, Mrs. Alexander, rode through the enemy camp in an "ornate barouche [which supposedly belonged to Blair's brother-in-law, Col. Franklin A. Dick] pulled by a high-stepping team" driven by Mrs. Blair's slave, "Peter." Henry Boernstein, a close associate of Lyon's who was there at the time, told a quite different, more mundane, story in his memoir. He described Lyon coming in from his reconnaissance the night before the attack on Camp Jackson "covered in mud and dirt" after crawling through "a ditch" at the camp. There is no mention of the details of the more colorful accounts.[40]

The next day, on May 10, with Harney out of the way, Lyon was free to execute his plan. That morning he sent for his men and formed them into columns. Throughout the morning, rumors ran rampant through St. Louis that Lyon had held a council of war the night before. Frost, hearing the rumors, was incredulous that Lyon would make such a rash, illegal move as to attack his military camp. Still, the incessant talk made him nervous, and he sent his chief of staff, Col. John S. Bowen, with a note to Lyon asking "whether there is any truth in the statements that are constantly poured into my ears." Lyon, of course, lied about the matter, as any good conspirator would, saying "positively that the idea [of attacking the camp] had never been entertained."[41]

That afternoon Lyon ordered his regiments to march across St. Louis. Col. Henry Boernstein, the commander of one of the regiments, described their organization. "General Lyon, with two companies of regular infantry; Major Backhof with six cannon; and the First Regiment (Col. Blair) marched down Laclede Avenue"; "the Second Regiment (Col. Boernstein) went down Pine Street"; "the Third Regiment (Col. Sigel) marched down Olive Street"; and "the Fourth Regiment (Col. Schüttner) followed the course of Market Street." Apparently, the units were sent in multiple columns for speed of execution and to allow for heightened impact if they made contact with an active enemy at the camp. A curious but oddly fearless mob followed the Germans through the town.[42]

At around 3:15 P.M., Lyon's men—all at once and as planned—converged on Camp Jackson and encircled it. Lyon's artillery, meanwhile, took up positions on the heights, threatening, as Boernstein said, to "pound [the camp] to a pulp." Under a flag of truce, Lyon sent Maj. Benjamin Farrar to Frost with a note demanding his surrender. The note told Frost that his camp was "evidently hostile toward the Government of the United States" and "plotting at the seizure of its property and the overthrow of its authority . . . [and therefore it was Lyon's] duty to demand . . . [its] immediate surrender."[43] Frost was given thirty minutes to comply. After reading the note, Frost, astonished and infuriated, wrote back: "Sir, I never for a moment having conceived the idea that so illegal and unconstitutional a demand . . . would be made by an officer of the United States Army, I am wholly unprepared to defend my command from this unwarranted attack, and shall therefore be forced to comply with your demand."[44] Some 689 out of the 891 troops at Camp Jackson surrendered, with 202 men having escaped before they could be captured.[45]

A throng of people now began hovering around the camp, becoming more and more agitated as they realized what was happening. When Lyon's men raised the Union flag and cheered, it was too much for the mob, and they began cursing and throwing clods of dirt, rocks, and tiles at the German soldiers. Out of a nearby house under construction, someone fired a pistol at the troops. Then, more shots erupted from men "hidden high in the trees" in a nearby wood. These shots struck several soldiers, one of them later dying. Colonel Boernstein's men, without waiting for orders, as Boernstein later insisted, fired on the crowd, and twenty-eight civilians soon lay dead or dying in the bloody street, while another seventy-five were wounded. Two women were killed. The crowd went wild with fear and flew in every direction. Frost said later that "a fire was opened upon . . . [my] troops, and a number of men put to death, together with several innocent lookers-on—men, women and children."

Amidst the chaos, it took Lyon until nearly six o'clock to get the prisoners in formation to march to the arsenal. To accomplish the feat, the First and Second Regiments were placed in columns on the right and left sides of the street with the prisoners between the two groups. Once the regiments and prisoners were formed, Lyon gave the order, and the columns moved forward. The arsenal was six miles away, and as the soldiers passed through the streets, the people gathered, screaming, "Hessian Mercenaries!" "Murderers!" and other insults. The fact that Lyon's troops were composed "almost exclusively," as General Harney said, of German immigrants especially galled the crowd. The reality of "foreigners," many of them barely able to speak the English language, shooting "Americans" infuriated them—and, yes, frightened them also. It appears in retrospect that Lyon would have been wiser to parole the prisoners where they were captured rather than stage such an elaborate spectacle, which only further agitated the crowd.

The next day, the *Missouri Republican* referred to the event as "Black Friday." The violence of the day alienated many Missourians and galvanized Southern support throughout much of the state and nation. The unofficial armistice between the North and South that had developed after Fort Sumter had ended on the bloody streets of St. Louis. The night after the attack on Camp Jackson, several Germans were murdered and their bodies placed in prominent places as a warning to the rest. Meanwhile, many of the people in St. Louis fled the town "by train, in buggies and on horse back."[46]

When news of the capture of Camp Jackson reached Jefferson City, the legislators passed within fifteen minutes a "military bill" placing Missouri on a war footing and installing the Missouri State Guard as its army. Shortly thereafter, Governor Jackson was authorized to take control of the railroads and telegraph lines. Meanwhile, Jackson sent Sterling Price to talk with General Harney, who had just returned to St. Louis. When Harney met with Price, he objected to Missouri's recent "military bill," which he said was an "indirect secession ordinance . . . and cannot and ought not to be upheld . . . by the good citizens of Missouri."[47] A Harney-Price agreement, nonetheless, was the result. It essentially promised that Harney would keep Federal troops in St. Louis if Price promised, on his part, to keep the peace in the rest of Missouri and ordered home the four thousand troops now assembled at the capital. By that time, however, Blair had received Lincoln's permission to fire Harney when he thought it "indispensable" to do so. When Blair learned from his spies that Gen. James S. Rains was recruiting secessionist troops in western Missouri, he promptly sacked Harney.[48]

On May 30, Lyon was made interim department commander in Missouri. In the meantime, Jackson, pushed by proslavery moderates to come up with some sort of accommodation with Lyon, set up a meeting for June 11 to discuss the Missouri situation with the former captain, now a general. Jackson was stalling for time. Distrusting Lyon, Jackson demanded an agreement from him giving his entourage safe passage to and from the Planter's House in St. Louis, where the two parties would meet.

Jackson arrived at the Planter's House on June 10 with General Price, now commander of the Missouri State Guard, and Thomas L. Snead, Jackson's secretary. On the other side of the table at the meeting were Lyon, Frank Blair Jr., and Maj. Horace A. Conant, Lyon's aide. During the meeting, Jackson offered to disband the state guard and forgo implementing the military bill if Lyon promised to disband the Home Guards and make no effort to occupy the state. After a four-hour meeting, Lyon finally rose to his feet and said,

> Rather than concede to the State of Missouri the right to demand that my government shall not enlist troops within her limits, or bring troops into the state whenever it please, or move its troops at its own will into, or out of, or through the state: rather than concede to the State of Missouri for one single instant the right to dictate to my government in any matter, however unimportant, I would rather [Lyon rose to his feet and pointed at the various Missourians] see you, and you, and you, and you, and you, and every man, woman, and child in the state, dead and buried.

He turned to Jackson and Price: "This means war. In an hour one of my officers will call for you and conduct you out of my lines." Then, Lyon strode brusquely out of the room, followed by his satisfied colleagues.[49]

Jackson, Price, and Snead returned to the railroad depot in St. Louis, entered their special railroad car, and sped toward Jefferson City, pausing along the way to burn the bridges over the Gasconade and Osage Rivers. Their train arrived in the capital at 2:00 A.M. on June 12. Jackson immediately summoned his staff and hurriedly boxed the state's records for evacuation. On the same day, Jackson, by proclamation, called up fifty thousand men from the various Missouri militias to protect the state from the Federal armies. Before noon the next day, Price sent orders to his various militia commanders to rally their troops and report to Boonville or Lexington, whichever town was closest to their mustering-in point. On June 13, 1861, learning that Lyon and a two-thousand-man force (in reality seventeen hundred men) were headed for Jefferson City aboard three steam boats, Jackson, Price, and Massey piled the state's records aboard the steamer *White Cloud*, grabbed the state seal, and headed for Boonville, a number of miles up the Missouri River.

Leaving St. Louis on June 13, Lyon followed rapidly on Price's trail, reaching Jefferson City at 2:00 P.M. on June 15, where he stayed overnight. On June 16, after leaving Col. Henry Boernstein and three companies of the Second Regiment, Missouri Volunteers, to occupy the Missouri capital, Lyon raced for Boonville, hoping to catch Price and Jackson before they headed south. Arriving within eight miles of Boonville that evening, Lyon disembarked and set up camp. The next morning, on June 17, Lyon advanced his force two miles westward along the river flood plain toward Boonville. His advance guard soon received fire from Jackson's pickets, so Lyon pushed forward rapidly. He overran Jackson's camp and seized some of his weapons and supplies. Lyon lost two killed, one missing, and nine wounded. Jackson, meanwhile, fled southward, accompanied by his nephew, Col. John S. Marmaduke, and Gens. Mosby M. Parsons and John B. Clark, commanders of the Sixth and Third Missouri Military Districts. Of the three hundred to four hundred men in his force, Jackson had lost some three men and twenty-five wounded during the engagement. Jackson now intended to link up with Gen. Ben McCulloch, commander of Confederate forces in Arkansas, who was somewhere in southwest Missouri. Though the Missouri State Guard had lost control of the river and railroad networks across central Missouri, the force was still intact.[50]

At about this time, Missouri lieutenant governor Thomas Reynolds and Jackson's personal emissary, Edward Carrington Cabell, were in Richmond attempting to convince Confederate president Jefferson Davis to support Missouri with armed force. President Davis, however, after learning of the Price-Harney agreement, was wary of Jackson. Davis feared that Jackson might be cutting a peace deal with Lyon. Finally, the punctilious Davis told the Missourians that he thought it only proper for him to deal with the same Missouri state convention that had been summoned in February and March 1861. Davis's adherence to legal proprieties seemed inappropriate at this point; the South was in a life-and-death struggle and needed every available ally, of which Missouri was one. Two days later, Davis came to his senses, and his secretary of war ordered Gen. Ben McCulloch to aid the Missouri State Guard in any way he could.[51]

By June 20, 1861, Jackson's military force had arrived at Syracuse on the Pacific Railroad, and on June 21, it passed through Cole Camp, where it picked up several companies of infantry. Shortly thereafter, the force entered Warsaw, where more men joined up, and the four-gun brass battery taken from the Liberty Arsenal on April 20 was added to its train. Twenty miles north of Carthage, Jackson's small army united with Brig. Gens. James S. Rains and William Y. Slack's forces. Meanwhile Price, McCulloch, and Gen. Nicholas Bart Pearce had joined forces at Cowskin Prairie near Maysville, south of Springfield. Col. Elkanah B. Greer would soon join them with his men.

On June 28, Col. Franz Sigel, who had been ordered to attack Jackson, passed through Sarcoxie in southwest Missouri with some two thousand men, hoping to crush Jackson between his force and Lyon's. He had learned that Jackson, with approximatley four thousand men, was some fifteen miles north of Lamar. Although Sigel was unaware of it, a number of Jackson's units were unarmed; some of General Rains' men, for instance, had no weapons and were used only "to present the appearance of a reserve corps." In addition, Col. R. L. Y. Peyton's Third Cavalry, Eighth Division, had only two companies armed with ammunition; his other six and one-half companies "could obtain none." The Missouri troops, moreover, carried poor weapons. Union major John M. Schofield maintained that most of the Missourians were armed with little more than "shotguns and common rifles" and "a few pieces of almost worthless artillery." He described the Missourians, uncharitably, as a "miserable rabble."

On July 5, Sigel made contact with the Missouri State Guard six miles north of Carthage and attacked them boldly, fighting outnumbered while holding the low ground. The Missourians responded by assaulting Sigel in great force, using their cavalry wings to threaten Sigel's flanks, rear, and baggage trains menacingly. These flanking movements forced Sigel into a frantic, hopscotching retreat into Carthage. Sigel skillfully used his artillery to protect his rear as he fled into the night, but he had failed to prevent the juncture of Jackson and McCulloch's forces and had done poorly against the so-called miserable rabble. Oddly, Lyon later commented on the "high appreciation" he had for Sigel's "generalship."[52]

On the same day, Col. James McIntosh from McCulloch's army surprised ninety-four of Sigel's men, commanded by Capt. Joseph Conrad, Third Missouri Infantry, at Neosho and captured them. Sigel claimed later that he had left Conrad at Neosho "for the protection of the Union-loving people [there] against bands of secessionists." When Conrad was captured and paroled, however, he reported that he left the town "with an escort of about 30 men . . . for our protection, the people of Neosho having threatened to kill us in the streets." Schofield claimed that Sigel stationed the soldiers at the town "with no apparent object." On July 6, Generals Price and McCulloch joined up with Jackson's men, and on July 12, Jackson left for Richmond, Virginia, hoping to obtain Confederate financial and military aid.[53]

Seeking to engage the Missouri forces in the south, Lyon, having arrived in Springfield early on the night of July 13, combined his forces into what he called the "Army of the West" as part of his "Southwest Expedition." Half of Lyon's force was composed of unpaid, three-month volunteers, many of whom would shortly be discharged. Lyon soon began jousting with the Confederate forces in the area, feeling them out with patrols and larger units to gauge their strength. Lyon appears to have been intimidated by the Southern forces, for on August 20, he sent a message to General Frémont saying, "I find my position extremely embarrassing, and am at present unable to determine whether I shall be able to maintain my ground or be forced to retire. I shall hold my ground as long as possible, though I may, without knowing how far, endanger the safety of my entire force." Lyon told Washington he was facing a rebel force of "30,000 [men] and upward," a wild estimate. On June 22, Lyon sent a plea to his new commander, Maj. Gen. George B. McClellan, for two more regiments, but no reinforcements were sent. Meanwhile, without telling headquarters, Lyon concentrated his force, composed of some 5,600 men, and planned a surprise attack against the combined Confederate force of 10,175 men situated somewhere near Cassville. The odds against Lyon's army were not as unfavorable as they might appear at first glance, for his army was considerably better armed, equipped, and trained than the Confederates. But the Missourians and their Southern allies, as they had demonstrated earlier to Sigel, were game.[54]

On the night of August 9, 1861, Lyon moved his army south of Springfield along the Cassville Road. At 1:00 A.M., he halted the march and ordered his soldiers to "lay on their arms till early dawn." Before daybreak, Lyon's army resumed the march and made contact with Confederate pickets at around 4:00 A.M., driving them in. The Confederate army, he discovered, was camped on the east and west banks of Wilson's Creek, twelve miles south of Springfield. The Confederates, now fully alarmed, had rallied to take the field.

Some time earlier, Sigel's twelve-hundred-man Union brigade, including Backoff's six-gun battery and companies of the First U.S. Cavalry and Second U.S. Dragoons, had moved as a separate column to a position at the rear and left flank of the Confederate army. At the first sound of "musket firing," Sigel was prepared to attack. Lyon, meanwhile, was three miles to the north, squaring off against the northern end of the Confederate camp. Because the Union army was outnumbered, Sigel's separation from the Union main force was especially risky. Also, Sigel was outside supporting range, rendering his position much more vulnerable if his battle went poorly.

At around 5:00 A.M. on June 10, serious skirmishing between the forces ensued, and Lyon sent Capt. Joseph P. Plummer's First Infantry Battalion across Wilson's Creek to secure the Union's left flank. Simultaneously, Capt. James Totten's Company F, Second U.S. Artillery, and supporting units went forward to anchor the Union middle, situated on high ground, later referred to as "Bloody Hill." A number of attacks and counterattacks ensued along the entire line, with both sides suffering heavy casualties. The Battle of Wilson's Creek was under way.[55]

At 8:30 A.M., Sigel's men, who had been attacking the Union's rear, were counterattacked by Lt. Col. S. M. Ham's men (of Col. Louis Hébert's Third Louisiana Infantry), members of the Missouri State Guard infantry, and Hiram Bledsoe and G. Reid's batteries. Sigel's men were routed and five of his six valuable guns were captured. Sigel's brigade now fled in total disarray, and many of the men were killed or captured. Inexplicably, Sigel fled all the way to Springfield rather than join up with Lyon.[56]

Back at the main battle, Lyon now attempted to rally the troops to the left of Totten's threatened battery on Bloody Hill. In the attack, Lyon's horse was killed and the general wounded in the leg and head. As he walked a few steps to the rear, someone heard him say, "I fear the day is lost." Ignoring his wounds, the brave Lyon remounted another horse, and "swinging his hat in the air," pressed valiantly forward, near the right center of his line, rallying troops from the Second Kansas and remnants of the First Iowa Cavalry, who had been shouting, "We have no leader! Give us a leader!" Within minutes, Lyon was killed as a ball struck him in the chest.[57]

Maj. Samuel Sturgis, hearing of Lyon's death some thirty minutes later, assumed command as the senior Regular Army officer on the field. At 11:30 A.M., after nearly six hours of continuous fighting, there was a supposed lull on the front. Sturgis, by now, had learned of Sigel's defeat. Saddled by huge numbers of wounded, he was aware that his troops had been without water since 5:00 A.M. and were nearly out of ammunition. Lyon had thrown in all the reserves, and now McCulloch was ready to bring his large Southern unit into the fray. Obviously, victory was beyond Sturgis's grasp, and total defeat well within it. Sturgis ordered 2d Lt. John V. Du Bois' battery to take up a defensive position on the next hill to the north to cover the Union retreat. Sturgis then ordered his forces to begin the long trek back to Springfield. The body of the brave Lyon, for reasons always inadequately explained, was left lying on the field of battle.[58]

As the Union army moved north and west across the rolling hills, cannon balls skipped, plunged, and exploded around its rear guard, marking the end of the Battle of Oak Hills (popularly known in Northern histories as the "Battle of Wilson's Creek"). Most of the Northern officers in their official reports, some of them word for word, concurred that they retreated after a lull in the battle. Brig. Gen. William M. Wherry, Sixth U.S. Infantry, Lyon's aide-de-camp, said that the Federals retrograded after "pouring a murderous, deadly volley [on the Southerners], which created a perfect rout" and that the Federals "continued to send a galling fire into the disorganized masses as they fled, until they disappeared and the battle was over."

Southerners tell a far different story, indeed. In his official report of the battle Gen. Ben McCulloch, commander of the Southern forces, wrote, "Our gallant Southerners pushed onward, and with one wild yell broke upon the enemy, pushing them back and strewing the ground with their dead. Nothing could withstand the impetuosity of our final charge. The enemy fled, and could not again be rallied, and they were seen at 12m. [Meridian, i.e., noon] fast retreating among the hills in the distance. Thus ended the battle." Brig. Gen. Nicholas B. Pearce said, "Our boys charged the second line with a yell, and were soon in the possession of the field, the enemy slowly withdrawing toward Springfield."

The Federals had lost 1,317 men out of 5,400 engaged, the Confederates 1,230 out of 10,200 engaged. The Northern account of the battle is the one invariably read and cited, but it is debatable whether it is the most accurate one.

Col. Franz Sigel, who took command of the Union forces when they reached Springfield, planned to retreat in the middle of the night with his crippled army toward the rail terminus at Rolla (carrying some "$250,000 in specie from [the] Springfield Bank," no doubt the property of local Southern farmers and businessmen).[59] Maj. John Schofield claimed that the plan was to begin the march at 2:00 A.M. "in order that the column might be in a favorable position for defense by daylight." However, when Schofield reported to Sigel at the time of departure that the column was ready to march, he found Sigel "asleep in bed" and his men "making preparations to cook their breakfast." Schofield said, "It was 4 o'clock before I could get them started."[60]

Unfortunately for the Federal forces in the west, the Battle of Wilson's Creek was not their only unsuccessful battle early in the war. By early September 1861, Price had "chastised" a desultory attack by Gen. James Lane and Col. James Montgomery, driving their scattered forces back to Fort Scott and beyond. Then, Price advanced north, receiving numerous reinforcements daily. When Price reached Warrensburg at 2:00 P.M. on September 11, he rested. The next morning, he advanced his huge army eastward toward Lexington, Missouri, to attack Col. James A. Mulligan's

3,500-man Union force. Mulligan was headquartered in the Masonic college in the town, where he commanded the local defenses and kept in safekeeping some $750,000 taken from the pro-Southern local bank.[61] (General Price maintained that the Federals had "stolen" some "$900,000" from the bank.)

When Mulligan learned that Price was coming, he sent frantic pleas for help to Gen. John C. Frémont, now commander of the Western Department in St. Louis. But the only result was a barrage of confusing messages, passed back and forth between Frémont, to whom nobody seemed to be listening and who acted slowly and indecisively; Union brigadier general Jeff C. Davis, the commander at Jefferson City and an inveterate user of alibis who received requests too late anyway; Gen. Jim Lane, who was busy marauding somewhere south of Harrisonville and usually ignored most orders; Brig. Gen. Samuel D. Sturgis, who appeared unable to cross the Missouri River; and Brig. Gen. John Pope, a disinterested observer at Palmyra. Ultimately, no relief arrived for Mulligan.

By September 13, Price's advance guard skirmished with Mulligan's pickets outside the town thereby initiating the Battle of Lexington. On September 14, with his main force of some fifteen to twenty thousand troops now concentrated, Price drove Mulligan's men behind barricades and invested the town. Capt. Henry Guibor, a Southern artillery commander, now bombarded the Union men, beginning a seven-day siege. On September 19, Brig. Gen. Thomas Harris, commander of the Second Division, Missouri State Guard, asked for Price's permission to build hemp bale breastworks that could be rolled toward the Union defenses in the attack.[62] On September 20, employing perhaps two hundred bales made wet with water to prevent their igniting, Price's men approached the Union defenses behind a wall of rolling bales. As they pushed the bales in successive ranks toward the Northern lines, the Southern men poured a hot fire into the Union troops, which caused Mulligan at 4:00 P.M. to order white surrender flags hoisted. Mulligan had attempted heated shot, exploding shells, grape, and canister against the bales, but they refused to ignite. Meanwhile, the "thundering" Federal artillery had broken almost all of the glass panes in the nearby buildings, "the earth trembled," and the garrison had run out of water. But, ultimately, Mulligan said, the "artifice" (the hemp bales) had been "destined to overreach us."

The "Battle of the Hemp Bales" was over, and Price had captured Mulligan's entire army as well as thousands of rifles and a large store of supplies. In what Generals Price, Harris, and Rains all referred to as an "almost bloodless victory" (the Missourians claimed less than 100 casualties, the Federals some 149), the Missouri State Guard had beaten the Union army a second time. Federal commanders in the U.S. Army's official records, however, claim that Price lost 1,400 killed and wounded in the battle. Such lying and exaggerations about casualties were common on both sides. Soon, however, the Union army became concentrated in the Lexington area and forced Price to retreat southward.[63]

***

Earlier, on July 30, the same men who had attended the conventions of February 28 and March 4, 1861, which had decided Missouri's position on secession were reconvened. This time, exceeding powers granted to them by the Missouri legislature when they were originally formed, the men adopted ordinances declaring the positions held by the duly elected governor, lieutenant governor, secretary of state, and members of the legislature null and void. In their place, they chose some of their own members to fill the slots: Judge Hamilton Gamble as governor, Willard P. Hall as lieutenant governor, and Mordecai Oliver as secretary of state, all unelected officials. These men held office until an election was held in November 1861 to select permanent state officers. In response, Jackson and his fellow refugees formed an opposition state government that remained organized until the end of the war but was recognized legally only by the Confederacy. The displaced Missourians located their capital in various parts of Missouri and then, when forced, moved their quarters to Arkansas and Texas until the conclusion of the war.[64]

On September 2, when Sterling Price began his advance north to attack Lexington, Missouri, he approached Drywood Creek, Missouri, east of Fort Scott. This was Price's threatening message to the Kansans concerning their vulnerability. Gen. James Lane and his fellow commanders, Cols. James Montgomery and Charles Jennison, both of southeast Kansas notoriety, advanced to meet Price with some two thousand infantry and cavalry. They were swept aside by the Missouri State Guard in a short skirmish.[65]

Lane's troops fought long enough with Price to gain an appreciation of his strength then disengaged and kept their distance thereafter. When Price passed northward, Lane, in the guise of shadowing the Missouri State Guard, crossed the border into Missouri and began one of the great marauding rampages of the Civil War.

Chapter 7

Jayhawker Invasion of Western Missouri

On June 19, 1861, Capt. Charles "Doc" Jennison arrived in Kansas City with one hundred Mound City Sharps Rifles Guards. Jennison claimed that he was there to assist Regular Army officer Capt. William Edgar "W. E." Prince in occupying the town, but there is no evidence that Prince requested his services. Soon, using the town as his camp, Jennison made a scouting expedition to Independence, where he compelled some of the local rebels, through armed threats, to swear allegiance to the Union. Afterward, he rode into Blue Mills Hills, broke up a guerrilla camp, and captured a single rebel. As the Jayhawkers rode back to Kansas City, the local people were startled by the appearance of two black soldiers armed with Sharps rifles in Jennison's ranks. George Caleb Bingham, the noted artist and Unionist, who lived in Kansas City at the time, said that Jennison and his men were ordered by Prince, the local U.S. Army commander, to leave the state shortly thereafter; Prince apparently considered the Jayhawkers a disturbing influence. Soon, however, Jennison and his men crossed the border again, skirmished with rebels, and returned to Kansas with plunder. A procession of freed slaves, who, Jennison said, "happened to walk off on their own accord," composed the rear of his formation.[1]

Conceiving western Missouri to be a ripe target, Jennison, with eighteen men, rode into the state again on July 4, 1861 (ten weeks before Price's attack on Lexington, Missouri). Some eight hundred Missouri Unionists joined up with the Kansan, and this small army raided along the roads and byways, stripping farmers of their personal property, livestock, and grain stores and burning their homes and barns. During this one-week exercise, three of Jennison's scouts were captured by secessionists and hung, the first serious resistance by Missourians to the wanton attacks. Gov. Charles Robinson of Kansas, remarking on the general climate on the border at this time, said that the "toxin of war was the signal for the resurrection of all the thieves, plunderers and murderers of territorial days." The U.S. Army, by this time, had become suspicious that the Jayhawkers were unsettling the area, perhaps inciting a general rebellion among the inhabitants.[2]

During Jennison's July 4 raid, he captured a wagon train and oxen. The

wagon train, it turned out, was going to Fort Arbuckle with military supplies and operated under a safeguard by Maj. Samuel D. Sturgis of the regular U.S. Army—a fact that must have been known to Jennison. This latest
outrage caused Captain Prince to send a fiery complaint to Jennison.

> By the Rules and Articles of War, all persons who shall force a safe-
> guard . . . shall suffer death. It is to be presumed that the persons
> engaged in the capture and detention of this train were actuated by
> the best motives for the interests of the country and ignorant of the
> degree of criminality attached to the offense, but . . . these acts [have]
> the sanction neither of the State or the Federal Government, and
> when exercised in this arbitrary manner without the color of any law,
> must be regarded as privateering.

Prince ordered Jennison to return the wagons "intact."[3]

On July 18, Jennison's Jayhawkers again rode into western Missouri, this
time arriving with some 45 men in response to a request for aid from Maj. R.
T. Van Horn, who reported that his 150-man Home Guard was being over-
powered by 350 secessionists at Harrisonville. Colonel Nugent, with several
hundred more Missouri Home Guards, also answered Van Horn's rescue call.
The Union men soon united their forces, and in recognition of Jennison's
acknowledged military reputation, the two Missouri militia commanders
waived their superior rank and made him commander. Under Jennison's lead,
according to Jennison's own account, the Union troops drove the secessionists from Harrisonville. Historian Richard Brownlee said, however, that when
Jennison arrived at the town, it "held not an enemy soldier" and that Jennison
"had most of the stores broken into and robbed before Van Horn's main
body arrived." The take was around $2,000 in money and goods. One of the
soldiers involved in the raid, in an unsigned letter to the *Leavenworth Daily
Conservative,* reported his booty as blank books, soap, drawers, a bridle bit, a
necktie, two hats, writing paper, and drugs and medicines—a seemingly pal-
try take, but perhaps good enough for a poor, young trooper.[4]

In his operations, the nearly illiterate Jennison kept his orders to his men
simple:

> When we're in camp, we're all boys together, but when in the field, it's
> generally understood that I run the machine.
> [*another example*] Hello, there, you, Mr. Man! Take a squad of men, and
> go down to yonder house, and burn it to the ground, as quick as the
> devil will let you.[5]

One of Jennison's leaders who fought in the last two Missouri actions
was Charles Metz, alias Marshall Cleveland, an ex-Missouri Penitentiary

Members of the Kansas Seventh Volunteer Cavalry, the "Jayhawkers," the scourge of western Missouri. The picture was taken at Butler, Missouri, in 1863. *The Kansas State Historical Society, Topeka*

convict, later a commander of a company of Jennison's Seventh Kansas Volunteer Cavalry. This force was soon to be dubbed "Jennison's Jayhawkers" or the "Southern Kansas Jay-Hawkers," as they preferred to call themselves. Cleveland distinguished himself in the Morristown operation by killing Rev. Martin White, the killer of Frederick Brown (John Brown's son, who was killed during Atchison's 1856 invasion of Kansas). Apparently, White's killing was not motivated by revenge; Cleveland merely sought White's mule and White refused it. Later in the summer, Cleveland and John Steward returned to Missouri to continue freelance plundering. As a result of these raids, by early July, James Montgomery reported contrabands (slaves) streaming into Kansas by "brigades."[6]

***

In April 1861, two months after Kansas became a state, a fierce battle ensued concerning who would fill the new U.S. Senate positions. The contests were between James Lane and Frederick P. Stanton for one seat and Samuel Pomeroy and Marcus J. Parrott for the other. Lane, after finding himself outvoted by Stanton in preliminary votes by the Kansas state legislature, which decided such matters, joined forces with Pomeroy. The two men, pooling their support, finally won the Senate seats, but not till 297 votes were cast.

In mid-April, the new senators traveled by train to Washington, arriving in that city about the time of the Fort Sumter bombardment. They found the town in violent turmoil and the populace stricken with terror, believing that the Southerners were about to take the city. Wild rumors circulated, one concerning the possible assassination of the president. In the spirit of patriotism (and self-interest), Lane responded by mustering in his Kansas cronies—a large number of whom had followed him to Washington hoping for patronage. Lane pressed the men, some 75 to 120 of them, into what he called his "Frontier Guards." The men, offering their services without pay, bivouacked in the sumptuous—for them—East Room of the White House. For the next two weeks, until May 3, they functioned as Lincoln's personal bodyguard and protected the bridge over the Potomac River. Beyond the bridge lay Virginia, the most powerful state in what would become the Confederacy. Lincoln, by now a friend of Lane, was impressed and grateful for the Kansan's initiative and service. When Lane later asked Lincoln to sign appointments, the president quickly scrawled his signature, not even examining the men's credentials. This was true of political appointments as well as military ones.

On June 19, 1861, Lane proposed to Secretary of War Simon Cameron that Lincoln should authorize him to form two regiments for the defense of Kansas with Lane himself as their commander. When Cameron brought the matter to Lincoln the next day, the president replied: "We need the services of such a man [Lane] out there at once; that we better appoint him a brigadier-general of volunteers to-day, and send him off with such authority to raise a force . . . [as] will get him into actual work the quickest. Tell him when he starts to put it through. Not be writing or telegraphing, but put it through." Lane's unit would be known as the "Lane Brigade." Although the governors of states usually appointed militia commanders, Lincoln allowed Lane to circumvent this ordinary convention and muster in his own brigade, independent of state authority.[7]

When Charles Robinson, Kansas's governor and one of Lane's bitter enemies, learned that the "Grim Chieftain" was now a U.S. senator as well as a brigadier general, he made it known publicly that Lane was violating the Constitution, Article 1, Section 6, which prevented a brigadier general of a state militia from representing the same state in the Senate. In typical fashion, Lane promptly had his personal friend, Gov. Oliver P. Morton of Indiana, appoint him a general in the Indiana militia, thus circumventing the law.[8]

In late July 1861, Lane began forming his brigade, composed of the following units and commanders: Third Kansas, Col. James Montgomery; Fourth Kansas, Col. William Weer; Fifth Kansas, Col. Hampton P. Johnson; Sixth Kansas, Col. William R. Judson; Seventh Kansas Cavalry,

Col. Charles R. Jennison; and Eighth Kansas, Col. Henry W. Wessels. From the start, Lane's Brigade had a southeastern Kansas personality, which boded ill for Missourians. Montgomery and Jennison, two of the brigade's mainstays, were already skilled marauders hated and feared in Missouri.

Company H, composed of many of Jennison's original Jayhawkers, became the most notorious unit in a notorious brigade. Ex-convict Marshall Cleveland, the captain of H Company, the "black horse company," has already been mentioned for his exploits in Missouri in early 1861. Many of Cleveland's colleagues saw him as an authentic swashbuckler. But his discipline was poor, and his tenure short in the brigade. In fact, he failed to survive its first formation. When Daniel Read Anthony called for a "dismounted parade" of the regiment, acting on Col. Charles Jennison's behalf, Cleveland turned out for the formation "in a somewhat motley garb—a soft hat, a regulation coat, drab trousers thrust into low-topped riding boots, a belt carrying a surplus of revolvers and a saber that seemed a hindrance." When Anthony censured Cleveland publicly for his incorrect uniform, Cleveland indulged in a loud shouting and cursing match with Anthony then mounted his horse and rode off to pursue his own freelance, no-holds-barred Jayhawking operations.

Cleveland was tall, erect, and a dead shot. One of his colleagues in Jennison's regiment, Simeon M. Fox, said that had Cleveland dressed the part, he would have been the "ideal of an Italian bandit." Fox described Cleveland as being thin of visage, "his complexion olive-tinted and colorless," with "black, piercing eyes, finely cut features, dark hair and beard, correctly trimmed, complet[ing] a *tout ensemble.*" Cleveland soon attracted a number of men to his gang from Jennison's old organization, all of whom, according to Fox, were "degraded ruffians," "dissolute and dirty desperadoes." One thing particularly remarkable about their appearance, he said, was that some of them had dyed their mustaches a "villainous metallic black," marking them as "irreclaimable scoundrels." Cleveland soon made his headquarters in Atchison, Kansas, where he dubbed himself the "Marshal of Kansas." He virtually controlled the town, using it as his base of operations for Jayhawking runs into northwest Missouri's rich farming communities and for robbing wagon trains and banks. On November 16, 1861, Cleveland's gang robbed the Northrup and Union Banks in Kansas City. Finally, he became such a pest to the army in Missouri *and* Kansas that Company E, Sixth Kansas Cavalry, surrounded him near the Marais des Cygnes River and shot him dead. His so-called "brevet wife" later placed a tombstone atop his grave in a St. Joseph cemetery with the epitaph "One hero less on earth/ One angel more in heaven."

Company K in Jennison's regiment also became well known. Its commander was John Brown Jr., the son of Old Brown, of Harpers Ferry infamy. The men of the company assembled each evening after a day's

Marshall Cleveland, who was "Wanted—Dead or Alive" by the U.S. Army in September 1861. His real name was Charles Metz, and he was a former penitentiary convict as well as one of the original officers of the Kansas Seventh Volunteer Cavalry. *The Kansas State Historical Society, Topeka*

march and surrounded Brown's tent. A chosen speaker would then exhort the men concerning some chosen theme, closing the talk by loudly chanting, "Do you swear to avenge the death of John Brown?" The men screamed rabidly in reply, "We will! We will!" The company then sang the "John Brown song," ending it in an accelerated last verse followed by "Then, three cheers for John Brown, Jr.!"[9]

But of all the Jayhawker commanders, the one with the most flagrant reputation for violence in Missouri was Lt. Col. Dan Anthony, the brother of Susan B. Anthony, the noted suffragette. Although Anthony was a man of high intelligence and surface cultivation, he was ruthless, violent, and immune from mercy. A rabid abolitionist, he came to Kansas in the first migration funded by the New England Emigrant Aid Company. Later, he became a fire and marine insurance agent, land speculator, publisher of the *Leavenworth Daily Conservative,* and after the war, a couple of times, mayor of Leavenworth, Kansas. Historian Stephen Starr described Anthony as "a man with a forceful personality, possessed of a violent temper and a bitter tongue, harsh, rigid, overbearing, insensitive, and impetuous." All of this he was, and more.

The Anthonys were Quakers (except for Daniel's mother), and the family had connections with most of the prominent abolitionist figures of the nineteenth century. Dan Anthony, on his own part, not only hated what he called the "Slave Power," but he also detested even the middle-of-the-road Democrats of his era and said, "I think Satan has a fast hold on them. . . . The whole party is as corrupt as Hell itself. . . . God almighty has written on their faces . . . the word Scoundrels." So radical, outspoken, and inflammatory was Anthony in his public utterances that during a speech in Leavenworth, he was shot at three times. In 1859, Anthony rescued a black barber named Charley Fisher from a U.S. marshal seeking to arrest him. For his felonious part in rescuing Fisher, Anthony was indicted, but the indictment was never acted upon. Like many abolitionists, Anthony only honored Federal authority or Federal laws when they were imposed on him by force. On June 13, 1861, Anthony was verbally attacked in a newspaper article by R. C. Saterlee, the editor of the *Leavenworth Herald,* who called him a "liar," a fairly commonplace practice in the politicized press of the day. When Anthony met Saterlee on the street the next day, he demanded a retraction. Saterlee drew a pistol and fired at Anthony, who returned the fire, killing the editor. After a five-day trial, Anthony was acquitted.[10]

***

In mid-August 1861, Lane traveled to Fort Scott with his staff, four former Garibaldi men from Italy and Sen. Samuel Pomeroy's young son. At Fort Lincoln, a fortification he had built twelve miles northeast of Fort Scott, Lane assembled more than twelve hundred men. With this relatively small force, it

Daniel Read Anthony, a member of the pioneer Emigrant Aid party to Kansas and one of the perpetrators of some of the worst crimes and atrocities in Missouri during 1861-62. *The Kansas State Historical Society, Topeka*

was clear to him that he could only make armed gestures against Price's ten thousand troops just across the border in Missouri. Price was still basking in his triumph over Lyon at Wilson's Creek/Oak Hills. Federal authorities ordered Lane to shadow Price's army closely and harass its rear and flanks as it moved north toward Lexington. But Lane's sole objectives from the start seem to have been to protect Kansas and to chastise Missouri. The Federal army's objectives were their own matter, and he disregarded its orders.

When Price learned that the Missouri counties east of Fort Scott were now "infested" with Lane's "marauding and murdering bands," he sent Gen. James S. Rains' cavalry to eject them from the state. On September 2, Rains skirmished with Colonels Montgomery and Weer at Drywood Creek, Missouri, ten miles east of Fort Scott, driving Lane's forces west into Kansas toward the fort. Price referred to the action as a "trifle," but it clarified in Lane's mind the dangerous strength of Price's army.[11]

When Governor Robinson of Kansas heard of the action at Drywood Creek, he became agitated and wrote General Frémont, explaining, "But what we [Kansans] have to fear, and do fear, is that Lane's Brigade will get up a war by going over the line, committing depredations, and then returning into our State." Robinson asked Frémont to "relieve us of the Lane Brigade, [and] I will guarantee Kansas from invasion from Missouri." Robinson believed that Lane's provocations and those of his followers could ultimately prompt a violent retaliation by Missourians (as they did by 1863). Robinson knew that Lane had recently threatened to "play hell with Missouri," and the governor appeared convinced that he was referring to the local, unarmed Missourians, not Price's powerful army. The editor of the *Topeka Tribune*, John B. Greer, also castigated Lane: "The return of Gen. Lane [from Washington] is the return of gasconade and humbug. He has filled our community with a thousand conflicting statements as to his authority and his appointment by the President, to do this thing and do that, none of which are true, or can be true, in the nature of the case. To suppose them true is to suppose the President and Secretary of War to be fools, fit subjects for the mad house." Nonetheless, most of the tales Lane was telling were quite true, and he had considerable "prestige and influence" with the president.[12]

U.S. Army authorities, by this time, had gotten wind of excesses by Lane's units operating in the central border counties and at Fort Scott. On September 9, 1861, Capt. W. E. Prince wrote Lane.

> I hope you will adopt early and active measures to crush out this marauding which is being enacted in Captain Jennison's name, as also yours, by a band of men representing themselves as belonging to your command. Captain Daniel W. Wilder will be able to give the details of their conduct at Leavenworth City, and doubtless their atrocities in other localities have been already represented to you. Please have a formal examination into the plundering of private and public buildings, which has recently taken place, as I am informed, at Fort Scott. It will be necessary for representation to higher authority.[13]

Lane ignored such messages.

When Lane's men had skirmished with Price's army at Drywood Creek, Lane had left some of Jennison's men behind to protect Fort Scott, Kansas. It was they who had ransacked and pillaged the town and to whom Prince was referring, in part, in his message to Lane. He was also referring to Jennison's attacks on Missourians in the central border counties. Prince's consequent opinion about Lane's men and their actions is evident from his coinciding description of them as "a mere ragged, half-armed, diseased, and mutinous rabble, taking votes as to whether any troublesome or distasteful order should be obeyed or defied."[14]

This "rabble" continued their behavior and soon had the opportunity to extend their actions in Missouri. Price had advanced on Lexington, and the way was clear for Lane to move into virtually undefended western Missouri. Lane now began implementing his planned projects. One was to destroy Osceola, Missouri, to be followed by the sacking of a string of towns as he proceeded north. On September 10, with an army of some fifteen hundred men, Lane started north on the military road (along the Missouri-Kansas state line), vowing to "pitch into" Butler, Harrisonville, Osceola, and Clinton, Missouri. After arriving at Trading Post on September 12, Lane veered southeast toward Osceola, burning and plundering everything in his line of march and looting a wide swath on his flanks. Lane said, "We believe in a war of extermination. . . . There is no such thing as Union men in the border of Missouri. I want to see every foot of ground in Jackson, Cass and Bates counties [in Missouri] burned over—everything laid waste." In a reference to marauding, he added, "Everything disloyal from a Shanghai rooster to a Durham cow must be cleaned out."[15]

By September 23, Lane's advance guard of skirmishers passed through Roscoe, Missouri, then reached Osceola. When Colonels Weer and Montgomery reached the outskirts of the town, they received sporadic fire from a small detachment of thirty Confederates commanded by Capt. John M. Weidemeier. The rebels, firing from the brush, were soon driven out and one Missourian was killed while several were wounded. Lane claimed that more Southern men were holed up in the courthouse, and he ordered Capt. Thomas Moonlight, his chief of artillery, to bombard the building to "shell them out." Soon, it became a roaring inferno. Within minutes, the entire business district of Osceola was put to the torch as well as all the homes except for a sprinkling of houses on the town's outskirts. Everyone was robbed, present or absent.

Meanwhile, Montgomery ordered the heads of 150 barrels of whiskey stored in a warehouse in the town busted, and the contents of the barrels surged down the street. Montgomery hoped to destroy the liquor before his men discovered it and became unmanageable. But he was too late. Many of the soldiers had already gotten hold of the whiskey, quaffed it, and now were staggering through the streets. As the liquor flowed toward the river, soldiers stooped and filled their canteens then cupped their hands and gulped down more. Before long, most of Lane's army was roaring drunk. The whiskey soon became ignited, like everything else in the town, and a stream of flaming spirits rushed into the ravine leading to the Osage River. Later, 300 besotted and helpless men, Lane's soldiers, were loaded aboard wagons and stolen carriages to be carried out of the town.

Alcohol was not the only spoil of war that the town offered. Rev. Hugh D. Fisher, one of Lane's chaplains, made off with the altar furnishings from the local church, which he intended to use to complete his own church, now being built in Lawrence, Kansas. Lane, not to be outdone, selected a fine carriage, piano, and silk dresses (for his wife, perhaps, or some other female or females, for Lane was an opportunist). At the outset of the raid, the Osceola bank was robbed of some four thousand to eight thousand dollars, as much as one hundred thousand dollars in today's money, a testimonial to the town's wealth, now completely obliterated.

When Lane left town, a long train of wagons followed him filled with booty: camp equipment, boots, shoes, clothing, tons of pig lead, kegs of powder, percussion caps, supplies of cartridge paper, 3,000 sacks of flour, 50 sacks of coffee, slabs of bacon, barrels of brandy, 500 pounds of sugar and molasses, assorted pieces of furniture, and other pleasant knickknacks and baubles. Behind these wagons plodded 350 horses and 400 cattle formerly owned by the locals. Then, there was the long train of wagons filled with drunken soldiers. And behind them, near the end of Lane's ragtag procession, plodded a column of 200 freed slaves, a situation that became a fixture in the plundering processions of the Lane Brigade. At the very rear of the column, a mile-long stretch of "appropriated" wagons was filled with slaves too young or old to walk as well as the blacks' belongings. The ex-slaves would be forced to travel in the dense dust cloud formed by the long train. Lane had said earlier, "Slavery would not survive the march of the Union Army"; in this case, Lane was fulfilling his prophecy.[16]

Eventually, most of the "loot" Lane stole found its way to Lawrence, Kansas, his home and base of operations. The citizens of Lawrence, had they thought on the matter, must have known that Lane and his men's booty were obtained through the pain, misery, and often death of their neighbors in Missouri, but few of them raised any cries of indignation at these depredations. But when their own town suffered a similar fate—when Quantrill stole some of the Missourians' looted property back in August 1863—then, their howls of "atrocity" were carried in most of the newspapers in the East.

As Lane proceeded north, his troops burned and plundered their way through rich farm country, turning it into a veritable wilderness. At a point midway to Kansas City, Rev. Hugh Fisher led the black contingent of Lane's party directly west toward Kansas. When his column reached the state line, Fisher turned to the ex-slaves, raised his right hand over his head, and pronounced in stentorian tones, "In the name of the Constitution of the United

States, the Declaration of Independence, and the authority of General James H. Lane, I proclaim you forever free!" Of course, there was nothing legal in this declaration; Lane and the Kansans oddly claimed to listen to a "Higher Law." Interestingly, when Frémont issued a public proclamation saying essentially the same thing as Fisher, Lincoln promptly fired him.

Historian Hildegarde Rose Herklotz said of the raid on Osceola:

> His [Lane's] troops were no better than an armed and organized banditti, and they had more power for evil than mere robbers and murderers, because their officers were acting under regular commissions from the Government which they used as a means of covering up their crimes. The destruction of Osceola was a case of wanton devastation. In this town about one-third of the people were Unionists and many were in the Federal Army. When Lane destroyed and appropriated the property there, he made no distinction between the Unionists and the Secessionists, but destroyed everything which came into his way."[17]

On September 16, during the march to Kansas City, Colonels Montgomery and Hampton P. Johnson skirmished the enemy near the town of Morristown, where Johnson was mortally wounded. As a result of this misfortune, seven Confederate prisoners, according to Simeon M. Fox, a Jayhawker who was present, were subjected to a "drum-head court-martial" and shot at the edge of their graves. Capt. Henry E. Palmer, another Jayhawker, said, "Their graves were dug, and they were compelled to kneel down by the edge of the graves, when they were blindfolded, and shot by a regularly detailed file of soldiers; the graves were then filled up and we marched away."[18]

When Lane's Brigade finally entered Jackson County, far to the north, it approached the farm of Solomon Young, the grandfather of Harry S. Truman, and a prominent man in Jackson County circles. Here, the Jayhawkers evidenced their normal mode of operation. But this time it was performed not against secessionists or Southern sympathizers but against a well-known Missouri Unionist family, which the Young family clearly was. Harriet Louisa Young, Harry Truman's grandmother, remembered well Gen. Jim Lane's visit to the Young farm. When Lane's men reached the farm, they broke formation and circulated around the place, shooting some four hundred hogs, cutting out their hams, and "leaving the rest to rot." Harriet Louisa was forced to bake biscuits for the men "until her hands blistered." Some of Lane's Jayhawkers relaxed on her best quilts, smearing them with mud from their boots. Other Jayhawkers amused themselves by "blasting away" with revolvers "at her hens."

Lane's men then looked for the "man of the place." When Solomon Young could not be found, the Jawhawkers began their tested, successful interrogation techniques on the best person available, Harrison Young, one of Solomon's sons. Seizing the boy, they demanded to know where his father was. Harrison answered truthfully that his father was conducting a wagon train out West. This answer failed to satisfy the soldiers, so a noose was thrown around the boy's neck, and he was hoisted off the ground, the usual Jayhawker interrogation technique. Harrison was left suspended for some time in this state, gagging and reddening from loss of oxygen; then, he was dropped to the ground and the rope loosened. Again, he was asked the same question, and the torture continued. (Usually, this torture was used by Lane's men to extract information about caches of money and jewelry.) After several suspensions, the soldiers finally decided that the exercise was useless—or they tired of an unprofitable game—and let poor Harrison loose. The Young's barn was then set ablaze. Finally, Lane's soldiers marched down the road toward Kansas City, chicken and geese feathers fluttering in their wake, carrying with them, among other things, the Young's "silver" and their "feather beds."

Later, because they were known Unionists, the Youngs made a claim against the U.S. government for $21,000, more than a quarter of a million dollars in today's money, though not for this encounter but for later appropriations by a Colonel Burris of "1,200 pounds of bacon, . . . 65 tons of hay, 500 bushels of corn, 44 head of hogs, 2 horses . . . and 30,000 fence rails." In addition, General Sturgis was responsible for taking some "150 head of cattle and a Captain Axline 13,000 fence rails, 1,000 bushels of corn, and 6,000 'rations.'" Eventually—*some thirty-five years later*—the Youngs were paid for it, likely with the aid of lawyers and litigation. Southern sympathizers in the area, of course, qualified for no claims, no matter their losses, and many were ultimately ruined.[19]

About this time, Lane had railed at his men:

> You sneaking thieves, what did you think of yourselves when you were invading the premises of that widow in the north part of town, and stealing her nightdress, her skillets and her chickens? Were you acting the part of soldiers then? Did you think we were at war with chickens and skillets? . . . So help me God, if the like occurs again, the guilty party, if found, shall suffer the extreme penalty of the law.

All of this, of course, was just shoptalk from a fellow who had just stolen a nice piano, carriage, and silk dresses in Osceola, and the men likely chuckled and sneered at Lane's insincere, fatuous ranting behind his back.[20]

Lane at last arrived in Kansas City on September 29, where he disputed with General Sturgis as to who was the ranking officer in the area. On October 1, overshadowing this quarrel, Lane and Sturgis were ordered to join Frémont at Warsaw, Missouri, in an effort to launch an attack on Price, who had by now retreated to southwest Missouri. As usual, Lane disregarded Frémont's orders and stayed in Kansas City to consider "political matters."

On October 18, three weeks later, he finally set out with Sturgis to join Frémont at Springfield. The two arrived on November 1 after the whole matter of an attack on Price was moot. Several months later, when Maj. Gen. Henry W. Halleck became the new commander of the Department of the Missouri, he heatedly expressed his disapproval of Lane's behavior in Missouri, and the complaint reached the desk of Abraham Lincoln. "I am sorry that General Halleck is so unfavorably impressed with General Lane," Lincoln responded, apparently in support of Lane.[21]

**

With this latest disappointment, Frémont had exhausted all his political and military stock and was fired. He had been in trouble with Lincoln for some time because of his failure to reinforce Lyon at Wilson's Creek, which was compounded by his sluggish response to Price's invasion. But Frémont had sealed his own fate, earlier, on August 30, when he had issued his Missouri Emancipation Proclamation without consulting Lincoln, thereby assuming, Lincoln thought, presidential powers. It took Lincoln some thirty days to determine how to sack the popular general and potent political star (Frémont had been the Republican presidential candidate in 1856). But Lincoln's trouble is understandable. He had been striving desperately since the outset of the war to hold the crucial Border States in the Union, so Frémont's emancipation edict fell on Washington and the Border States like a bombshell. At the same time, Frémont had become involved in a feud with Lincoln's pet, Frank Blair Jr. Blair had become so vocal in his opposition to Frémont that the general had had to arrest him twice for "undermining his authority" and influencing the president against him. There was also the question of Frémont's awarding government contracts for the building of the defenses around St. Louis to his old cronies from California rather than letting them to Blair's supporters from St. Louis. But it was the emancipation proclamation that convinced Lincoln to sack Frémont.

In his proclamation, Frémont had decreed martial law throughout Missouri; ordered that all armed and hostile men taken within the Federal lines were to be court-martialed and shot, if guilty; and that the "real and personal property of those who shall take up arms against the United States, or who shall be directly proven to have taken an active part with their enemies in the field, is declared confiscated to public use, and their slaves, if any they have, are hereby declared free men." Lincoln was fighting two rebellions: one was composed of the unified South; the other consisted of radicals and fanatics within his own party, of which Frémont was a leader.[22]

Lincoln, highly perturbed, on September 2 wrote Frémont:

> I believe that there is a great danger that the closing paragraph, in relation to the confiscation of property and the liberating of slaves of

traitorous owners, will alarm our Southern Union friends and turn them against us; perhaps ruin our rather fair prospect for Kentucky [keeping it in the Union]. Allow me, therefore, to ask that you will, as of your own motion, modify that paragraph so as to conform to the first and fourth sections of the act of Congress entitled: "An act to confiscate property used for insurrectionary purposes," approved August 6, 1861, and a copy of which act I herewith send you.[23]

Lincoln signed a relief order for Frémont on October 24 and sent it to Gen. Samuel R. Curtis, who was to relieve Frémont "subject to these conditions": that he had not "fought and won a battle," "shall then be actually in a battle," or shall then "be in the immediate presence of the enemy in expectation of battle." Clearly, Lincoln was a shrewd political tap-dancer. The firing seemed reminiscent of Harney's sacking by Blair, another cutely contrived and orchestrated firing by one of Lincoln's agents. While Lincoln took such action against Frémont for his order, he apparently ignored the fact that Lane's Brigade had been continuously freeing slaves and appropriating slave owners' properties for over four months—and Jennison and Montgomery *for over three years!*[24]

***

Around the second half of September 1861, Jennison was organizing his new regiment, and he spent part of the time in Leavenworth and some of the rest in Kansas City. Since his new regiment, the Seventh Kansas Volunteer Cavalry, was not officially to be mustered in until October 28, Jennison was accompanied to Kansas City by units of his Mound City Sharps Rifles Guards. At about this time, in nearby Independence, some of the Unionists living in the town (there were but few) were being harassed by the predominantly secessionist majority. William Miles, the town's city marshal, realizing that help was as close as Kansas City, raised a deputation of the local citizens and traveled to Kansas City to obtain allies. There, he met the ready ear of Charles Jennison

Soon, Jennison and his Jayhawkers were in their saddles and riding across the rolling Missouri farmland toward Independence, some twelve miles away, to chastise the "secesh." To decrease the possibility of opposition, Jennison started at daybreak and arrived at the town at 7:00 A.M. The Jayhawkers quickly surrounded the town to prevent anyone's escape. The local men, hearing a commotion, attempted to hide and rushed into cellars, attics, and relatively inaccessible places. Jennison's troopers, nonetheless, ferreted them out, yanking them from garrets, barns, sheds, and crawl spaces. The Southern men, some three or four hundred of all ages, were brought down to the courthouse square, guns at their backs, and "corralled." The rest of Jennison's troops were fast at work gathering all the personal belongings of the people: carriages, wagons, buggies, horses, mules, fine furniture, jewelry, firearms, clothes, and household items, anything moveable and valuable. They piled the booty against the iron fence that bordered the courthouse. At the same time, they harnessed up the citizens' vehicles and wagons and placed them along the dirt street that ringed the square.

Jennison, astride his horse, then pulled out a long list from his pocket and unfolded it. The list contained the names of most of the men in town, nearly all of whom were supporters of the South. Jennison ordered Miles, the local marshal, to pick out the men as he called their names and herd them into a group. He warned Miles that if he picked out even a single Union man, he would strike the lawman in the face with his saber. Throughout, the Kansas cavalrymen rested their carbines on their right legs, smugly snickering as they watched the proceedings. After reading the list, Jennison apologized to the small number of Unionists for their inconvenience and told them to gather their property and take it home.

The "head Jayhawker" wore his favorite hat for this performance, a tall fur one that made him look a foot taller than his unusually short height. Jennison then harangued the crowd for over a half-hour, reciting to them their sins and shortcomings and warning them that for every Union man killed in Jackson County hereafter, he would ensure that "ten of the most prominent secessionists of Jackson County should suffer death." After the Sacking of Independence, Jennison ordered the wagons, buggies, and other vehicles formerly owned by the pro-Southern people of Independence to be loaded with all their worldly belongings. The Jayhawkers filled "twelve to fifteen wagons." Jennison now gave the order, and a procession of wagons filled with plunder creaked steadily out of the town. Unionist historian Wiley Britton said that the black children and women sitting atop the Jayhawked wagons heaped with Jayhawked booty made "an amusing picture." It is unclear in what sense Unionist Britton found this "amusing." Meanwhile, the once-proud citizens of Independence, one of the wealthier communities in western Missouri, slunk home. But they would remember this day bitterly, and so would their sons, many of whom would soon take up the role of guerrillas.

A Jayhawker captain, Henry E. Palmer, described Jennison's men when they arrived back at their base. "Returning from their first raid into Missouri, they marched through Kansas City nearly all dressed in women's clothes, old bonnets and outlandish hats on their heads, spinning-wheels and even gravestones lashed to their saddles; their pathway through the country strewn with (to them) worthless household goods, their route lighted by burning homes." Jennison sometimes referred to his regiment as a "Self-Sustaining" one. Perhaps, it was more than self-sustaining; Jennison remained a wealthy man throughout his life, mostly as the result of this sort of "military" service.[25]

The action at Independence, if it is worthy of the appellation, was the last for Jennison personally. Hereafter he delegated nearly all of the field duties of the Seventh Kansas Cavalry to his subordinate, Lt. Col. Daniel Anthony, and Maj. James D. Snoddy. These officers organized the regiment at Leavenworth, largely in Jennison's absence, and formally mustered it in on October 28, 1861. Though Jennison was nominally in command, he spent nearly all of his time near Squiresville, Kansas, playing poker with associates while his men were in the field. Anthony told a correspondent in a letter of March 1, 1862: "Col Jennison had been col [colonel] of this regiment six months and has yet to give the first command to them—I have always commanded them—Have been with them in all their expeditions into the enemy's country except one time Jennison went to Independence."[26]

Anthony, in a letter, told his brother Merritt that as late as October 1, the regiment had not received its horses, and the men were stationed in "brick dwellings" and "brick stores" in Kansas City. For the next couple of weeks, Anthony and his men served as provost marshals, or military police, in the town. After a relatively quiet time in Kansas City, Anthony finally equipped and mounted his men. He then learned of a large rebel force camped south of Westport, Missouri, along the Little Blue River. Upton Hays, an irregular officer, commanded it. Hays had been enlisting men and was now preparing to take them South to join the regular Confederate army. Anthony decided it was time to wage war.

On November 10, A, B, and H Companies (some 150 men armed with Sharps rifles), the ordinary advance guard of the Seventh Kansas Cavalry and its best-armed units, pushed south from their camp on Alexander Major's farm (Eighty-third Street and Stateline Road in present-day Kansas City) to intercept Hays. The Missourians were camped thirteen miles away. Anthony surprised the rebels early the next morning, but Hays responded quickly, dropping his men back into the rocky hillside and brush along the Blue River, where they took up nearly impregnable positions and began firing. Instead of flanking Hays and forcing him to withdraw to more easily assailable ground, the rash Anthony, an aggressive military novice, made a headlong, frontal charge, losing 9 men and 32 wounded in a short, desperate fight. Anthony told his father later that he received during the fight a "Colt revolver bullet" that "struck on the hilt of my sabre." Anthony, somewhat sobered, returned to Kansas City.[27]

Several days later, Anthony took the Seventh Kansas Cavalry on a foray to Pleasant Hill, Missouri, where he recaptured a large wagon train that had been taken by guerrillas several days before. During the trip, one of his enlisted men, Pvt. James C. Murphy, drew a revolver and pointed it at one of the regiment's officers, Lt. Isaac J. "Shag" Hughes. Hughes killed him. Anthony wrote his father, in reference to the killing, "No complaints—." Anthony also reported matter-of-factly to his father, "Last night one of

our men stole some property and he is to be shot this morning at 9 A.M."
On the same day, Joseph Raymond, a Mexican, was executed for raping a
prostitute in Kansas City. During the foray around Pleasant Hill, Anthony,
in reprisal for the guerrilla capture of the Union wagon train, had his men
burn and pillage houses and property in a wide swath around Pleasant Hill.
Thirty years later, in a written history of the area, the event was referred to
as "Jennison's Day" although Anthony was the author of the attack.[28]

For the next four months, Daniel Anthony's Seventh Kansas Cavalry,
with a force numbering from five hundred to eight hundred men in size,
traveled around Cass and Jackson Counties in Missouri. Sometimes, the
Jayhawkers moved in full force; at other times, they traveled in small
patrols. Anthony wrote his father on November 24, urging him to send
Merritt, Daniel's brother, to Missouri, saying, "I could give him a chance to
make money fast." To his friend Aaron, on December 3, Anthony wrote:

> I have taken a Secesh [Missourian's] Stallion worth $1,000, and a Grey
> horse worth 200. I now have three tip top horses—
> Don't you want a captaincy or a majorship in the army—or don't you
> want to come out here and speculate in cattle—horse and mules—
> There is a good chance to buy cheap—and stock a large farm here at
> little expense—
> There is money in it to any one who will attend do it—

On December 22, 1861, Anthony reported to his father, "We took 150
mules & 40 horses—129 Negroes and gave the Negroes 60 Horses &
mules a lot of oxen, 10 waggons & two carriages and all loaded down with
Household Furniture—The Negroes train into Kansas was over a mile
long." On the day after Christmas 1861, Anthony reports: "I have selected
a fine house for my Head Quarters—the owner is in the Secesh army—
(this letter is written on Secesh paper taken at Harrisonville, Mo) . . . I have
four colored individuals for servants—one to take care of House—One
body servant one cook and one waiter." He repeated the news about his
"four colored servants" to his sister, Susan B. Apparently, Anthony was
becoming well practiced in the Union version of black servitude. Anthony
also told his sister that he had had a post-Christmas dinner of "splendid
biscuit—coffee—roast goose & chickens & Butter and Molasses—with
plenty of secesh crockery. . . . I never ate a better dinner anywhere." Likely,
most of this meal was commandeered from Missouri farmers.

On December 26, 1861, Lt. Col. Dan Anthony was in command of
"1500 men" and "3 pieces of artillery" at Morristown, near present-day
Freeman, Missouri, eight miles west of Harrisonville, at what they called
"Camp Johnson." His adjutant at the time was Lt. George H. Hoyt "of
Boston," who had been one of John Brown's lawyers in the Harpers Ferry
trial. Hoyt later became infamous as the Red Legs' field commander, and

famous even later as the attorney general of post-Civil War Kansas. Also present in Anthony's command was Richard J. Hinton, the radical abolitionist journalist. It was Hinton and Hoyt (see chapter 5, footnote 30) who had conspired to break John Brown out of jail before he was executed.

At this time, some of Anthony's men visited the home of Robert Allison Brown Sr., called "Wayside Rest," near Harrisonville, Missouri, one of the finest plantations in the area. Brown, earlier in 1861, had been a representative in "the convention called to consider the relations of Missouri to the Federal Union. . . . When the great question came up in the convention, Mr. Brown noted that Missouri should not dissolve her connection with the Federal Union." This stance, however, was to serve as no protection for him from Anthony's men. Elizabeth "Lizzie" Brown Daniel, Brown's daughter, wrote that

> Every day some of his [she thought Jennison's, actually Anthony's] troops were at our house for dinner and spying around. . . . On Christmas day [1861] three of the men came to take dinner, very sociable and friendly . . . two officers and one *high* private. The Captain said, "Mr. Brown, I see you have a great deal of silver and valuables around, and I'd advise you to be on your guard. Our boys are in and out of here a good deal and some of them are pretty bad and would take things." Father was always prepared for answers [cautious responses] and said, "Oh, the boys wouldn't take anything from us." After a hearty meal

The Robert Allison Brown home near Harrisonville, Missouri, one of the few surviving antebellum homes in western Missouri. Nearly all were destroyed before, during, and after Orders No. 11. *Courtesy of Arba E. Gilmore Jr.*

they remarked, "Well, we know where to get another turkey dinner next Sunday." Father said, "Welcome to our home any time."

The men left late, and instead of heading toward Morristown, the site of their camp, they rode toward Harrisonville, which struck Brown as odd and suspicious. Elizabeth Brown Daniel recounted:

About midnight there was a knock at the front door. Mother answered, and of course Father was up and dressing. Mother asked who it was and the answer "a friend." She insisted on knowing who the friend was, but he[,] changing voice, only said he wanted to speak to Mr. Brown. By that time Father [Robert Brown Sr.] was there with his pistol (but he never fired it that time). There was a light moon on the ground and he could see two men [framed by "light snow on the ground"] and knew they were of the three who had dinner. After a few words with them he knew what they wanted, and turning to Mother said, "Mary, go ring the bell and awaken the inmates of the house." That frightened them, and they turned to leave, one saying, "Wake the inmates and be damned," then fired one shot back at Father and it struck a brick to the right "west" of the door. The hole is to be seen today [Note: mortared up, but visible in 2003]. They left and Father didn't return the fire. The rascals were coming and going all the time spying and getting ready for their *big haul.*

The men were reported to be "Capt. Pardue, Black Horse Co. F, and Hogan or Hay."

Later that week, according to Lizzie,

Smith from Kansas (called Seegle by the men) and the man who killed Col. Hurst, with five others came and ordered dinner and horses fed. After dinner they swung their guns and searched the house, broke open trunks, drawers took all the powder and ammunition they could find, took Father's and Walter's pistols and a fine topcoat of Mr. Park Lee's. . . . One morning before we had breakfast . . . the yard was full of men, and four empty wagons were driven up to the back gate. An old man by the name of Slota (or something) headed a band of Negroes and white men arrested Father and took him out in front guarded by two Negroes and two white men, while they went to work robbing the home, smokehouse, work house and everywhere. They took one big Santa Fe wagon and forcibly loaded the servants [slaves] that had been left, George, Jane, Maria and small children and their belongings into it, then drove one of their wagons down to the smokehouse and filled it with meat, lard, sausage, molasses, kraut, apples and other food. Then to the workhouse and took all the tools, wagon and oxen, seven horses, four saddles, two saddle bags, stair carpet, bed clothing, window curtains, two fine new table linens, plated silverware (others were buried in the barn under the corn crib with other valuables). . . . They were like hungry wolves. . . . I can see a big yellow *nigger*, pistol in hand, stirring things around in Mother's top dresser drawer, picking up any little trinket that suited his fancy . . . a silver dirk, Grandfather's gold watch and long gold fob, a lovely beaded bag filled with little bits of treasure, old daguerreotypes of herself and friends. Mother asked him to please leave things alone that would be of no use to him. He quickly turned to her saying, "Will you keep your God damned mouth shut," pointing his pistol at her. She [Lizzie's mother] turned to the old sanctified rascal who was in charge and standing in front of the fireplace looking on, only giving him a look. He said, "Madam, war is a terrible thing."

In the summer of 1862, the Jayhawkers were not as lucky in their raid. About midnight, the Browns were aroused, again by someone at the door. Mrs. Brown went to the door and asked who it was. One of them answered, "I want to see Mr. Brown." Lizzie Brown said, "By that time Father was there armed and ready for them." Robert Brown told Mrs. Brown to "keep the boys [his son, Bob Brown, and a friend, Jim Sabens] back and upstairs.

Brick apartments occupied by house slaves and skilled black mechanics on the Robert Allison Brown plantation north of Harrisonville, Missouri. The apartments had wood floors and individual fireplaces. This plantation house was one of the few in Cass County, if not the only one, to survive Orders No. 11. *Courtesy of Arba E. Gilmore Jr.*

He knew too well what it meant." One of the men lunged at the door, but it failed to give. Then, Lizzie Brown described, the man

> stepped back, and with an oath said, "I'll get him this time." But father's bullet was too quick for him, and he fell and they took him off the porch. . . . All was quiet for awhile . . . but during the quiet Mother opened the east door of the kitchen and let Brother Robert out [Lizzie's brother]. There was a shot fired at him, striking and knocking a hole in the brick just about an inch from Mother's breast.

The Browns were afraid to let the other boy outside, so they placed him in a cellar beneath the kitchen floor and covered the trapdoor leading to it with a "flour chest," fearing the boy would be killed if they lost the contest. Around "two or three o'clock in the morning" a large unit of soldiers from Harrisonville descended on the Brown home. Lizzie Brown continued: "It was sprinkling rain and when it would lightning we could see the front fence lined with horses. The men had dismounted and suddenly the whole command fired at him [Robert Brown Sr.]." Finally, they approached the portico of Brown's home and demanded entrance. Brown refused to open the door. Lizzie Brown explained, "Father could see them, the portico full of them, and one big fellow swore he'd get the damn rascal and a flash of lightning showed him up [through one of the vertical side windows that framed the door] as he made another unsuccessful lunge, and when he started the last time, Father shot him, and he fell dead."

Lizzie Brown related that her mother hid in a closet behind the front stairway, loading guns for her husband during the Jayhawkers' attack. Around daybreak, Brown "said goodbye," and made a successful dash to safety out the front door as "the whole command fired at him." Later he was exonerated for his part in the gunfight. Brown had been robbed an estimated "ten times" during the war, and the front door, its frame, and the side window of the Brown home still show signs of a spray of bullet holes about .36 caliber in size, as well as indications of filled-in bullet holes in the masonry. After this last episode, Brown was forced to take up residence in Lexington, Missouri, and conducted business from Judge Ryland's office in that town. Perhaps the only reason he survived these altercations with the Federals was because of his prestige and political connections in Harrisonville and western Missouri. Robert Allison Brown Sr. was the son of Brig. Gen. John Brown of the Kentucky militia. His grandson, Robert A. Brown III, who preserved this history, said, "One reason for narration of happenings in Western Missouri immediately prior to, during and following the Civil War is to tell of happenings that have not and will not appear in history books written and controlled by those who have reason to be ashamed of their treatment of an outnumbered and mistreated people."

The Brown family would not be the last to suffer such treatment at the hands of Anthony and his men. On January 1, 1862, Anthony took two hundred men and his twelve-pounder howitzer to Dayton, Missouri. Anthony said that he quickly concluded that the town had been "used voluntarily by its inhabitants as a depot for recruiting and supplying the rebels," so "it was burned [forty-six houses and buildings] except the one belonging to the Union man." He said he also "captured a lot of stock belonging to the rebels." On January 9, Anthony sent a Capt. Clark S. Merriman with fifty men to look for rebels near Columbus, Missouri. When he left the town, Merriman said that he was fired upon by rebels, and five of his men were killed. Merriman returned later with reinforcements, found no rebels in the town, and burned it to the ground. He also "captured 60 head of horses, mules, and cattle, and young stock." On January 14, it was reported by Col. Frederick Steele that Anthony had visited Rose Hill and "burned forty-two houses in that vicinity and robbed others of valuables and driven off stock."[29]

On January 18, Union major general Henry Halleck addressed the adjutant general of the army, Brig. Gen. Lorenzo Thomas, and complained that Jennison (actually Anthony in command) and his men were "no better than a band of robbers; they cross the line, rob, steal, plunder, and burn whatever they can lay their hands upon. They disgrace the name and uniform

Today, the door of the Robert Allison Brown home north of Harrisonville, Missouri, still shows signs of Jayhawker attacks in the form of a spray of bullet holes. The present owner, a descendant of the original Brown, has left the holes as a reminder of the Jayhawker reign of terror. *Courtesy of Arba E. Gilmore Jr.*

of American soldiers and are driving good Union men into the ranks of the secession army. . . . If the government countenances such acts by screening the perpetrators it may resign all hopes of a pacification of Missouri." The assistant adjutant general wrote Anthony on January 20 concerning the destruction of Dayton and Columbus. "The general commanding finds no evidence in either report of a state of facts sufficient to warrant these extreme measures. Your reports therefore are disapproved and held in reserve for further consideration and action," he communicated. Nothing, however, was done about the matter.[30]

The enlisted men of the Seventh Kansas Cavalry tell an even more candid story about their regiment's exploits and provide a clearer picture of the violence and brutality it perpetrated. Fletcher Pomeroy, a new recruit in Company H, described his experience the following way:

> Company H was advance guard, marching about one fourth of a mile in advance of the main column. . . . As we marched along, we suddenly discovered a building on fire a short distance in advance. . . . We wondered how it got afire, but we soon learned. We had gone but a little further when a turn in the road brought us in sight of a house. Women and children were fleeing to the woods while members of the advance guard were smashing in the windows and firing the house. Across the street were several stacks of wheat and oats; these were also fired.[31]

Some historians and commentators might minimize this experience by this Missouri family, but the psychological trauma created by such events—and the incidents were very widespread—must have endured a lifetime for the children and adults involved. When this experience is multiplied by dozens, even hundreds of families, it explains why so many of Missouri's young men joined the ranks of the guerrilla bands.

Ordinary security in western Missouri had become virtually nonexistent. Webster Moses, of Company D, Seventh Kansas Cavalry, described his visit to a wealthy Missouri farmer's residence.

> When we were at Lone Jack[,] A. Downing and about 10 of us went out Jayhawking. We went before breakfast and stopped at a rich secesh and told them we wanted some breakfast while they were getting breakfast we caught their horses and took the best ones when we came to breakfast they did not have dishes enough the negroes sayed that they had them hid we asked the Gentlemen where they were and he told us. We found some silver ware among the rest. I got the cupps. Two silver Ladles and two sets spoons. They sayed that the spoons belonged to the children and I gave them back. I gave Downing one ladle and the other to Capt Merriman. . . . Some of the boys got in some places about $100.00 worth of silver and some got considerable money.[32]

A contemporary account by George Caleb Bingham refers to a Missourian who was murdered by Jayhawkers in an "altercation growing out of his refusal to supply his murderer with liquor." Bingham also mentions another case where a man tried to protect three valuable mules by swimming them across the Missouri River and was deliberately shot and killed for his audacity. On December 12, 1861, a Maj. H. H. Williams crossed over into Missouri and burned Papinsville and Butler, returning into Kansas with freed slaves and stock, continuing the unending, daily litany of theft and arson. At this point in the war, through the actions of Lane, Jennison, Montgomery, and Anthony, the towns of Osceola, Dayton, West Point, Morristown, Columbus, Butler, and Papinsville, Missouri, ceased to exist; along the major byways of Missouri, little more than solitary, charred chimneys decorated the landscape; millions of dollars' worth of personal and slave property had been extinguished; and virtually every town and hamlet and a multitude of farms in western Missouri had experienced a raid or suffered outrageous intimidation. The Jayhawkers had become a pox, and everywhere they traveled or stopped, for a radius of several miles in every direction, the area became blighted and despoiled. The people, whether living in town or in the country, now lived in a state of continual terror. William Voran Powell related that his grandfather, Charles Jonathan Powell, who lived southwest of present-day Belton, Missouri, near the Kansas border, said, "The only time you could travel was at night."[33]

In November, further exacerbating the chaos in Missouri, Lane's chaplains Hugh D. Fisher and H. H. Moore went into Missouri and escorted from the state 160 wagons loaded with blacks, distributing them in labor-poor southern Kansas. By 1863, Missouri would lose 35 percent of its valuable slave property through these illegal and criminal actions. From the point of view of most Missourians and many army men, the situation was becoming an intolerable nightmare.[34] General Henry Halleck complained:

> The conduct of the forces under Lane and Jennison has done more for the enemy in this State [Missouri] than could have been accomplished by 20,000 of the enemy of his own army. I receive almost daily complaints of the outrages committed by these men in the name of the United States, and the evidence is so conclusive as to leave no doubt of the correctness. It is rumored that Lane has been made a brigadier-general. I cannot conceive of a more injudicious appointment.... [It] is offering a premium for rascality and robbing generally.[35]

Gov. Hamilton Gamble, the man who replaced Jackson as governor of Missouri, also complained to Washington repeatedly concerning the "wanton outrages" suffered by Missouri's citizenry, both secessionist and

Unionist. Other prominent Missouri Unionists also joined their voices to the clamor that something must be done. Secretary of War Edwin M. Stanton answered Missouri representatives James S. Rollins and Thomas L. Price, saying,

> GENTLEMEN: I have the honor to acknowledge the receipt last evening of your letter . . . respecting the outrages alleged to have been committed against Union men in Missouri by a force under Colonel Jennison [actually Anthony]. . . . I beg you to be assured that no effort on the part of the Government will be spared to protect the Union men and loyal citizens of Missouri from all illegal forces and lawless violence, come from what quarter it may.

Finally, the persistent cries of Missourians appeared to have captured the attention of President Lincoln. But he would do nothing directly about it.[36] As long as Missouri was successfully being held in the Union by force of arms, Lincoln looked the other way.

When Schofield had commanded the army in Missouri, Lincoln had warned him not to take political sides, to "Beware of being assailed by one and praised by the other," referring to the quarreling radical and conservative Missouri Republicans. Now, by the spring of 1862, through shrewd manipulations, Lincoln and the War Department either removed or acquiesced in the removal of Lane, Jennison, and Anthony from operations in Missouri. First, the Seventh Kansas Cavalry was reassigned to Humboldt, Kansas, well away from the Missouri border. The pretext for the reassignment was that the Humboldt area needed defending, which it did not. Then the Seventh Kansas Cavalry was included in plans for a projected Southwest Expedition to New Mexico, seemingly a thinly veiled attempt to banish the unit as well as the Lane Brigade from the area.

Finally, Jennison lent a hand in his own departure through his pique at not being promoted to brigadier general, which he had expected although he had never done anything to earn it. In an assembly of his regiment, he told the men that he was resigning; he added that he intended to start his own "independent force" and invited them to join. This, in the perception of Regular Army officers, was tantamount to insubordination and the incitement of mutiny. What is worse, 20 percent of Jennison's men promptly took him up on the proposition, and he "furloughed" them. On November 20, 1862, Dan Anthony, possibly seeing an opportunity to rise at the expense of his old boss, informed on Jennison to Brig. Gen. Samuel D. Sturgis, a rigid, Regular Army officer. Sturgis, disregarding Jennison's high-geared political clout with abolitionists in Kansas and the nation (he was, after all, in many respects, their darling), boldly sent an eleven-man deputation to arrest Jennison and his henchman George Hoyt, John Brown's lawyer at Harpers Ferry and soon the leader of the Kansas Red Legs. By 9:00 P.M., Sturgis had both men shackled, transported across the Missouri River under guard, and placed aboard a train headed for the Fifth Street Military Prison at St. Louis.

When Sturgis's guards arrived at the jail with their prisoners, Jennison and Hoyt were placed under the custody of the provost marshal, B. G. Farrar, who was given a special note from Sturgis offering this advice:

> I send Col. Jennison, of the Seventh Kansas Cavalry Volunteers to St. Louis, in order that he may be placed in such close custody as will place his escape beyond the pale of possibility—and I hope you will send him at once to Alton. He is charged with very grave offenses,— such as disorganizing his regiment, and inducing his men to desert so that he can place himself at their head when the expedition leaves the State for New Mexico, &c., and become the leader of a band of outlaws whose object is to be "plunder." . . . You will find him an exceeding plausible and shrewd man, which renders him the more dangerous to this already distracted community—and if not well guarded he will escape and return to this country, where he knows every lane and bush, and all the troops in the State will be unable to recapture him.[37]

Jennison's powerful abolitionist friends prevented him from being court-martialed and eventually enabled his parole. Jennison's official pillaging days were over—but only for a while.

Because Anthony followed the same program of pillaging rebels and freeing slaves as Jennison, the abolitionists protected him also. However, Anthony was apprehensive when Jennison first came under attack by the U.S. Army. He told his father in a letter, "He [Jennison] talked very foolishly about the regiment disbanding &c and said harsh words of the officers and President—which he said might cause his arrest—If they have charges against him for his Missouri Policy—we are all in the same boat—."[38]

Anthony survived Jennison's debacle and ultimately led the Seventh Kansas Cavalry in operations in Mississippi. According to Anthony, incompatibility with his commanding officer, Gen. Robert B. Mitchell, his one-time subordinate, forced him to resign on August 7, 1862. Anthony was actually pressured out of the service by his superiors for ignoring, then violating, army slave policies in the South as well as for "allowing his men to rob and steal from private families, and for allowing his men to break into private houses and break open wardrobes, closets, etc.," according to Capt. J. H. Odlin, Gen. William S. Rosecrans' acting assistant adjutant general. This reason is not nearly as pleasing an explanation for his dismissal as the one Anthony concocted.[39] George Hoyt ended up in Mississippi, too, but resigned officially on September 3, 1862, and returned to Kansas. Once Lane pulled his brigade out of Missouri, it was given no further role in military operations along the border, so Lane returned to the Senate. By the end of 1862, Lane, through the power of the patronage he wielded, decided the elections for the new governor of Kansas, Thomas Carney, and Kansas's representative to Congress, A. Carter Wilder, both from Leavenworth, Kansas. Anthony, by 1863, would become the mayor of the town.

***

The Missouri counties fronting Kansas bore the brunt of the Jayhawker invasion. But the second tier of counties in Missouri, those thirty to fifty miles eastward, in the interior of Missouri, were not immune. Not only did some of the Jayhawker units pass through these counties, but they had equally oppressive Missouri militia units stationed in their principal towns, and these units practiced many of the same policies as the Seventh Kansas Cavalry. What was particularly odious about the actions of the local militia units was that they were examples of Missourians tyrannizing Missourians. The bullying, plundering, and killing done by the militias was fully sanctioned, too, by the U.S. government.

Fortunately for the historical record, we have some extant diaries from this period, one of which was kept by Willard Hall Mendenhall, a thirty-year-old farmer and carriage maker from Lexington, Missouri, a town some sixty miles east of the border. Mendenhall kept a diary off and on for three years and left a perceptive account of what occurred in his area. Lexington, Mendenhall's hometown, was a thoroughly Southern town, occupied early by Kansas and then Missouri Union militias. Lt. Col. Bazel F. Lazear of the Twelfth Missouri State Militia, in a letter to his wife in 1863, left a good description of what he called the "red hot Secesh town" of Lexington. He wrote, "It is very different soldiering here to what it was in South East Mo [Missouri] where the people were ignorant and knew nothing. Here the people are rich and refined and in fact a good deal aristocratic. I have invitations every day to go somewhere to dinner or tea or to hear music as almost every house has a piano and somebody to use it."[40]

The following paragraphs are entries and partial entries from William Mendenhall's diary; they provide a vivid account of what was happening east of the border counties.

> *January 13, 1862:* I heard a rumbling noise like the sound of many wagons, in a short time I found it was a train of army wagons accompanied by a file of men armed. They went as far the Wallace haystacks, took the fence down, drove all the teams in. I thought they would take all they had left to live on this winter . . . Nine teams went on, in a few hours the nine teams came back loaded with corn, and hay, with two farm wagons

loaded with meat, and seven horses tied behind their wagons . . . We are very much afraid the soldiers will get our mules.

January 14: The soldiers have been searching nearly all the houses in town, taking guns, pistols, sugar, coffee, flour, nuts and anything they could get.

January 15: This is a reign of terror. [Charles] Jennison's Kansas [regiment] is in the neighborhood. I am told they have burned two hundred private residences and shot several men.

January 18: The troops sent out twenty-three wagons today. They returned all full. I think the country out this road must be destitute.

January 20: Today twenty-three wagons went out foraging, returned all loaded. . . . A newspaper made its appearance in town this morning, printed there by the soldiers, called the Kansas 1st . . . . It gives no news except what they make.

January 22: I called Mrs. [Lucinda] Henderson. She is very angry at the way the soldiers are conducting themselves here. They have levied a tax on the seccessionists of this military post. They are classed off. First class secessionists pay $20—second class $10 etc. What the money is for I do not know. It appears to me they are determined to take everything out of this country . . . For money they levy a tax. If not paid the next day you are cast in prison.

February 13: As Mollie [Mendenhall's wife] and I were going home [from a funeral] we met a number of soldiers and learned that they was from Col. Jennison's command of Jayhawkers (*thieves*). A short time after I arrived home two of them came to the door and pounded. I went to the door, I found they was soldiers. One of them demanded in a very boisterous manner the guns and revolvers I had in the house and said that he had been told that I was [a] secession [ist]. And that I was recruiting, etc . . . told him that I had no guns in the house. He did not appear satisfied until I told him to search the house (that was what he wanted so they could scatter over the house and steal). . . . They took a bottle of wine out of their pocket, called for a glass, drank it and left us.

February 14: I had not been in town long before a great number of my acquaintances in with complaints of outrageous depredations. At Mr. Sam'l Sawyer's they robbed them of bed clothing, all of his clothing, several bottles of wine, their horse, etc, and threatened to shoot Mrs. Sawyer if she followed them about the house. At Mr. Thos. Callaway's they demanded his money with their guns pointed at him, took many things there, threw his surveyor's compass in the fire. Went to John Ewing's, broke their furniture, took his and his wife's clothes, then set the house on fire. At Thos. Shields's (they have nearly everything taken from them) they looked at their piano, said they had broken many of them since they left Independence. They must thank them if they did not break theirs. They forced Mrs. [Susan] Trigg to play for them while they danced, as they left the house one of the men remarked to Mrs. Thos. Shields, (who is quite a fine looking young woman) that they liked her looks and would come back that night and stay with her. At Col. [Caleb] Bellis's they took his horse, gold watch, some money. I do not know how much, and abused his wife shamefully, felt of her person, and used insulting language. The outrages are too numerous to write. After the men took all they wanted from Col. Bellis they scattered them about the room and set it on fire.

February 19: A few soldiers of Col. Stevenson's command went to Doc. [William] Bulware's home and stole several of his fine chickens. He heard of it and met them with the chickens and demanded them. They resisted and cut at him several times with a knife. Doc drew his pistol and shot him in the neck. Did not kill him.

March 3: I heard that Col. Stevenson had a guard placed around the Episcopal Church yesterday and would not let Mr. [G. K.] Dunlop (the preacher) have service because he omitted "the President of the United States" in his prayer.

March 14: Mr. Sam'l Sawyer and Wm. Limrich are lying in jail arrested by the military here. They have never been in the army south or made treasonable speeches. We do not know what they are arrested for.

Sunday, March 30: When we arrived [in town] we learned that Col. Stevenson had closed the churches, there are eight churches in town. There was a service in but two of them, Catholic and Campbellite.

He has also closed the schools, and Baptist and Presbyterian female seminaries. There is nothing strange [in] these times. This has been the land of the free, and the home of the brave, it appears the object of the Federal Government is to free the Negro and enslave the white man in the South.

April 6 and 7: No news of importance except the soldiers in town are still swearing [in] citizens. They take oath only by force. If they do not they are sent to jail.

May 24: Col. Houston visited the prisoners after he arrived here. Had Mr. Martin Slaughter put in irons and chained in a dungeon.[41]

July 17: Mr. Gasper passed here yesterday evening on his way home and was shot a short distance from here. He was a curious man. It is supposed he was shot on account of his politics. A lot of cavalry passed as we were eating supper with a lot of prisoners.

July 21: We hear of acquaintance being shot every few days by both parties. The jail and Arcana Hall are full of prisoners.

August 21: Last night Mr. Wallace was here a short time. When he went home he found a wagon in front of his house, on inquiring found the soldiers in his house demanding his bed clothes & mattresses. They took them off with them.

August 22: Foraging parties go out every day, as the country around town is stripped of corn, hay & everything else, they go several miles in the country. They kill all the chickens, turkeys, geese, ducks, etc. that come in their sight. Last Saturday I gave up my fine Navy revolver to the military authority. I regret it very much as I have no arms in my house.

August 30: Drove to the shop. . . . I went in and found that it was taken possession of by the Federal troops for a commissary store. They went in and ran out my carriages without saying a word to me about it. At night some troops came to our house for my team, but fortunately the mules had jumped out of the pasture and I did not know

Union soldiers "living off the land" in Missouri at the expense of the local farmers, most of whom were never paid for their losses. *The Kansas State Historical Society, Topeka*

exactly where they were. They took all they could find in the neighborhood.

November 3: Today one squad of soldiers brought in 100 prisoners from Dover [a tiny town near Lexington]. The best citizens in that part of the country. This is a perfect reign of terror.

December 8: We were all invited to take tea at Mr. Wallace's this evening. When we were about done eating there was a rap at the door. Mr. Wallace went to the door, found there was ten soldiers. They demanded whiskey. Mr. Wallace asked what authority they had to come there at that hour of night (8 o'clock) for anything. One of them drew his pistol and pointed it in Mr. Wallace's face, saying d—— you that is my authority and will use it if necessary. . . . The worst of it is that they will not be known or punished.[42]

After the war, Mendenhall moved his family to Houston, Texas. However, what he had considered a "reign of terror" was only a pale imitation of what had been happening in the border counties of Missouri west of Lexington.

***

By mid-1862, the Lane Brigade had exited Missouri, Lane had adjourned to the Senate, Anthony and Hoyt had been removed from Missouri and deposited unceremoniously in Mississippi with the Seventh Kansas Cavalry, and Jennison had temporarily been jettisoned from the U.S. Army. Now, a new marauding unit of some thirty to one hundred men formed and began operations in western Missouri. Who was its leader? Not surprisingly, Charles Rainsford Jennison, Missouri's old menace. By summer's end, the unit's field commander would be George H. Hoyt, one of Jennison's former Seventh Kansas Cavalry officers and John Brown's old attorney. The new unit was called the "Red Legs" or "Red Legged Scouts." In 1863 a writer described Hoyt at a public meeting in Paola, Kansas, "dressed in a suit of black velvet, red sheepskin leggin[g]s reaching to the knees, a red silk handkerchief carelessly thrown around his neck, and a military hat with a flowing black plume. At his waist was an embossed morocco belt carrying a pair of ivory-mounted revolvers."[43] Unionist George Caleb Bingham's painting, *Order No. 11,* shows a Red Leg intimidating an elderly man after killing his unarmed son. The killer is dressed in typical Red Leg attire, his right hand on his revolver. Homes are being burned and plundered in the background.

While some historians are vague about the origin of the Red Legs, Kansas historian William Elsey Connelley said that they were organized by Gens. Thomas Ewing Jr. and James G. Blunt "for desperate service along the border." The Red Legs "received usually the salary of a commissioned officer whose uniform they were authorized to wear." Once they were formed, however, they became "fatherless children." No one, neither Blunt, who commanded the District of Kansas, nor Ewing, who commanded the District of the Border, wished to own them officially. Historian Stephen Starr said, "The Red Legs were not the kind of military body that keeps records and makes reports," and added, they "stole, robbed, burned, and killed indiscriminately, and not in Missouri alone." A Red Leg, "Sore-eyed" Dan, once complained when Jennison shot and killed an elderly man: "By G—d that is the first time I ever saw a dog killed that had no teeth."

Writing from Leavenworth, Kansas, C. M. Chase, a Union journalist for the *True Republican and Sentinel,* of Sycamore, Illinois, defined the Red Legs and the various forms of Jayhawkers who operated in Missouri and Kansas:

> Jayhawkers, Red Legs, and Bushwhackers are everyday terms in Kansas and Western Missouri. A Jayhawker is a Unionist who professes to rob,

burn out and murder only rebels in arms against the government. A
Red Leg is a Jayhawker originally distinguished by the uniform of red
leggings. A Red Leg, however, is regarded as more purely an indiscriminate thief and murderer than the Jayhawker or Bushwhacker. A
Bushwhacker is a rebel Jayhawker, or a rebel who bands with others for
the purpose of preying upon the lives and property of Union citizens.
They are all lawless and indiscriminate in their iniquities. Their occupation, unless crushed out speedily, will end in a system of highway robbery exceeding anything which has existed in any country. It excites the
mind, destroys the moral sensibilities, creates a thirst for wild life and
adventure which will, on the restoration of peace, find gratification in
nothing but highway robbery.[44]

Demonstrating how difficult it is to penetrate the misinformation surrounding many of the events and circumstances of the Border War,
General Blunt proclaimed the following to one of his commanders:

All operations against rebels must be directed by the legal military
authorities. This injunction is to apply especially to an organization
known as the "Red Legs," which is an organized band of thieves and
violators of law and good order. All such persons found prowling over
the country, without a legitimate purpose, must be disarmed; and if they
shall be caught in the act of thieving or other lawlessness, or in the possession of stolen property, for which they cannot give a good and sufficient reason, they shall be shot upon the spot. And as there is reason to
believe that officers in the military service are implicated directly or indi-
rectly, in the offenses committed by "Red Legs" and other lawless bands,
therefore, upon the evidence that any officer has failed or neglected to
carry out the foregoing instructions in reference to such offenders, they
will be dishonorably dismissed the service of the United States.[45]

In his message, General Blunt disavowed any affiliation with the Red
Legs. He even referred to them at another time as the "Forty Thieves." We
know, nonetheless, that one of the leaders of the Red Legs was the infamous "Captain Tough" (W. S. Tough), Blunt's own chief of scouts! Josiah
C. Ury, who was a "captain of scouts from 1862 until the close of the war,"
served under Blunt, where he wore "red and tan-colored buckskin leggings" as part of a squad of fifteen to twenty men called the "Red Legs."
Blunt was not the only authority who was known to support members of
the Red Legs. When Dan Anthony became mayor of Leavenworth, the Red
Legs used the town as a place to dispose of stolen property. They also had a
headquarters in Lawrence, Kansas, where regular public auctions were held
selling the stolen horses and property of Missourians. Jennison, after 1862,

operated a shipping business, Losee and Jennison, in Leavenworth, where he used many of the horses and property stolen by the Red Legs and other thieves from Kansas in his business. The people of Lawrence, according to historian Albert Castel, were "either unable to drive these bandits out or were indifferent to their presence." Likely, most of the people of Lawrence were not only indifferent to their presence, they also sanctioned and approved of it. The Red Legs used the Johnson House hotel in Lawrence as their hang-out, and buildings made of straw sprawled along a ravine near Massachusetts Avenue, where they kept stolen Missouri goods before auctioning it off and housed runaway slaves. Writer Lucien Carr called Lawrence a "mere fence-house for stolen property" once owned by Missourians.[46]

General Ewing wrote to Anthony on July 20, 1863, warning him that he had declared martial law in Leavenworth County and adding, "I will not abate or surrender my military jurisdiction, which extends to both arrest and punishments, in favor of a civil jurisdiction extending only to arrests, nor allow any town in my district to become a city of refuge within whose precincts the pirates of the border may escape the swift process of martial law." One of the reasons General Ewing placed Leavenworth under martial law while Anthony was mayor appears to have been because of his concern with illegal operations emanating from the town. Historian Stephen Starr said, "It was generally believed that he [Anthony] was hand-in-glove with the Red Legs and brigands of all descriptions who infested the eastern counties of Kansas as much as they did northwestern Missouri."[47]

Despite Ewing's attempt to remove the Red Legs from Lawrence and the surrounding areas, they remained. George W. Martin, secretary of the Kansas State Historical Society, writing in 1910, dispelled any doubt as to those who controlled the Red Legs.

> During the war on the border there was a legitimate organization of Union scouts called the "Red Legs." . . . There were never less than 50 of them, nor more than 100. The organization was formed in December, 1862 or January 1863. . . . They were employed by the generals in command, and were carried on the pay rolls at seven dollars each per day. Cyrus Leland, Jr., who was an officer on Gen. Thomas Ewing's staff says that Ewing always had several of them in his employ. . . . Thomas J. Anderson, of Topeka, who was a member of General Blunt's staff, tells me that Blunt also had many of them on the pay roll . . . so the red leggings seem to have been a badge of desperate service in the Union Army, furnished from headquarters.

Martin continued, "The Red Leg was a terror in Missouri. All their witnesses say that the Red Leg was a way above the average man in ability. They were recognized by the government as fully as any captain, colonel or general." Albert Greene, a soldier in the Ninth Kansas Cavalry, said that "The exigencies of the border warfare demanded the organization of a company of picked men, capable of independent action, . . . who would act on an instant on their own initiative, without waiting for orders from superior authority and the cumbersome machinery of military etiquette."[48]

Among the members of the Red Legs, besides Jennison and Hoyt, were such notables as William F. "Buffalo Bill" Cody, James Butler "Wild Bill" Hickok, Theodore Bartles, William Sloan Tough (known as "Captain Tough" or "Tufts"), Jack Harvey, Walt Sinclair, "Red" Clark, and "Jeff Davis" (actually Capt. Joseph Bloomington Swain, of New York). Some of the Red Legs had bizarre names like "Sore-eyed Dan," Sam "Pickles" Wright, "Pony" Searl, Charles "One-eyed" Blunt, "Yellow Tom" Cullinan, and "Beauregard" Jack Bridges. The headquarters of the Red Legs was Six Mile House on the road from Kansas City to Leavenworth. They also had a headquarters in Fort Scott. Another of their headquarters was Lawrence, Kansas, where they often nested, rested, and stored their loot. Buffalo Bill Cody admitted that as one of the Red Legs, he raided Missouri farms and settlements, adding "Few of us ever returned empty-handed. . . . We were the biggest gang of thieves on record." "Willie" (as his sister referred to him), after he joined the "Red Legged Scouts," told his sister upon returning from his duties that he had been "out with his Scouting Co." on a "Scouting Tour."

The Red Legs were well and widely known by those whom they stayed among in these small towns. When Quantrill's guerrillas fled Lawrence in August 1863 after sacking and burning the town, their pursuers captured some of the young guerrillas and turned them over to Hoyt, the field chief of the Red Legs, who promptly and personally executed them. Obviously, the Kansas authorities knew the Red Legs only too well.[49] Three years after the Civil War—noting how interwoven the crooked and unlawful were with the sanctioned and legal in Kansas—George Hoyt, the putative field leader of the Red Legs became the attorney general of Kansas, and Jennison became an elected state representative. Anthony continued to be elected mayor of Leavenworth.[50]

Leverett W. Spring, a New England English professor and historian, said this of the Red Legs:

> Early in the struggle an organization appeared known as "Red Legs."
> . . . It was a loose-jointed organization, with members shifting between twenty-five and fifty, dedicated originally to the vocation of horse-stealing, but flexible enough to include rascalities of every description. At intervals the gang would dash into Missouri, seize horse and cattle—not omitting other worse outrages on occasion— then repair with their booty to Lawrence, where it was defiantly sold at auction. "Red-legs were accustomed to brag in Lawrence," says one

William H. "Buffalo Bill" Cody, a known Red Leg, admitted his part in their operations, stating, "We were the biggest gang of thieves on record." *The Kansas State Historical Society, Topeka*

who was familiar with their movements, "that nobody dared to interfere with them. They did not hesitate to shoot inquisitive and troublesome people. At Lawrence the livery stables were full of their stolen horses. One day I saw three or four Red-legs attack a Missourian who was in town searching for lost property. They gathered about him with drawn revolvers and drove him off very unceremoniously. I once saw Hoyt, the leader, without a word of explanation or warning, open fire upon a stranger quietly riding down Massachusetts Street. He was a Missourian whom Hoyt had recently robbed. The gang contained men of the most desperate and hardened character, and a full recital of their deeds would sound like the biography of devils.

Spring said that either the people of Lawrence were unable to drive out these desperate men, or "they thought it mattered little what might happen to Missouri Loyalists." Gov. Charles Robinson, a man of some ethical standing, attempted to rid Kansas of them and became the object of an assassination attempt by Red Legs "which barely miscarried."

D. W. "Webb" Wilder epitomizes the Jayhawker interlude in Kansas history best. The editor of the *Leavenworth Conservative,* who held the Franklin Medal from the Boston Latin School, the Bowdoin Gold Medal from Harvard, and a position in the Boston bar, exemplifies the fanaticism and corruption of the abolitionists of this period. He said: "Jayhawking was got up in Kansas. It's one of our things. It works well; we believe in it, we are going to have it. It don't make any difference whether the authorities, civil or military, believe in it or not. Kansas don't care much for authorities; never did, never will."

Wilder reveals the undiluted truth. Years of breaking the law, avoiding the law, and defying the U.S. government and its agents had created a truly lawless breed of men, fanatics with a brazen disregard for law and order. And it was precisely these lawless, unprincipled men who often held top positions in Kansas government.[51]

Gov. Charles Robinson of Kansas, as noted earlier, was correct when he predicted that the upshot of Kansas Jayhawker raids into Missouri would be the emergence of a group of Missourians seeking revenge and retaliation. A dynamic Missouri guerrilla movement erupted in late 1861 that would seek to protect Missourians and obtain revenge for the many crimes, outrages, and indignities suffered by the citizens of Missouri through the actions of the Jayhawkers and their political and military allies. The guerrillas would have a long memory, and it would not be a single crime that fired their animus, as advocates of Kansas often propose, but a sorry multitude of them.

Chapter 8

Nemesis: The Emergence of Quantrill

The heyday of the worst Jayhawking was over. But the effects of the Jayhawking had opened a Pandora's box of retribution. Because of the Jayhawking raids into Missouri from 1858 through 1861, the carnage by the Lane Brigade in 1861 and early 1862, and the continuation of various forms of marauding by the Red Legs and the Missouri Union militias in Missouri, a guerrilla movement germinated and began to flourish in western Missouri. Many historians, today and in the past, emphasize that the Kansas invasions into Missouri from 1858 through 1865 were in response to incursions by Missourians into Kansas during the territorial period. If there were such a connection, the devastating raids into Missouri must have been one of the most disproportionate responses in history.

Missouri raids into Kansas during the territorial period had been relatively controlled, largely sanctioned by the U.S. government, of short duration, and a response to real threats posed by abolitionists in Kansas to Missouri property. In contrast, the invasions by Kansans of Missourians from 1858 onward were largely gratuitous examples of total war, the attempt by an enemy, through armed force, to liquidate the capital resources of an enemy, destroy homes, properties, businesses, towns, farms, lives—everything—in order to impoverish, vanquish, and destroy that enemy. The campaigns into Missouri were continuous, to a considerable degree uncontrolled, often without quarter, and motivated primarily by greed, with sometimes a patina of rabid abolitionism as a specious pretext.

The invasion of Missouri was further exacerbated by the drought in Kansas in 1860, which even the copious and generous aid sent to the area from the East failed to alleviate. The result was that thousands of previously poor and now impoverished hungry Kansans, some of whose children wore Sam Pomeroy grain sacks for clothing, many of whom had cultivated a well-established disdain for law and order for over six years, now coveted the well-stocked pantries, flocks, herds, stores, and rich possessions of Missourians. When the war broke out, there was nothing to restrain this restless group from crossing the border and helping themselves, which they did violently, disgracing, according to several Union generals, the United States uniforms they wore. The natural and expected reaction by

Missourians to this incessant carnage was to add a terrible new dimension to the struggle between the two states in the form of virulent guerrilla warfare, certainly the direct result of the earlier carnage.

For the sake of coherency, the last chapter focused largely on the actions of Kansans in western Missouri, touching only lightly on the guerrilla response (principally, Upton Hays' resistance to Anthony on the Little Blue River south of Westport, Missouri, on November 10, 1861). Actually, when the war broke out and Missouri's elected government was driven south, there was widespread secessionist resistance, both unorganized and organized, in Missouri, and not just in the west. By late 1861, the guerrillas in western Missouri began to form into small bands of twenty to thirty men. They later developed the ability to combine, when the need arose, into a dangerous, small army numbering some three hundred men. During their early operations, William Clarke Quantrill led the guerrillas. Due to the demonization of Quantrill in histories, an examination of the man is imperative.

Quantrill was not a native Missourian. He was born in Canal Dover, Ohio, on July 31, 1837, of middle-class parents. Quantrill's grandfather, Thomas Heiser Quantrill, a blacksmith, had been a captain in the War of 1812, and his father, Thomas Henry Quantrill, a tinner, minor inventor, and later, the principal of the Canal Dover Union School. Nothing much of violence is found in Quantrill's early background. This absence of childhood trauma forced some of his detractors, like Kansas historian William Elsey Connelley, the author of the book *Quantrill and the Border Wars,* an early, influential history, to go to considerable lengths in order to concoct a childhood considered "traumatic" enough to justify his later accusations that the young Ohioan was doomed to criminal depravity from his earliest existence. Connelley was reduced to dredging up stories about the young Quantrill shooting holes in the ears of pigs, throwing small snakes at girls, and locking a young lady in a belfry for amusement. These boyish antics and others like them, according to Connelley, were a sign of Quantrill's incipient depravity and showed that he was "cruel and heartless . . . idle and worthless." Even Quantrill's family closet of ancestors was emptied in a quest for skeletons. As in most families, some were found, one a supposed pirate. The demonization of Quantrill, exemplified by Connelley's portrayal of him, continued through the Civil War and remains quite virulent today. Some historians have even commented on the sinister sound of Quantrill's name, an odd form of attack since he had a conventional, more or less English one.[1]

Because of the incessant campaign to demonize Quantrill and his importance to the subject of the Border War, the author has chosen to examine Quantrill's life before he became the leader of the guerrillas. Quantrill was a handsome boy, who from the time he was sixteen, worked off and on as a schoolteacher. Wanderlust and the persuasion of friends,

William Clarke Quantrill, the demonized leader of the Missouri guerrillas. *State Historical Society of Missouri, Columbia*

however, convinced him in 1857, when he was twenty, to go to Kansas to stake a claim. He traveled to that territory with several Canal Dover men, Harmon V. Beeson; Beeson's son Richard, a friend of Quantrill; and Col. Henry Torrey, Quantrill's life-long mentor and supporter. The two older men paid Quantrill's fare in return for specified acts of labor to be performed by him when they arrived. For the next six months, Quantrill did minor farming and developed his claim, which was located close to the Marais des Cygnes River near Stanton in Miami County. Later, he moved to Tuscarora Lake, where he had a falling out with the Canal Dover men over petty thefts, allegedly committed by Quantrill, and Quantrill's counter-claim, at least partly legitimate, that he had been dispossessed by one of the Canal Dover men.

In the spring of 1858, Quantrill's wanderlust came to the fore again, and he signed aboard Henry Clay Chiles' army provision train at Fort Leavenworth, bound for Utah. Quantrill was hired as a "bull whacker" or herder. Many of the men engaged for the expedition were a rough lot, "the outscourings of the slums," some said; others were "enterprising young men." Quantrill, because of the blazing red shirt he wore and the coarse nature of many of his vulgar companions, came to be called "Red Shirt." Quantrill always seemed to make a splash, to be noticed somehow. The expe-dition, conducted by Brig. Gen. Albert Sidney Johnston, had as its object the pacifying of the Mormons. The six hundred 6-mule teams were soon organ-ized into twenty-six wagon trains and left Leavenworth around June 1, 1858. Upton Hays, mentioned earlier as the Missouri guerrilla who led the battle against Anthony's Seventh Kansas Cavalry near the Little Blue River in 1861, was a member of Quantrill's wagon train to Utah, as well as a number of other Missourians. Contacts with these men during the expedition likely influenced Quantrill's decision to take up arms on behalf of Missouri after the war broke out. Certainly, they proved valuable contacts to Quantrill a few years later, when he became the principal guerrilla chief in Missouri.[2]

Before arriving in Utah in early September 1858, Quantrill stopped for a time at Fort Bridger. R. M. Peck described the dapper Quantrill at this time: "A pair of high-heeled calf-skin boots of small size; bottom of trousers tucked into boot-tops; a Navy pistol swinging from his waist belt; a fancy blue flannel shirt; no coat; a colored silk handkerchief tied loosely around his neck; yellow hair hanging nearly to the shoulders; topped out by the inevitable cow-boy hat."[3]

For a couple of months, while the expedition stayed in Utah, Quantrill became a cook for twenty-five men. During his idle hours, he indulged his appetite for reckless gambling. Soon, Quantrill decided to join a gang of men going to Pike's Peak, Colorado, to try their luck at gold mining. After spending some forty-seven days in the gold fields, Quantrill ended up vir-tually empty-handed, finding only $54.34 of the glittering metal, which failed to cover his expenses. During this period of his life, Quantrill assumed the sobriquet Charley Hart for unknown reasons, perhaps only because of his innate secretiveness. The trip west among rough companions seemed to mature Quantrill, harden him, and make him bolder, faster thinking, shrewder, more cunning, and, yes, devious, all qualities that would serve him well as a guerrilla chief.

During his Pike's Peak adventure, Quantrill also appears to have suffered traumatic, personal misfortunes. In a letter to his mother, Caroline Quantrill, from Lawrence, Kansas, dated July 30, 1859, Quantrill wrote,

> I have seen some pretty hard & scaly times, both from cold weather & starvation & the Indians & I am one of 7 out of a party of 19 who started from Salt Lake city for the Gold Mines of Pikes Peak, which are talked of all over the country. . . . I am now in Lawrence after having spent over $300 & many a day & night when I expected to be killed or freeze to death & all that saved my head was I was out hunting away from the camp about a mile and a half & hearing the firing hurried to camp in time to see the Indians driving off our horses & my friend lying on the ground apparently dead but still breathing with difficulty—having been shot 3 times, his leg broke below the knee, shot in the thigh with 7 iron slugs & last shot through the body with an arrow which I first thought would kill him but he lives yet.[4]

Quantrill's experiences as a teamster on the wagon train to Utah, his time in Mormon country, and his hard life in Colorado and on the Plains appear to have prepared him to some extent for the perils that followed in his life. During this period, he learned to carry and use a gun, to deal with tough people in complex interactions, and to suffer and prevail over adversity. As Quantrill told his mother in a letter on January 26, 1860, "I have seen a little of the world. I know how others manage to keep moving in the vast crowd which is moving ahead."[5]

On March 23, 1860, Quantrill wrote his sister cryptically, "You people of the crowded city can form no idea of what men go through and how they have to struggle to keep from the grasp of grim Death, who apparently stares them in the face as they move along." He told his mother also of the "excruciating pain" he suffered in Colorado from snow blindness and of a night in the mountains when their guide, discovering that he had lost the way, told the men, "Well boys my heart is almost broke when I think that we may all die here tonight." Later, Quantrill confessed apprehension about the situation on the border, telling his mother, "There is no news but hard times, and harder still coming . . . for the devil has got unlimited sway over this territory." Obviously, Quantrill was no longer a simple country schoolteacher.[6]

Earlier, in a letter to his mother from Stanton, Kansas, on January 22, 1858, Quantrill had shown the influence of the political philosophy of the Kansans living around him:

> About the last elections here is this 10,126 votes against the Lecompton swindle & 6,000 for it, of which 3000, if not more were illegal. I saw Ohio Democrat here yesterday which had some what I call D___n lies about Kansas & I would like to tell the editor so to his face. He said Jim Lane, (as good a man as we have here), was fighting U.S. Troops at Ft. Scott, he was there but did no fighting; his presence is enough to frighten 100 Missourians.[7]

But two years later, in a letter to his mother on January 26, 1860, Quantrill had changed his views dramatically:

> You have undoubtedly heard of the wrongs committed in this territory by the southern people, or proslavery party, but when one knows the facts they can easily see that it has been the opposite party that have been the main movers in the troubles & by far the most lawless set of people in the country. They all sympathize for old J. Brown, who should have been hung years ago, indeed hanging was too good for him. May I never see a more contemptible people than those who sympathize for him. A murderer and a robber made a martyr of, just think of it.[8]

From this point on, Quantrill remained generally aligned with the Southern cause.

In the fall of 1859 and spring of 1860, Quantrill had returned to Stanton, Kansas, and taught a six-month term of school. One of his female students, years later, described him as "a good teacher; had large blue eyes, a Roman nose, light complexion, light hair . . . peculiar eyes . . . like no other eyes . . . upper lids heavy . . . he took no part in affairs . . . a very quiet man, secretive and peculiar." His other students, when questioned about him later in life, all said, "He was a good teacher and that he had no trouble whatever in his school." During this time, Quantrill stayed with John Bennings, a proslavery man, and his son, Adolphus, a friend and companion of Quantrill on his trip to Utah. Quantrill must have had a reasonably good reputation to be allowed to teach school in this close-knit community.[9]

By summer 1860, Quantrill had moved to Lawrence under his assumed name, Charley Hart, where he lived on the Delaware reservation. One of his friends in Lawrence, Nathan Stone, the proprietor of the Whitney House, the hotel where Quantrill sometimes stayed, knew that his real name was William Clarke Quantrill, but most did not. Holland Wheeler, a civil engineer who lived in Lawrence at the time, described Quantrill when he arrived in town. "He was dressed with corduroy pants tucked into his boots, woolen shirt, slouch hat, and carried an oilcloth grip. He was about five feet nine inches in height, [actually five feet ten] bow-legged, weighed about 150 or 160 [perhaps 171] pounds, sandy hair, rather hooked nose, and had a peculiar droop to his eyelids . . . had a lady friend who was in town at times. Saw him riding with her in a carriage several times. . . . He was somewhat of a horseman, and only a fair shot." Quantrill was known, however, as a good judge of horseflesh. The people around Lawrence at this time believed that he was a detective for the Delaware Indians.[10]

From this point on in his life, Quantrill assumed an entirely different persona. This change was foreshadowed in a letter he sent to his mother in February 8, 1860. In the letter, he wrote, "I can now see more clearly than ever in my life before, that I have been striving and working really without any end in view. And now since I am satisfied that such a course must end in nothing, it must be changed, and that soon, or it will be too late." For the next six months, Quantrill was involved in endless intrigues with the proslavery and abolitionist gangs that hovered around Lawrence.

One of Quantrill's more intimate Lawrence "friends" was Capt. John E. Stewart, a Methodist minister and rabid abolitionist from New Hampshire, who owned a farm four miles south of Lawrence in the heavily wooded bottomland along the Wakarusa River. Stewart had built a fort there, which he used as a base of operations for raids into Missouri and for a place to harbor "stolen" and runaway slaves before sending them along the underground railroad. Stewart had longstanding ties with John Brown and James Montgomery in their Linn and Bourbon County operations. Among Stewart's gang at Lawrence were Walt Sinclair, who later became a Red Leg, and Barclay Coppoc, one of John Brown's followers at Harpers Ferry, who escaped arrest by Federal authorities. Stewart's fort was used also to hide stolen horses and cattle seized in raids into Missouri and in forays on proslavery Kansas farmers. He periodically sold the stock, and he and his gang kept the proceeds. The authorities around Lawrence knew of Stewart's activities and winked at them slyly. Authorities in the state of Missouri, various Missouri counties, and private individuals also knew about Stewart and offered a standing bounty of one thousand dollars for his death, a fact of which Quantrill was aware. Stewart accepted Quantrill for he portrayed himself to Stewart as a rabid abolitionist.[11]

While Quantrill cozied up to Stewart, he developed even closer and apparently more legitimate ties with the proslavery gang in the Lawrence area, men who usually hung out around the Kansas River ferry and were led by Jake Herd. Herd was feared, considered a "terror raiser" by the Free Staters around Lawrence, and given a wide berth by all. Herd's main pursuit was kidnapping the slaves freed by Stewart and carrying them back to

Missouri, where he collected fees from the slave owners for his expenses and the risks he incurred. The abolitionists all considered Herd's operation a strictly mercenary one, but the great danger surrounding his operations suggests that he was motivated in part or, more likely, a great deal by ideology. It was Herd who captured John Doy, "the slave stealer" mentioned in an earlier chapter, a very dangerous enterprise. Herd's accomplices were Thomas and Jacob "Jake" McGee, Henry McLaughlin, Esau Sager, Jack Eliot, John Stropp, Jay Vince, Frank Baldwin, Quantrill, and others.[12]

Since Quantrill networked with both the Free Staters and the proslavery supporters, some Kansans believed Quantrill was one of the proslavery party's spies in Lawrence. John Dean, who owned a wagon shop in Lawrence, an active abolitionist and close friend of Quantrill's until his proslavery agenda became apparent, wrote,

> Quantrells [sic] occupation while living at and near Lawrence was that of a "spie" or detective in the interests of Slavery, and it may possibly be of the then Gov't. One of the Coppic boys that was at "Harper's Ferry" with Old John Brown was in "Kansas", and some with me about that time, and the U. S. Gov't was looking for him. After the mask had been removed and the light of truth let in to those heretofore uncertain matters, there could be no other conclusion than that Quantrell was acting the part of detective or spie in the pay or interest of the South, and put his time in in the best way to "make," not always governed in his actions by the plumb line of "right" [sic].

Dean also told W. W. Scott, an early biographer of Quantrill, that he (Quantrill) "proved himself to be a member of a pro-slavery secret society of Missouri western border notoriety and also a secret agent of said society."[13]

W. L. Potter, a proslavery advocate who lived at Paola when Quantrill was in Lawrence, told Quantrill's biographer and boyhood friend, W. W. Scott, that Quantrill had close associations with the proslavery party. Potter, who acted at times as a deputy U. S. marshal, deputy sheriff, deputy jailer, and deputy constable near Paola said he knew Quantrill as "Bill" Quantrill and that, in the fall of 1860, he was involved in a meeting held at the Union Hotel in Paola in which only men opposed to Jayhawking attended "by special invitation." Some of the attendees at the meeting were "George W. Miller EX Circuit judge [later] of Denver Colorado"; lawyers E. W. White, Robert White, and "Massey"; "Goodwin Taylor a Merchant, Allen T. Ward a Merchant, Thos. Kelley, General Seth Clover, Indian agent & Col Torrey [Quantrill's friend and confidant]." Quantrill attended the meeting and proposed to the men "that he wanted to get Jennison in a Place where he could either capture or Lawfully kill him." He also told the men of a planned "Raid on Paola" by Jayhawkers and a planned robbery of some "$30,000" to be carried aboard the Kansas City, Paola & Fort Scott Stage as a gold shipment to Col. Seth Clover, the agent for the Miami Indians. As a result of Quantrill's warning, according to Potter, a company of U.S. infantry accompanied the money to Paola.[14]

So the question with Quantrill is whether his connection with the proslavery party was official and orchestrated or a personal campaign. If a connection existed between Quantrill and the Southern men, it goes far in explaining how an outsider like Quantrill, a Northerner in fact, was able to achieve an ascendant position in the Missouri guerrilla movement by 1862. Pro-Southern Missourians were especially fearful of spies intruding into their organizations. Whether or not he was a spy or counterspy, his actions were consistent with one. But admitting him to be such would take away much of Quantrill's alleged venality and undermine the argument of many historians, so this data is unstated in those works. But whatever Quantrill's failings, he clearly was bold, cunning, intriguing, and resourceful.

No matter Quantrill's affiliations, one thing is also certain: his involvements in Lawrence were extremely dangerous and criminal. In the several months in that town from the summer to fall of 1860, he was involved in a number of perilous and allegedly criminal situations, including the conspiracy to murder a free black barber, Allen Pinks; a raid with Walt Sinclair and Barclay Coppoc on proslavery farmers in Salt Creek Valley, north of Leavenworth, where the men stole a large number of cattle and horses, leading them to Stewart's fort; a turnabout raid with Herd's men on Stewart's fort to capture escaped slaves; a raid into Missouri with Lawrence men for cattle, during which Quantrill turned coat and attempted to help the Missouri farmers regain their livestock; an alleged theft by Quantrill of the Ridenour & Baker powder house on the banks of the Kansas River; an alleged theft by Quantrill of ponies from the Kickapoo Indians; and his alleged complicity in arson and the kidnapping of a fugitive slave. Quantrill had a busy summer. Many Kansans during this period believed that Quantrill's paramount objective throughout this time was to induce Stewart to make a raid into Missouri, which would give Quantrill an opportunity to capture him, obtain a huge reward, and make a name for himself. Stewart, however, while friendly with Quantrill, was wary of him and, besides, took pride in planning and conducting his own raids.[15]

By late November 1860, Quantrill's position in Lawrence became untenable. The Douglas County Court found indictments for his arrest for theft of horses and cattle, burglary, kidnapping, and arson. Soon thereafter, upon seeing Quantrill strolling down Massachusetts Avenue, Sheriff Samuel Walker deputized George Earl and attempted to arrest the wanted man. Aided by his unwitting friend John Dean, an abolitionist, Quantrill escaped from the town, momentarily ending his escapades in Lawrence. He would be back.

Around this time, a number of transplanted Iowans now living in Pardee, Kansas—Edwin Morrison, Albert Southwick, Charles Ball, and Chalkley T. Lipsey—were planning an expedition into the Cherokee Nation to free slaves. The four young men, of Quaker parentage, were from Springdale, Iowa, and members of its secret abolitionist society. Springdale was one of the main stations along the underground railroad, and John Brown had been a frequent guest there, attending secret meetings in the town. Brown also had drilled his men at Springdale before the Harpers Ferry raid. The young Iowans recently had formed a secret lodge of their own in Pardee (a town named after Pardee Butler, mentioned earlier in reference to his being tarred and cottoned, who was Chalkley Lipsey's minister).[16]

Recently, three freed slaves from the Cherokee Nation, who now lived in Springdale, had contacted the Pardee men for help in freeing their families, who were held as slaves by Indians in the Cherokee Nation. The Pardee men agreed to help them and went to Lawrence to enlist John Dean's help. Rev. J. J. Lutz of Springdale, Iowa, later justified the young men's abolitionist activities, saying, "I think that most men on the higher planes of thought and feeling recognize at times a conflict between human enactments and that higher law of their being; and so reserve the right to owe their highest allegiance to the *higher law* [emphasis added], and suffer the human penalties." (The "higher law," unfortunately, had acquired a poor reputation in Kansas and Missouri as inducing theft, murder, and mayhem.) Dean, whose help the young men sought, was a known abolitionist with a reputation for making successful raids. Because Quantrill had been agitating for some time to be included in Dean's abolitionist enterprises, Dean now turned to him for assistance, muscle, and know-how. Meanwhile, the abolitionists left one of their companions back at Pardee to prepare a cabin for the freed slaves when the expedition returned.[17]

Around December 1, Quantrill set out for Osawatomie, Kansas. Several days later, he was followed by Dean; the Pardee men, Morrison, Southwick, Ball, and Lipsey; John S. Jones, known as "Mr. Baker"; and the three black men, William and John Thompson and John Martin. The men traveled to Osawatomie in a wagon driven by William Partridge. It was assumed that other abolitionists would help the men once they arrived at Osawatomie. When the men arrived at that town, they acted in a secretive manner, and Dean quietly attempted to enlist Capt. Ely Snyder, a well-known Jayhawker and abolitionist, to join them in their expedition. Snyder, however, said the plan was impractical (later, he said that he distrusted Quantrill; he had been on earlier Jayhawking raids with him into Missouri). Finally, the expedition to the Cherokee Nation fell through, and the three blacks wished no further connection with other abolitionist plots.

Quantrill, however, agitated for a raid on a Missouri plantation of which he knew, one that had many slaves and whose master had lots of gold. Quantrill's plan was to raid Morgan Walker's plantation, a nineteen-hundred-acre farm with close to thirty slaves and large herds of horses and mules. The Walker house, a two-storied affair with nine rooms, had slave quarters, cribs, and barns to its rear. The farm was situated three miles northeast of Blue Springs, Missouri, and seven miles generally east of Independence. The young abolitionists fell in quickly with the scheme, feeling that they had already committed themselves to some sort of abolitionist enterprise.

By this time, Partridge had returned to Lawrence with his wagon, so Quantrill was forced to find another. For this purpose, he sent Dean and Southwick to Lawrence to obtain one from his friend Nathan Stone. The wagon would be used to help carry the slaves and other assorted plunder. Other wagons could be obtained at the Walker's. The plan was for Southwick and Ball to arrive at the Walker place at a predetermined time with a wagon from Lawrence to carry off slaves and booty.[18]

Quantrill, accompanied by Morrison, Ball, and Lipsey, now crossed into Missouri near Indian Creek, just inside the state, where the men camped the first night close to the ford. To curb the suspicions of Missourians, the men left their shotguns and Sharps rifles behind and carried only knives and revolvers. For the next couple of days, they walked in a northwesterly direction toward Blue Springs. If stopped along the way by authorities, they planned to tell them that they were on their way to Lafayette County to work on the Missouri Pacific Railroad, then in progress. As they neared the Walker home early the next day, they passed Morgan Walker, a Jackson County pioneer, in the road on his way to Independence. Quantrill, either not knowing who he was or pretending not to know, asked him the way to Morgan Walker's place. Walker replied, "I am the man!" Quantrill then inquired the way to his son Andrew J. Walker's house. When Quantrill and the men arrived within a mile of young Walker's home, they camped in a thicket.[19]

Around 11:00 A.M., Quantrill left the camp and went to the home of Andrew Walker, who lived a quarter-mile from his father. Quantrill told Walker that he was a member of a gang of Jayhawkers sent from Kansas to rob his father and steal the family's slaves and property. He said his partners were in the bush and had sent him to reconnoiter the Walker place in preparation for a raid. Quantrill offered to help Walker defend his property; Andrew fell in with the plan. Quantrill told Walker that his scheme was to return that night with his companions. Walker, as part of Quantrill's plan, would meet them with an armed reception committee (at the appropriate moment). Quantrill, then, would fight along with Walker's men. Soon, the two men had worked out the fine details.

Walker soon contacted John Tatum, Lee Coger, D. C. William, and Clark Smith to assist him. At nightfall, these men, armed with shotguns heavily loaded with buckshot, positioned themselves in a harness room adjoining Walker's front porch (just to the right of the porch, when facing the house). Mrs. Morgan Walker's loom was on the right side of the porch, and Andrew Walker and one of his men hid behind it. The night was dark, so Walker and his friend were hidden from view. The harness room, where the three other men hid, had a side door opening onto the porch. The men positioned themselves near the door, which they planned to open at the opportune time and fire on the abolitionists. The plan was for Quantrill and the abolitionists to enter Walker's house, demand Morgan Walker's slaves and money, and then leave the house by the porch to gather up the slaves. Quantrill was to stay in the house and pretend to guard Morgan Walker.

About ten minutes before Quantrill and his men arrived at Walker's home, the elder Walker returned from his trip to Independence, so Andrew Walker explained the plan to his father. By this time, John Dean and Albert Southwick had arrived from Missouri with a wagon to carry off the slaves. At 7:00 P.M., Quantrill approached the Walker home with the abolitionists in tow. He had Dean hitch their wagon some distance from the house. The five men then strode in the darkness toward Walker's house, which faced east. Morrison was stationed outside the door as a guard, and Dean took up a position in the yard. Quantrill, Ball, and Lipsey walked to the front door and knocked loudly. Ball, acting as the group's spokesman, greeted Morgan Walker with a gun and quickly came to the point. He told the elder Walker that they were abolitionists and had come to free his slaves and take his money, horses, and mules. Moments later, it was decided that Quantrill "would take care of the old folks" (guard them), while Ball, Lipsey, and the others collected the slaves and loaded them aboard wagons.

After this was decided, Ball and Lipsey walked out the front door onto the porch. The sky was dark, but with the aid of the light coming from the front door and a candle that had been placed in a nearby window, Andrew Walker and the man next to him saw the clear silhouette of the abolitionists, raised their guns, and fired. Morrison fell on the porch dead; Lipsey, wounded in the thigh, cried for help. Ball, firing at his adversaries wildly with one hand, grabbed Lipsey around the waist and stumbled with him into the darkness. The men from the harness room now rushed onto the porch, raised their shotguns, and fired a thundering volley at the dark shapes in the front yard. Dean was struck in the foot by the buckshot. He and Southwick staggered toward the wagon, hurriedly boarded it, and brought the horses to a gallop. They hardly looked back until they reached Lawrence. Southwick later claimed not to have been present at the affair, but clearly he had been.[20]

Ball, realizing their friends had abandoned them, dragged Lipsey through the darkness to a nearby farm, where they hid all night in a thicket, nearly freezing in the cold night air. The next morning, Ball extracted buckshot from Lipsey's thigh, dressed his wounds, and administered an herbal poultice to his injury. Two days later, a local slave, hunting for hogs, found the two men. After talking to the men, the slave promised to help them escape in return for his freedom. Instead, he reported their whereabouts to his master. The word was passed on to Morgan Walker and his two sons, who, accompanied by Quantrill, promptly sought out the abolitionists.

Several stories exist concerning the ensuing confrontation. John Dean later said that Ball, when confronted by his enemies, valiantly raised himself to his feet and shook "his revolver at Quantrill, dar[ing] him to come out in fair sight and range." When Andrew Walker subsequently shot Ball in the head with his buffalo rifle, according to Dean's story, Quantrill ran up to the remaining abolitionist, and, "putting his revolver into the mouth of Lipsey, who lay helpless, fired and killed him." Historian Albert Castel repeats a somewhat similar version: "Quantrill ran up to the helpless Lipsey and shot him through the head with a pistol. Now there would be no embarrassing revelations on his part!" The whole problem is that Dean, known to be an unreliable witness, was not present and could not have known what transpired.

Andrew Walker, Morgan Walker, and Andrew's brother *were* at the killing, as was Quantrill, all probably the only firsthand witnesses to the event. In a letter to historian William Elsey Connelley dated February 3, 1883, Andrew Walker wrote, "Two days later a Negro man saw them [Lipsey and Ball] in the woods, and told his master who told my father. My father, brother, Quantrill and myself went out where they were. They drew their pistols and my father and myself fired on them killing them both. Quantrill did not kill either of them. . . . They had stolen a horse the night before and had it tied in the brush near by. They were to leave that night." Multiple, differing accounts about the same event are common in history; nonetheless, firsthand accounts, though sometimes not as melodramatic as others, are hard to confute by hearsay. In this case, Walker's story is clearly not conducive to the demonization of Quantrill, nor, more importantly, was there any reason for him to lie.[21]

The abolitionists' raid on Walker's place created a great stir in the neighborhood, and the next day, dozens of concerned local farmers rode to the Walkers to view Southwick's remains. The locals were aghast at the audacity of the Jayhawkers and worried about the security of their own slaves, herds, and property. There was a general belief that something must be done to protect them. The locals were puzzled also by Quantrill's part in the affair and queried him sharply. That is when he concocted the story that he and his brother had been attacked on the plains by thirty of Montgomery's Jayhawkers, robbed of everything, and his brother killed. At the same time, Quantrill told the men, he had been wounded in the chest and leg. The story was long winded and elaborate, told of Quantrill's great suffering, and related that Quantrill had sided with the Walkers in order to kill some of the men who had killed his brother. Quantrill, in addition, said that some time ago he had joined up with the Jayhawkers for the purpose of killing all the men who had killed his brother; thus far he had killed eighteen of the men without their becoming suspicious. The story, although a complete fabrication, seemed credible and was filled with colorful and emotional details that appealed to the listener's sentiments. Missourians believed the story for years, even long after the war.

A sheriff soon arrived and arrested Quantrill and took him to Independence for questioning. Andrew Walker accompanied Quantrill, and when they got to town, he explained Quantrill's part in the raid to the sheriff, who kept Quantrill in a cell until nightfall *for his own safety*. At 8:00 P.M., he was turned loose a free man, and he and Andrew Walker turned in for the night at the local hotel, sleeping in the same room.

The next morning, when the story of the Walker raid became general knowledge, a fiery mob assembled in Independence. On learning that one of the raiders was in their midst and unpunished, they became enraged and sought to lynch Quantrill. When Walker, who was at the stable to retrieve his horse, got wind of the development, he returned quickly and interceded. He explained the situation to the mob and closed by telling them that if they killed Quantrill, it would "be over his [Walker's] dead body." This quieted the mob.

Later that day, Andrew Walker bought Quantrill a new suit of denim, and the following day, Morgan Walker gave him a thoroughbred horse named "Black Bess," as well as a saddle, bridle, and fifty dollars. A local justice of the peace, Squire Lobb, gave Quantrill another ten dollars. When Andrew Walker and Quantrill returned to the Walker farm, the family decided that it was best for Quantrill to leave, but he was invited to return when things cooled down. The Walkers were afraid that if Quantrill stayed, the Jayhawkers would return to revenge themselves on him and perhaps torch Walker's house, steal his property, and kill his family.[22]

Quantrill spent most of the rest of the winter of 1860-61 in the employ of Marcus Gill, a plantation owner who lived near New Santa Fé (Little Santa Fé), on the Kansas-Missouri border. Historian William Elsey

Connelley said that Quantrill "was a great favorite" of the Gills, who owned one thousand acres of land and a large number of slaves. The proximity of Gill's place to Kansas made the plantation owner extremely vulnerable to raids, and Gill's great-great-grandson, Byron C. Shutz, believed that his forebear hired Quantrill because he wanted somebody that "was good with guns and a good rider." In the spring of 1861, Quantrill traveled to Texas with Gill, probably as a guard to protect his slaves and those of a Mr. Lipscomb while in transit. Many western Missourians at this time were moving their slaves South for safekeeping, and Quantrill, during this period, formed further ties with elite Missourians.[23]

In early 1861, during his term of employment with the Gills, some of Quantrill's time was spent in Kansas. He made several trips to Paola to visit his old friend Col. Henry Torrey, who, historian Connelly said, "fêted" him and treated him as an "honored guest." He was "caressed by the family." His old friend W. L. Potter also made much of Quantrill, the "hero." Also during this time, Quantrill made three dangerous trips to his old haunts near Stanton, specifically to the home of his friends Adolphus Bennings and Albert Bennings and their father John. He also visited a female friend.

His appearances did not go unnoticed. William Strong, an enemy of Quantrill, heard of his presence in the area and notified Capt. Ely Snyder, the Osawatomie Jayhawker. Snyder directed both Strong and Peter Hauser, the son of Samuel Hauser, the justice of the peace at Stanton, to watch for Quantrill and to report to Snyder when Quantrill next visited. Meanwhile, Snyder looked for some pretext to murder him.

When Quantrill visited Stanton again, both Strong and Hauser rode to Osawatomie, some twelve miles away, to inform Ely Snyder. Upon receiving word of Quantrill's presence, Snyder formed two parties of "desperate men" and headed for Stanton to catch him. Snyder said later that he wanted to give Quantrill "justice with a inch roap [sic]." Snyder hoped to have the senior Hauser put out a warrant for Quantrill's arrest for burglary, kidnapping, and horse stealing. Once the warrant was issued, Snyder's men would volunteer to be Hauser's posse. If Quantrill resisted arrest or attempted to escape, which Snyder expected, the Jayhawkers would have had an excuse to kill him.

But, as it turned out, Justice of the Peace Hauser refused to sign a warrant, and Snyder enlisted the local constable, E. B. Jurd, to sign it. Jurd, accompanied by Snyder and his posse, rode to the home of the Bennings, where Quantrill was staying. Three Osawatomie men had already reached the house: Elias Snyder (no relation to Captain Snyder), John S. Jones, and W. M. Martin. They had encircled Bennings' house to prevent Quantrill's escape.

At daylight, the men attempted to gain entrance to Bennings' house, but Quantrill warned them away, telling them that he intended to fight to the death rather than be captured. He was certain that if Snyder's men apprehended him, they would kill him. After a parley with Jurd, the constable, Quantrill was disarmed and promised protection. Jurd intended to take Quantrill to his office at Stanton, where he believed Quantrill would be safe. As he left the house, Jurd held Quantrill's revolvers aloft to show that he was disarmed. Bennings, however, secretly had handed Quantrill another revolver, which was hidden from view. Adolphus Bennings, recognizing Quantrill's peril, ran to the stable and rode to Paola for help.[24]

Once Jurd and the posse reached the constable's office in Stanton, which was upstairs in T. R. Wilkerson's store, Quantrill demanded his revolvers, saying that he feared being "shot down like a dog" by Snyder and his men. Jurd, before taking Quantrill into his office, deputized a number of the local residents to help protect his prisoner. The Reverend Robert Shearer, one of the men deputized by Jurd, said that he was outside the constable's office when he was made a deputy and that five of Snyder's men immediately approached him with Sharps rifles. Shearer threatened to shoot them if they raised their weapons. One of Snyder's men pointed his gun at Quantrill, and Shearer said that he "knocked [the] gun up and drew my revolver and said whats up?" Quantrill was rushed into the constable's office and told to ascend a ladder and pass through a hole in the ceiling into the upstairs. Shearer followed him and yelled down at the men below that "the first man that stuck his head above the trap door I would kill."

When Adolphus Bennings got to Paola, he went to the house of W. L. Potter, who quickly raised a force of some fourteen men, hearing, he said, that that was the size of Snyder's band. George White, one of the members of the group, said, "I went to the livery stable & got a Team & three seated Hack[.] I called on Lawyer W. W. White, Lawyer Robert White, Lawyer Massey, Dr. W. D. Hoover, Tom Kelley, Goodwin Taylor merchant, Lon Light, and several others. . . . We went there in a sweeping trot in Hacks, Buggies & on Horseback." Historian Connelley said that Potter's posse "descended upon Stanton with that brazen assurance, loud profanity, and vulgar swagger then common to the border-ruffians in their attitude and intercourse with the Free-State Settlers." Obviously, these men, based on their professions, were prominent elites of Paola and not border ruffians as Connelley defined the term, i.e., "white trash."

When the men had dismounted, Potter walked up to Quantrill and the constable, extended his hand to Quantrill, and said cheerily, "How do you do Bill? What are you driving at now? Stealing horses?" Quantrill replied, "Well they charge me with it," to which Potter answered, "Oh certainly they are all honest men that prefer the charge against you I suppose. They know nothing about stealing Horses & Niggers, robing [sic] & Burning

Houses, & murdering citizens, from one end of the Land to the other." A three-seated hack was waiting at the door, and Potter handed Quantrill a revolver and led him to the hack. Potter told Quantrill that "if they [the Jayhawkers] fired one shot, that I would shoot Snyder in the face & keep shooting, as long as there was one left, & for him to do the same." With a double-barreled shotgun in one hand and a revolver in the other, Potter ordered the crowd to disperse. As Snyder's Jayhawkers watched dejectedly, the Paola men rode out of town.

Once Potter and his men arrived in Osawatomie, the lawyers present submitted a writ of habeas corpus. The local Republican probate judge, Thomas Roberts, Quantrill's landlord when he was a schoolteacher, released him. After he had secured a quick lunch of "cake, bread and butter and sandwiches," Quantrill left town on his black horse, only minutes before the arrival of a posse from Lawrence with a warrant for his arrest. Leading the posse was Capt. Ely Snyder and Maj. H. H. Williams, the sheriff of Lykins County (now Miami County). Williams was the same person who, with his cohorts in May or June 1861, broke down the door and robbed a store in West Point, Missouri, an act that began the Kansans' wartime incursions into Missouri. Later, on December 12, 1861, Snyder would attack and burn Papinsville and Butler, Missouri. Sometimes, in Border War history, it is difficult to identify the "upright" and the "degenerate," as they frequently prove to be the same individuals in different accounts.[25]

After evading the posse led by Snyder and Williams, Quantrill returned to the plantation of Marcus Gill. He conducted Gill's slaves to Texas in spring 1861 (as previously mentioned), then Quantrill journeyed north as far as Arkansas, where he lived for awhile with Joel Mayes, the head chief of the Cherokee Nation. When the Cherokees, at the outbreak of the Civil War, joined forces with the Confederates at the Battle of Wilson's Creek, Quantrill fought with an Indian company as a cavalry private. Later, when Sterling Price advanced north on Lexington, Quantrill participated in the action at Drywood Creek. John Newman Edwards, a major and adjutant in Gen. Jo Shelby's cavalry, reported that Quantrill performed heroically at Lexington although no special mention is made of him in Price's record of the battle. After Lexington, Quantrill drifted back to visit his old friends in Jackson County.

Around October 1, 1861, Quantrill reported to Andrew Walker that marauders were raiding the Stone neighborhood, some four miles north of Blue Springs and not far from Walker's place. In a letter to Connelley on February 3, 1883, Walker said, "Some Kansas men came into the neighborhood robbing. I got 11 men together, Quantrill with me and we started on the hunt of them. Coming on to them we fired into them. It was near old Mr. Thompson's house." The Jayhawkers, who were wearing

Union uniforms, had attacked the De Witt and Strawder Stone farms. Mrs. Stone, according to Walker,

> got angry with them and talked pretty sharp to them and one of them struck her on the head with his pistol. We overtook them just as they were coming out of Mr. Thompson's house [the bluecoat's third raiding destination], a quarter of a mile from Mr. Stone's house. They had just mounted their horses. We put spurs to our horses when we saw them, and as we neared them, fired, killing the man who struck Mrs. Stone with his pistol. Two others were wounded, both of whom, it was reported died at Independence subsequently. We then dispersed.

The bluecoats scurried into Independence to report on the guerrillas. This was the first operation by what would become Quantrill's guerrillas.

The next day, the local constable, Squire Hightower, took Strawder Stone and Billy Thompson, the victims of the marauders, to Independence and charged them with murder. Quantrill went to Hightower, told him that neither Stone nor Thompson had anything to do with the killings and informed him that he and others were responsible for the deaths. Stone and Thompson were exonerated. This selfless act made Quantrill a hero in the area. Walker said, "He [Quantrill] was at that time just like the rest of us. He was content to be one of the privates. I was, in fact, during the fight at Stone's farm, the leader." Walker said shortly thereafter, however, that Quantrill became "the leading spirit among the guerrillas," and from this point on, Federal officials sought Quantrill's arrest.

Around Christmas 1861, a renegade Southern soldier, George Searcy, began stealing horses and mules from the local farmers, some of them "Union men." Quantrill's men captured Searcy, according to Walker, "and took him to a point on the Little Blue River and hanged him," with Walker's help. The horses, mules, and goods stolen by Searcy were returned to their owners. By this time, Quantrill had enrolled a number of guerrillas: Perry Hoy, Joe Vaughn, James and John Little, George Todd, Joseph Gilchrist, Harrison Trace, and William Haller. Within days, William H. Gregg and John W. Koger also joined up. This was the nucleus of what would become a band of over three hundred men. Quantrill's earlier experience as a Jayhawker, soldier, and rugged miner had served him well.

Shortly thereafter, a Union collaborator, Riley Alley, who owned a farm east of Blue Springs, invited a number of the guerrillas to a ball held at his home. Quantrill suspicioned a trap and warned his guerrillas. When the festivities were approaching their peak, a Federal cavalry unit surrounded the house, broke in the front door, and declared all the partygoers under arrest. The young men were sequestered upstairs, the ladies downstairs. After it was discovered that few guerrillas were present, the young people were held in the house more than twenty-four hours in hopes that more guerrillas would arrive. Finally, the captured young men, including Riley Alley (as a cover), were hauled in wagons to Independence. Alley left the vicinity later, fearing retribution. Sol Basham, one of the few guerrillas present, was sentenced to the Rock Island Penitentiary for the remainder of the war.

On January 22, 1862, Quantrill's men skirmished with Union troops outside the home of Moab McAlexander of Sni-a-Bar Township. The Sni-a-Bar neighborhood was to become a hotbed of guerrilla activity throughout the war. In this instance, three ordinary, unarmed civilians, Crocket Ralston, John Frisbee, and John Barnhill, were in McAlexander's home consorting with the guerrillas when the house was surrounded by Union troops. The guerrillas, seeking to resist the Federals but also wishing to protect the civilians, sent the noncombatants out of the house. Ralston and Frisbee departed and were promptly captured and shot. The guerrillas Gregg and Haller and the innocent Barnhill raced from the house amid gunfire, somehow escaping. One guerrilla was shot.[26]

Quantrill and his men continued to be Union targets. During an expedition to the Blue Springs area, Capt. William S. Oliver sought to make quick work of Quantrill's guerrillas. In a message to his commander, Brig. Gen. John Pope, on February 3, 1862, Oliver reported that the "infamous scoundrel" Quantrill and "his gang of robbers" had been robbing mails, stealing the coaches and horses, and committing "other similar outrages." Oliver claimed to have killed nine of Quantrill's men and wounded one of some "18 or 20" guerrillas encountered. This would have been a most serious setback for Quantrill, losing 50 percent of his men to casualties, that is, *if* the report were actually true. Oliver claimed he lost one man killed and one wounded but was able to recapture "6 or 7 wagon loads of pork and a quantity of tobacco" recently captured by Quantrill from the Federals as well as a "valuable stagecoach with two of their horses." Oliver reported, however, that Quantrill continued to drive out Union supporters in the Blue Springs area: "I hear of him to-night 15 miles from here, with new recruits, committing outrages on Union men, a large body of whom have come in to-night, driven out by him. Families of Union men are coming in the city [Independence] to-night asking of me escorts to bring in their goods and chattels, which I duly furnished." The guerrillas did not appear particularly affected by Oliver's alleged decimation of their ranks.[27]

While Quantrill had not been operating for a considerable length of time, he was beginning to attract notice of more prominent figures. Col. Robert H. Graham, commander of the Eighth Kansas Infantry, wrote

Gen. Henry Halleck, who was instrumental in creating the extermination policy against the Missouri guerrillas. The policy brutalized Missouri guerrillas, and many of them became violent as a natural response. *State Historical Society of Missouri, Columbia*

Maj. Gen. Henry Halleck, commander of the Department of the Mississippi, on March 19 of a raid by Quantrill on March 7 in Johnson County, Kansas, near Aubry. Graham said that Quantrill's men had "murdered several citizens at Aubry, in said county, and carried away quite an amount of property." Graham sent Capt. John Greelish, of Company E, Eighth Kansas Volunteer Regiment, to intercept the guerrillas. A first lieutenant Rose of that command skirmished with "about 30 men" of Quantrill's "company" and claimed his men killed two partisans and wounded several others. Nonetheless, Quantrill, in his "retreat," "drove a family from their home and burned their house." Graham claimed he lost no men. But he also asked for reinforcements of "several companies of cavalry."[28]

During the raid on Aubry, 2d Lt. Reuben A. Randlett, who was heading home on sick leave, had been staying at the local tavern for the night. He slept in the same room as Abraham Ellis, Quantrill's old superintendent of schools when he was at Stanton. On the morning of the seventh, the innkeeper awakened the men at dawn, warning them that guerrillas were storming the town. Ellis heard the cry, "Cutthroats are coming!" He said, "Men were screaming & swearing like Devils." The windowpane was frosted, so Ellis looked through a clear part of the pane near its margin. At that moment, Quantrill saw him and fired his revolver. The bullet crashed through the window frame and struck Ellis in the middle of his forehead, imbedding itself. He fell to the floor, blood streaming from the wound.

Randlett, seeing they were impossibly outnumbered, went downstairs and turned his revolver over to the first guerrilla who entered the tavern. Quantrill soon arrived. When Ellis came downstairs, blood running down his face, he staggered into Quantrill and the guerrilla chief said, "Why, Ellis, is that you?" Ellis said that Quantrill "washed my face & said he did it himself & was dam-d sorry for it." Ellis was released, but Randlett, who told the guerrillas his name was R. A. Brown, was made a hostage for the next three weeks to be offered as an exchange for a captured guerrilla. While Randlett was a captive, the guerrillas received word that the Red Legs were burning homes in Cass County. Randlett rode along with the guerrillas and watched from a hilltop with his assigned guard as the guerrillas skirmished with the marauders at a point near the state line east of Paola. Several Red Legs were wounded. Later, when an exchange of prisoners failed, Randlett, whom the guerrillas generally liked, was freed by Quantrill.[29]

On March 19, 1862, Gen. Henry Halleck, now general in chief of the Union army, issued an order outlawing guerrillas and requiring their extermination on capture. This order established an entirely different dimension to the conflict in Missouri. If young Missourians wished to participate in the Civil War now, they must do so in regular units or risk being hung or shot on capture. Upon hearing of Halleck's move, Quantrill gathered his guerrillas together and explained to them the new situation. Should they continue as guerrillas, he warned, they would no longer be in any way protected by ordinary civil and military laws. He asked if any of the men wished to drop out of the organization. Some twenty did so. Before long, however, they were back in the ranks. They discovered that it was even more dangerous for young men to remain at home than in the bush. Under the new order, farmers who remained at home, if it was believed that they had "harbored and fed such miscreants as guerrillas," would be "put under heavy bonds and security for their future good conduct or confined until they give such bonds, etc." The new order also put a serious onus on the female members of guerrilla families, who were now subject to arrest and imprisonment. After Quantrill explained to the guerrillas the new extermination order, he turned to Randlett and said, "What do you think of that, lieutenant?" Randlett answered, "I could not blame you for shooting me now." Quantrill replied, "Not a hair of your head will be harmed."

For the guerrillas, the new order meant that to surrender was tantamount to inviting execution. From their perspective, if their lives were to be forfeit, then why should the lives of their hated enemies be inviolable? In the bush, beyond all restraints, anything was possible, they knew. If they were to be shot down like dogs, they thought it high time to strike back in kind.[30] Indeed, such "extermination" orders have seldom produced the desired effect and have historically served only to create more guerrillas.

On March 22, 1862, Quantrill's band, thirty to forty in number, moved west from Independence along the road to Westport. When they arrived at the Blue River Bridge, they disarmed an unnamed " 'Dutch' [German] Federal sergeant" who acted as a bridge guard and halted a civilian called "Allison" and his son. Quantrill, in line with the new Federal extermination policy, believed that from now on it was to be tit for tat. He tried and convicted the soldier on the spot. Then he allegedly shot both the soldier and the civilian and had their bodies thrown on the bridge and the structure set afire.

Afterward, the guerrillas stopped at the farm of the prominent Alexander Majors to eat. Having eaten, they pushed south, arriving at the home of David Tate, a secessionist, by nightfall. Quantrill and twenty-seven men lodged at Tate's for the night, making their beds on the floor. The rest of the guerrillas scattered to other homes in the area. Meanwhile, Col. Robert B. Mitchell's Second Kansas Cavalry was hot on their trail. When Mitchell arrived at New Santa Fé at 10:00 P.M., he sent Maj. James A. Pomeroy with cavalry companies D and E to the Tate house, three miles away, to arrest its owner. Tate was known to be a guerrilla collaborator. The size of the detachment sent to arrest Tate suggests that Mitchell was suspicious that the guerrillas were at Tate's house or that he knew they were there. When Pomeroy approached Tate's home, Quantrill's pickets either failed to give the alarm or the cavalry advanced so rapidly that the guards were overrun before they had a chance to warn their friends, and the cavalry troop quickly surrounded Tate's house.

Major Pomeroy boldly walked up to Tate's front door, banged on it, and demanded the surrender of the occupants. Shots were fired through the door, some say by Quantrill, but the shots harmed no one, according to the official army report. However, they may have struck Pomeroy. The guerrillas now blockaded the door with furniture and began shooting out of the windows of the house. The Union soldiers returned their fire in thunderous volleys. When Tate's wife and children, who were inside the house, screamed, the firing ceased, and the noncombatants were allowed to leave the house. At this time, two guerrillas crawled out a window and surrendered. Then, the firing continued in an explosive roar. By this time, Capt. Amaziah Moore of Company D had assumed command, replacing Pomeroy, who had been wounded some time after knocking on Tate's front door. Meanwhile, Moore sent one of his men to New Santa Fé for reinforcements. Moore now ordered some of his soldiers to set Tate's house afire, and soon flames and smoke billowed from the cabin.

By this time, Quantrill had discovered that part of the rear of the log cabin was composed of only weatherboarding, and he ordered his men to knock a hole in the wall. When this was accomplished, he lined up his men in single file and gave them directions. They dashed through the hole into the darkness, firing their revolvers in every direction. Within moments, most of the men had disappeared into the woods behind the house and found safety. Two men, the Rollen brothers, however, were killed as they fled the house. Another guerrilla, Perry Hoy, was struck on the head and captured. The army's official report stated that another six guerrillas were captured in the operation. Mitchell said in his official report, moreover, that five dead guerrillas were "distinctly seen in the flames" inside the house. Later, Tate's property and livestock were hauled away by a Lieutenant Aduddell and fifteen men. The guerrillas had lost twenty-five horses and twenty sets of equipment.

Four months later, Perry Hoy, in a largely trumped-up trial by a military commission (see note), was sentenced to die before a firing squad. The verdict violated Army General Orders No. 71, which specified that the president must sign all execution orders. Hoy was convicted of being an accessory in the killings at the bridge and of violating "the laws and usages of war." The *St. Louis Tri-Weekly Missouri Republican* of August 1, 1862, described Hoy's execution:

The prisoner [Hoy] was marched on to the grounds by the soldiers; he wore a black suit and a felt hat; his arms were pinioned. Hoy was brought to the place where he was to be shot, made to kneel and his hat removed. A detachment of soldiers stood about twenty yards distant, and the moment the guard left, the command to fire was given—twelve volumes of fire leap[t] from the rifles, and Hoy [was] dead. He fell over upon his face and died without a struggle. One ball went through his head and two through his body. . . . [He] was placed in a coffin and borne to the military burial ground. The soldiers marched off, the band playing a lively air.[31]

Hoy received better treatment than the guerrillas would in the future. They were generally left where they fell.

Chapter 9
Trial by Fire: The Tempering of the Guerrillas

By March 31, 1862, Quantrill and his guerrillas were again in the Blue Springs area, at Pink Hill, nineteen miles east of Independence, on the farm of Samuel C. Clark. Capt. Albert P. Peabody, commanding a squadron of the First Missouri Cavalry, had been dispatched to locate and destroy them. He searched for them in the area but was unsure of their exact whereabouts, so Peabody divided his force, sending Lieutenant White and Company C in one direction with thirty-five men, while he took thirty troopers and Second Lieutenant Gurnee of Company D with him. When Peabody's men passed a two-story log house perched on a hill near Pink Hill they received heavy fire. His men fired back, injuring guerrilla Ed Koger, who had just ridden up to the house and was hitching his horse. Guerrilla William Gregg had been cutting one of his comrade's hair and fled for cover. Assigning some of his men as horse holders, Peabody dismounted and advanced toward the house, ordering his men to fire at the open windows and doors.

Quantrill and eight guerrillas manned the first floor of the cabin; George Todd and other partisans defended the upper story. Gregg had taken up a position in the slave cabins nearby. Peabody's men continued firing at the house for over an hour and a half, avoiding a foolhardy direct assault on the guerrillas' protected position while they prudently waited for reinforcements.

Farmers living in the area, learning of the attack, rallied in support of the guerrillas and fired their muskets at the soldiers from behind trees and bushes and from the hilltops. According to Maj. Charles Banzhaf's official report of the action, the farmers wielded "mostly Sharps rifles," a highly dubious claim, since even the guerrillas lacked such fine weapons. The farmers, more likely, were armed with a motley collection of shotguns and outdated rifles.

In the midst of the fighting, Peabody had sent a messenger to Lieutenant White for help, but before White arrived with reinforcements, the defenders had swelled incredibly from "sixty" to "150 men," according to Banzhaf. Historian William Connelley reported a more likely number in the fight: about thirty guerrillas and no more than thirty other supporters. The guerrillas, meanwhile, had knocked out the chinking between the logs of the cabin and were using the holes for gun ports to deliver heavy fire. When White finally arrived, as recorded in the official U.S. Army report of

William H. Gregg, one of Quantrill's lieutenants. Gregg became a deputy sheriff of Jackson County after the war. *Kansas State Historical Society, Topeka*

the battle, Peabody charged the log house and his men killed "6 of the enemy . . . instantly" and wounded "many," driving the guerrillas from their protected position into a "timbered, rough, and hilly country, where pursuit was not an easy task." William Gregg said the guerrillas lost no one. But Peabody captured some twenty horses and equipment (saddles and bridles) left behind by the guerrillas—the second such loss for them in nine days. Peabody had suffered three wounded soldiers but none killed.[1]

Another fifty men under Captain Murphy, "with 2 lieutenants, 3 sergeants, 5 corporals, and 41 privates," had been called to Pink Hill to support Peabody. When they arrived in the area of the Little Sni River, they found the guerrillas in a well-entrenched position "on a high bluff . . . [in] breastworks of rocks." The guerrillas had retreated there after the fight with Peabody; the guerrillas claimed later that their attack on Murphy was an ambush. As was their practice, after exchanging fire with Murphy's men, the guerrillas melted into the brush. Murphy, who had been firing from an exposed position, claimed only two casualties and said that he killed five guerrillas, wounded six, and captured one. Because the guerrillas were at some distance and carried away any killed or wounded, the Union officer reporting the action, Capt. John B. Kaiser, had no way of knowing their exact number of casualties, and those reported are highly doubtful. Kaiser claimed Union casualties of one dead and one wounded. That a force fighting from an open, exposed position against an enemy securely ensconced behind breastworks should suffer fewer casualties than its opponent flies in the face of all combat experience in the Civil War. When he filed the official report of the action, Kaiser said, "The Union people here are suffering greatly from the hands of these ruffians. They are daily driven from their homes and many of them are caught and either hung or shot. No Union man is safe 1 mile from camp unless a force is with him."[2] The same thing, of course, could be said for the safety of Southern families when jayhawkers or the Union militia were around.

By this time, the guerrillas had adopted their distinctive uniforms, usually a flat-crowned, wide-brimmed hat with curving brim, or a hat with the brim pinned up on one side by a star or ornament. The hat was usually replete with a black plume. Atop their full shirts, they wore a "guerrilla shirt," a pullover garment, sometimes with a scooped-out neck and four capacious pockets, where the guerrillas kept their extra, loaded revolver cylinders and ball ammunition. Their sweethearts and mothers often embroidered their "shirts" with elaborate, colorful designs. Stuffed into their belts and attached to their saddles were from three to six multishot revolvers, which gave the guerrillas overwhelming firepower at close range but rendered them vulnerable to long-range rifle fire.[3]

After tracking Quantrill and his guerrillas for five days, the scouts of Lt. Col. Egbert B. Brown located them along the Santa Fé Trail, twelve miles east of Independence. At daylight on April 14, a cavalry detachment of thirty men led by Lt. G. W. Nash, First Missouri Cavalry, had positioned themselves to attack Quantrill at dawn. Brown, in his official report of the action said, "The night was dark, and a heavy rainstorm raged until 4 o'clock in the morning." The storm concealed Nash's advance. At dawn, the Union patrol reached a log house two miles off the road, where the guerrillas had found cover during the storm and were asleep. For the third time in succession, the guerrillas negligently had assigned no pickets, this time because they believed no one would be afoot in the driving rain. They were dead wrong. At dawn, Nash charged the guerrillas, surprising them completely, firing at them as they were "flying to the brush, about 20 rods from the brush, killing 4, wounding 4, and capturing 5 prisoners, all the horses, accouterments, most of their arms and clothing [leaving them] barefooted and coatless." These were grievously amateurish and deadly mistakes. The guerrillas were either going to have to learn to fight more intelligently or they soon would be destroyed.[4] Fortunately for them, they proved to be quick learners.

The guerrillas heretofore had maintained an adequate, surreptitious source of gunpowder, pistol caps, and lead, sending their sisters and others not attracting suspicion into Kansas City and Independence to purchase them. But by May 1862 the Federals caught on to the practice and carefully monitored and suppressed distribution of munitions. For that reason, Quantrill and George Todd, now acting as the guerrilla chief's right-hand man, set out on two plug horses for Hannibal, Missouri. Within a few days, they had purchased fifty thousand pistol caps, sold their horses, and returned to St. Joseph by railroad. Hiring a hack at "St. Jo," the two men traveled to Kansas City and made their way safely through the Federal guards with their contraband.

By June 11, the guerrillas had reformed and regained their confidence, attacking a twenty-four-man mail escort traveling from Independence to Pleasant Hill. The escort, commanded by Capt. J. F. Cochran, was assaulted only ten miles from Independence. Cochran had assigned "six men riding by file" as an advance guard. The guerrillas attacked the guard, killing two men and dangerously wounding three. Cochran, who had been "50 yards in the rear with 18 men," pursued the guerrillas, "but the villains made good their escape," he said, apparently without casualties. When the mail finally arrived at Pleasant Hill, the carrier refused to make the return trip to Independence. Lt. Col. James T. Buel, the army commander at Independence, refused to send more of his men with the mail, unwilling to have more of them murdered. Henceforth, he said, secessionists would carry the mail, and he "would hold them accountable for its safe transmittal." Although this was a clear violation of the practices of war, it was probably effective; later, the Rules of War would ban such practices. Four days later, on June 15, Lieutenant Colonel Buel reported that Captain Spellman's command had encountered Quantrill and "killed two and wounded three of the robbers."[5]

The guerrillas were now attacking traditional guerrilla targets, the enemy's lines of communication: trains, wagon trains, mail wagons, telegraph lines, and riverboats. By doing so, the guerrillas were obtaining weapons, ammunition, supplies, and food as well as depriving their enemies of the same. They also were severing communications between the enemy army's headquarters and its isolated units around western Missouri. Eventually, the army would be forced to man cavalry stations at twelve-mile intervals in every direction throughout western Missouri in an attempt to control the situation. The army hoped that, by employing continuous cavalry patrols in search-and-destroy operations, the number of guerrillas in the area would be reduced. At the same time, however, they were using up significant manpower, which would now be unavailable to fight main force Confederate units in the South. Such was the South's intention in using the guerrillas. For every fielded guerrilla, at least ten Union soldiers were required, a pretty standard measure, applied as recently as the Vietnam War in the twentieth century.

On June 23, Capt. James Breckinridge, commanding thirty men of Company B, Seventh Missouri Volunteer Cavalry, advanced on the J. R. Lowe farm near Raytown. As he moved through the area, he noticed "suspicious-looking persons." Leaving his horses and their guards at the Lowe farm, Breckinridge and his men set out through the brush. He found a recently abandoned camp, with bridles, blankets, and a lariat littering the area. Breckinridge deployed his men as skirmishers and pushed forward through the dense, almost impenetrable brush, leading the way with a four-man advance guard. After Breckinridge and his men had traveled three-quarters of a mile, they saw a picket and fired at him. The young guerrilla dropped his coat and ran for cover. Instantly, guerrilla pistols roared, spitting fire at Breckinridge and the Union front from the bushes and brush. Wounded in the leg, Breckinridge commanded his men to retreat to their hitched horses. When he got back to the horses, Breckinridge discovered that one of his men was missing, killed by the guerrillas.[6]

On the same day, at Pink Hill near Blue Springs, Maj. Eliphalet Bredett, Seventh Missouri Cavalry, led 108 men of Companies K and F on an excursion to the Sibley and Pink Hill area. As he passed through Wellington, Missouri, he sent his men around the town, where they collected 54 prisoners, believing, he said, that they had been "aiding and abetting the rebellion." Then, he went to Napoleon, Missouri, and rounded up another 25 prisoners, 3 of them recently returned from Southern battlefields. Bredett then divided his unit into three columns and pushed toward Sibley. A Lieutenant Wrightman, in command of one of the columns, captured 7 more prisoners, one of which had a pistol with the name of "a notorious bushwhacker and guerrilla" inscribed on it, sufficient reason, in Wrightman's view, to send him to Independence for trial. Bredett said, "Several others of this lot of prisoners were strongly suspected of connection with the bushwhackers." Such arrests, like kidnapping really, became commonplace in Missouri. Since Lincoln had suspended habeas corpus for his own illegal seizure of political opponents, he did not censure his lower-ranking field commanders for following suit.

Reinforced by an additional eighty men, in the manner of a wolf hunt, Bredett now scoured the country with a long line of skirmishers, during which he drove a couple of unknown men, presumed to be guerrillas, before him. But, as often happens in such drives, the men escaped through holes in the line. What was done with Bredett's prisoners is not revealed in his report. If not imprisoned or murdered out of hand, all would have made excellent candidates to become guerrillas, provided they were not already.[7] Such "sweeps" were often the guerrillas' best recruitment tools and pushed many fence-sitters into their camp.

The indiscriminate harassment and killing of individuals presumed to be guerrillas steadily continued. On July 6-9, First Lieutenant White, Company C, and Second Lieutenant Gurnee, Company D, First Battalion, First Missouri Cavalry, set an ambush for the guerrillas, hoping "to beat the bushwhackers, if possible, at their own game." White reported bagging three of them and "capturing four horses and one mule."[8] Whether these men were actually guerrillas or simply unfortunate farmers is impossible to determine.

In mid-June, Upton Hays returned to Jackson County in western Missouri to recruit a regiment for the Confederate army. He discovered that Quantrill had so stirred up Jackson County that it was impossible to perform his recruiting mission. The area was crawling with cavalry patrols. To improve the situation, Hays suggested that Quantrill proceed southeast into the northern part of Henry County to decoy the Federals while Hays recruited his regiment. Quantrill quickly repaired south and as promptly attracted the attention of Federal troops. Had Quantrill been merely the common criminal and freebooter many historians have claimed, he hardly would have cooperated so freely with regular Confederate forces, especially when it increased his personal peril.

At 8:00 P.M. on July 8, Maj. James O. Gower, commander of the First Iowa Cavalry, sent Companies A, G, and H—under the command of Lieutenants R. M. Reynolds, Bishop, Foster, and Whisenand—to search for Quantrill's guerrillas. The soldiers, ninety-four in number, were to search for the rebels at a reported camp along Sugar Creek, near Wadesburg in Cass County. Gower planned for his unit to move against the guerrillas at night then attack them at dawn, a standard military practice.

At 6:00 A.M. the next morning, on July 9, Lieutenant Bishop's Company

A, performing as the advance guard, rammed into Quantrill's guerrilla camp and was quickly repulsed. The main column, led by Lieutenant Reynolds and his men, pushed forward to take up the fight, advancing on the guerrillas aggressively. The guerrillas threw Reynolds back also, during which he lost one man killed and three wounded.

When the Union detachment returned to Clinton, Major Gower sent for reinforcements from Butler and Warrensburg, requesting that all available units be sent to the Lotspeich Farm in Cass County. Meanwhile, Gower, at 5:00 A.M. on July 10, marched to the farm with 75 enlisted men and 4 officers of Companies A and G. Gower and his men reached the farm at 11:00 A.M., where they were joined by 65 men from Butler commanded by Capt. William H. Aukeny. Another 65 men from Company G were present from Harrisonville, commanded by Capt. W. A. Martin, and 60 men under the command of Capt. Martin Kehoe arrived from Warrensburg. Gower now had 265 men in his command, as many men as the guerrillas, he believed.

The troopers now took up the hunt, and at 2:00 P.M., Kehoe, acting as Gower's advance guard, discovered Quantrill's trail at Lincoln Ford on Big Creek. He pursued him, passing along the bottomland at the margins of the creek. Finally, Kehoe overtook Quantrill at 7:00 P.M. and informed Gower of the guerrillas' location. Apparently, Quantrill and his men had stopped to have dinner, so Gower, finding his men exhausted and hungry also, decided to do the same, having traveled some fifty miles that day. Gower directed his men to obtain food and forage at the local farmhouses.

The next morning at 10:00 A.M., Kehoe, impatient to engage Quantrill and irritated at Gower's slowness in rousing the rest of the men, left the camp with his troopers in pursuit of the guerrillas. Capt. Henry J. Stierlin, commander of the First Battalion, First Missouri Cavalry, said in his formal report that Gower had tarried in setting out that morning and that Kehoe, anxious to pursue Quantrill, had told his commander that he was leaving, informed him in which direction he was going, and promised to send a messenger to Gower when he made contact with the guerrillas. Stierlin said, moreover, that Kehoe set a slow pace, hoping that Gower would catch up with him. Gower, however, moved out of camp an hour behind Kehoe and beyond supporting range. In his own report, Gower told an entirely different story, saying that Kehoe "marched without my knowledge in the morning, and in direct disregard of [my] orders." This after-the-fact finger pointing indicates the unfortunate development of this engagement.

Four miles west of Pleasant Hill, after following a "zigzag" path and "passing over the most inaccessible route that could be found," Kehoe ran into Quantrill's pickets on the Searancy farm and fired at them. This time, the guerrillas, after recently being surprised several times, had adjusted to the necessities of battle and assigned guards to warn them of an enemy's approach. When Quantrill heard the firing, he yelled, "Saddle up!" and guerrillas specially assigned to the task led the horses to the rear and hitched and equipped them.

Kehoe approached the guerrillas and, seeing their preparations to burn down the Searancy house, ordered his troopers to attack. William H. Gregg, one of Quantrill's lieutenants, said that when Kehoe approached, the guerrillas were ordered to hide behind a fence and hold their fire until the Union soldiers approached to within forty to sixty feet. The unsuspecting Kehoe was riding directly into an ambush.

In the blazing fire, Kehoe's horse was shot out from under him, and Kehoe himself received a "ball in his right shoulder." His advance guard was blown out of their saddles, six men killed outright and nine wounded, including Lieutenant White—a striking example of how dangerous close fire by guerrillas was. Gower was still an hour behind Kehoe, so Kehoe's troopers, after retiring some distance, attempted to stand off the guerrillas at long range with their muskets until help arrived. During the fight, guerrilla John Hampton was killed and George Mattox and William Tucker wounded. In response, Quantrill led the guerrillas in a charge on the Union troopers, killing two of them. Again, the guerrillas were dangerous up close, vulnerable at a distance.

Gower finally arrived at 11:00 A.M., and his men drove the guerrilla pickets back into Quantrill's main force. The guerrillas retreated for a half-mile, and entered a shallow ravine or "gulch." Capt. W. A. Martin, Company G, drove the guerrillas from this low, dense thicket in a heated hand-to-hand struggle, where "saber-stroke was parried with clubbed gun." Running out of bullets, some of the guerrillas resorted to throwing rocks, it was said.

Three out of four of Gower's commissioned officers were wounded in the fray. Gower reported later that he had lost "11 killed and 21 wounded" in the "three skirmishes." While no bodies of guerrillas were found, Capt. W. A. Martin claimed that the guerrillas had lost some twenty-three to twenty-five killed and wounded and carried their casualties with them. Martin also believed that Quantrill had been shot in the leg (actually, he was shot in the groin), and he reported that the Union troopers captured thirty horses and abundant saddles, blankets, coats, one mailbag, horse equipment, and a spyglass suspected to be Quantrill's.

In retrospect, William Gregg, years later, called the one-and-one-half-hour battle at the Searancy house and nearby Lotspeich farm "a wonderful fight." He claimed the guerrillas lost only two men and a small number of wounded (likely an exaggeration on the low side). Of those wounded, however, was Quantrill, who was forced to nurse his wounded thigh as well as fight off a bout of erysipelas brought on by his wound. W. A. Martin, on his part, thought that the Federals had "finally cut to pieces this lawless band of marauders," an overly optimistic assessment as it turned out. The guerrillas had learned that they could stand up to a Union force if necessary. But Quantrill understood that head-on encounters, due to the relatively small number of guerrillas, were ordinarily to be avoided. At the Lotspeich farm, the Union soldiers had had a tough fight, more than they had bargained for.[9] The guerrillas' learning curve was increasing in each engagement.

Less than two weeks later, Lieutenant Dewolf, Seventh Missouri Volunteer Cavalry, skirmished with a band of guerrillas near Columbus, Missouri, on the Blackwater River. The commander of the subdistrict, Col. Daniel Huston Jr., reported that Dewolf killed four of "the miscreants," wounded eight or ten, and "captured 13 horses, 10 guns, and 6 pistols, besides a quantity of ammunition." Dewolf had one wounded trooper and "1 horse killed and 3 horses slightly wounded." Huston said that the guerrillas were pursued until "darkness compelled our men to give up the pursuit." The official army reports of these sorts of encounters are ordinarily the same: the guerrillas are supposed to have taken a drubbing; the Union men are said to come off almost unscathed. And yet, the guerrillas continued to operate, seemed to gain in strength, and ordinarily became more formidable with each encounter.[10] The conclusion that the Union commanders routinely "cooked the books" regarding these engagements is inescapable, as the truth did not read as well.

In late July, the town marshal of Independence, Jim Knowles, alerted Lt. Col. James T. Buel of a ford crossing the Little Blue that was a common rendezvous site for guerrillas. Knowles piloted Buel to the location, near Blue Cut, and an ambush was set. Soon, guerrilla George Todd and his friends John Little and Ed Koger rode into the stream to water their horses, chatting to one another as they did so. A thunderous volley rang out and smoke filled the air. Little and Koger rolled dead from their horses into the muddy stream. Todd, without thinking, drove his spurs into his mount, scrambled up the opposite bank, and miraculously rode off untouched. Psychologically, however, he had been struck to the quick. Though he had no great reputation for violence up to this point in the war, henceforth, he would fight with an animal ferocity and show little mercy. When Federal actions did not kill or capture a guerrilla, they often resulted in creating a more deadly, determined foe.

Meanwhile, Gen. Thomas Hindman of the Confederate army sent several colonels to western Missouri to recruit men to fulfill Southern manpower needs after the recent Confederate loss at the Battle of Pea Ridge, called by Southerners the Battle of Elkhorn Tavern, and the transfer of the Missouri State Guard east of the Mississippi. The colonels assigned the task were Gideon W. Thompson, Joseph Porter, John T. Poindexter, and John T. Hughes. The irregular soldiers recruited by these men created so much agitation and turmoil that, for a time, it threw the leading Union officers into panicked responses. Porter, for instance, organized a one-thousand-man force in northern Missouri that threatened to unhinge Federal control of that area. After several bloody confrontations with army units in the area, however, his force was virtually destroyed, and he was killed. Quantrill's guerrillas were now the largest and most powerful partisan force in Missouri. They remained potent because they avoided direct collisions with Federal forces unless they outnumbered them.

These sorts of actions unnerved the U.S. command in Missouri; they feared that they were losing the state to the insurgents. In an attempt to regain a semblance of order in Missouri, Brig. Gen. John M. Schofield, on July 22, 1862, published General Orders No. 19, specifying that all able-bodied men in Missouri were to be impressed into Missouri militia units "for the purpose of exterminating the guerrillas that infest our state." This order would force young Missourians to choose sides. Many would choose to fight with Quantrill rather than unite with "Yankees" to exterminate their own people. Others threw in their lot with the Federals. Positively affecting the Union cause, the orders placed a huge number of Missouri men in uniform to stave off the guerrilla challenge. At the same time, it allowed Federal soldiers recruited in the North to be used where they were needed most, in battles against the powerful Confederate army in the southern and eastern theaters, rather than being relegated to Missouri in large numbers to fight guerrillas.

On August 1, 1862, John T. Hughes, now a brigadier general, moved into Jackson County with seventy-five men to recruit a brigade for the Confederate army. After the Confederate defeat at Pea Ridge on March 7-8, many Southern men from Missouri had straggled home. Hughes hoped to reenlist these ex-soldiers and enlist other men of recruitment age. But his eye was set primarily on mustering men in the area north of the Missouri River. Hughes and the Confederates, therefore, needed to seize Independence, Missouri, which would secure an area of safe passage for the men when they were marched south. Hughes set up a recruiting camp on the Charles Cowherd farm near Lee's Summit, where he erected a tall flag-pole that sported the Confederate Stars and Bars. On a clear day, his camp could be seen from the top of the courthouse in Independence. This should have sent a chilling message to Buel, the local army commander. Curiously, Buel seemed unconcerned about the danger. Hughes, on his part, planned to either capture Buel or expel him from Independence by force.

With this goal in mind, Hughes contacted Quantrill and Col. Upton Hays for men and support. Hays rushed to Hughes' aid with three hundred men; Quantrill offered another twenty-five. The guerrillas in western Missouri had been operating in the almost impenetrable woods and thickets that blanketed much of the area. Thus, they could remain hidden from Buel's scouts until they emerged for a raid, during which time, small bands might coalesce into a small, compact army capable of lightning strikes.

At Independence, Buel had under his command no more than five hundred men. But because he was responsible for patrolling the area and for providing escorts for the mail and wagon trains, his command in Independence was composed normally of a smaller force than that, often less than four hundred men. Buel's command in Independence was composed of three companies of the Seventh Missouri Cavalry commanded by Captain Breckinridge; Capt. W. H. Rodewald's company of the Sixth Regiment of Missouri Enrolled Militia; and two companies of Colonel Neugent's (or Newgent's) Second Battalion, Missouri Provisional Militia, commanded by Capts. Jacob Axline and Aaron Thomas.

Buel's headquarters staff was stationed in the Southern Bank building on Lexington Street, at the southwest corner of Independence Square. Rodewald was situated across the street in a two-story building. Acting provost marshal Lt. Charles W. Merrihew (or Merryhew) was positioned at the jail, one block north of the northeast corner of the square, on North Main Street. Buel's vulnerability came from his placement of the bulk of his men a half-mile south of the square in a cavalry encampment. The camp was situated in a low-lying, open cow pasture, with the only defensive structure being a stone fence that lay about one hundred feet west of the encampment and extended for a half-mile. The trouble with this sprawling disposition, of course, was that it made mutual support of the various components of the command quite difficult.

Captain Breckinridge, only a few days earlier, had returned from an eleven-day scout and informed Buel that he had encountered no guerrillas or other troop concentrations. In this report, Buel heard exactly what he had wanted to hear—that there was simply nothing at all to fear. Meanwhile, Morgan Mattox, one of Quantrill's men, entered Independence in the guise of a farmer selling pies and onions to soldiers. He cased the town thoroughly, pinpointing the likely number of troops and their exact deployments. As they frequently did, the guerrillas had already won the intelligence-gathering battle.

At about 10:00 P.M., Sunday, August 10, a Mrs. Wilson, a Union supporter who lived three miles north of Blue Springs, rushed into Buel's headquarters and informed him that word was out that he would be attacked that night by a large force presently camped near Blue Springs as well as by another force from the Sni. In fact, she had seen the Blue Springs men, and there were some one thousand to twelve hundred of them. Rodewald and Thomas were present, and Rodewald listened intently.

When Mrs. Wilson finished her excited speech, Buel answered sarcastically: "We have heard such reports several times lately, and don't you see we are here yet!" He told Mrs. Wilson "she had better go home, or go and stay all night with some friend, and go home in the morning." As Mrs. Wilson left Buel's headquarters, she ran into Captain Rodewald again and retold her story. She then asked him to direct her to the home of General Lucas, a local Union supporter. After she told Lucas her story, he went to Buel and remonstrated that he should place his men on high alert and insisted that Mrs. Wilson was a highly reliable witness. The supremely confident Buel answered him that "he wished that people would stop bringing in such reports—'on that we always know how to take care of ourselves.' " Lucas, his feelings ruffled, turned on his heel and left. Buel told Captains Rodewald and Thomas that they might as well go to their homes in town that night, not stay close as they often did during emergencies. No extra precautions, moreover, were given to the men at the camp. Mrs. Wilson's warning, however, had impressed the more prudent Rodewald, and he alerted his men of a possible attack and ordered them to load their carbines and be ready.

At 3:50 A.M., one of Rodewald's guards screamed, "Halt! Halt! Halt!" and fired at men approaching him. Quantrill and his men, acting as the advance guard, shot all such sentinels on Spring Street (or Spring Branch Road or Big Spring Road), near Burford's gate at the east end of town. Offering full support, Hughes and his men were immediately behind Quantrill. The rebels stopped at the courthouse square and hitched their horses then marched in double-quick time toward the army camp to the south. The square quickly filled with Confederates, and Rodewald's men began firing at them from the second story of their quarters in the bank. One of the Confederates cried out, "For God's sake don't fire, it's your own men." This ruse caused the Union fire to stop temporarily. Rodewald, meanwhile, brought his men out of the building, placed them into line, and ordered them to fire at the Confederates riding through the square toward the military camp. The first volley struck Col. Kit Chiles, killing him in front of the bank. Rodewald held his position at the corner of Lexington and Liberty Streets until 6:00 A.M., repulsing three charges. Buel then ordered Rodewald's men into the headquarters building, where they took up more-protected defenses in the windows on the first and second stories. He also stationed men in the west yard, the side of the building without windows. Quantrill and his guerrillas now manned the building across the street from the headquarters building and rained a steady pistol fire through the windows of the headquarters.

Once the Federal soldiers were ensconced in the headquarters building, Buel now questioned Rodewald on the location of the U.S. flag, and Rodewald told him that it was at the company quarters across the street. Buel wanted to hoist the flag to signal the men at the camp that he was still in the fight. Rodewald's sixteen-year-old bugler, William O. Buhoe, volunteered to retrieve the flag and rushed barefoot through heavy fire and obtained it, returning miraculously unscathed. Because there was no flagstaff on the building, two of Rodewald's men attempted to fasten the Stars and Stripes to the chimney. Both men were killed in the attempt.

Then, a recently captured Confederate lieutenant and one of his men were ordered to place the flag. Despite this violation of the laws of war, they did so successfully as the guerrillas recognized them and carefully held their fire. Quantrill's orders for the raid had been to pin down Buel and to picket the town after the raid was completed. He had accomplished the first chore by boxing in Buel.

Meanwhile, acting provost marshal Merrihew, who was stationed at the jail, fired a volley at the enemy, dashed out of the building with fourteen men, and fled toward Kansas City, arriving there that afternoon. The guerrillas immediately took possession of the building. When George Todd entered the jail, he looked into one of the cells and stepped back in amazement. There was Jim Knowles, the guide who had led Buel to the ambush that had killed Todd's friends, John Little and Ed Koger, at the Little Blue River near Blue Cut. Knowles, ordinarily the town marshal, had been put in jail recently for the intemperate killing of an Irishman, who had been drunk and only "cutting up a little," it was said. Todd emptied his revolvers into the unfortunate Knowles in a paroxysm of anger.

Earlier, two columns of rebels, one led by Colonels Thompson and Chiles and the other by acting brigadier general Hughes, had dismounted at the square. Thompson, now that Chiles was dead, marched with the men down Lexington Avenue; Colonels Hughes and Hays' column went down Walnut Street. The Federal camp was sandwiched between these two streets. When the Confederates moved into position to the north and west of the camp, they fired into the Federal tents at a range of one hundred feet, surprising the Union soldiers and decimating them. No pickets had been placed on duty. Captain Breckinridge, one of the commanders in the camp, thoroughly intimidated, shouted, "Boys, we are completely surrounded, and we had better surrender." His fellow officer Captain Axline had a different view of the matter and shouted, "Boys, get your guns and ammunition and rally behind the rock fence," by far the cleverest Federal decision of the day.

The rebels, once they entered the abandoned camp, began to plunder it and lost much of their focus and momentum. This departure from the planned attack allowed Axline to regroup his men behind the stone wall and prepare to resist. At daylight, Hughes and a number of his men attempted to flank the Union troops and turn the tide of battle, but Hughes was shot in the forehead and killed. The stone wall had turned out to be an excellent extemporaneous field fortification. Some rebels, however, took up enfilading positions south of the wall and made it hot for the Union men.

Confederate colonel Gideon Thompson next assumed command and sensibly attempted to turn the Federal right, but he was wounded in the knee. Colonel Hays then assumed command and wisely avoided frontal attacks. The fight now degenerated into a sharpshooting match, and Hays was wounded in the foot but continued to fight. To eject Axline without flanking him on the right now seemed impossible. Axline, meanwhile, ordered Lieutenant Harrington to report to Colonel Buel's headquarters to receive instructions. Harrington, instead, put discretion ahead of valor and repaired to Kansas City à la Merrihew and was out of the fight.

At 9:15 A.M., Buel ordered his men to cease firing and sent his adjutant, Lieutenant Preble, with a flag of truce (a bed sheet rapped around a ram-rod) to the commanding officer of the Confederates, who by now was the wounded Hays. About 11:00 A.M., Hays returned with Preble, and the two commanders, Hays and Buel, worked out surrender terms. Rodewald's company of ninety-one men subsequently stacked their arms in front of the Union headquarters. Twenty-five minutes later, Axline's men marched onto Independence Square to do likewise. Colonel Thompson, though wounded, now paroled the Federal officers, enlisted men, and prisoners. Twenty-six Federal soldiers had been killed in the initial attack on the camp, and seventy-four Union troops were wounded, eleven of whom later died. In comparison, nine rebels were mortally wounded and the Confederates lost twenty-three men killed, ten of whom were officers. These officers were a high rate of relative casualties and a sign that the Union sharpshoot-ers were maximizing their fire by targeting Confederate commanders.

At five o'clock that afternoon, the Confederates left Independence, set-ting off in the direction of their camp near Lee's Summit and carrying with them some "fifteen wagonloads of arms, ammunition, and quartermaster and commissary stores." On August 16, Quantrill returned to Independence and obtained several wagonloads of gunpowder, which he hid in a cellar on the Morgan Walker farm. Meanwhile, the paroled Union men were ordered to Benton Barracks, where they were mustered out of the service. With some merit, Quantrill and his men claimed credit for the victory. The plan to raise a Southern brigade, however, ended with Hughes' death.[11]

After the Battle of Independence, Quantrill and his men went to the Morgan Walker farm but did not stay long. They returned to the Walker farm on April 12, then moved to the Ingraham farm six miles west of Lone Jack. On April 15, Col. Gideon W. Thompson mustered Quantrill and his partisans into the Confederate service "under the auspices of the Partisan Ranger Act of 1862." Elected as officers were Quantrill, captain; William Haller, first lieutenant; George Todd, second lieutenant; and William H. Gregg, third lieutenant. Quantrill's men were now officially members of the Confederate army, although not recognized by the Federal army.

About this time, a military confrontation developed between the Confederate and Union forces in western Missouri. The Union forces con-sisted of Maj. Emory S. Foster and detachments from five companies of the Seventh Missouri Volunteer Cavalry, which included details from three companies of the Sixth Cavalry, Missouri State Militia; two companies of the Eighth Cavalry, Missouri State Militia; one company of the Seventh Cavalry, Missouri State Militia; three companies of Colonel Neugent's Second Battalion Cavalry, Missouri State Militia; and a section of the Third Indiana Battery (with two six-pounders), under Lt. J. S. Develin. In all, Foster commanded a Union force of 806 men. In addition, Col. FitzHenry Warren, First Iowa Cavalry, was ordered to join Foster at Lone Jack, Missouri, by no later than the morning of August 16. Gen. James Blunt's force from Kansas was also expected to join up with Foster, but his reinforcements were uncertain. Ultimately neither of the latter two forces arrived in time to aid Foster at the Battle of Lone Jack. Warren mistakenly took the wrong road to the town and arrived after the battle. No field officers (rank of major and above) accompanied the force, Major Foster said, because of "jealousy in regard to rank."

The Confederate command was composed of Col. John T. Coffee, with twelve hundred men, and Col. Vard Cockrell, with the regiments of Cols. DeWitt Clinton Hunter, Dick Hancock, John C. Tracy, Gideon W. Thompson, Upton Hays, Bohannon, and S. D. Jackman, besides a smattering of Quantrill's partisans. The Confederates were believed by the Union army to have four thousand men.

On the morning of August 15, Foster set out with his army toward Lone Jack, arriving at that town at 9:00 P.M. after a hard and hot thirty-five-mile march. Foster said he attacked the enemy concentrated near the town and "routed" them. After the fight, Foster arrested Lieutenant Develin for "being drunk" during the skirmish. Then, Foster settled down for the night, with his men in line, hopefully awaiting reinforcements. Though outnumbered, he had a two-gun battery to augment his well-armed infantry and wielded a small but quite formidable force. In addition, Foster had a *bois d'arc* hedge on two sides of his position, which would limit the effectiveness of Confederate charges from those directions and inhibit attempts to flank him. Moreover, a deep stream, always a considerable obstacle for an enemy, was under his control to his rear. His scouts now determined that he was facing up to three thousand rebels.

Once the attack opened, on August 16, the Confederates found themselves weakened by their lack of artillery. The Union battery sprayed the compact Southern lines with deadly canister, or grape shot, and musket fire, upsetting their initial attack. The Confederates now concentrated on disabling the Union's artillery component, their principal aggravation. As a result, they shot the horses hitched to the artillery pieces and made an assault on the men protecting the guns. In this encounter, Foster and 60 men led a desperate Union counterattack to protect the guns and drag them to safety. Only 11 men reached the guns, all of them wounded, but they managed to drag the pieces to the rear. Foster was shot in the charge, and eventually, the weapons were abandoned, one being spiked. Finally, after receiving 25 percent casualties and losing another 44 men missing, the crippled Union force, now led by Capt. Milton H. Brawner, marched back to their base at Lexington, "unmolested" their report said, reaching that town about 7:00 P.M. Brawner believed the Confederates had lost 118 killed. More of Quantrill's guerrillas arrived at the battlefield as reinforcements, but not until the defeated Brawner was on the road to Lexington.[12]

After the battle of Lone Jack and before he went south to join the Southern army, Upton Hays turned over the hated Federal lieutenant Levi Copeland of Neugent's regiment to Quantrill. He had been captured at the Battle of Lone Jack and was wanted by the guerrillas. William Gregg, Quantrill's third lieutenant, said that Copeland had "murdered numerous old men, among them two of the Longacres of Johnson County." Copeland was taken to Quantrill's camp, four miles northeast of Lee's Summit, and put under guard. One night, two men known to Quantrill, Charles Cowherd, the owner of the farm where Quantrill and Hays were staying, and William Howard, brought the guerrilla chief a copy of the *St. Louis Republican*. Gregg waited his turn while Quantrill read the paper, seemingly with great interest. Then, Gregg noted a dramatic change in Quantrill's expression. He dropped the newspaper, pulled a small piece of paper from his pocket, and scribbled a few words on it. He folded the paper and handed it to Gregg. "Give this to [Andy] Blunt," he said. Quantrill told Gregg that the article referred to the execution of guerrilla Perry Hoy. Before he carried the note to Blunt, Gregg opened it and read it. It said, "Take Lieut. Copeland out and shoot him, get two prisoners and shoot them." Now, as should have been expected, the extermination policy was working both ways.[13]

Quantrill's new course of action did not deter the Union troops. On August 17, Lt. Col. John T. Burris, Tenth Kansas Infantry, marched to Independence from Fort Leavenworth with around three hundred and fifty men and occupied the town. Maj. Wyllis C. Ransom, Sixth Kansas Cavalry, accompanied Burris. Ransom reported that when he arrived at the town, he arrested "McCarty, the editor of the *Border Star*. . . a lying dirty sheet. . . . I ordered the type of the office to be destroyed." In his report, Burris described the newspaper as "a treasonable sheet." Burris and Ransom soon left Independence in pursuit of "Colonels Thompson, Hays, and Quantrill." Ransom and Burris pursued the guerrillas toward Harrisonville and, after receiving information from a black spy of the guerrillas' whereabouts, set a trap for them along the way with their artillery. But Ransom, who accompanied Burris, said no artillery rounds were fired at the guerrillas because they were "in a deep ravine utterly impracticable for artillery." Meanwhile, Burris burned down the house and outbuildings of Charles Cowherd. Ransom claimed he also burned "30 stacks of wheat, about 800 bushels of threshed grain, [and] 3,000 bushels of corn." After traveling to Hickory Grove, Burris caught up with Quantrill and Hays and ordered his artillery to fire on them. He claimed this caused them to be "thrown into confusion," and he watched the guerrillas as they receded from sight. He then returned to Kansas City with "a considerable number of horses" and "80 loyal colored persons," apparently freed slaves (perhaps eight hundred thousand dollars worth of chattel property in today's dollars). Burris claimed to have killed twelve guerrillas, wounded several, and captured two prisoners. Ransom, on his part, said twenty Confederates were wounded in a force numbering some "1,200."[14]

On September 6, Quantrill and 140 guerrillas rode to Olathe, Kansas. On the way, according to William Gregg, they killed 10 more men to revenge the death of Perry Hoy. Historian William Connelley also claims that before entering the town, the guerrillas killed Frank Cook as well as John J. and James B. Judy, who had recently enlisted in the Twelfth Kansas. When they reached the outskirts of Olathe, Gregg and 60 men cordoned off the town to prevent anyone fleeing. Then, Quantrill and the rest of the men rode to "Court Square," the center of town, dismounted, and hitched their horses. According to Gregg, they "found 125 soldiers drawn up on the sidewalk south of the square." Quantrill quickly conceived a plan and informed the men. The guerrillas walked behind their horses (using them as barricades),

Histories refer to the mythical Missouri guerrillas' black flag. Shown is an actual flag dropped by the guerrillas in Olathe during a raid. It appears to be a clutched white fist on a field of blue, replete with alternating red and white stripes. *The Kansas State Historical Society, Topeka*

drew their revolvers, and ordered all present to surrender. Only one soldier resisted and was shot, as well as a couple of townsmen. A townsman bitterly commented that the men were shot "like so many hogs."

After Quantrill and his men took control of Olathe, historian Connelley said, they shot Hiram Blanchard of Spring Hill, Josiah Skinner, and Phillip Wiggins, citizens, not soldiers. Then Quantrill brandished his commission as a captain in the Confederate service before the townsmen. When he met an old friend from Paola, Judge E. W. Robinson, he chatted with him for an hour, while his men looted the stores, took horses and wagons, and "everything of wearing apparel." The next morning, on September 7, Quantrill paroled the men captured at the town and rode back to Missouri. In comparison with the future, the guerrillas showed great restraint.[15]

On September 8-23, 1862, Burris and his Kansans, over 300 men, made another excursion from Fort Leavenworth into Missouri. This time, Burris trailed Quantrill through Jackson, Cass, Johnson, and Lafayette Counties, maintaining a relentless pursuit. Finally, Burris's advance guard, 50 men led by Capt. Daniel H. David, Fifth Missouri Cavalry, found the approximately 150 guerrillas ranged to their front in line of battle. They were near Smithfield, five miles north of Pleasant Hill. Burris ordered his force to attack, and the guerrillas, after a short, heated exchange of gunfire, retreated, leaving 1 man dead, Young Simmons of Westport, and 3 believed to be wounded. The Federals suffered the same number of casualties. Burris, nonetheless, did well on this venture into Missouri, capturing "100 stand of arms, 10,000 rounds of ammunition, nearly 100 head of horses, 4 yoke of oxen, 5 or 6 wagons, a number of tents and other camp equipage, also a considerable haul of dry goods, groceries, &c," said to be booty from the guerrillas' Olathe raid.[16]

While Burris was still pursuing Quantrill, on September 22, 1862, Abraham Lincoln, in the wake of the Battle of Antietam in Maryland, published his first Emancipation Proclamation. In the proclamation Lincoln called for the freeing of slaves in "designated States and parts of states," all in the South but not including the entire South. He also stated, through "military necessity," that former slaves were to be "received into the armed service of the United States to garrison forts, positions, stations, and other places, and to man vessels of all sorts in said service." A careful caveat is that no mention is made of blacks being used in regular fighting units (as they were already in Kansas at this time), *and there was to be no abridgment of slavery in the Union,* including Missouri, Kentucky, and the other Border States.

On October 5, 1862, Captain David left Independence on a scout with eighty-eight soldiers. Four miles outside town, he arrested several suspicious men. Looking for signs of guerrillas, he then traveled east to the Walker farm near Blue Springs and camped there for the night. The next day, David searched the area between "Fire Prairie and Snibar," toward

Sibley, Missouri. As he rode, he noticed pickets atop some of the hills in the distance, one named Big Hill, a high promontory; he suspected that a guerrilla camp lay ahead. Approaching Sibley, he divided his force into two columns. One of the columns captured two horses with "Government equipments" at a Mrs. Garrison's place. David's own column moved toward Big Hill, where he planned to wait until reinforcements arrived. He believed a guerrilla force of perhaps one hundred fifty to three hundred men was in the area. As he proceeded toward the hill, some guerrillas fired on him then fled into the woods. David followed them and in a firefight mortally wounded Col. Dick Chiles and captured three horses as well as equipment. Chiles, new to Quantrill's command, had been told to arrange an ambush, but the trap backfired on him, and he was shot through the lung and killed. Another guerrilla, Pat O'Donnell, was wounded. When David returned to the main road, he discovered he had lost one killed and two wounded (one mortally). He said that in his unit were "many others with holes shot through their clothes and hats, which shows that they were standing close up to their work." Two of David's men, however, had fled at the start of the fight.

The next morning, David's artillery battery fired canister at the guerrillas, causing them to retreat, as he put it, "through the worst brush thickets that I ever saw, they scattering and concentrating alternately during the day." David then returned to camp "almost exhausted from fatigue. . . . We do not believe," he concluded realistically, "the guerrillas can ever be taken by pursuit; we must take them by strategy."[17]

Around mid-October, the guerrillas decided to make another Kansas raid, this time on Shawneetown, a small village near the Kansas state line. As they rode toward the town, they encountered an escorted wagon train. No pickets had been posted, and the soldiers accompanying the train, about thirty in number, were mostly asleep. The guerrillas attacked the escort in force, killing half the men and driving off the rest. After their raid on the wagon train, the guerrillas galloped into Shawneetown on October 17, robbing it of household goods and horses, killing seven citizens, and burning the town. What the Jayhawkers had been doing for years in Missouri was now happening in Kansas, albeit on a more modest scale.

On November 3, the guerrillas headed for Texas, their winter home, passing southwest along the Harrisonville-Holden Road. On the way, they came upon a train of thirteen U.S. Army wagons escorted by Capt. W. M. Newby, commander of Company G, Sixth Regiment Cavalry, Missouri State Militia; the train was headed for Sedalia. When the soldiers saw the guerrillas, they tried to circle their oxen-drawn wagons, but the guerrillas descended on them so rapidly that they were surrounded and unable to resist. Some "4 soldiers and 6 teamsters [were] killed," as well as "2 soldiers and 1 teamster" wounded. In addition, Lieutenant Newby was captured.

Col. Edwin C. Catherwood, Newby's commander, earlier had received reports of Quantrill's presence in the area and had become so apprehensive about the safety of the wagon train that he had begun to race to its aid. When he arrived at the wagon train, he realized that he was too late. Nonetheless, he set out after Quantrill, aggressively overrunning his rear guard and rescuing "Lieutenant Newby and 1 private." Catherwood reported "killing 6 and wounding 25 of the enemy."[18]

After Quantrill's engagement with Catherwood, he proceeded south and on November 5, 1862, ran into Col. Warner Lewis's three-hundred-man Southern unit. Lewis persuaded Quantrill to join him in an attack on the Union garrison at Lamar, Missouri. The plan was for Quantrill to attack the town from the north, while Lewis attacked from the south. At the pre-arranged time, 10:00 P.M., Quantrill's guerrillas drove in the pickets at the edge of the town. They carried on a two-hour gun battle without success, losing two men. Lewis, inexplicably, failed to appear.

When the guerrillas arrived in Arkansas, most of Quantrill's men became part of Gen. Joseph O. "Jo" Shelby's brigade and fought with him in several engagements, including Cane Hill on November 28. In the meantime, Quantrill and two of his men, Andy Blunt and Higbee (first name not known), went to Richmond, Virginia, to obtain a colonelcy for Quantrill and the right to raise a regiment under the Confederate Partisan Ranger Act. According to an account by Gen. Lewis T. Wigfall, as related to John Newman Edwards, Quantrill told the Southern leadership that he wished to wage all-out war, to raise the "black flag." This curdled the Confederate leaders' blood. Apparently, they still wished to wage orthodox warfare. Quantrill's detractor, historian William E. Connelley, nonetheless granted that if Pres. Jefferson Davis failed to make Quantrill a colonel at this time, then Gen. Sterling Price may have done so. Connelley said that this was "a common procedure in the Confederate service west of the Mississippi." Most Border War historians, however, have resisted this promotion of Quantrill, refusing the guerrilla chief this modest recognition. But in a letter to exiled governor Thomas C. Reynolds from Maj. Gen. Sterling Price, the general repeatedly referred to Quantrill as "Colonel Quantrill." Assistant Adjutant General MacLean's letter to Quantrill, written on the same date, was surmounted by the title "Col. William C. Quantrill" and addressed him as "Colonel." Quantrill may well have been a colonel, albeit without a regiment. But most historians have remained unwilling to grant him this recognition without a specific document of proof in hand.[19]

***

Now that the Missouri guerrillas were under siege by Federal troops and Missouri militias, what had become of the Kansas Red Legs? Apparently, aside from their normal raiding activities into Missouri, they were now in the business of freeing slaves in Missouri and mustering them into Kansas units. In a statement addressed to Abraham Lincoln on September, 8, 1862, a number of prominent Missouri Unionists complained "that unless these negro brigades and regiments are disbanded and disarmed, and those men who have been instrumental in organizing them are severely dealt with by the Government, the most serious difficulties will take place between Missouri and Kansas—two loyal States—the end of which no man can see."

At the same time, Edward M. Samuel of Liberty, Missouri, attached his own remarks to the same protest letter to Lincoln:

> About 15 days ago some 15 persons from the State of Kansas—white men—under the command of a man calling himself Jeff. Davis, but whose real name is said to be Swain [a well-known Red Leg, mentioned earlier], and who is reported as a desperately bad man, came into the county of Clay, as Swain said, to "recruit Negroes for General Lane's Negro brigade." They took forcible possession of some 25 Negro men and about 40 horses from persons indiscriminately, and started to cross the Missouri River with them over into Kansas. Hearing of it, Captain Johns, of the Missouri State Militia, then in command at Liberty, sent out about 50 men to capture or shoot the men and retake the Negroes and horses. His company of militia succeeded in capturing 8 of the Jayhawkers and recovered all the Negroes and horses. The Jayhawkers were lodged in the jail at Liberty, where they were when I left home, on the 4th. A day or two afterward a white man presented to the officials at Liberty a written demand for the release of these 8 Jayhawkers, signed by Colonel Jennison, with a threat that he "would hold the county responsible if they were not released and given up." The demand of course was refused.[20]

How these sorts of activities could occur in Missouri under Federal army control is explainable by the fact that Maj. Gen. Henry Ryan Curtis, commander of the Department of the Missouri, had "military and administrative policies highly favorable to the radical factions of the Republican Party in Missouri and Kansas." By June 1863, Lincoln had removed Curtis for his inability to maintain a middle ground in Missouri politics, replacing him with Maj. Gen. John Schofield. That general then divided the old military district existing along the border in Kansas and Missouri into (1) the District of the Frontier, which "consisted of Kansas below the thirty-eighth parallel, the Indian Territory, and the western tier of counties in Missouri and Arkansas south of the thirty-eight parallel," all under the authority of Brig. Gen. James Blunt and (2) the District of the Border, to be commanded by Brig. Gen. Thomas Ewing Jr. and comprised of "all of

Kansas above the thirty-eighth parallel and the two western tiers of counties in Missouri north of the parallel and south of the Missouri River."

After taking command, Ewing, based in Kansas City, complained about the "men in Kansas who are stealing themselves rich in the name of liberty. . . . Those persons who are influential by reason of boldness, position or talent, have long been engaged in distorting the honest sentiment of the State, and giving respectability to robbery when committed on any whom they declare disloyal." Before long, these very men would be placing extreme political pressure on Ewing to do their bidding.[21]

***

Throughout 1862, the Missouri guerrillas had been learning by means of the hard school of experience how to conduct guerrilla operations. At the same time, through Gen. Henry Halleck's extermination order, they had learned how little value Union men placed on their lives. This lesson was not lost on them, and they increasingly came to place much less value on the lives of Union men. Out of the forge of adversity, the guerrillas had been slowly but surely tempered into a formidable, extremely dangerous, and deadly force.

Chapter 10

The Guerrillas' Identity, Extermination, and Trauma

There are two sides to the issues behind the Border War, but few writers/historians point that out. Among others, Don R. Bowen of the University of Illinois has defined the sides, noting that pro-Union accounts of the war portray Quantrill and his men as "essentially murderous thieves, utterly devoid of any social or political ideals, who took advantage of the turmoil of the times to enrich themselves at the expense of their neighbors." (Bowen correctly observed that that is how virtually all guerrilla movements are described by the dominant elite who oppose them.) The "second, pro-guerrilla" position maintains that the Southern "insurgents rose in defense of their homes and families as well as in the name of the Southern cause against the savage depredations of an alien, occupying army."[1] That they were violent, deadly men is unarguable. Who they were and how they got that way, however, are issues that deserve more attention than they have thus far received.

It is worth noting that no books on the Border War published in the last twenty-five years—new publications or reprinted versions of books with revised introductions—have mentioned the two seminal articles by Bowen on the Border War. These articles, analytical studies of *Missouri Census of 1860* data, destroy the notion that the Missouri guerrillas were lowlife thugs involved in the war for blood lust and booty. Bowen's study demonstrates, beyond rational doubt, that the Missouri guerrillas and their close supporters were the sons and daughters of the western Missouri elite, not the sort of young men expected to form en masse a "bandit army" of three hundred men.

The Missouri guerrillas, during and after the Civil War, became the victims of a thorough character assassination. This denigration began as soon as they mounted their horses and resisted Federal authority. The propaganda attacks occurred in newspapers, books, and in U.S. Army official correspondence. First, the guerrillas were called "thieves" and "robbers," then the verbal attacks degenerated into references to "demons" and "devils." And this tradition continues today in the titles of a recent motion picture, *Ride with the Devil,* and a book on Quantrill, *The Devil Knows How to Ride: The True Story of William Clarke Quantrill and his Confederate Raiders* (1998).

Despite their loaded titles, both the film and book mentioned are more enlightened representations of the guerrillas and Quantrill than most recent creations of their type. But demonizing the guerrillas has always had commercial value in newspapers, movies, books, and historical articles; incorporating the term "devil" into titles, for instance, is a more certain method of generating commercial success.

The most important and influential early history to demonize and distort the characters of the Missouri guerrillas was by the acknowledged dean of Border War historians, William Elsey Connelley, a Kansan, in his 1910 history, *Quantrill and the Border Wars.* Connelley witnessed firsthand to which class of people the guerrillas belonged. He talked with former guerrillas, dined with them, interviewed them for his histories, then misrepresented them, saying:

> They [guerrillas and their families] scarcely pretended to raise anything more than a scanty patch of corn; and when they could not put on their tables the flesh of the almost wild razorback hog which roamed the woods, they made meat of woodchucks, raccoons, opossums or any other "varmint" their gun could bring down. They did not scorn hawks or owls if hunger demanded and no better meat could be found.

> It was this "White Trash" [Connelley's capitalization] which added so much to the horrors of the war, especially in Missouri, and so little to its real prosecution. Wolflike in ferocity, when the advantages were on their side, they were wolflike in cowardice when the terms were at all equal. They were the Croats, Cossacks, Tolpatches, Pandours of the Confederacy—of little value in battle, but terrible as guerrillas and bushwhackers. From this "White Trash" came the gangs of murderers and robbers, like those led by the Youngers, Jameses, Quantrills and scores of other names of criminal memory.[2]

This characterization of the Missouri guerrillas is not only inaccurate, it is also patently absurd, as Bowen's census data reveals. If it were not for the indelible, pervasive, and stultifying influence Connelley has had on generations of historians, his words might be ignored. But his misrepresentations live on.

Quantrill, in particular, was a favorite target and butt of Connelley's vituperative remarks. Even Quantrill's family lineage was maligned by Connelley, who said:

> But this union of this couple [the marriage of Quantrill's mother and father] produced him that shed blood like water, a fiend wasteful and reckless of human life. They endowed him with depravity, bestowed

"A guerrilla raid in the West," a drawing from an 1861 *Harper's Weekly*. The propagandistic nature of the drawing is obvious and typical of the prevalent perception of the Missouri guerillas. *The Kansas State Historical Society, Topeka*

upon him the portion of degeneracy. In cruelty and a thirst for blood he towered above the men of his time. Somewhere of old his ancestors ate the sour grapes which set his teeth on edge. In him was exemplified the terrible and immutable law of heredity. He grew into the gory monster whose baleful shadow falls upon all who share the kindred blood. He made his name a Cain's mark and a curse to those condemned to bear it.[3]

Connelley, who was for some time the secretary of the Kansas State Historical Society, continually maligned Quantrill, saying, "A character capable of such baseness is incomprehensible. Depravity in such a form and carried to such an extent bewilders, becomes a mystery." Quantrill, according to Connelley, "betrayed and murdered his friends and drenched a border in blood"; he "had no convictions, stood for no principles, was in favor of no State or party, had no choice of communities, could not comprehend honesty, was an utter stranger to loyalty, and did not know such a thing as friendship."

Thomas Goodrich, who skillfully compiled archival material into less biased books on the Border War, felt somehow compelled to observe, "Even his name had a strange, surreal sound—Quantrill!" Even if one agrees with Goodrich's peculiar claim, which seems to have no substantiation, this is a particularly odd criticism since the guerrilla leader had no choice in his paternity.[4]

Another writer who has done much to damage Quantrill's reputation through innuendo is Jay Monaghan, the author of one of the few modern books devoted exclusively to the Border War. Monaghan referred to "lascivious lipped Quantrill with his ready smile and gang of mix-bloods." He described a "man of liquor and women, reckless when in command with his slant-eyed crew." Monaghan also writes, "Quantrill's longhorn mustache paralleled the brim of a low-crowned black hat garnished with gold band and tassels. Four pistol butts raised their ugly heads above his belt. This Short-cropped hair emphasized the smallness of his head on a giraffe neck—a pervert among unkempt followers." On the next page, Monaghan includes, "Quantrill's broad, voluptuous lips sneered." These almost clownish examples are obviously attempts to taint Quantrill as an inveterate "criminal type" by means of invective. Such descriptions are similar to the racist propaganda employed during World War II to demonize America's Japanese enemy by emphasizing racial features and stereotypical behavior. Referring to one of Quantrill's lieutenants, Dave Poole, as "the freebooting comedian" is Monaghan's backhanded way of labeling all the guerrillas as freebooters, for Poole was only typical. Monaghan's contention that Quantrill was "reckless in command" is especially absurd; his actions were almost always epitomized by great care, deliberation, and caution.[5]

Other writers, such as Albert Castel, author of *A Frontier State at War: Kansas 1861-1865* and *William Clarke Quantrill: His Life and Times,* are subtler in their attacks. Castel wrote, "It is extremely unlikely, too, that men of the Quantrill-Todd-Anderson ilk were motivated more than slightly by any higher purpose than plunder and murder. In a strict sense they were not even Missourians, and their careers show that they were as ready to rob and slay Confederate adherents as they were Union." Nearly all of this is untrue, unproven, or ill considered. None of these men at any stage in their careers as guerrillas were "ready to rob and slay Confederates" as they would Union men. Their guerrilla peers never would have allowed it. As far as the motivations of these three men are concerned, Castel has incorrectly identified what moved them. For these men to risk their lives daily, sometimes hourly, they would have had to have been "motivated more than slightly" and firmly believed in the cause for which they were fighting. No amount of money could have induced them to voluntarily submit to such suffering, and none of the guerrilla chiefs became rich through obtaining what Castel calls "plunder," as did the Jayhawkers Lane and Jennison. Indeed, Jennison was a much more likely candidate for demonization had Castel and the others been motivated to turn their pens on a figure who, though Northern, was truly worthy of their censure.

Furthermore, why Castel believed that it is necessary to be a Missourian to fight for the South, and inferentially, a Northerner to fight for the North, is quite puzzling because it is widely known that both Northerners and Southerners fought on both sides in the Civil War. In the battle of Chickamauga, for instance, Southerners in the Deep South acted as guides for the Northern army, while a Northerner, Bushrod Johnson, led the Confederate assault that broke the Union line and won the battle for the South. While Castel is even handed in comparison to some historians, this single example is meant to show the subtle nature of some of the bias employed, consciously or unconsciously, against the Missouri guerrillas. Moreover, it masks the central question: what terrible atrocities by Union forces caused normal young men to turn into violent killers? The answer to that question is particularly embarrassing for Union apologists to answer, so they simply don't.

It is important to note that Quantrill, although he was far from the bloodiest of the guerrillas, has invariably served as the lightning rod for indirect attacks against the guerrillas as a group, the inference being that if the leader of the guerrillas was a so-called rotten apple, then so was the bushel (the guerrilla organization) of which he was a part. Castel, Monaghan, and others, in a multitude of instances, referred to the guerrillas as "bushwhackers," a term with obvious negative connotations of which the writers must have been aware. Modern guerrillas, such as the

Vietcong of the Vietnam War, are never referred to as "bushwhackers."[6] Such use of terms is historical propaganda.

What, then, did Quantrill's "friends" say about him? Frank James said, "I will never forget the first time I saw Quantrill. . . . He was full of life and a jolly fellow. He had none of the bravado of the desperado about him. We loved him at first sight." After one of his battles, a woman who saw him for the first time said, "I saw Quantrill . . . after the fighting was over, when he rode to the house to look after his wounded. He looked as little like the horrible bloodthirsty bandit . . . as it is possible to imagine. Instead of this, he was a modest, quiet, good-looking man, with blue eyes . . . , gentle of manner and courteous as well." His lieutenant, William Gregg, who became a Kansas City lawman after the war, said of him: "History after history has been written about Quantrill and his men, none of which can be characterized as true. . . . One thing I do know however, and that is, that he was a soldier and not afraid to die, that he was equitable and just to friend and foe up to a certain period of the war." Another of Quantrill's captains, who disliked him, Charles F. "Fletch" Taylor, said, "Q. was a good commander and a brave man and all the men had confidence in him. Don't think he was cowardly, although I never saw him in a close place, as the men preferred to go in the lead, and let him manage, as we did not want to lose him."[7]

So who were these guerrillas, who were so maligned by most historians and writers for more than 130 years? In the 1970s, Don R. Bowen examined demographic data from the *Missouri Census of 1860* for Jackson County, Missouri, to determine the guerrillas' background in relation to the following:

(1) Age; (2) state, territory or country of birth; (3) number and order of siblings; (4) residence in 1860; (5) occupation, if any; (6) marital status; (7) number of children; (8) value of real property owned, 1860; (9) value of personal property owned, 1860; (10) number of slaves owned, if any; (11) regular military service in either the Missouri State Guards or the Confederate States Army; and (12) regular military rank.

Bowen also determined in relation to the guerrillas' parents, their:

(1) occupation, (2) value of real property owned, 1860; (3) value of personal property owned, 1860; (4) number of slaves owned, if any.[8]

These are relatively objective, unbiased criteria for establishing the true social position of the guerrillas. In Bowen's thorough, but largely ignored study, he concluded that one-third of the guerrilla leaders owned slaves; three-quarters of their parents did so. Of the guerrilla followers, one-tenth owned slaves, while half of their parents owned slaves. Because slave owning was rare in the general population, it is easily seen that many of these young men were from the more prominent, affluent families in the area. Bowen determined that the guerrillas were not only better off than the general population of Jackson County, they also were, generally speaking, "very much better off," in fact, "in terms of the times, wealthy people."

Buttressing the assumption of the social prominence of the guerrillas and their families, Bowen also demonstrated that, at some time, three-quarters of the guerrilla leaders were lieutenants or above in the army of the Confederate States or the Missouri State Guard. According to Bowen, the leaders of the guerrillas were the kind of men who, in ordinary times, would have filled leadership positions in their communities. In addition, they were well-socialized members of their communities, an extremely important feature for guerrillas, who depend ordinarily on local support to survive.

Bowen concluded that the guerrilla leaders were largely "the sons and heirs of an established local elite." Over 90 percent of the guerrillas' fathers held middle- to upper-class positions in the community, and their slave property alone was worth "double the county-wide mean." All of this, of course, negates Connelley's contention that the guerrillas were "White Trash" and makes the assertion that they were ordinary thieves highly questionable.[9]

Bowen contends that the Union occupation of western Missouri threatened the property of the guerrilla families, their status, and, in some cases, their lives. According to Bowen's search of the index of the U.S. Army's *Official Record*, the guerrilla families, in respect to the Federal army, suffered "search of property, seizure of property (livestock, crops, slaves, etc.), destruction of property (burning of buildings, shootings of horses, etc.), arrest or detainment of persons, forced bail or bond giving, forced removal of families, summary execution, [and] execution by court martial." According to Bowen's count, ninety-three guerrilla families were subjected to the above sanctions during the war. The threat to the property of the young guerrillas' families by the Federal forces was also a menace to the young guerrillas' own future estates and status. In response, and largely for that reason, the young guerrillas waged war on the Federal army and its allies, the Missouri militias—not for plunder, as many historians maintain.[10]

Once the guerrillas left their homes and took to the bush, their lives were totally disrupted. Their ordinary ways of supporting themselves disappeared, and they were forced to sustain themselves, as all guerrillas do, by obtaining food, forage, and shelter from the local people, usually voluntarily but, if necessary, through some measure of coercion. The guerrillas' preferred source of sustainment, of course, was taking what they needed from their enemies—the Federal army, Union supporters, and spies in the area. It should be obvious that the guerrillas did not receive ordinary payments for their services as did the Union soldiers and Missouri militiamen.

What should be equally obvious is that the guerrillas had to support themselves by whatever means necessary, as all guerrillas do.

Some historians have referred to guerrillas "stealing" and "plundering."
When the Federal armies practiced the same behavior on a *massive scale,*
such writers called it "appropriating" or "living off the land." Obviously,
the Federal army never paid for any appropriated Southern property, and
it was lost to the owners forever, whether it was called "theft" or "appropriation." From a Southerner's perspective, the Union army was "plundering," and there was no real distinction between the actions of guerrillas and
Yankees—except in magnitude. The guerrillas received most of their forage and food, however, from friends. The justification the Union army
used for their appropriating of property was to defend it by the then-cur-
rent "Laws of War." But these laws possessed no moral validity and
expressed no moral imperative; they were merely the codification of military and governmental expedients against an enemy. Even property appropriated by the U.S. Army from Union farmers was often not paid for or
paid for only when, as in the case of the Solomon Young family (mentioned earlier), several decades had passed and lawyers were summoned to
attempt to enforce payment.

But even what the army called its official "Laws of War" cannot be used
to justify the Jayhawker invasions of Missouri in 1861-62 and the Red Leg
and Missouri Militia atrocities that succeeded them. These "Laws of War,"
promulgated on April 24, 1863, at the direction of Abraham Lincoln, were
encompassed in General Orders No. 100, *Instructions for the Government of
Armies of the United States in the Field.* Some of the articles specified:

> Article 16. Military necessity does not admit of cruelty—that is, the
> infliction of suffering for the sake of suffering or for revenge, nor of
> maiming or wounding except in fight.

> Article 22. The principle has been more and more acknowledged that
> the unarmed citizen is to be spared in person, property, and honor as
> much as the exigencies of war will admit.

> Article 25. In modern regular wars of the Europeans, and their
> descendants in other portions of the globe, protection of the inoffen-
> sive citizen of the hostile country is the rule; privation and distur-
> bance of private relations are the exceptions.

> Article 28. Retaliation will, therefore, never be resorted to as a mea-
> sure of mere revenge, but only as a means of protective retribution,
> and moreover, cautiously and unavoidably; that is to say, retaliation
> shall only be resorted to after careful inquiry into the real occurrence,

and the character of the misdeeds that may demand retribution.

Unjust or inconsiderate retaliation removes the belligerents farther and farther from the mitigating rules of regular war, and by rapid steps leads them nearer to the internecine wars of savages.

Article 44. All wanton violence committed against persons in the invaded country, all destruction of property not commanded by the authorized officer, all robbery, all pillage or sacking, even after taking a place by main force, all rape, wounding, maiming, or killing of such inhabitants, are prohibited under the penalty of death or such other severe punishment as may seem adequate for the gravity of the offense.

A soldier, officer, or private, in the act of committing such violence, and disobeying a superior ordering him to abstain from it, may be lawfully killed on the spot by such superior.

Article 46. Neither officers nor soldiers are allowed to make use of their position or power in the hostile country for private gain, not even for commercial transactions otherwise legitimate. Offenses to the contrary committed by commissioned officers will be punished with cashiering or such other punishment as the nature of the offense may require.

Article 47. Crimes punishable by all penal codes, such as arson, murder, maiming, assault, highway robbery, theft, burglary, fraud, forgery, and rape, if committed by an American soldier in a hostile country against its inhabitants, are not only punishable as at home, but in all cases in which death is not inflicted, the severer punishment shall be preferred.

Clearly, the Jayhawkers led by Lane, Anthony, and Jennison; their confederates, the Red Legs; and the Missouri militias ran criminally roughshod over these articles in the most flagrant ways.

Though Union forces illegally participated in many guerrilla-like activities, they eagerly punished the Missourians for such behavior. Arrayed against them were thousands of Union soldiers based at cavalry posts at roughly twelve-mile intervals throughout western Missouri. The primary objective of these troopers was to seek out and destroy the young guerrillas, killing them and obliterating their operations in the area. For this purpose, patrols were sent out continuously, and when contacts were made, manhunts were begun, and men captured were killed.

This continual, unending pursuit of the young men hardened them, upset their psychological equilibrium, filled them with fear and dread, and ultimately made them violent—much the same way it would transform an innately brave but ordinarily docile German Shepherd into a fierce and dangerous animal if it were beaten daily. The guerrillas witnessed their friends falling by enemy fire, tumbling from their horses, riddled with bullet holes. Their bodies were left to rot in the brush, where they were ravaged by the creatures of the Missouri and Kansas wilderness. Because it had been ordered that they were to be exterminated upon capture, the guerrillas soon felt they had little to lose by killing their hated tormenters, and they did so, eventually with relish. After awhile, they wore the captured uniforms of their enemies, rode up to them unannounced, and killed them by stealth. Or they set up ambushes and killed their enemies. The guerrillas also suffered ambushes, which is how the notorious William Anderson was finally killed. But the guerrillas' tormentors never have been called "bushwhackers."

No writer understood the guerrillas better than John Newman Edwards, Gen. Jo Shelby's adjutant, who knew many of the guerrillas personally and understood their feelings and thoughts. In his book, *Noted Guerrillas,* written shortly after the end of the Civil War, Edwards described the guerrillas' inner turmoil and raison d'être:

> Civil War might have made the guerrilla, but only the excesses of civil war could have made him the untamable and unmerciful creature that history finds him. When he first went into the war, he was somehow imbued with the old-fashioned belief that soldiering meant fighting and that fighting meant killing. He had his own ideas of soldiering, however, and desired nothing so much as to remain at home and to meet its despoilers upon his own premises. Not naturally cruel, and averse to invading the territory of any other people, he could not understand the patriotism of those who invaded his own territory. Patriotism, such as he was required to profess, could not spring up in the market-place at the bidding of Red Leg or Jayhawker. He believed, indeed, that the patriotism of Jim Lane and Jennison was merely a highway robbery transferred from the darkness to the dawn, and he believed the truth. Neither did the Guerrilla become merciless all of a sudden. Pastoral in many cases by profession, and reared among the bashful and timid surroundings of agricultural life, he knew nothing of the tiger that was in him until death had been dashed against his eyes in numberless and brutal ways, and until the blood of his own kith and kin had been sprinkled plentifully upon things that his hands touched, and things that entered into his daily existence. And that fury of ideas also came to him slowly, which is more implacable than the fury of men, for men have heart, and opinion has none. It took him likewise some time to learn that the Jayhawker's system of saving the union was a system of brutal force, which bewailed not even that

which it crushed; that it belied its doctrine by its tyranny; stained its arrogated right by its violence, and dishonored its vaunted struggles by its execution. But blood is contagious as air. The fever of war has its delirium. When the guerrilla awoke, he was a Giant! He took in, as it were, and at a single glance, all the immensity of the struggle. He saw that he was hunted and proscribed; that he had neither a flag nor a government; that the rights and the amenities of civilized warfare were not to be his; that a dog's death was certain if he surrendered even in the extremest agony of battle; that the house which sheltered him had to be burnt; the father who succored him had to be butchered; the mother who prayed for him had to be insulted; the sister who carried food to him had to be imprisoned; the neighborhood which witnessed his combats had to be laid waste; the comrade shot down by his side had to be put to death as a wild beast—and he lifted up the black flag in self-defense and fought as became a free man and a hero. . . . Desperate and remorseless as he undoubtedly was, the guerrilla saw shining down upon his pathway a luminous patriotism, and he followed it eagerly that he might kill in the name of God and his country. The nature of his warfare made him responsible, of course, for many monstrous things he had no personal share in bringing about. Denied a hearing at the bar of public opinion, the *bête noir* of all the loyal journalists, painted blacker than ten devils, and given a countenance that was made to retain some shadow of all the death agonies he had seen, is it strange in the least that his fiendishness became omnipresent as well as omnipotent? To justify one crime on the part of a Federal soldier, five crimes more cruel still were laid at the door of the Guerrilla. His long gallop not only tired but infuriated his hunters. That savage standing at bay and dying always as a wolf dies when bayed at by hounds and bludgeoned by countrymen, made his enemies fear him and hate him. Hence, from all their bomb-proofs his slanderers fired silly lies at long range, and put afloat unnatural stories that hurt him only as it deepened the savage intensity of an already savage strife. . . . Man for man, he put his life fairly on the cast of the war dice, and died when the need came as the red Indian dies, stoical and grim as stone.[11]

On March 19, 1862, when Gen. Henry Halleck, commander of the Department of the Mississippi, issued his order outlawing guerrillas and commanding their execution upon capture, it was passed down the chain of command to Brig. Gen. James Totten, who, on April 21, 1862, published Special Orders No. 47. In the order, Totten stated that western Missouri had become the "haunts of these outlaws and the farmers generally in these neighborhoods are said to be knowing to and encouraging the lawless acts of these guerrillas." Totten claimed that western Missouri had been "reduced to a state of anarchy" and declared that henceforth guerrillas "will be shot down by the military upon the spot when found perpetrating their foul acts."

The guerrillas, in response and protest, began reprisal killings of Union soldiers. When captured guerrilla Jim Vaughn was to be hung on May 29, 1863, by Gen. James Blunt's men in Leavenworth, Col. Ben Parker, a partisan leader from northwest Missouri, threatened to execute four captured Union soldiers. Blunt, however, followed a policy of no compromise and no communications with the guerrillas, and Vaughn was hung. Before the trap door opened, Vaughn said stoically, "This is my last look—let her slide." Later, Parker executed five Union prisoners, one more than his warning—the fifth for good measure.[12]

Halleck, who ordered the exterminations, had been a student of the "Laws of War" and had authored a book on the subject, *International Law; or, Rules Regulating the Intercourse of States in Peace and War.* Halleck's views on the treatment of guerrillas in war were inspired by Napoleon Bonaparte's treatment of guerrillas in the Continental wars of the early nineteenth century. In 1863, Halleck had the opportunity to further refine his interests in the "Laws of War," when he promulgated General Orders No. 100, *Instructions for the Government of Armies in the Field.* This document was a revised version of the concepts found in Francis Lieber's book, *A Code for the Government of Armies* (1863). Lieber had fought in the Prussian Army against Napoleon during the Napoleonic Wars. Orders No. 100, called "Lieber's Code," was a derivative of Lieber's earlier work and contained the codification of the U.S. Army's "Laws of War" (excerpts of which can be found earlier in this chapter). These "laws" were applied to guerrillas in Missouri as well as to the Confederate army.

Lieber and Halleck were in no way exceptional in their admiration for the great French general. Indeed, their military education was based on Jomini's *Art of War,* his classic distillation of Napoleon's tactics. What one might question, however, is whether Napoleon's policy toward guerrillas should have been an exemplar of humane treatment of enemies in war. Napoleon, it will be remembered, had a guerrilla problem in his peninsular campaign in Spain and Portugal that became so costly it nearly unhinged his other Continental military operations. Almost the entire *Grande Armée* finally became involved in the struggle, but the war remained unwinnable. Ultimately, Napoleon's policy was to send armed French patrols into the Spanish countryside after guerrillas, where the French showed no mercy, often murdering indiscriminately. This became the precise American policy.

In Spain, the peasant insurgents answered violence with violence. As Robert B. Asprey, author of *War in the Shadows: The Guerrilla in History,* described the war, "Cruelty answered cruelty; terror escalated, the French in particular practicing a frenzied rapine. . . . During Marshal Soult's assault, swarms of Portuguese civilians were left floundering in a river by a collapsed bridge. The oncoming French battalions cold-bloodedly fired into this mass until . . . planks were laid on the pile of dead bodies that arose from the river; the French passed over, and carried the batteries of Villa Nova."[13] Such was the Napoleonic example chosen for American counter-guerrilla operations in the Civil War.

Clearly, the more severe the attempt to suppress guerrillas, the more virulent their response. The application of extreme violence to subdue guerrillas, modern armies have discovered, is not a winning formula for destroying them. In such situations, a sort of reciprocal chain of violence develops, and it often accelerates and intensifies over time. Lt. Col. Edwin Kennedy Jr. (U.S. Army, retired) said that today, "The U.S. Rules of Land Warfare generally prohibit killing guerrillas, even though they are violating the normal rules of land warfare [for instance, not being in uniform]." Kennedy added, "The reason we refuse to execute guerrillas today is partly because of the reciprocal violence we can expect in return. Also, we choose not to enflame the general populace and cause them to go over to the enemy."

The opposite course of action produced the carnage that took place in Missouri, 1861-65. At first, in his confrontations with the Federal forces in Missouri, Quantrill attempted to exchange prisoners, as in the case of Randlett, and to parole prisoners, as in the case of prisoners at Olathe. Even in late 1864, when Quantrill seized a Federal camp at Tuscumbia, Missouri, he paroled the entire camp of Federals. But the Federals consistently refused to exchange prisoners and refused to parole guerrillas. In fact, they outlawed guerrillas and sought to exterminate them in every instance. This was an open invitation for the guerrillas to reciprocate: to kill captured Union soldiers rather than paroling them; however, Quantrill, so frequently demonized as a "devil," often did not conform to such a policy.

Not unexpectedly, the guerrillas who sacked Lawrence in 1863 were not the sunny warriors of late 1861 and 1862. By August 1863, the guerrillas were prepared psychologically to annihilate 150 citizens of Lawrence, Kansas, "men and boys," in an orgy of violence. (Usually not mentioned is that some of the guerrillas were "boys," too.) The Federal soldiers who pursued the guerrillas from Lawrence were prepared also to shoot captured and wounded guerrillas and to allow, they say, the "Indians" accompanying them to scalp them. After the raid on Lawrence, the townsmen dragged a guerrilla, a former minister, through the town behind a horse, threw rocks at the body, and then tied it in a tree, where they used it for target practice. Afterwards, the body was thrown in a ravine, where wild animals devoured it and scattered the bones. By 1864, the guerrillas under the command of William (now called "Bloody Bill") Anderson took up the same practice of scalping, attaching human trophies to their bridle reins, and committing atrocities on Missouri militia troops at Centralia. However, before the raid on Centralia, some of Anderson's men were scalped by Missouri militia troops, so the violence was never one sided although many of the histories endeavor to make it sound so.

None of this behavior is unique to this period in American history. During the American Revolution, the American insurgents committed atrocities and terrorist acts on the British, and in the South, British commander Banastre Tarleton committed even worse things on American civilians. During the Vietnam War, Lt. William Calley became a scapegoat to atone for more widespread atrocities by Americans against the Vietcong and North Vietnamese army soldiers. Many American young men now suffer posttraumatic stress disorders because of the extreme violence they were subjected to and sometimes perpetrated during that war. As John Newman Edwards said in the 1860s, "blood is contagious."[14]

Many Americans might be surprised to hear these charges. The Vietnam War, according to author Paul Fussell, was "systematically sanitized and Norman Rockwellized, not to mention Disneyfied. . . . No matter how severely wounded, Allied troops are never shown suffering what was termed, in the Vietnam War, traumatic amputation; everyone has all his limbs, his hands and feet and digits, not to mention expressions of courage and cheer."[15]

A soldier relating his experience of Vietnam said, "Well, at first, I mean, when I just come there, I couldn't believe what I was seeing. I couldn't believe Americans could do things like that to another human being . . . but then I *became* that. We went through villages and killed everything, I mean *everything,* and that was all right with me." Another soldier said, "War changes you, changes you. Strips you, strips you of all your beliefs, your religion, takes your dignity away, you become an animal. I know the animals don't—the animal in the sense of being evil. You know, it's unbelievable what humans can do to each other. I never in a million years thought I would be capable of doing that. Never, never, never." Yet another soldier said after losing his closest friend in Vietnam, "And it wasn't that I couldn't be killed. I didn't care if I was killed. . . . I just didn't care if I lived or died. I just wanted blood. I just wanted revenge, and I didn't care. I didn't see myself going home. No . . . Nope, I didn't."[16]

More than a few soldiers in Vietnam—like Anderson and George Todd in their rampages late in the Civil War—went "berserk." One soldier said, "I don't know what I did with the bolt of the [M]16, but I got it to fire, and I emptied everything I had into him. Then I saw blood dripping on the back of my hand and *I just went crazy.* I pulled him into the paddy and carved him up with my knife. When I was done with him, he looked like a rag doll that a dog had been playing with." Another veteran of Vietnam explained about losing a friend in combat: "And I cried and I cried and I cried. . . . And I stopped crying. And I probably didn't cry again for twenty years. I turned. I had no feelings. I wanted to hurt. I wanted to hurt. And I wanted to hurt."[17]

Herbert Hendin and Ann Pollinger Haas, in their book, *Wounds of War: The Psychological Aftermath of Combat in Vietnam,* remarked that there was little public awareness of the context in which American soldiers became violent in Vietnam, that little was said "of the common occurrence that is seared in the memory of many combat soldiers: a captured American tied to a tree, his genitals cut off, and stuffed in his mouth. The sight of the mutilated body, intended by the Vietcong to create fear in our soldiers, was at times used by American officers to create rage and ferocity in them instead."

Tony Swindell, a veteran of the 11th Infantry Brigade, Americal Division, in the Vietnam War in 1968-69, said of his experiences:

> From my personal experience, the real psychological damage from combat doesn't come from one isolated firefight or rocket attack. It involves a sustained period of terror over weeks and months with no refuge or safe place. You first become numb with fear, knowing you can get killed asleep or awake, and then you become full of anger and hatred when you start to lose buddies. Your enemy no longer has a human face. At its worst, you lose respect for life, and you don't care if that body in front of you is a civilian or NVA. "Kill 'em all and let God sort 'em out." Only one rule, stay alive.

Swindell continued, "There are some things that are still impossible to articulate except maybe to another ex-grunt. I saw things I couldn't explain even to myself."[18]

At the peak of American involvement in the Vietnam War, the Americans probably outnumbered the Vietcong and North Vietnamese forces in South Vietnam by a ratio of 10 to 1. In Vietnam, American troops also had a hugely disproportionate advantage in firepower. In contrast, in western Missouri, over the period of the war, the Federal forces outnumbered the guerrillas, in the whole, by at least 25 to 75 to 1! The guerrillas fought valiantly against these overwhelming odds, but not without great cost and suffering. If American troops suffered trauma in Vietnam when they had a distinct advantage in numbers, an overwhelming advantage in firepower, and participated in relatively short one-year tours, think what must have been the experience of Missouri guerrillas from 1861 through 1865 when conditions were dramatically the reverse.[19]

This is the face of war that most people do not understand but which often became the Missouri guerrillas' experience. It is a psychological realm, a dimension of feeling and being that everyday men and women have not experienced, imagined, or fathomed. But this is the fearful reality, sometimes, in bitter military struggles. Young, patriotic men must live and endure this "reality" and hope they emerge from the experience alive and with a scintilla of sanity. Not all of the Missouri guerrillas succumbed to the stress of daily combat over the more than three years they fought, but many, understandably, did.

Chapter 11

"Hell in Their Neck": The Guerrilla Response[1]

In the spring of 1863, the guerrillas returned to Missouri from Texas stronger, more numerous, and exceedingly dangerous. They had gotten their baptism by fire during their operations in 1862 and had learned how to fight. Now, when a band of them crossed a road on horseback, they dragged branches over their tracks or threw blankets on the road and rode over them, leaving little trace. When they were afoot and crossed a path, they walked in the same set of footprints to hide their numbers. Advancing as a large body, they sent out vedettes—mounted, advance scouts—to report enemy dispositions to their front. They also recruited local farmers, who sent signals to them concerning Federal troops in the area. Because they knew most of the bridle paths and roads where they traveled, they moved rapidly to attack, retreat, or disperse.

The guerrillas also had refined other tactics, emulating in many respects the way Indians waged war on the frontier. When outnumbered, the partisans attacked the Federals from concealed positions, fired volleys at them, and then fled down remote pathways. When pursued, they broke up into smaller units, forcing the Federals to do likewise. Then, in accordance with preconceived plans, they reformed and attacked the smaller, now divided Federal units. Whenever possible, the guerrillas approached the Federals stealthily and attacked them violently, at a full gallop, screaming their eerie, rebel cries, falling on the bluecoats before they had an opportunity to form and fire. Armed with four to eight .36-caliber Colt Navy revolvers, aimed instinctively and loaded with light rounds for accuracy, they fired rapidly, at close range, in an explosion of devastating fire that often panicked Federal troops. Once the Union soldiers broke formation, the guerrillas fell on them individually or in small groups, like wolves upon prey, and destroyed them. Mobility, stealth, and overwhelming, close-range firepower were the keys to their tactical successes.

The guerrillas' favorite tactic was the ambush, which they used in several variants. Sometimes, they would send out a single guerrilla or a small band of partisans as bait. These men would fire a few rounds at a larger Federal patrol or unit then flee to a prearranged killing ground established by the guerrillas. As the decoyed Union troopers charged to this position, the guerrillas would fire a volley into their ranks from behind cover and then charge them on horseback. When outnumbered Union soldiers met the guerrillas in the open field, their greatest chance was to break the guerrilla charge at long range, with volley fire. To minimize the effects of volleys, the partisans would lean over and clutch the necks of their horses or twist their bodies over the sides of their horses, away from the incoming fire, in the Indian manner. If the outnumbered Federals failed to halt the guerrilla charge, they were faced with possible destruction by the overwhelming, close-in firepower of the guerrillas' revolvers.

Guerrillas seldom attacked fortified positions, and when they did, they usually regretted the experience. Ordinarily, they chose to fight in their own element, in the dense woods they knew so intimately and in situations where they outnumbered the enemy. In this respect, they emulated most irregular warriors around the world, from Fabius in ancient Rome down through the ages to Mao and Giap. Because their enemies invariably outnumbered them in the aggregate, the only way the partisans could fight effectively and survive over time was through attacking smaller units than their own, preferably through surprise. Frank James, a guerrilla (later a notorious bandit), said he was confused at first by guerrilla fighting. After his experience with the Confederate army, the idea of firing and running seemed strange, almost cowardly. But he soon realized that it was the only way guerrillas could survive. If they met their enemies head-on, they would be decimated, eventually exterminated, because of their lack of numbers. For this reason, the guerrilla commanders generally sought relatively low-risk, high-success scenarios. When the guerrillas were massed, any inferior-sized Union unit was extremely vulnerable to total annihilation, as they would be at the Baxter Springs and Centralia massacres (see following chapters). Outnumbered soldiers, fighting on foot with single-shot muzzle-loaders, were extremely susceptible to the lightning strikes, explosive firepower, and shock of guerrilla cavalry.

The guerrillas' strategy was based on the principle of mobility. They tried to remain in motion, thus keeping their enemy off balance. This continuous attacking and retreating created havoc among the Federals. Telegraph lines, small garrisons, couriers, convoys, wagon trains, mail shipments, patrols—no one and nothing was safe. At any time a whooping band of rapidly firing partisans might erupt from the brush and attack the Federals with a frenzy of violence and a storm of bullets. The guerrillas, by 1863, also had the overwhelming support of the people of western Missouri and could depend on them for intelligence, food, and forage, as well as succor if they were wounded.

All Missourians of army age were required to enlist in the Missouri Union militias, so the guerrillas often wore captured Union uniforms to delay detection. Only a man dressed in Federal blue was safe from Union cavalry troopers on the roads and byways of western Missouri. Since the partisans were already outlawed and marked for extermination, wearing Federal uniforms in violation of the laws of war posed no additional threat to their lives. Sometimes, the partisans would casually ride up to small Union outfits while dressed in their captured Union uniforms, hail them in a friendly manner, then open up a murderous fire on them at close range, killing as many of them as possible. In this treacherous environment, whether a farmer, guerrilla, or Union soldier, it was difficult to determine friends or enemies. Guerrillas posed as Union soldiers; Red Legs and Federal spies posed as guerrillas. Civilians unable to determine the true identity of strangers and respond accordingly were often killed.

Meanwhile, the sisters of the guerrillas and their older male relatives continued to venture into the towns of western Missouri to buy supplies (pistol caps and powder) and spy on the Federals. They returned to the guerrilla camps with reports of Union manpower, artillery pieces, and the layout of camps. John Noland, a free black man and guerrilla, acted as a spy in Lawrence. When Federal spies ultimately infiltrated the guerrilla movement, Quantrill and his chiefs, for everyone's safety, kept crucial elements of their plans secret from the men, informing them only of what they needed to know as late in an operation as possible.[2]

For that reason, during the raid on Lawrence in 1863, it is doubtful that any of the guerrilla rank and file knew where they were headed until they crossed into Kansas. Had they known earlier, a Federal spy or spies hidden in their midst would have known also, fled the guerrilla column, and blocked the invasion. Gen. James Blunt, in a letter to Maj. Gen. Samuel R. Curtis on April 17, 1863, confirmed the presence of spies in the guerrilla groups: "I have a man who joined the Knights of the Golden Circle [a secret pro-Southern organization] some time since in Missouri for certain purposes. He has been for some time with [George] Todd's band of guerrillas in Jackson County." Though the guerrillas knew they had spies in their organization and were vigilant concerning them, killing any upon discovery, they were still affected by them.[3]

By May 5, 1863, Quantrill had returned to western Missouri and reassembled his guerrilla force. In a report to his commanding officer, Union lieutenant colonel Walter King reported Quantrill's appearance:

> An hour has elapsed since penning the foregoing paragraph, spent in interview with "John DeCourcy," my most trusted spy, who reached here, and I gather the following: Quantrill is here; he came from Price to conscript; he came with 40 men; he has joined [General John?] Reid's, [John] Jarrett's, [George] Todd's, [Cole] Younger's, and Clifton's gangs to his own, which give him from 125 to 150 men . . . has orders from Price to stop bushwhacking and horse stealing . . . Quantrill is

to annoy Kansas and Western Missouri; intends to conscript all of military age; has secret notice among Southern men to come to his camp and get property taken by mistake; came here to stay, not take away any recruits; seems to be rather elevated in his purposes by his six or eight months' experience with the regular forces.

From this report, it is apparent that Quantrill avoided taking property from pro-Southerners and that he was not operating as a freelancer but under the general control of the Confederate army. This was clear to his enemies, if it is not to some historians.[4]

As operations commenced in early summer 1863, much of the power within the western Missouri guerrillas was concentrated in the guerrilla chiefs, who operated under Quantrill's direction in large operations but acted more or less independently the rest of the time. In early May, Richard F. "Dick" Yeager, one of Quantrill's chiefs, conducted a raid into Kansas that signaled the vulnerability of that state's defenses. Yeager, leading a group of guerrillas, remained undetected in that state until he reached Council Grove, some one hundred miles west of Missouri, in the heart of eastern Kansas. Yeager's intention was to burn Council Grove, but when he suffered a severe toothache, he was forced to go into that town to find a dentist, a man he knew, Dr. J. H. Bradford. The doctor, a former Missourian, while extracting Yeager's tooth, persuaded him to save Council Grove. Yeager agreed and headed back to Missouri along the Santa Fé Trail, burning and pillaging his way eastward.

The local lawmen seemed paralyzed by Yeager's unexpected presence. Finally, the United States marshal at Leavenworth, James L. McDowell, pursued Yeager with a posse. Encountering the partisans northwest of Emporia, near the Cottonwood River, he attacked and captured twelve of them. In typical guerrilla fashion, the remainder dispersed and made their way back to Missouri singly or in small groups. McDowell's captured prisoners were turned over to John E. Stewart, the Jayhawker who had been Quantrill's ally in Lawrence before the war. According to the *Kansas City Journal of Commerce*, the guerrilla captives attempted to escape and "the guards fired upon them and the whole number were killed." Likely, they were summarily executed.

Yeager and eight of his men, undeterred, continued raiding across the state. On May 8, they captured the Rock Springs stagecoach depot and killed a soldier, George N. Sabin. Near Lawrence, at David Hubbard's store, they questioned the proprietor about his political affiliations and then attempted to kill him. Hubbard, who survived the attack, reported later, "One bullet went through my lungs, the other two missed." After looting the store and robbing some of the locals, Yeager and his band continued eastward, stopping next at Black Jack, where they robbed a stage and its passengers then unharnessed and took the horses. The warning left by Yeager's raid was clear: the security of Kansas was in jeopardy.[5]

On June 16, 1863, another ominous event occurred. A 150-man detachment of the Ninth Kansas Cavalry, which had been out all day looking for guerrillas, approached its base at Westport, Missouri. As it neared the village, Lt. George Todd and a band of screaming guerrillas rode from the woods and attacked the column with a barrage of deadly fire, panicking it. Once the Federals broke formation, the guerrillas rode through their ranks, killing twenty troopers and wounding many others. The Federals fled wildly into Westport, much sobered by the experience. This successful attack demonstrated that the guerrillas were reaching a peak of killing proficiency and learning the value of rapid, violent charges.[6]

Prior to these summer attacks, Brigadier General Ewing began a policy of arresting and imprisoning the sisters of known guerrillas. He used their alleged "spying" as a pretext for these illegal arrests, and the women were held without trial, bail, or legal recourse. John McCorkle, a guerrilla scout, said that his sister, Mrs. Charity Kerr, and his sister-in-law, Mrs. Nannie McCorkle, were arrested by Ewing's soldiers for driving into Kansas City an oxen-pulled wagon filled with wheat to be ground into flour. One of their Unionist neighbors, Anderson Cowgill, had alerted Ewing that the girls were rebels and obtaining food for the guerrillas. Upon Cowgill's word alone and with no corroborating evidence, the girls were promptly arrested and thrown into jail with other young women of their kind. Earlier, Bill Anderson's sisters had been arrested at gunpoint, taken as hostages, and removed to Kansas City. The plan was to send the girls to a prison in St. Louis, a catastrophe for women in those days. Meanwhile, the multistory, ramshackle building where they were held shook periodically, swayed and shuddered, frightening the young girls. The shaking was caused by a dangerously weak foundation that was ignored by Federal officials even though the prisoners complained incessantly about it. The building finally collapsed, killing and injuring a number of the young girls and women.

The *Kansas City Post* in May 2, 1910, described the event:

> There were nine of these girls in the prison at 1409 Grand Avenue, when it [the building where the young girls were imprisoned] fell. One of these was Josephine Anderson. Her two sisters, Mollie, aged sixteen, and Janie, ten years old, were also prisoners with her [actually, Josephine, Jennie, and Mary], and it was these three especially that the Union soldiers wanted to kill because they were sisters of Bill Anderson, the guerrilla. The others were Mrs. Susan Vandiver, Mrs. Armenia Whitsett-Gilvey and Mrs. Christie McCorkle Kerr, all of who were killed and Miss Mollie Cranstaff, now Mrs. William Clay,

Miss Sue Mundy, now Mrs. N. M. Womacks of Blue Springs [Missouri] and Mrs. Nan Harris McCorkle. The last three escaped with serious injuries.

A controversy exists today as to what caused the building to collapse. George Caleb Bingham, a prominent Kansas City Unionist, owned the building; however, General Ewing, commander of the District of the Border, had appropriated the building for army use, in this case, apparently, as an act of spite against Bingham, his political enemy. Ignoring the fact that the women were illegally held as hostages of war, Kansas historian William Connelley argued that the girls "caused the walls to be undermined" by digging under the foundation in an attempt to escape. Connelley does not explain how they accomplished this from their prison rooms in the building's *upper* floors. He said pigs also "rooted up along the walls," undermining the foundation to such an extent that during a windstorm the building collapsed. Connelley admits that Ewing was "negligent" but implies that he was not culpable.

Some commentators, like the author of the above newspaper account, suggested that the soldiers guarding the building deliberately undermined its foundation, causing the building to collapse in a heap of blood and masonry. The same writer also claimed that the merchants occupying the lower stories of the building recently moved "out their stock of groceries and whiskey which they took to a safer place." Meanwhile, the girls were left in the imperiled building, where plaster continually fell from the ceiling. The girls, the writer added, were "in a panic" over the situation. When the building finally caved in, according to this account, "Janie" (probably Mary) Anderson leaped out one of the second-story windows of the building, but the "twelve pound ball that had been chained to her ankle held her back and both her legs were broken. . . . There were groans and screams for a long time, and Josephine Anderson could be heard calling for someone to take the bricks off her head. Finally her cries ceased." Historian Albert Castel said a surgeon who watched over the prisoners alerted Ewing of the danger but was ignored. Charity Kerr, Josephine Anderson, Susan Vandiver, and Armenia Gilvey died in the collapse. Mary Anderson remained a cripple for the rest of her life. The guerrillas were enraged, and Bill Anderson, whose three sisters were in the building and who was already a violent killer, likely became psychotic in reaction to the event, for his most notorious depredations were committed after the girls were killed or injured.[7]

But the collapse of the building in Kansas City was only one of a series of events that inflamed the Missouri guerrillas about this time. Some writers have claimed that the burning of Osceola was the culminating event that precipitated the attack on Lawrence, Kansas, in August 1863. But the attack on Osceola took place in 1861, so this would have been a rather belated reaction to say the least. Other writers attributed the attack on

Lawrence to the killing of the sisters of the guerrillas. Realistically, however, the assaults perpetrated by Kansans against the people of western Missouri from 1858 through the summer of 1863 contributed to the attack on Lawrence. All of these provocations produced a psychological "boil," festering and ready to burst in an explosion of violence. It would take little in mid-1863 for something to further ignite the furor of the guerrillas, to enrage them to such an extent that they would risk their lives in what Quantrill himself called a "forlorn hope"—a last-ditch, perilous, frantic act of revenge—an attack on well-defended Lawrence, Kansas.

On August 18, 1863, at Ewing's direction, Maj. Preston B. Plumb, Ewing's chief of staff, promulgated General Orders No. 9 and General Orders No. 10. Among other things, General Orders No. 9 stipulated:

> I. Lieutenant Colonel Walter King, Fourth Missouri State Militia, will . . . make and certify a list of all such Negroes at each of such [military] stations, and of all the persons by whom the disloyalty of their master can be shown, and will deliver one copy of such list to the commander of such station and forward one to this headquarters.
>
> II. Commanders of such stations will furnish from time to time, as they may be called for by commander of escorts, copies of the list so prepared and filed with them, and will issue rations, where necessary, to Negroes named in such list who are unable to move from such station or to earn a living there, until escort can be furnished them to a place of safety where they can support themselves.
>
> III. Commanders of companies or detachments serving in that part of Missouri included in this district will give escort and subsistence, where practicable, to all negroes named in such certified lists to Independence, Kansas City, Westport, or the State of Kansas, sending direct to these headquarters all such Negroes fit for military duty and willing to enlist.

What was being enacted in General Orders No. 9 was (1) that the slave property of western Missourians, their expensive human chattel, was being taken from them irreversibly; and (2) their freed slaves, perhaps many of them, were to be enlisted into the U.S. Army to fight for the North, possibly against their old masters.

Then, propounding the injury, General Orders No. 10, promulgated at the same time, was designed to deliver the *coup de grâce*. It stated:

> I. The teams of persons who have aided the rebellion since September 25, 1862, will be taken to help such removal [of former slaves

A raid into Missouri by a black union unit. In a state where slavery was still legal as late as 1865, such raids sent shock waves through the elite class and ordinary citizens in Missouri. *The Kansas State Historical Society, Topeka*

to freedom], and, after being used for that purpose, will be turned over to the officer commanding the nearest military station, who will at once report them to an assistant provost-marshal or to the district provost-marshal, [the military police] and hold them subject to his orders.

II. Such officers will arrest, and send to the district provost-marshal for punishment, all men and all women not heads of families who willfully aid and encourage guerrillas [meaning the sons and daughters of slave owners and others], with a written statement of the names and residences of such persons and of the proof against them. . . . The wives and children of known guerrillas, and also women who are heads of families and are willfully engaged in aiding guerrillas, will be notified by such officers to remove out of this district and out of the State of Missouri forthwith. . . . If they fail to remove promptly, they will be sent by such officers, under escort, to Kansas City for shipment south, with their clothes and such necessary household furniture and provision as may be worth removing.[8]

The final gauntlet had been flung. Ewing, earlier, on August 3, 1863, had suggested to his commander's adjutant general that "the worst rebel families" be placed "in colonies on the St. Francis and White rivers in

Arkansas, with only their clothes and bedding to accompany them." General Orders No. 9 and General Orders No. 10, which came on the heels of this proposal, were a modification of that suggestion, with other measures to boot. Such draconian measures as Ewing's would be rightfully classified as war crimes in the twentieth century, yet they were ignored or glossed over by the Lincoln administration and by subsequent historians of the Border War. Only the savage act that they clearly precipitated— the Lawrence raid—has been perpetuated by most historians. The guerrillas, members of a proud class of Missourians, were aware of this new escalation in the conflict, and it surely influenced their resolve to mount a reprisal raid on the hotbed of abolitionism, Lawrence, Kansas, the home of Jim Lane and headquarters of the Red Legs.[9]

Quantrill had been agitating for a raid on Lawrence for some time. Now, in early July 1863, he called his captains together for a war council. Several accounts exist concerning what was said at the gathering; probably the most reliable one comes from William Gregg, Quantrill's adjutant. Gregg said that Quantrill exhorted the men to "go to Lawrence," saying, "It is the great hotbed of abolitionism in Kansas, and add the plunder (or the bulk of it) stolen from Missouri, [which] will be found stored away in Lawrence, and we can get more revenge and more money there than anywhere else in the state." (A number of historians usually cite the above quote as demonstrating that the guerrillas went to Lawrence for plunder, failing to note that the plunder mentioned was the former property of Missourians.) When some of Quantrill's men raised questions regarding the great risk of the operation, Quantrill answered, "I know, but if you never risk, you will never gain." It took but little effort for him to convince his lieutenants of the justification for the raid. Ominously, Anderson was especially eager.

The desire for a reprisal raid against Lawrence had been high in all their thoughts. A final council of the guerrilla chiefs, during which the details of the raid were settled, took place on August 15 at the Garrol farm south of Oak Grove. John Noland, the free black man, and Fletcher Taylor had been on spying expeditions to Lawrence, and at one of these councils, Taylor suggested that the town was ripe for an attack. The streets were wide with extensive spaces between the houses, ideal for a cavalry assault. In addition, the military personnel stationed in the town, even with the help of the townsmen, appeared insufficient to defend it if the town were attacked by surprise. It was not at all clear that a surprise was possible, however, as it meant a long, perilous ride deep into well-protected Kansas with the omnipresent likelihood of detection. Finally, the raid was agreed upon, and the various chiefs returned to their respective camps and ordered their men to clean and oil their pistols, prepare a large supply of ammunition, and mend their "war-harness." According to Gregg, the leaders "did not tell the men of the contemplated raid," doubtless to hide

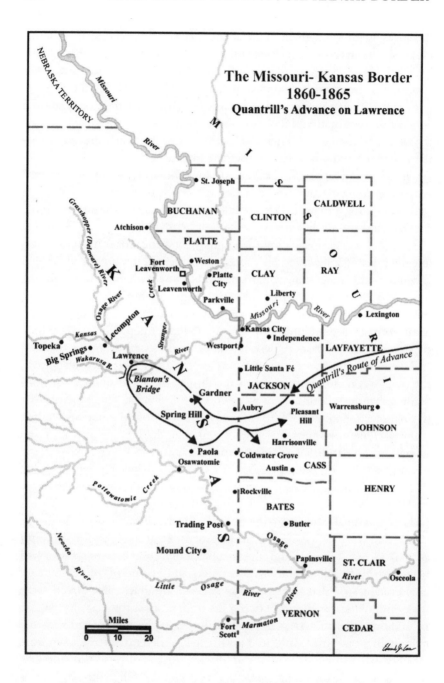

The Missouri- Kansas Border
1860-1865
Quantrill's Advance on Lawrence

the information from the spies they knew festered within their ranks.[10]

A rendezvous of the guerrillas was set for the evening of August 18 at the farm of Captain Pardee (or Perdee) on the Blackwater River in southwest Saline County. Late on that day Quantrill's band left its camp at the Cummings settlement along the Sni and headed for Pardee's farm, "twenty-four miles southeast of Independence." Guerrilla bands from Lafayette and Johnson Counties arrived at the bivouac area during the night.

The next morning, on August 19, 294 guerrillas mounted their horses and set out westward for Lone Jack. Supply and ammunition wagons and ambulances trailed the force as it wound through wooded lanes, stirring a large cloud of dust. Quantrill sent out vedettes (mounted scouts) to probe his front and flanks for signs of the enemy. The scouts returned continually with reports. Local farmers along the trail also sent signals to the partisans warning them when danger lay ahead. The column moved slowly, stopping and starting often, arriving only as far as Lone Jack by noon, a distance of only ten miles. There, the men stopped to eat and obtain forage for their horses.

After refreshing themselves and finding the area to their front relatively quiet, the guerrilla column advanced again, passing through Chapel Hill then swerving toward the southwest. Traveling in a column of fours, the men gradually picked up their pace. Soon, the sun went down and night settled in, but the guerrillas plodded steadily on through the darkness. At 7:00 A.M. the next morning, August 20, they arrived at the middle fork of the Grand River, in dense woods, just south of modern-day Belton, Missouri, at the site of a small cattle-loading enterprise called Harrelson, named after its owner. There, the exhausted guerrillas tied up their horses, made camp, and curled up and fell asleep.

Earlier that day, south of the Big Blue River, the guerrillas had been joined by 104 men under the command of Col. John D. Holt, who had just returned from recruiting men in northern Missouri for operations in the South. Taking advantage of this chance meeting, Quantrill persuaded Holt to join up with the guerrillas for the attack on Lawrence. It would "christen" his men, Quantrill promised him. Another 50 guerrillas from the Osage and Grand River valleys joined up with Quantrill at the camp on the Grand. The guerrillas, now 448 in number, were less than four miles from Kansas, which lay just to their west.[11]

At around 3:00 P.M., the guerrillas saddled up and wended westward in a column of fours, penetrating the Kansas state line approximately two miles south and three miles east of the Federal army post at Aubry. The time was around 5:00 P.M. Capt. Joshua A. Pike, commander of Company K, Ninth Kansas Volunteer Cavalry, and Company D, Eleventh Kansas Volunteer Cavalry, was reported to have one hundred men at the post. Controversy exists over why Pike did not attack the guerrillas when they entered Kansas, or failing that, why he neglected to dog and harass them after they passed into the interior of the state. Gregg said Pike's men "rode out on the prairie formed, and looked at us pass," making no attempt whatever to stop the guerrillas.[12]

Pike, however, tells an entirely different story. In his account he said

Quantrill passed into Kansas five miles south of Aubry and none of his scouts saw the guerrillas. Moreover, instead of one hundred men at his post, he said he had but "twenty-one" able to fight, a low figure that has not been substantiated. Though Pike may have been unaware of the guerrillas' presence earlier in the day, at 7:00 P.M. a local farmer reported to Pike that "seven to eight hundred men in the [guerrilla] command . . . had passed his house." The farmer said that Quantrill had posed as a Union commander and told him that his unit was on its way to Paola. (Many of Quantrill's men wore Union uniforms, so this ruse was possible.)

Later, when Pike was criticized for not attacking Quantrill as he crossed into Kansas, he claimed an attack against Quantrill would have been "suicide," the incontrovertible truth. Clearly, Pike's comparatively small force would have been annihilated by Quantrill's guerrillas had it contested them. Nonetheless, Pike was made one of the principal scapegoats for the success of the raid, primarily for his failure to warn the interior towns of Kansas, especially Lawrence, of the guerrilla threat.

Pike, once he heard of Quantrill's presence, sent a courier to his commander, Lt. Col. C. S. Clark, at Coldwater Grove twelve miles to the south, who also had troopers further south at Rockville and Chouteau Trading Post. Pike sent another courier to Capt. Charles F. Coleman at New Santa Fé, twelve miles north of Aubry along the Military Road, informing him of the guerrillas' arrival. Coleman had two companies of cavalry, or eighty men. He subsequently relayed Pike's message to Ewing at Kansas City, but Ewing was absent. Preston B. Plumb, Ewing's chief of staff, however, received the message around midnight and answered the call by mustering thirty men at Kansas City and Westport. Coleman, meanwhile, set out for Aubry, joined his forces with Pike's, and, as the senior commander, took up Quantrill's trail. Several attempts by various parties were made to warn Lawrence; all of them failed either to reach the town at all or to reach it in time.[13]

As the Federal forces scrambled to react to the incursion, Quantrill's partisans continued westward across the rolling hills of eastern Kansas, fully six hours ahead of their pursuers. After advancing ten miles into the state, Quantrill stopped at the Sims farm for supper. When it became dark, the guerrillas pressed on, traveling a little south of west for ten miles until they passed through Springhill. There, a few soldiers were spotted but ignored. Then, the partisans turned northwest toward Gardner, eight miles away, on the Santa Fé Trail. At 10:00 P.M., the moon went down, and a carpet of darkness descended on the guerrillas. The night was black and the path through dense timber was difficult to determine.

Three miles north of Gardner, sometime after midnight, Quantrill's force entered a wild area described as a "maze of creeks [and] tributaries," where it was easy to get lost. Quantrill seized local farmers one at a time to serve as guides. Guerrilla lieutenant Gregg reported that at least ten guides were taken. All eventually were shot and killed for various reasons: some lost the way; others turned out to be maverick Missourians. Once their usefulness was questioned, they were killed, partly to prevent their spreading the word of the attack in progress. As the guerrillas moved through the countryside, they periodically consulted their "death list," names of hated Kansans to be killed. Several Kansans whose names were on the list were killed, but many luckily escaped. At the home of Joseph Stone, a refugee Missourian, Stone was recognized as the man who had caused Todd to be arrested in Kansas City early in the war. Todd wished to kill Stone, but Quantrill thought the noise would alarm the area. Todd, undeterred, sent for a rope to hang him. When none could be found, a musket was brought instead. Todd made short work of Stone, beating his brains out. While at Stone's place, Quantrill took a boy, Jacob Rote, as his final guide. After traveling northwestward through a wooded maze for ten miles, the partisans neared the Wakarusa River.

When the guerrillas crossed the river at Blue Jacket Crossing, the birds twittered, announcing the dawn. The column continued to advance along the winding road to Franklin, a small village just outside Lawrence. It was becoming light, and they were getting close to Lawrence. Recognizing the need to move faster, Quantrill ordered the horses to a thundering gallop in a column of fours. Between Franklin and Lawrence, on elevated ground, Quantrill halted the troop and sent Gregg and a detachment of five men into Lawrence to test its defenses. The town, composed of more than three thousand people, was concentrated in a square mile of territory. At this point, Quantrill warned the men not to attack women, blacks, or children. Teenagers from fifteen to sixteen years old, however, were considered fair game; some of Quantrill's men were little older than that themselves.

After sending Gregg forward across the treeless prairie, Quantrill sensed that apprehension existed in his ranks, and he rode along the column yelling, "You can do as you please. I am going into Lawrence!" This said, he spurred his horse and trotted to the front of the column. The men followed eagerly. Near the southeast corner of Lawrence, two of Gregg's men met Quantrill with a report: the way was clear. Quantrill's daring venture had achieved complete surprise. Shortly thereafter two men were sent down a pathway leading to the home of the Reverend S. S. Snyder, the commander of the Second Colored Regiment. Snyder was on the guerrillas' death list with two counts against him: he was an abolitionist minister and the organizer of a black military unit. The team sent after Snyder found him milking his cow, and an explosion of pistol fire sent him sprawling dead in a pool of milk and blood.

William Gregg, Quantrill's adjutant, said that when the guerrillas entered Lawrence, Quantrill urged them, "Give the Kansas people a taste of what the Missourian has suffered at the hands of the Kansas

Jayhawkers. . . . Kill, kill and you will make no mistake."[14]

The guerrillas entered Lawrence diagonally, from southeast to north-west, crossing vacant lots and avoiding obstacles. At Quincy and Rhode Island Streets, according to a preconceived plan, some of the guerrillas left the column to form a cordon around the town. Another detachment of eleven headed to Mount Oread, a high, then-barren hill overlooking the town that gave a perfect view to the east for fifteen miles. They were to report any approaching Federals.

Quantrill's main force now surged toward Massachusetts Street, the main street in town and the site of the business district. The two military camps in Lawrence, spaced two hundred yards apart, were encountered just south of the business district and adjacent to Massachusetts Street. Encamped there were the Second Colored Regiment (ordinarily command-ed by Capt. S. S. Snyder, the man just killed), and the Fourteenth Kansas, a white unit. Gregg came upon the white unit first. The unit was housed in tents while other soldiers were asleep on the front porches of the local houses on this warm August morning. Gregg, passing the white unit, raced into the black camp and opened fire. Quantrill and the rest of the force supported him, and the main column divided and encircled both military camps. At the first firing, the men in the black camp streaked in every direction, concentrating later in hidden places in the willow brakes along the river until the raid was over. Quantrill's guerrillas charged the tents of the twenty-two white recruits, riding their horses through the guy ropes and toppling tents. Their reins clutched in their teeth, the partisans fired rapidly at point-blank range with both hands, killing every soldier visible or bulging from under the collapsed canvases. Only four or five soldiers escaped, and those miraculously. The Union soldiers had posted no guards, and their weapons had been foolishly stored more than a block away.

One of the guerrillas dismounted in front of the wrecked tents and yanked an American flag from its mooring. Tying the banner to his horse's tail, he mounted and with a loud whoop galloped up the street, trailing the Stars and Stripes in the dust.[15]

After the camp was destroyed, one of the guerrillas yelled, "On to the hotel! On to the hotel!" and the rest of the men picked up the chorus. Quantrill and Gregg, firing to their right and left, rode down Massachusetts Street and stopped at the river. Then they turned back up the street. As the main column pushed down Massachusetts Street, smaller columns went down the back streets, sealing off the business district. There was to be no escape. Designated guerrillas snipped the ferry cable joining Lawrence to the military camp on the opposite bank of the Kaw River. Nothing was overlooked.

The only chance for the soldiers and civilians of Lawrence was to obtain weapons at Palmer's gun shop on Massachusetts Street, where many of the soldier's weapons were being repaired, or at the town arsenal, in a vacant storeroom on Massachusetts Street between Winthrop and Pinckney Streets. According to Robert Gaston Elliott, "All citizens [in Lawrence] capable of service were organized into military companies and supplied with Springfield muskets." Obviously, the people of Lawrence were not "helpless" and "unarmed citizens" as some historians have claimed. They were well-armed members of home guard companies and decently trained. There was, however, considerable disorganization on the part of their leaders in Lawrence in rapidly supplying weapons to those who needed them. In retrospect, it appears that Lawrence's military leaders had been criminally negligent: the leaders of Lawrence had posted no guards; no workable contingency plan existed in case of a surprise attack; and the townsmen responded slowly and sluggishly to the threat. Quantrill had simply outgeneraled Lawrence during the raid. This humiliation has given rise to all sorts of strained excuses and alibis, which have become part and parcel of the demonization of Quantrill.

As the onslaught continued, some of the guerrillas dismounted and raided the liquor stores along Massachusetts Street. Breaking the necks from bottles, they sent the stinging liquid down their parched throats, which eased their nerves but made them more bellicose and intractable. William Bullene, looking out at the carnage from the upstairs window of

The sacking of Lawrence, Kansas, April 21, 1863. Using cavalry in its premier function—shock—Quantrill overwhelmed the town, killing 150 citizens and burning the downtown and much of the residential district. *The Kansas State Historical Society, Topeka*

his father's store, watched as one of the partisans rode his horse up to John Speer, the eldest son of the editor of the *Kansas Tribune*. The guerrilla asked Speer some questions, then pointed his revolver at him and killed him. Dismounting from his horse, the guerrilla rifled Speer's pockets. Moments later, Billy Wilkins was shot on New Hampshire between Winthrop and Henry Streets. A German returning home with a package of meat was gunned down. A carpenter, J. W. V. Thornton, who lived on the south side of Winthrop, was shot thrice, once in the shin, a second bullet in his hip joint, and a third in the face. Then, his assailant attempted to maul the man by riding over him with his horse, but Thornton's wife intervened. Guerrillas rode up and down the street "at a mad gait, firing at everyone they saw running," and screaming, "Jennison!" "Osceola!" "Butler!"[16]

Robert Gaston Elliott, who was staying in the Eldridge House at the time, later analyzed the situation:

> It had been held that only an organized army of considerable strength would dare bring its forces within striking distance of Lawrence. . . . The rapidity of their [the guerrillas'] movements and the extent of their occupancy within so short a time multiplied every estimate of their numbers; and the boldness of the invasion, the confident man- ner of the leaders, with the abandon of recklessness that everywhere marked their followers, impressed everyone with a sense of a force impossible to resist. . . . The calamity had burst upon all with such sudden and unconceived force and flashed with such terror that the will was subdued and the emotions paralyzed.[17]

The question that echoed in each man's mind was "What were [the enemy's] numbers? . . . What was this body?" The people of Lawrence had bragged that with fifteen to thirty minute's notice, they could resist and defeat any Missouri force. But they had been assaulted precipitately, with- out warning, and by overwhelming force. Elliott said, "One glance was enough to reveal the character of the catastrophe. . . . Dead bodies could be seen along the sidewalks; men pursued and shot down; any attempt at escape only provoked a fatal shot from a revolver." Elliot thought that the "the sudden dash [of the guerrillas in entering the town] cut off all chance of arming or defense, and the falling victims proved that merciless slaugh- ter had been planned as the prelude to the tragedy."

Erastus D. Ladd, another shrewd witness to the raid, said, "When they [the guerrillas] rode into the main street and commenced their hellish work, they immediately broke into squads and rushed through all the streets, killing every man they saw, probably in order to prevent any concentration or organization on our part for defense." All of these varied circumstances acted to enervate the men of Lawrence. Quantrill's principal tactic in attacking the town was to strike it hard, violently hard, using his cavalry in its most devastating manifestation—shock! Elliott said, "What had been conceived as impossible had happened." And it had happened by design, not accident.[18]

With the streets of the city under their control, the guerrillas began to congregate on the corner of Winthrop and Massachusetts in front of the Eldridge House, a four-story hotel and the frontier town's gem. Inside the hotel, some of its sixty-five occupants had earlier been roused by the gunfire. The night watch or clerk had "sounded a gong with a prolonged roll," alerting the lodgers still slumbering. As the early-morning attack had begun, Robert Stevens, a lawyer, looked out his window and heard someone shout, "Kill every damned man!" Then, he saw two men shot and killed as they tried to escape from the hotel. Stevens had looked across the street where "the two Range boys, & two other Germans, lay asleep on the plank walk, under an awning." Seconds later, horsemen rode by and shot "all 4 dead." Stevens had glanced at his watch; it read "15 minutes after five." Some of the lodgers, strangers to Lawrence, men from the East, had thought they were witnessing some sort of Wild West demonstration, but painfully it dawned on them that they were participants in a massacre. A witness said these Eastern men "paced the corridors, upbraiding the authorities for not suppressing the riot, and besought 'someone to call upon the mayor to surrender the town and stop the butchery.'" They were slow in understanding the situation.[19]

However, the guerrillas, milling about on horseback, were quick to realize that the hotel was the key to the capture of Lawrence, for the building doubled as a fort. Finally, one of the partisans rode up to the door of the hotel and screamed: "All you god-damned sons of bitches come in front! Come right out here!" A feverish conversation developed inside as to what should be done. A few thought that nothing should be done; they should remain silent and see what developed. Finally, assuming a leadership role, Alexander Banks, the provost marshal of Kansas, with the support of most of the others, concluded they should surrender—but only on condition that their safety was to be guaranteed. Banks pulled a sheet from one of the beds and draped it over the windowsill as a gesture of surrender.

Guerrillas soon poured into the hotel. Robert Stevens, who had stayed the night at the hotel after a railroad meeting, said, "Four bandits came up [stairs] & demanded watches, money, &c., which generally were given up." Stevens, cannily, had handed over his valuables to a Mrs. Bancroft, who was not searched. Some of the holed-up inhabitants, mostly the new visitors to the town, had locked their doors. The guerrillas blasted holes in the locks, burst their way inside, and robbed them. The newcomers were beginning to understand the enormity of the situation.

Still, there was no sign of Quantrill. The hotel was afire and Robert Stevens became concerned that he and the other inhabitants would be burned alive. He approached one of the guerrilla guards, an older man, and revealed a Masonic sign. When a secret sign was returned, Stevens appealed to the old man to go for Quantrill, which he did. Soon, Quantrill rode up to the hotel on a magnificent gelding captured from Col. James T. Buel at the Battle of Independence. He dismounted and with several guerrillas at his side strode into the hotel. The guerrilla chief wore a low-crowned black hat with a gold cord encircling it for a band. His shirt was of brown wool and his gray trousers were stuffed into cavalry boots. His pale blue eyes, calm and steely, looked out from under drooping lids. His hair was sandy, and he sported a dashing imperial moustache and reddish sideburns on a face that was sun beaten, dirty, and unshaven from his long ride. Four .36-caliber Colt Navy revolvers were stuffed in his waistband.

Stevens, who had previously represented Quantrill in a law case in Lawrence, "took him by the hand, led him aside, & finally got from him a promise of protection for the whole crowd"—a haven at the Whitney House, a nearby hotel. Banks demanded safe passage, which Quantrill readily agreed to. As the prisoners walked out of the hotel, chemicals in the Prentiss & Griswold drugstore on the first floor of the hotel exploded. The prisoners were marched quickly to a grassy area to the "east," where some of the guerrillas fired on them "but did no harm," according to Robert Elliott, one of the prisoners. Screaming guerrillas surrounded the prisoners, though, and demanded they be killed.

This dangerous commotion caused Stevens to call for Quantrill again. When the somewhat annoyed guerrilla chief returned, he assigned George Todd, an imposing and fiery six footer, to guard the prisoners and escort them north and east to the Whitney House (the City Hotel). Todd noticed Banks's resplendent, blue uniform and ordered him to take it off and exchange clothes with him. Now dressed in a striking Union tunic and smart trousers, Todd marched the prisoners to the Whitney House. Quantrill went along and used the hotel for his headquarters. The hotel was owned and managed by Quantrill's old friend, hotelkeeper Nathan Stone, and Quantrill wished to protect him from violence. When a general outcry to kill the prisoners arose from the guerrillas outside the Whitney House, Quantrill, according to prisoner Robert Elliott, "swore that he would do it [protect the prisoners] if he had to kill every man that interfered."[20]

Still seeking to revenge themselves on the city of Lawrence, the guerrillas attacked the Johnson House hotel, the headquarters of the Red Legs, on the west side of Vermont Street. As it developed, the Red Legs were out of town. This absence failed to dissuade the guerrillas from their need for revenge, and they attacked the house, "holding the inmates of the house responsible for them [the Red Legs]." Earlier, a black man had run down the street yelling, "The secesh are here!" Frightened by this alarming cry, some of the employees of R. C. Dix, who owned a wagon shop next door to the hotel, took refuge in the Johnson house—even Dix's own brothers, Stephen and Frank. This was not a good choice. When the guerrillas stormed the hotel, Stephen Dix was shot in the head as he retreated down the back stairs. His brother Frank was shot three times and left for dead. Frank finally crawled into a well for safety but nearly died of blood loss and exposure. R. C. Dix stayed next door at his business in an attempt to protect his employees. Soon, the guards watching over Dix and his men began firing at them. All the men fell, "seven of them dead [including Dix], and one, Mr. Hampson, wounded but feigning death."[21]

Those men were not the only ones to make a fatal mistake by hiding from the guerrillas. Lawrence's mayor, George W. Collamore, at the outset of the raid, found he and his friend Pat Keefe surrounded in Collamore's home in the northwest part of Lawrence. When guerrillas approached the mayor's front door, Keefe and Collamore dashed into a back room and descended into a dry well to hide. When the house was burned, the two men were asphyxiated. Later, J. G. Lowe lowered himself into the well by a small cord in an attempt to rescue the two men. The rope broke and he fell to the bottom of the well and also died of the noxious fumes.

As the raid progressed, the guerrillas robbed and burned nearly all the stores in Lawrence and burned many of its houses. At the home of Dr. Jerome F. Griswold, at the corner of Indiana and Winthrop Street, the doctor and his boarders, Harlow W. Baker, J. C. Trask, and S. M. Thorpe, were robbed and ordered into the street, ostensibly to be marched to the Eldridge House. The guerrillas had promised the men safe passage in return for their surrender. On the way, however, the men were shot and left for dead in the street. George H. Holt and J. L. Crane, who owned a shoe store in Lawrence, were detained and shot when one of the raiders screamed, "They have been in Missouri killing our people!"

William Gregg, Quantrill's adjutant, said, "This wholesale killing [by the guerrillas] was repugnant to many of the men, and also to many of the officers, but forbearance had ceased to be a virtue[;] our own loved ones had been murdered, robbed and insulted, there was a price upon the head of Quantrill and Anderson's sister had been murdered, and any day any of our sisters were liable to be murdered." Gregg said that when he rode to the southern part of downtown Lawrence, he found "40 shanties, built, three sides board, the fourth a hay stack, and covered with hay[;] all of these shacks were filled with household effects stolen from Missouri, much we recognized, many of these were featherbeds, quilts, blankets, &c. stacked in them higher than I could reach, fine bedsteads, sideboards, book cases and pianos that cost thousands of dollars." Lawrence was widely known as "a fence-house for stolen property" from Missouri.[22]

When the notorious James Lane, who had profited from the looting of Missouri property, heard the first racket made by the partisans, he leaped from

Rev. Hugh D. Fisher, Gen. Jim Lane's chaplain, who was on the guerrillas' "death list" when they sacked Lawrence in August 1863. After hiding in various parts of his house during the raid, including the cellar, his wife dragged him free of his burning home hidden in a rug. *The Kansas State Historical Society, Topeka*

his bed, flew to the front door of his new brick house, and removed the number plate from his front door. Lane's residence at the west edge of town was visited early in the raid. He was naturally on the death list. But since spies had informed the guerrillas that Lane was not at home, their only objective was to see his house burned to the ground. When the partisans arrived at Lane's front door and pounded on it roughly, Lane dashed out the back door and raced west into a nearby cornfield in his nightshirt, his long, bony knees pumping for all they were worth. Meanwhile, the guerrilla squad burned his house to the ground, probably including the piano he stole in Osceola.

At a nearby farmhouse, Lane located some ill-fitting trousers, a straw hat, old shoes, and an unsaddled plow horse. Riding southwest, he mobilized eleven farmers to pursue the partisans when they left town. Lane hoped to follow Quantrill, augment his numbers as he went along, and wait for army reinforcements to arrive, when they might successfully challenge the guerrillas. [23]

Lane's Jayhawker chaplain, the Reverend Hugh D. Fisher, who had freed so many Missouri slaves and was despised by the Missourians, had his home on the northwest corner of South Park visited repeatedly. Fisher, after hiding in the cellar of his brick home and suffering several close scrapes, finally escaped from his burning home hidden under a rug, dragged out of the house by his wife. Fisher hid in the bushes with a rug over his head until the guerrillas left town.[24] Many other people from Lawrence concealed themselves in the area of town called Central Park, which was west of the business district, along a brushy ravine that divided the northwest part of the town from west Lawrence. Others huddled in corn patches west of town and under high banks along the river.

Around 9:00 A.M., the raid ended. Guards atop Mount Oread reported a telltale plume of dust emanating from Captain's Creek, some twelve miles to the east. Capt. Charles F. Coleman was advancing toward the town with a large cavalry force. Quantrill ordered his men to assemble at South Park in the south-central part of town; meanwhile, Gregg was told to gather up drunks and stragglers. The rest of the men were ordered to obtain fresh horses, saddle up, and secure their plunder. They were to assemble at Blanton's Bridge, three miles south of the town on the Wakarusa River, and be ready to ride down the Fort Scott Road. Quantrill, as a parting gift, gave Jacob Rote, the young boy who had guided him to Lawrence, a horse and a new suit of clothes for his helpful efforts.

As the partisans left town, four stragglers headed for the Whitney House to settle a score with Nathan Stone and his daughter. Earlier, in an altercation between Stone's daughter Lydia and one of the guerrillas, Larkin Skaggs, Lydia's diamond ring had been stolen. When she had complained to Quantrill, he had ordered Skaggs to give it back. Skaggs did so but warned the Stones that they had not heard the last of the matter. Now that Quantrill had left town, Skaggs and his men returned to the hotel and commandeered it. Robert Stevens, who was at the hotel, said, "Four of his [Quantrill's] gang came back, (stragglers) two of them drunk, swearing they would kill young Stone, Lydia Stone, & Stevens [himself]." Stevens continued, "Young Stone & I jumped out of the window & got under the bank of the river." Meanwhile, the elder Stone was killed.[25]

After leaving the Whitney House, Skaggs stopped at the home of Mrs. Fred W. Read and attempted to burn it down. He was drunk, and as he left the house, he told Mrs. Read prophetically, "I have staid here so long I fear I shall be killed!" As Skaggs raced from town, several soldiers and some Indians began chasing him. They had crossed the river from the military camp on the opposite bank and were looking for stragglers.

Meanwhile, William Speer, the son of journalist John Speer and the brother of the recently slain John Speer Jr., had been given a gun by John Jr.'s mother and told to "go out and kill some of the guerrillas." Speer and his friend Frank C. Montgomery hid behind a hedge in the south part of town, waiting for a straggler to pass. Soon, Skaggs raced down a road toward the hedge where the two boys were hidden. Soldiers and Indians pursued him. Speer poked his gun through the hedge and fired at Skaggs, and the guerrilla fell from his horse wounded. Before Speer could approach Skaggs, White Turkey, a young Delaware Indian who had been chasing Skaggs, dismounted, shot him in the heart, and scalped him (one of the first instances of scalping in the Border War).

Larkin Milton Skaggs had been a Baptist minister before the war, and his family, historian William Connelley said, was a "good one." When journalist Charles M. Chase entered Lawrence after the raid on the town, the first thing he witnessed was "a negro rushing through the streets on horseback, dragging the dead body of a dead rebel, with a rope around his neck hitched to his saddle. A crowd was following pelting the rebel with stones." The body Chase saw was likely that of Larkin Skaggs. Later, it was said, some black people unsuccessfully tried to burn the body. Evidently, one of Skagg's fingers was sawed off to obtain his gold ring, and his body was tossed in a ravine, where his bleached bones were noticed several years later. Other accounts refer to Skaggs' body being tied in a tree and used for target practice.[26]

Some 150 male inhabitants of Lawrence were killed in the raid, and much of the town was burned to the ground. On August 23, 1863, the *Leavenworth Daily Conservative* reported the loss to the town as two million dollars in property and two hundred thousand dollars in cash. It described Massachusetts Street, the main business artery, as "one mass of smouldering ruins and crumbling walls. . . . Only two business houses were left upon the street—one known as the Armory, and the other the old Miller block. . . . About one hundred and twenty-five houses in all were burned, and only one or two escaped being ransacked, and everything of value carried away or destroyed." A supposed "spy," John Calloo, was hung on April 27, 1863, six days after the raid. He was said to have made a "confession," after which he was killed. Despite the overwhelming violence of the raid, historian Albert Castel, without minimizing that violence, called the sacking of Lawrence, from a purely military standpoint, Quantrill's "masterpiece," a "perfect combination of timing and execution."[27]

***

At midnight on August 20, Maj. Preston Plumb had left Kansas City in pursuit of Quantrill. He arrived in Olathe at dawn. By that time, smoke could be seen rising from Lawrence, some twenty-five miles away. Five and one-half hours later, at 10:30 A.M., Plumb joined up with Coleman's force some six miles southeast of Lawrence. Plumb, the ranking officer, took command of their combined forces. By this time, both officers saw a large cloud of dust and smoke rising into the sky south of Lawrence. Quantrill had advanced some six miles south of the town and was burning houses along his path. Plumb believed that Quantrill intended to strike the Santa Fé Trail on his way back to Missouri, so he turned his men obliquely in a south-westerly direction and moved across the open prairie to intercept him.

Meanwhile, James Lane was leading a ragtag group of thirty-five farmers and a handful of soldiers in Quantrill's wake. The "Grim Chieftain" had placed the men under the command of Lt. John K. Rankin, but Lane acted as Rankin's "guide." Lane's men had made contact with Quantrill as he burned the village of Brooklyn, Kansas, south of Lawrence, and they now fired sporadically on his rear guard. Lane's Kansans were poorly mounted and armed, but the senator's only purpose at this time was to maintain contact with the guerrillas, to harass them until he was reinforced. Lane's men were fleabites to Quantrill; at any time, he could reverse his course and annihilate them. But Quantrill and his guerrillas had no time to dally. They must push eastward if they were to avoid the host of Union units now converging on them from all over Missouri and Kansas.

When Lane neared Prairie City, he learned that Plumb and his men were nearby. Quantrill, meanwhile, had left the Santa Fé Trail and turned south down the Fort Scott Road for half a mile. Quantrill likely changed roads to avoid contact with Plumb or to seek a less-expected route back to Missouri. Lane sent a messenger to Plumb telling him that he was attacking Quantrill's rear guard and asking for Plumb's support. In response, Plumb sent Coleman across Ottawa Creek with two companies of cavalry to help Lane. Plumb stayed on the east side of Ottawa Creek, his object being to cut off Quantrill before he reached Ottawa Crossing, a difficult fording point that lay ahead of the partisans. Plumb's intention was to attack the front and rear of Quantrill's column simultaneously and bring on a decisive battle.

When Quantrill learned that his rear guard was being attacked, he gathered some of his men together and personally counterattacked Lane and Coleman's weak force, causing it to fall back in disarray. Quantrill led the charge, "riding recklessly, the bridle-reins on the saddle-horn, firing rapidly with revolvers in both hands." When Plumb heard the loud barrage of gunfire caused by Quantrill's fierce attack, he feared for the safety of Coleman and Lane's men and reversed his course, wisely marching to the sound of the guns and abandoning his plan to cut off the guerrillas. For his trouble, he later was accused of cowardice. Quantrill, after clearing the Federals from his rear, returned to Ottawa Crossing and managed the crossing of the river.

After fording the river, Quantrill chose sixty of his best men and formed a rear guard. For the rest of the way back to Missouri, Quantrill employed a classic cavalry tactic, placing thirty of his men at fifty-foot intervals across the rear of his force in a long skirmish rank. Another thirty-man skirmish rank was positioned parallel to the first rank but four hundred feet behind it. When Plumb's force eventually charged the guerrillas, the rear-most skirmish rank, when pressed hard, fired volleys at the bluecoats until it expended its ammunition, then it rode through the rank of thirty men behind it, reloaded, and remained in reserve until needed. The men continued to rotate in this way all afternoon. It was not often necessary for the rear guard to fire, however, because Quantrill's horses were fresher than those of his pursuers as most of the guerrillas had found new mounts in Lawrence to replace their weary ones. Quantrill told the rear guard, "Fall back on me whenever it may be necessary, but whatever you do, don't let them break your line." Periodically, the rear guard halted, which forced the Union soldiers to form into line of battle. Then the rear guard would fire a volley and ride off. This tactic gave the guerrillas in the main body a chance to rest.[28]

For the rest of the day, the grinding pursuit continued with minor skirmishing between Plumb's advance guard and Quantrill's rear guard. Plumb had given Lt. Cyrus Leland Jr. the command of the Union's advance guard. Given the more experienced men and the stronger horses, Leland harassed the guerrilla rear. These attacks, however, were largely ineffectual. Even when Leland was able to approach the guerrillas closely and challenge them, he was quite vulnerable, for Plumb and the rest of the Union troopers, mounted on tired horses, lagged far behind, out of supporting range. Because of the intense heat and their exertions, several men on both sides died of heat stroke. A number of horses also died that day, and many of the remaining horses died a few days later from the rigor of the march. They had been ridden relentlessly for over seventy-five miles in intense heat. Both forces had been active for more than twenty-four hours with no opportunity to eat, sleep, or rest. The guerrillas, to lighten their loads and speed their progress, had jettisoned much of their plunder, leaving an assortment of litter sprawling behind them.

Around sundown, the guerrillas neared Paola. Their scouts informed them that a Union force at Bull Creek blocked the way ahead. Leland was also aware of this Union force, and he ordered his men to charge the guerrillas. Quantrill, aware of the impending threat to his front, responded to the one in his rear by calling for a massive counterattack on Leland. This threw the Kansans into a wild retreat. William Gregg, Quantrill's adjutant, said the Union cavalry was driven "pell mell like a drove of sheep for half a mile or more." The rest of the Union force, commanded by Plumb, lagged so far to the rear by this time that they were of no consequence. In his official report of the sacking of Lawrence, General Ewing outrageously described this particular episode by claiming, "A skirmish ensued, the guerrillas breaking and scattering." Clearly, the guerrillas did nothing of the sort and no one pursued them as they made their way toward Bull Creek.

Quantrill now turned his men left and north along Bull Creek in the waning light. When they reached a pond, some of the guerrillas rode into the water until it covered the sides of their horses. They reached their hats down and filled them, raising the cloudy, sallow liquid to their mouths and drinking it—their first water since early that morning. Darkness now covered the prairie. After traveling several miles north, Quantrill crossed Bull Creek at Rock Ford, where a flat rock slab forms the bottom of the river. This ford provided easy passage for the wagons and ambulance. On the other side of the river, the men tethered their horses and gathered around a small knoll and along the hillside to rest. Many of the men fell asleep instantly.[29]

Meanwhile, Plumb and his men turned in for the night at Paola, surviving a somewhat harrying experience when they crossed Bull Creek, where they were almost fired on by Lt. Col. C. S. Clark's men, who had difficulty identifying them. At Paola, Plumb turned over command of the assembled forces to Clark, who was now the ranking officer. Between 1:00 A.M. and 2:00 A.M. on August 22, some of Clark's scouts returned to camp with word that the guerrillas were bivouacked at Rock Ford. Clark, however, refused to pursue Quantrill until the next morning. The guerrillas, after their early morning contact with the Union scouts, moved on in the darkness and soon brushed into Union lieutenant colonel Walter King's scouts of the Fourth Missouri State Militia Cavalry. The guerrillas, however, stole away in the darkness and pushed on into Missouri.

The Cass County Home Guards accompanying Clark the next morning, mounted on fresh horses, soon overran Quantrill's rear guard near the state line and captured three of his men. George Hoyt, the resident Red Leg, took one of the captured men aside and questioned him. After interrogating the young man, Hoyt expressed disgust at the cheap trinkets the man had stolen at Lawrence—"marbles, jewsharps, mouth organs, toys, shoestrings, cheap buttons." Hoyt shot him, saying, "I will just kill you for being a damned fool!" Apparently, Hoyt, applying his decadent standards, considered the guerrillas low-grade thieves. Hoyt, as mentioned earlier, was destined to become a future attorney general of the state of Kansas, the state's chief legal officer. Incidents like this gave him ample training in areas of jurisprudence such as judge, juror, and executioner, but gave him little practice in the finer points of the law.[30]

The guerrillas were so beset during the morning of August 22 that they were forced to abandon their ambulance, which earlier had traveled with Quantrill's advance guard under Dick Yeager. The partisans, encumbered and imperiled by the ambulance's slow speed of advance, concealed it down a wooded lane, absent its horses but filled with its wounded. The Federals quickly discovered the wagon and captured the wounded partisans. One of the wounded men, Jim Bledsoe, asked that his wounded comrades be carried out of the ambulance and placed on their knees to face their enemies as they were being executed. "Do not shoot us from behind," he requested. The Kansans complied and killed the wounded soldiers as they faced them. Kansas historian William Connelley said that "Indians" accompanying the Union force then scalped the dead prisoners (a second instance of Border War scalping). Upon hearing of this atrocity, Bill Anderson, soon to be called "Bloody Bill," would have his own grisly reply.[31]

By this time, Union forces were converging on Quantrill from every direction. The guerrillas pushed on toward Grand River, near their camp of August 20. There, Quantrill divided his force, sending half the men south down the Grand River, the rest eastward through the rolling, wooded hills toward Pleasant Hill. When the latter column of guerrillas arrived near Big Creek, west of Pleasant Hill, they ran into Lt. Col. Bazel F. Lazear's Missouri First Cavalry. The partisans melted into the woods, each man responsible for his own safety and escape. Later, Lt. Cyrus Leland Jr. captured three guerrillas near Lone Jack. He hung them from a tree at such a height, it was said, that a horseman riding underneath them could not touch their heels. Before he left the site, Leland posted a sign on the tree warning, "Don't cut them down!" The U.S. Army claimed to have killed one hundred of Quantrill's guerrillas after the raid on Lawrence, perhaps one-third of his entire force. Within six weeks, however, Quantrill annihilated eighty-seven of Gen. James Blunt's men at Baxter Springs in an engagement with a one-hundred-man detachment led by the general himself—a considerable accomplishment *if* the above Union casualty figures were accurate.[32]

Later historians have, of course, trumpeted the Lawrence raid as the worst atrocity of the entire war. Certainly murder and mayhem were the order of the day for the guerrillas. However, if the raid is placed within the context of the depredations suffered by Missouri civilians from 1858 onwards, Quantrill's opinion that "Lawrence had it coming" makes considerable sense from the Missourians' perspective.

Chapter 12

Retribution: General Orders No. 11 and Quantrill's Reply

On the evening of August 22, 1863, a day after the raid on Lawrence, Sen. James Lane met with Brig. Gen. Thomas Ewing on the Missouri border at the point where Quantrill had emerged from Kansas. Their subject of discussion was the border situation, and it was far from a pleasant encounter. At the meeting, according to one eyewitness account, Lane accused Ewing of "a milk-and-water administration of the military affairs along the border." At the conclusion of their meeting, Lane told Ewing, "You are a dead dog if you fail to issue that order as agreed between us." Considering Lane's continuing influence over Abraham Lincoln, Ewing would not have considered this an idle threat.

Nonetheless, the promulgation of the notorious General Orders No. 11, just three days later, on August 25, 1863, appears to have had no direct connection with this meeting. Orders No. 11, or something like it, was a scourge Ewing and his commander, Maj. Gen. John Schofield, had been mulling over for some time. Faced with the realization that until that point in the war their counterguerrilla policies had proven to be bankrupt and ineffective, the two men could concoct no better remedial measures than to further escalate the violence and brutality against guerrilla families and the general population. Orders No. 11 was the natural outgrowth of General Orders No. 9 and 10, issued in mid-August, but it raised the brutality to a much higher level.

The raid on Lawrence made it easier for Ewing and Schofield to institute the new, more severe policy. The Union commanders were responsible for the security of the border and eastern Kansas, and Quantrill's raid had exposed their efforts as inadequate, to say the least. Therefore, local Unionists and leaders in Washington would expect them to take immediate, dramatic, and in this case, violent corrective action. Indeed, Schofield penned a message to Ewing on August 25, the day Ewing promulgated Orders No. 11, suggesting a nearly identical, but even harsher, policy. Because the relations between Schofield and Lane were frigid at best, and Schofield was in complete military charge of the border, Lane's intimidating meeting with Ewing probably had nothing to do with the origin of Orders No. 11. It may have had a lot to do, however, with the *severity* in which the order was enforced.[1]

Ewing, on August 25, 1863, from his headquarters in Kansas City, issued General Orders No. 11, which specified in paragraph I,

I. All persons living in Jackson, Cass, and Bates Counties, Missouri, and in that part of Vernon included in this district, except those living within 1 mile of the limits of Independence, Hickman Mills, Pleasant Hill, and Harrisonville, and except those in that part of Kaw

Brig. Gen. Thomas J. Ewing, commander of the District of the Border and one of the army commanders who instigated Orders No. 11. *The Kansas State Historical Society, Topeka*

Township, Jackson County, North of Brush Creek and west of the
Big Blue, are hereby ordered to remove from their present places of
residence within fifteen days from the date hereof. . . . Officers commanding companies and detachments serving in the counties named
will see that this paragraph is promptly obeyed.

In this part of the sweeping order, Ewing banished the vast majority of
citizens of the border counties—probably twenty thousand souls—from
their traditional homes and farms, as only a handful of people lived in the
small towns of western Missouri at the time. It was also stipulated in the
order that those who proved their loyalty were exempt, but that likely
excluded at most only 20 percent of the population of the area. Moreover,
this exception was not always recognized, meaning that some of those
swearing allegiance to the Union suffered as well as those termed disloyal.
The people of western Missouri, loyal and branded as disloyal, were forced
to leave their homes, their crops, their forage, and any other items they
could not remove from the area by September 9, 1863. Because most of
their horses and oxen had been appropriated or stolen earlier, this left them
with few resources for conveying goods and belongings from the area.[2]
Later, in the twentieth century, similar ruthless acts would justly receive
international censure and be termed "ethnic cleansing." Since that concept
had yet to be invented, Ewing's action would simply be referred to in its
day as "military expediency."

The rationale behind the order was that guerrillas, in order to thrive, must
have a sustaining population to support, harbor, and feed them. It was
thought that by removing most of the people of western Missouri from
their homes and farms, the guerrillas might be eliminated from the region.
The order was an open admission that the guerrillas worked hand in glove
with the local population in their operations and received extensive popular
support. This admission provides further evidence that the claim made by
Connelley and other historians describing the guerrillas as simply bandits or
common criminals preying on both sides is without foundation.

Gen. William Halleck, general in chief of the U.S. Army, assured Ewing
that the measure fell "within the recognized laws of war" and cited
Wellington's adoption of the procedure in Portugal and the employment of
the same expedient by the Russians in the 1812 campaign.[3] Although the
orders bear some similarities to the brutal acts committed during the
Napoleonic Wars, they may be more closely compared to the deadly action
perpetrated by the British command in South Africa during the Boer Wars.
In that example, British forces attempted the same thing—to isolate enemy
combatants from the support of the local civilian population. To accomplish this objective, Britain forcibly relocated Boer families to what they
termed "concentration camps," with deadly results.

At the same time that Ewing was promulgating Orders No. 11, a number of Kansans were planning and promoting more thoroughgoing measures to revenge themselves upon the Missourians. Daniel Anthony and Jim Lane, the leaders of the movement, proposed sending an armed expedition into Missouri to regain "stolen property" taken from Kansans during the raid on Lawrence. Of course, such a rash venture could not be controlled, as all the principal U.S. Army commanders clearly understood. Had Kansans been allowed to cross the border, they would have considered themselves granted a license to kill and plunder, taking whatever they desired and killing whomever they wanted. This time, however, the U.S. Army would be held responsible for the excesses and atrocities. Schofield was far too clever to be dragged into such an obviously disastrous situation. Ewing and Schofield felt that banishing western Missourians—divesting them of their homes, their livelihoods, and much of their livestock and property—would be sufficient punishment for them, serve the needs of the army occupation force, dissuade guerrillas from infesting the area, and wash better with public opinion in the North than a public massacre and spree of thievery.[4]

Nonetheless, a large rally was held by Daniel Anthony and Sen. Jim Lane in Leavenworth on August 26, during which it was planned to meet again at Paola, Kansas, on September 8 "armed and supplied" for a fifteen-day campaign into Missouri "to search for their [the Kansans'] property and retaliate upon the people of Missouri for the outrages committed in Kansas." On September 8, the Paola meeting was held in the rain. Only a few hundred people attended, and they listened to Lane's hoarse, eccentric harangue, sometimes amused, but more often bored. The audience quickly determined that the whole affair was a joke. U.S. Army officers and their men attended the rally, too, and they intended, if need be, to suppress anyone attempting to do more than talk. Their attendance put a decided damper on Lane's windy oratory, which became less vigorous and shakier the longer he ranted. The meeting was a complete fiasco and led to nothing.[5]

In western Missouri, however, the enforcement of Orders No. 11 created a furor—and not just among the Southern sympathizers and Unionists directly affected by it. Prominent Unionists such as George Caleb Bingham of Kansas City confronted Ewing personally and railed at the "severity of the order" and demanded that it be "recalled." Bingham, a famous artist and Missouri's state treasurer, had ridden through western Missouri "unarmed and unguarded" while it was being evacuated. He had witnessed instances of men who "were shot down in the very act of obeying the order; one in which their wagons and effects were seized by their murderers; and one in which long trains of wagons loaded with spoils were heading toward Kansas." Missourians could not even defend themselves from such injustice. When Union supporters went to the military post in

Harrisonville to ask for arms to defend themselves, they were refused summarily, an act that Bingham had also witnessed.⁶ It was the Jayhawking of 1861 all over again. Bingham reported, "Large trains of wagons, extending over the prairies, and moving Kansasward were freighted with every description of household furniture and wearing apparel belonging to the exiled inhabitants." He said the raid put "an end to predatory raids of Kansas Red-Legs and Jayhawkers by surrendering to them all they coveted and leaving nothing that could further excite their cupidity."⁷

The greatest impropriety in Ewing's Orders No. 11 was not even the severity of its provisions but the people Ewing assigned to enforce them—his native Kansans, men bent on revenge. Gen. Henry Halleck believed that "all Missouri and Kansas Troops should have been removed from the border and troops from other states put in their places." Had such a logical and humane practice been instituted, much of the brutality associated with Orders No. 11 would have been eliminated. However, it was Ewing's prerogative to assign those who implemented the order, and his choice may have been due to the intimidation he received at the hands of James Lane. Because Ewing was a man with powerful political ambitions, he was susceptible to political pressures applied by Lane, the "King of Kansas politics."⁸

The practical result of Orders No. 11 was the imposition of great violence

The painting *Order No. 11*, by Unionist George Caleb Bingham. Ewing is shown on horseback in the painting, while Jennison, wearing red leggings, is shown shooting a helpless Missourian and intimidating an elderly man. *State Historical Society of Missouri, Columbia*

George Caleb Bingham, a famous Unionist artist who hounded Ewing about his inhumane treatment of western Missourians. After the war, he worked against Ewing's election to public office in Indiana. *State Historical Society of Missouri, Columbia*

and hardship on western Missourians. Martin Rice of Jackson County was one of those individuals who was loyal to the Union but experienced some of the violence directed toward residents of western Missouri. Rice read of the new order in an article in the *St. Louis Republican,* dated August 30. By the time he received word of Orders No. 11, he had already lost five precious days, time that he badly needed to remove his family and belongings and prove his loyalty. When he went to Pleasant Hill to prove his loyalty to a military official in order to gain a certificate and permit to remove his belongings to a military post, he waited all day without receiving it. Indeed, it was not until September 5 that he received the certificate. After receiving the certificate, he set out on the five-mile trip to his new home in Johnson County, near Basin Knob, but along the way a squad of the Ninth Kansas Regiment arrested him. A number of his neighbors, John S. Cave, Benjamin Potter, William Hunter, David Hunter, and Andrew Ousley, were also arrested at the same time.[9]

After questioning Rice, Capt. Charles F. Coleman, the arresting officer (the same Coleman who commanded at New Santa Fé when Quantrill crossed into Kansas several weeks earlier), told Rice brusquely: "Travel!" As Rice moved on with his wagon, he heard a series of shots and returned to learn what had happened. Upon his arrival, he found the dead bodies of his former neighbors, victims of a military atrocity. They had been accused of feeding Quantrill's men the night before. Rice likely provided the guerrillas with bread also, but he was a Unionist and apparently immune to the same punishment.

In November, Rice returned to his old home and found the neighborhood dogs acting like wolves and preying on the local livestock. Many of the local farmers, because they could not carry all their valuable property with them, buried some of it to preserve it. When one woman, Amanda Fields, returned to her home later, she found it burned, as well as her barn, outbuildings, and fences.

Bates County, some fifty miles south of Kansas City, became almost barren of population. Historian Ann Davis Niepman said that when the people of the county finally returned in 1864, "the county court tried to preserve its organization but could transact no business, there were no court sessions, no real estate transfers, no records, no taxes assessed or collected. As far as records or legal proceedings were concerned, Bates County had ceased to exist from September 1863, to the close of the war." All across the border counties stood solitary, blackened chimneys surrounded by burnt timbers, the remnants of homes and plantation houses—an entire way of life destroyed. Untended cattle, hogs, and sheep ran confusedly through the woods. Wildfires ran unchecked. The western counties became known as the "Burnt District." Such devastation as was visited upon the people of western Missouri makes even William T. Sherman's notorious March to the Sea in 1864 seem merciful

CIVIL WAR ON THE MISSOURI-KANSAS BORDER

in comparison. Nevertheless, while Sherman's march has gone down in
history as the ultimate example of his famous "War is Hell" remark, a
truer "Hell" already existed on the Missouri border a year earlier.

Lt. Col. Bazel F. Lazear, who hated Southern men, described the situation to his wife:

> It is heart sickening to see what I have seen since I have been back here.
> A desolated country and women & children, some of them almost
> naked. Some on foot and some in old wagons. Oh, God. What a sight
> to see in this once happy and peaceable country. There is no punishment
> on earth great enough for the villains who have brot [sic] this Rebellion
> about. We have put a good many of them out of the way lately. I yester-
> day had one publically [sic] shot. He was a prisoner we took the evening
> after we had the fight with Quantrill and was in the Lawrence raid. He is
> the second prisoner I have had shot and I will have every one of them
> shot I can get hold of, as such inhuman wretches deserve no mercy and
> should be shot down like dogs where ever found.[10]

It is interesting that Lazear felt no personal responsibility for what was
happening to these people, nor any culpability by the U.S. Army or the
United States; it was the enemy's fault, and the victims themselves were
blamed for their deadly predicament.

Despite its success in ridding the border counties of their inhabitants,
the military value of Orders No. 11 was questionable. There were still great
stores of grain in various parts of the border counties in 1864, and pigs,
cows, sheep, and chickens ranged the area. When the guerrillas were present, they seldom lacked food and forage. On January 14, 1864, by order of
Gen. Egbert B. Brown, supposedly "loyal" people were allowed back into
the area, and the guerrillas had access to even greater resources. The raids
against Kansas largely ceased in 1864, but this was because the guerrillas
were now being employed as scouts for the Confederate army in diversion-
ary missions and in railroad destruction in north-central Missouri as part
of Price's great raid into Missouri.

***

If the annihilation of guerrillas after the raid on Lawrence was as
thorough as Federal officers described in their reports, Quantrill should
have commanded a much weaker force when he set out in early October
1863 for the guerrillas' traditional winter home in Texas. Instead, on the
morning of October 2, Quantrill advanced toward the Grand River with
somewhere between four hundred and five hundred highly motivated
men, including the men under Col. John Holt who had participated in

the raid on Lawrence. Quantrill was likely now a full colonel (despite dis-claimers) in command of what he called the First Regiment, First Brigade, Army of the South. The command set out from Captain Pardee's farm and rode to the Grand River, where the guerrillas bivouacked for the night. The next night, the guerrillas camped near the Osage River. Then they followed the Fort Scott and Fort Gibson Road (the old "Fort Scott Military Road") toward Baxter Springs. Near that town, a crude military encampment, Fort Blair, was garrisoned by the Second Kansas Colored Infantry, commanded by R. E. Cook, and Company D, Third Wisconsin Cavalry, commanded by Lt. John Crites, who was also the garrison's overall commander. On October 5, James B. Pond had arrived at the post with part of Company C, Third Wisconsin. Crites was absent at the time, so Pond, with date of rank over the other lieutenants, assumed command of the camp.

Fort Blair consisted of a one-hundred-foot-long log structure that acted as a barracks. It was situated with the long axis running north and south and doors on the west façade. Abutting the barracks on the north and south ends and extending for some distance west were four-foot-high embankments formed of logs and dirt. They formed a three-sided, U-shaped enclosure. The west side of the encampment, where the open end of the U was located, had been part of the enclosure, but the wall had been removed recently to make room for more men and tents. A stream running east toward Spring River was just south of the encampment.

On October 6, sixty men had left the camp to forage, which left only sev-enty black troops and twenty-five white soldiers to man the camp. On the same day, Dave Poole, a guerrilla lieutenant, led the advance guard of Quantrill's force, while William Gregg commanded the rear guard. Earlier, Poole had captured a Union wagon train near Spring River. He had approached the train wielding a U.S. flag then launched a surprise attack. The captured teamsters told Poole of a Union encampment ahead, Fort Blair, and Poole sent word to Quantrill. Around noon, a portion of the guerrillas descended on Fort Blair in a charge led by Poole and Gregg. Riding into the camp, they found the soldiers eating in a kitchen area out-side the embankment south of the fort. Poole attempted to cut the soldiers off from the fort, but the men dashed helter-skelter through the mounted guerrillas, most of them making it back inside the enclosure. Lieutenant Pond, who was in his tent outside the embankment when the attack ensued, ran to the fort, commanded a howitzer, and fired on the guerrillas, disrupt-ing their charge. Some of Pond's men took up defensive positions around him. Quantrill, who reported the action later to the Confederate command, said in his report, "the negroes [of the Second Kansas Colored Infantry] took shelter behind their quarters" and "my men were compelled to fall back." About this time, Gregg heard firing to the north and galloped in that direction to discover the source. After ascending a hill to the north, he saw Quantrill arrayed in line of battle against a considerable Union force.

Purely by coincidence, Maj. Gen. James Blunt had ridden into the maelstrom. Blunt's escort, consisting of some one hundred men of Company A, Fourteenth Kansas, and Company I, Third Wisconsin Cavalry, had been traveling down the Fort Scott Military Road toward Fort Smith, Arkansas. As Blunt's unit approached within four hundred yards of Fort Blair (just

Gen. James Blunt, who narrowly escaped being killed by Quantrill at Baxter Springs. Nearly all of Blunt's men were killed in the fight. Blunt, however, escaped the battle scene on a blooded horse. *The Kansas State Historical Society, Topeka*

out of sight, over a rise in the ground), the general stopped to organize his band for a martial entrance into the post—a grand display with instruments playing and flags waving. It was Blunt and his entourage that Gregg saw facing Quantrill.

Quantrill's line of horsemen, one hundred in number, dressed in Union uniforms, faced Blunt across two hundred to three hundred yards of open prairie. Blunt first thought the partisans were Pond's men. He sent "Mr.

Capt. William S. Tough, a Red Leg (on the right), who served at times as a scout for Union army units, especially General Blunt's. That general often claimed he was searching for Red Legs to arrest; however, he commonly worked closely with them. *The Kansas State Historical Society, Topeka*

Tough" (Captain Tough, Blunt's scout, a notorious Red Leg) to determine whose force they were facing. Tough returned quickly and told him that it was the enemy. Blunt began forming his men into line of battle and closing up his headquarters train. He managed to get sixty-five of his men into regular firing formation when two of his men ran for cover. Maj. Henry Z. Curtis, Blunt's assistant adjutant general and son of Maj. Gen. Samuel Ryan Curtis, ordered the men back into line. They bolted again, followed this time by another eight men.

This was enough for Quantrill. Noticing the wavering Federal line to his front, he commanded a charge, and a thundering horde of screaming partisans descended upon the Federals. When the partisans neared the Federals, an explosion of gunfire rang out. Behind the first wave of guerrillas, a previously hidden wave of at least two hundred partisans galloped out of the timber and raced toward the Union troops. Union Company A disintegrated, the men flying in every direction. When the guerrillas neared the Third Wisconsin Cavalry, they also broke and ran, fleeing for their lives. General Blunt said his men were "completely panic-stricken" and described their actions as a "disorderly and disgraceful retreat." It was simply a rout. At a nearby ravine, many of the Union cavalrymen, in an attempt to flee the scene, attempted to leap across a deep gully, and failing that, fell into the gorge with their horses and were slaughtered.

General Blunt and Major Curtis, fleeing as well, were in the group escaping across the ravine. Curtis's horse was shot in the hip as it leaped. It faltered and the officer was tossed out of his saddle and shot in the head. Blunt, riding a fine horse, as generals are wont to do, or maybe because he was a greater horseman and smaller in stature, made the leap successfully. Blunt landed on his horse's neck then slowly squirmed his way back into the saddle and rode for his life. Apparently, he did not consider his own actions, as he had that of his men, as "a disgraceful retreat."

The members of the band, after being asked to surrender by William Bledsoe, an older guerrilla, turned on him, shooting and killing the man. Lieutenants George Todd and William Gregg, outraged at the act, approached the bandsmen. They began "waving their white kerchiefs in token of surrender." Gregg and Todd killed them all.

During the battle, a Union sergeant Jack Splane "received five balls, one in his head, one through his chest, one through his bowels, and the others in his leg and arm." As a guerrilla shot Splane, he cried out, "Tell old God that the last man you saw on earth was Quantrill." Splane miraculously survived; however, eighty of Blunt's men were killed, and another eighteen were wounded. The guerrillas lost only two men killed, while they captured two men, one a black barber named Zack, whom Todd knew personally, and another black named Jack Mann, who was killed later. Quantrill, in his official report of the battle, wrote, "We have as trophies two stand of colors, General Blunt's sword, his commission (brigadier

general and major general), all of his official papers &c. belonging to
headquarters." Blunt was ordinarily a formidable opponent; clearly, this
was not his day. Lieutenant Pond withstood the attack on his camp at Fort
Blair, and in his official report, in the racist language that was commonplace in his day, in the North and in the South, said that "his darkies
fought like devils."

After the Battle of Baxter Springs, Quantrill, who usually drank little,
became drunk and said, "By God, Shelby could not whip Blunt; neither
could Marmaduke, but I whipped him." Quantrill believed erroneously that
he had killed Blunt and Captain Tough.[11]

After the raid, on November 2, 1863, Quantrill received a message from
Major General Price through his adjutant general, MacLean, congratulating
him on his victory over Blunt. Price, through his adjutant, asked for a
report of the battle and requested that Quantrill describe

> the treatment which the prisoners belonging to your command
> received from the Federal authorities; also the orders issued by General
> Blunt or other Federal officers regarding the disposition to be made of
> you or your men if taken or vanquished. He [Price] has been informed
> that orders of a most inhuman character were issued. . . . [Price wish-
> es that] the Confederacy and the world may learn the murderous and
> uncivilized warfare which they [the Federals] themselves inaugurated,
> and thus be able to appreciate their cowardly shrieks and howls when
> with a just retaliation the same "measure is meted out to them."[12]

After leaving Fort Blair, the guerrillas made their way south, crossing
Colbert's Ferry over the Red River and continuing on to Sherman, Texas,
their traditional winter camp. After staying in Sherman a few days, they set
up camp at Mineral Creek, some fifteen miles northwest of the town. Soon,
dissension broke out in the guerrilla ranks. Apparently, the wild ways learned
by the guerrillas in their border warfare were hard for Quantrill to curb once
the men reached Texas. Many of the partisans, moreover, were resentful with
the way spoils had been distributed after the raid on Lawrence. They believed
that Todd and his men had received the lion's share. Because the guerrillas'
"spoils" were equivalent to their "salaries" and were important in sustaining
them, the inequitable distribution was a critical point of contention. The
guerrillas' dispute over this point likely led to their Christmas raid.

That Christmas, some of Quantrill's guerrillas cowed the town of
Sherman. W. L. Porter, who lived ten miles northeast of Sherman,
described the event:

> The men [the guerrillas] first got started at a House of their friends
> on Egg Nogg. They then got hold of some Whiskey & were like all
> other men on a christmas spree. Soon became wild & full of Reckless

fun . . . Some two or more rode on the Porch in the Hall [of the hotel], & the Main reception room discharged their Revolvers in front of the Hotel. Their Horses feet broke some few of the flooring in the Hall of the Hotel & they were done some damage to the furniture Mr Christian [the owner of the hotel] said the Men were his Friends & would settle for whatever damage they done to him & all others, which was done in a few days afterwards.

The guerrillas rode through the streets recklessly, screaming and firing their pistols at the local church steeples, filling them full of holes. In addition, they blasted the lock off the post office door, and after having their pictures taken at a local studio, dismantled the place. The guerrillas also rode their horses into the local grocery stores, where they allowed their mounts to break into bags of flour and eat from them.[13]

But their activities were not all just violent horseplay. About two miles south of Sherman, John Ross, Jim Crow Chiles, Andrew Walker, and Fletcher Taylor robbed and killed a Colonel Alexander. A man living on the Red River north of Sherman, a Major Butts, was also killed by guerrillas and robbed of "his Watch and Pocket Book." Both men were Confederate soldiers. Quantrill was faced with a crisis in his command. Because he was in a relatively settled area, this sort of violence could not be tolerated or condoned. Soon, some of Quantrill's men informed him that a "Lieutenant T" in his command (apparently Fletcher Taylor) had killed Butts. Quantrill arrested Taylor and some four others whom he suspected of complicity in the murders. He sent a message to Brig. Gen. Henry McCulloch, the brother of Confederate general Ben McCulloch, who had been killed at Pea Ridge, and the commander of the Sub-District of North Texas, requesting authority to court-martial the guilty party or parties. Meanwhile, the men who were guarding the prisoners deliberately allowed them to escape with their horses and equipment.[14]

Quantrill, thoroughly incensed, summoned his men and asked those who had been robbing people in Texas to step forward. He told them to "acknowledge their guilt & Promise that they Would Never again repeat it & that they could remain in the command the same as ever & He would not Permit them to be punished for it." He also said that "if they did not acknowledge it [their guilt] then & there, & if it was afterwords Proved against one of them that they Were Guilty of Violating the Law, that he would not shelter them." None of the partisans stepped forward. Quantrill then told the men that "if there was any Man or any Men in his Command, that did not like his style of commanding them, or if any of them wished to withdraw from his command, they could take their Horses, & Weapons and they were Welcome to leave and go where they pleased." Anderson, who had defended the prisoners from the outset, and may have been instrumental in their escape, immediately replied that he, for one, didn't approve of Quantrill's style of leadership. Anderson and eight of his men promptly rode out of the camp. Quantrill's command was disintegrating.[15]

Meanwhile, Bill Anderson, Fletch Taylor, and some of Anderson's men went to see General McCulloch at Bonham, Texas. In a private interview with the general, Anderson lied to him, telling him that Quantrill had ordered Taylor to kill Butts and that he was the spirit behind the lawless, violent behavior of the guerrillas. McCulloch, who had never been friendly toward Quantrill, summoned him to Bonham. When Quantrill arrived in town for the meeting, McCulloch, instead of asking Quantrill for his side of the story, as most commanding officers would have out of respect for a high-ranking colleague, simply informed him that he was under arrest and would be placed on trial. Then, oddly enough, McCulloch invited Quantrill to accompany him to dinner. Quantrill, shocked and livid with rage, answered, "By G—d, I do not care a G—d d—n if I never taste another mouthful on this earth." McCulloch left Quantrill under the guard of two privates and dined alone.

Quantrill, in the custody of these two men, likely was escorted to the office of the general. Pretending to cross the room to get a drink of water, Quantrill leaped on one of the guards and seized his weapon. Then, he disarmed the other guard. Locking both men in the room, Quantrill rushed down the stairs into the street. There, he ran into two more guards and disarmed them as well. Quantrill shouted to his men across the street: "Mount Your Horses Men We are all Prisoners here." As the partisans raced out of town, Quantrill sent one of his best-mounted men ahead to alert Todd of their situation. He was to bring ammunition and camp equipment and meet Quantrill and the rest of the men along the Sherman and Bonham Road near Bois d'Arc Creek.

In the meantime, McCulloch ordered Colonel Martin's regiment to capture Quantrill and "bring him back to Bonham dead or alive." Bill Anderson and Fletcher Taylor and their men joined up with Martin in pursuit of their old commander. At Bois d'Arc Creek, Anderson ran into Todds' men in the timber along the river. When Anderson and Taylor approached, Todd ordered his men to fire at their old comrades. When Anderson recognized Todd's men, he called out "that if they [Todd and his men] were not a damb [sic] set of cowards, to come out of the Timber in the Open Prairie and fight him like men." Todd remained in the woods and shouted back, "You have the Most Men and if You are not a set of God Damb cowards, come in here and take us out." Anderson wisely declined. Martin's force finally caught up with Quantrill and Todd, but just as they crossed the Red River, out of McCulloch's jurisdiction.[16]

Quantrill's feud with Taylor and Anderson was not the only instance of dissension within the guerrilla ranks. When the partisans had arrived from

Missouri, William Gregg had had a falling out with George Todd, Fletcher Taylor, James Little, and John Barker, whom Gregg had earlier called "thieves" for their failure to divide the spoils after a raid at Plattsburg, Missouri, where six thousand dollars was taken. Cole Younger and John Jarrette had warned Gregg that Todd would kill him. Gregg, however, refused to back down, and when he arrived in Sherman, he went to Quantrill's camp and asked him for a leave of absence so that he could report to department headquarters for a new assignment; he thought the guerrilla force was unraveling and had spent itself. The next morning, Gregg passed his enemies in Sherman and heard Todd say to Taylor, "There goes that S—of a B—; now kill him." Taylor replied, "I will not kill Gregg. He is a Southern man, and he has been a good soldier and officer. If you want him killed you will have to kill him yourself." Gregg subsequently joined Shelby's brigade and became a captain in Company I, Shank's Regiment.[17]

The discord in Quantrill's ranks continued to grow. Todd, who had functioned as Quantrill's right-hand man, had grown in the esteem of the rank-and-file guerrillas to such an extent that he now overshadowed Quantrill. Todd, an aggressive, natural leader, was fearless in battle to the point of foolhardiness and was much admired by the young guerrillas. Now, he was impatient to hold the dominant position in the guerrilla movement despite Quantrill's exhibited strengths as a commander. Consequently, Todd's followers elected him as captain of the guerrilla company. Quantrill's only pretension to power now was as the commander of a nonexistent regiment. The guerrilla force had lost its cohesion and solidarity, and its centralized command structure was faltering.

Chapter 13

End Game: Price's Raid and
the Death of the Guerrilla Chiefs

During the middle of March 1864, earlier than their usual migration north, Quantrill and his men left Texas with the intention of renewing the guerrilla war in western Missouri. Though the winter had proven to be a disaster for the guerrilla bands, the summer and fall of 1863 had seen their greatest triumphs. They had been able to strike almost at will. Lawrence and Baxter Springs had demonstrated they not only could take the war to the enemy, but when conditions were right, they could also defeat large Federal formations. But the winter camp in Texas had witnessed the crumbling of discipline and the falling out of the principal leaders. Having been in the bush for most of 1863, the men desperately needed rest and recuperation. They didn't get it. Still exhausted by their exploits of the previous year, the guerrillas trudged northward and reengaged in the seemingly unending war. Quantrill's personal ranks were depleted, and only forty or fifty men accompanied him north. Gregg was no longer with him, and Bill Anderson and Fletcher Taylor were hostile to him and had struck out on their own. As Quantrill and his men proceeded, they found little food or forage either in the bleak Texas countryside or on the route north. Constantly mounted on horseback, they swam the Red River and most of the other rain-swollen streams between Texas and Missouri. When they arrived in Johnson County, Missouri, their horses were jaded and the men hungry, exhausted, and discontent. They met local militias that were well mounted and rested, and the militias assailed them furiously. The chase was on.

The problems faced by the guerrillas were compounded by the internal strife of the small band. William Gregg stated that after the guerrillas' first day back in Missouri, Todd and Quantrill had a falling out that ruptured their relationship permanently. Gregg said, "[Quantrill] trusted Todd and Todd betrayed him." Evidently, Quantrill and Todd had been playing seven-up (pitch) for one hundred dollars a game, very high stakes, when an argument broke out between the two men. Quantrill accused Todd of reneging, to which witnesses agreed. When the argument intensified, Quantrill said that he was "not afraid of any man," whereupon, Todd drew his pistol, stuck it in Quantrill's face, and demanded that Quantrill admit he was afraid of him. Those watching the altercation thought Todd wished to kill the man and this was his pretext for doing so. Apparently, Quantrill believed so too, for he backed down prudently and became estranged from Todd thereafter. Quantrill spent most of the summer of 1864 in Howard County with Kate King (a.k.a. Kate Clarke), his young, attractive lover (some say common-law wife), and Todd soon reported to Gen. Sterling Price that he, Todd, was in charge of the guerrillas. When Price and Shelby refused to support Quantrill in his claim to leadership of the guerrillas— possibly in reaction to the great public outcry against him after the Lawrence raid—the guerrilla chief became embittered toward them.[1]

Despite the fallout, the guerrillas' activities continued uninterrupted, and Todd resumed his usual activities. On July 6, he attempted an attack on Brig. Gen. James Totten, inspector general of the Department of the Missouri, who Todd believed was traveling on the road from Independence to Pleasant Hill. Totten, however, had changed his route at the last minute and instead traveled through Hickman Mills. Todd, as he traveled down the Pleasant Hill Road in search of Totten, ran headlong into Capt. Seymour W. Wagoner's Company C, Second Colorado Cavalry, which was scouting two miles south of the Little Blue River. Gunfire erupted and Wagoner and seven Union men were killed and one wounded. Federal accounts say Wagoner, who commanded only twenty-five men, killed eight guerrillas out of an alleged force of one hundred. No guerrilla bodies, however, were left behind to support the claim. William Gregg, in contrast, reported that it was the guerrillas who were "outnumbered" and that the Colorado troops were "worsted."[2] Dual, usually conflicting Southern and Northern accounts are commonplace in Civil War reports.

The manhunt for the guerrillas continued relentlessly. A week after Wagoner was killed, on July 14, a 150-man Union unit led by Col. John G. Phillips entered the small town of Wellington, Missouri, near the Missouri River in Lafayette County. It was 10:00 A.M. on a Sunday morning. Phillips questioned a local "contraband" (freed slave) concerning guerrillas in the area and was informed that a marriage ceremony was in progress at Warder's Church nearby and that partisans were participating. One of the guerrillas, apparently, was getting married. Phillips sent 50 men to the church.

In his official army report, Phillips mockingly described the scene at the church when he arrived, saying that the Union soldiers found "a Hardshell [minister who] was in the habit of preaching to the 'Brushers' the riches of good whisky and guerrilla warfare." As the troopers approached the church, Phillips said,

> The cry of "Feds" "Feds" thundered from the audience. . . . The women and children screamed with terror, and rushing wildly from the church, exhibited a method in their madness by throwing themselves

in front of the rebel outlaws. [Union] Captain H. [Henslee], whose
presence of mind is equaled only by his gallantry, rode out and commanded the women to "squat." Five bushwhackers were killed outright, the sixth mortally wounded, and one or two, despite all vigilance,
made their escape amid the furore [sic] and confusion.

Col. Egbert B. Brown, the Union district commander, bragged later that
one of the guerrillas, Wilhite, "had twenty-eight balls through him and in
him, and another guerrilla eighteen, no person but the guerrillas was hit by
our men." Then, he added cynically, "The guerrillas, people, and priest
seemed to be worshipping together as innocent as lambs."[3] How many of
the dead were actually guerrillas or whether they were merely unfortunate
wedding guests is impossible to determine.

Conditions were even more unsettled north of the Missouri River, in the
northwest section of the state, than south of the river. Red Legs and
Jayhawkers, now officially sanctioned Union forces, had tormented the area
since 1862, and the other Union forces allotted to the area had been unable
or unwilling to contain them. To relieve the people of the area, General
Schofield had mustered into service Enrolled Missouri Militia units composed of ordinary, loyal Missourians. But even these units were insufficient
to quell the disorder. Governor Gamble, apprised of the problem, suggested to Schofield that he muster in formerly "disloyal" Missourians, former
members or deserters of the Confederate army, to fill the necessary manpower requirement.

The danger in mustering in these men was that soldiers were being armed
who might not remain loyal under all circumstances. Should Gen. Sterling
Price lead a raid into Missouri or attempt to reoccupy the state, for instance,
such militiamen might join him. Schofield and Gamble nonetheless authorized the enrollment of the Eighty-first and Eighty-second Regiments,
Missouri Enrolled Militia, and the men were armed for northwest Missouri
duty under General Orders No. 24. Schofield placed the soldiers under the
command of Col. James H. Moss, at that time commander of the Forty-
eighth Regiment, Enrolled Missouri Militia, a man thoroughly qualified to
lead them. The choice, however, was unsettling to many Unionists. Moss, it
became known, was the second cousin of Pres. Jefferson Davis of the
Confederacy, and his brother-in-law was Confederate colonel John C.
"Coon" Thornton, a Southern recruiter who was known to be currently
recruiting in northwest Missouri dressed in a Confederate officer's uniform.
Soon, Moss's regiments were called derisively the "Paw Paw Militia" for
their tendency to cozy up with the local partisans. Around June 30, 1864,
Moss was removed from his command, but much damage, from the Union
perspective, had already been done.[4]

Brig. Gen. Clinton B. Fisk, the commander of the Northern District of

Missouri, became so alarmed by the Paw Paws' activities that he ordered all the men enrolled in the Eighty-first and Eighty-second Regiments to turn in their arms at the St. Joseph Armory. Many of the men enrolled in the regiments, however, fled with their guns. Exacerbating the situation, in June 1864, "twenty-three kegs and 150 cans of gunpowder were discovered on the premises of four of the first families of St. Joseph." The powder, it was learned, was the same as that stolen from Camp Jackson three years earlier. Meanwhile, during June, Paw Paw militiamen allowed seven guerrillas to escape from a St. Joseph jail. Because 50 percent of Fisk's militiamen were Paw Paws, he believed they were thoroughly unreliable.

When Maj. Gen. William S. Rosecrans (who had been relieved of his field command after losing the Battle of Chickamauga in September 1863) replaced Schofield as commander of the Department of the Missouri, he finally addressed Fisk's plight and asked him for a report detailing the precise status of the Paw Paws. In his report, Fisk told Rosecrans the Paw Paw militias had allowed Confederate colonels John H. Winston and John Thornton to recruit at will in northwest Missouri. While Winston had been captured in March 1864 by Captain Kemper, Ninth Cavalry Missouri Militia, Thornton continued to operate free of all interference. By June 1, Thornton had enlisted five hundred men, all of whom remained in the northern border counties awaiting orders to move south to join the Confederate army.

On July 10, 1864, Thornton's men raised the Confederate flag over the town of Platte City, some fifteen miles north of Kansas City, and tore down the American flag, cutting it into swatches which they "fastened to their horses' heads." Meanwhile, five companies of Paw Paw militia in Platte City threw in their lot with Thornton. Soon, nearly every man in town was dressed in Confederate gray. St. Joseph's Paw Paw militia also joined up with Thornton, giving him some eight hundred men, a sizable, though inexperienced, force. This dramatic incident awoke Union commanders in the district to the crisis. Rosecrans, in response, assigned more Federal troops to the area, and Missouri's new governor, Willard P. Hall, sent Missouri militia units. The Federal commanders knew something had to be done about the insurgents in northwest Missouri immediately since both Union commanders and Paw Paw militiamen were aware of a rumored, impending attack into Missouri by Gen. Sterling Price.[5]

On July 13, a Union force "700 to 1,000 men strong," commanded by Col. James H. Ford of the Second Colorado Cavalry, marched out of Weston, Missouri, and attacked Thornton and three hundred of his men near Camden Point, Platte County, in a surprise attack, killing ten rebels and scattering the rest. A Clay and Platte County historian said that Ford shot three Southern soldiers in the attack, captured another then shot him, and took three other men prisoners, Andrew Smith, Peter Clements, and

Jesse Wytes, who were subsequently "shot—murdered without even the form of a court-martial." Ford said that soon after attacking Thornton's men at Camden, he "killed 25 [more]." Ford said he had "killed no civilians, although many of them need killing." Thornton's recruits, now said to be fifteen hundred in number, were hunted down like wild animals. For this purpose, Fisk divided the northwest counties into sectors, and the loyal militiamen drove Thornton's men ahead of them, as in a traditional wolf hunt, forcing them south toward the Missouri River. During this drive, Federal forces allegedly killed some two hundred men and captured one hundred. On July 17, Captain Moses, after an intense fight seventeen miles northwest of Liberty, killed "16 and wounded 21" of Thornton's men, losing "6 killed, [and] 4 wounded." Many of Thornton's men, nonetheless, managed to cross the Missouri River to relative safety.

Colorado militia/volunteer units like Colonel Ford's became notorious during the war, as some of their brethren perpetrated the infamous Sand Creek massacre in which dozens of Cheyenne men, women, and children were mercilessly gunned down without provocation. The Coloradan's commander, Chivington, when asked if his men should spare the Indian children, remarked callously, "Nits breed lice," and sanctioned the murders. Now Colorado troops were also guilty of murdering Confederate POWs in Missouri.

During this series of attacks, twenty houses in Camden Point were burned and the "principal part" of Platte City was destroyed. Along the way to Platte City, Ford's men, jointly commanded by Jennison, killed "Mr. Geo. M. McCuer, one of the oldest and most highly esteemed citizens in the county." Though he "had taken no part whatever in the war, [Union soldiers] shot him down in his own door." The father of A. R. Jack, the cashier of the bank in Platte City, was shot at in his front yard. Only the Christian Church in Platte City was saved since Jennison, who was directing the attack, favored it because of his wife's membership in that denomination. As Ford and Jennison traveled to Platte City, they also killed John Rogers, a man named Masterson, a boy named James Redman, and a Mr. Hall and Abram Estes, two farmers. As Jennison and Ford plundered their way through the country, they took "horses, wagons, harness, saddles, household goods, wearing apparel, meats, provision of all kinds—everything that a foraging party of thieves would be expected to lay their hands on. . . . They had over 100 head of horses with them, and a regular caravan of plunder. . . . They loaded 400 pounds of bacon into a wagon from Bradley Cox's smokehouse and carried it off to relieve the grasshopper sufferers in Kansas."[6]

***

The rumored raid by Price into Missouri became a reality in August 1864, when Gen. E. (Edmund) Kirby Smith, after a conference and interview with

Maj. Gen. Sterling Price, commander of the District of Arkansas, sent instructions to him on August 4 and 11 ordering him to invade Missouri. Price promptly commanded Brig. Gen. Joseph O. "Jo" Shelby to attack "Devall's Bluff and the railroad between Little Rock and the White River." The purpose of this attack was to divert the attention of Union forces while Price took the preponderance of his army across the Arkansas and White Rivers and marched north to Missouri. Shelby performed the mission with his usual éclat, capturing four hundred Federals and killing and wounding three hundred.[7]

By September 15, the various components of Price's army, called the "Army of Missouri," had joined him at Powhatan, Arkansas. From that town, they marched north to Pocahontas, Arkansas, 18 miles away, arriving there on September 16. Price, at this point, divided his army into three columns of three divisions, ordering them to converge on Fredericktown, Missouri, some 140 miles to the north-northeast. The army was sent by separate columns to ensure that forage and subsistence were obtainable for horses and men as they moved through the rugged hills. The columns passed into Missouri through Ripley County, in the southeast part of the state, led by Shelby on the left with two brigades, Brig. Gen. James F. Fagan in the center with four brigades, and Maj. Gen. John S. Marmaduke on the right with two brigades. Once the divisions arrived in Fredericktown, Price spent two days obtaining arms, shoes, and clothing for them and mustering in new recruits.[8]

According to Price's assistant adjutant general, Maj James R. Shaler, Price's army, at the outset, contained seven thousand men, two thousand of them unarmed, "mostly deserters." Price, however, said that he had "8,000 armed to 4,000 unarmed men," but this tally may have been taken later. The army's artillery included fourteen guns. The expectation was that great amounts of arms and supplies would be captured along the way and the army would become much larger in size through mustering in Missourians loyal to the South as they proceeded. Gen. Kirby Smith's orders to Price were to fill "the weak [skeletonized] brigades" and "scrupulously avoid the organization of any new brigades."

At a court of inquiry convened after the completion of Price's raid, Major Shaler said, "There was no discipline [in Price's army] when it began and during the campaign, and at its conclusion there was all the disorder that must necessarily obtain in an undisciplined command." Shaler said that because the army was composed of "conscripts, absentees without leave from their commands and deserters, and but a few volunteers," and because the army enlisted conscripts in relatively large numbers along the way, "as many as 10,000," "it was impossible to inaugurate any system of discipline." Price's army, therefore, was a loose-knit one, nearly a mob, and subject to breakdowns and confusion. Capt. T. T. Taylor, Price's assistant adjutant general, when he was asked to what he attributed the "bad discipline of the army," answered, "Two-thirds of the army were deserters from commands south of the Arkansas River and to the want of the enforcement of discipline by subordinate generals."[9]

Gen. Kirby Smith told Price at the outset of the raid: "[Your] object should be, if you cannot maintain yourself in that country, to bring as large an accession [of new recruits] as possible to our force." Smith added, "Make St. Louis the objective point of your movement, which, if rapidly made, will put you in possession of that place, its supplies, and military stores, and which will do more toward rallying Missouri to your standard than the possession of any other point." Kirby Smith offered one final suggestion to Price: "Should you be compelled to withdraw from the State, make your retreat through Kansas and the Indian Territory, sweeping that country of its mules, horses, cattle, and military supplies of all kinds." Historian Edgar Langsdorf has cited another implicit purpose behind Price's raid. He said, "Price as a practical politician was undoubtedly hopeful that his occupation of the state would have a considerable effect on the forthcoming Presidential election, in which the South ardently desired the defeat of Lincoln by George B. McClellan." McClellan, it was hoped, would negotiate a peace with the Confederacy and end the war. Besides the above reasons, a raid into Missouri would divert troops from the Eastern battlefields or troops on the way to those battlefields to the trans-Mississippi theater of operations, relieving pressures on the Confederate army in the East and South.[10]

Price's first objective in Missouri was the capture of Pilot Knob and nearby Fort Davidson. Once Price's movement north was reported, Brig. Gen. Thomas Ewing Jr. assumed personal command of the fort and its defenses. To ensure that no further Federal troops interfered with his army while it seized the fort, Price sent Shelby's division to the areas adjoining Pilot Knob in order to destroy the railroad and burn the bridges at Irondale, Big River, and Mineral Point, thereby slowing or preventing the arrival of Union reinforcements. To accomplish his mission, Shelby moved rapidly forward and charged into Potosi, driving its 150 defenders into the cover of the courthouse. Shelby brought up his artillery and "five rounds brought the white flag," he said.[11]

By September 27, Generals Marmaduke and Fagan had closed on Pilot Knob and Fort Davidson. A Southern artillery officer, after examining the fort with a telescope from nearby Shepherd's Mountain, discovered that it was an "irregular, octagonal earthwork" emplaced with seven heavy guns: "four 32-pounder siege guns and three 24-pounder howitzers en barbette." The post, the Confederate officer concluded, was "over garrisoned" and contained some fifteen hundred men. Capt. T. J. Mackey of Price's corps of engineers believed the fort contained "no bomb or splinter-proof shelters for the troops," thus it could be brought to its knees easily by artillery. An all-out bombardment of the fort, however, was found to be unrealistic. Ewing, the Southerners claimed, "had forced Southern residents [of the area], old and young, including boys, into the works from the college of Arcadia" to help protect the fort against bombardment.[12] If that claim was correct, Federal commanders in Missouri once again had illegally resorted to using civilian hostages, a clear violation of the "laws of war," which Halleck supposedly held in such high regard.

Two guns, twelve-pound Napoleons, from Marmaduke's division were placed on the east end of Shepherd's Mountain. They were used sparingly against the fortifications, however. At about 2:00 P.M., Price's artillery opened fire at a range of twelve hundred to fifteen hundred yards, and the Battle of Pilot Knob was joined. As the big guns exploded, Fagan and Marmaduke's divisions charged the fort en masse. In response, the Union artillery units outside the walls of the fort fired double-charged canister at the Southerners. As the Confederates approached within one hundred yards of the fort, the Union artillery began displacing into the fort. In the process, the lead horse of one of the foremost teams was shot down, and the gun had to be abandoned. During the chaos, the rest of the Union horses stampeded and had to be shot to prevent their carrying off the guns and carriages to the enemy. Some forty horses were wounded or killed in this way. When the Southerners drew to within "thirty paces" of the fort, the Union fire became so intense that they were forced to turn back, which caused them to suffer heavy casualties (the usual result in forced retreats). The Union troops, too, received heavy casualties.

Around midnight, recognizing the futility of continuing to defend the fort and expecting the Southerners' next charge to carry it, Ewing had his remaining cannons spiked and a long fuse run to the fort's magazine. Between 2:00 A.M. and 3:00 A.M., February 28, the Union soldiers abandoned the fort, and the fuse to the magazine was lit. Ewing ordered the entire garrison to march down the Caledonia road toward Webster, some thirty miles away, where he encamped that night. The soldiers were miles away before the fuse ignited the magazine. Evidently, Price had posted no guards because he had not expected Ewing's retreat. As a result, Ewing and his force were able to slip away initially unnoticed and unmolested. This was a serious oversight since the Confederate commanders had expected to launch a successful charge against Ewing's troops the next morning.[13]

Shelby, who had been conducting operations at Potosi, now marched his men toward Pilot Knob. On the way, Shelby received word from Price that he should join Marmaduke in the pursuit of Ewing. On Thursday, September 29, about 10:00 A.M., the two generals overtook Ewing and attacked him fiercely. Ewing, to prevent being flanked, proceeded down mountain ridges, finally arriving at Harrison's Station near Leasburg at sunset. Frantically, his men began unlimbering the artillery and building fortifications from available rail-road ties. Ewing reported, "A cut for the railroad track gave shelter for the horses." The Confederates continued their attack the next day, but Ewing's position was relatively impregnable unless the Confederates were willing to take heavy casualties, which they were not. On October 1, hearing of the advance of Union general John B. Sanborn's cavalry from Rolla, thirty-five miles away, Shelby and Marmaduke abandoned the area at midday. Ewing had received 20 percent casualties during the entire engagement and had narrow-ly escaped disaster.[14]

Though Ewing was ill-matched for Price's force, the Union army had made some preparations for the Confederate advance. As early as September 6, in anticipation of Price's move north, Gen. William S. Rosecrans had wired Maj. Gen. Henry Halleck asking him to divert Maj. Gen. J. Smith's division—then passing through Cairo, Illinois, on its way to Sherman's army—to help fight Price. Once these troops were relocated and their movement had come to Price's notice, the Confederate general realized that St. Louis was no longer a viable target, and he moved his forces west-ward, taking the German American enclave of Hermann on October 5 and advancing on Jefferson City, the state's capital, two days later with the inten-tion of seizing it. In the meantime, anticipating Price's objective, the deft Rosecrans had ordered Brig. Gens. John McNeil and John B. Sanborn, who were stationed at Rolla, to move their forces north in defense of the capi-tal. With their arrival, Brig. Gen. Egbert B. Brown, the commander at Jefferson City, had seven thousand defenders, as well as formidable rifle pits and earthworks in place. Besides Sanford and McNeil's units, Rosecrans sent another forty-five hundred men of the Third Division, XVI Corps, after Price from St. Louis, commanded by Brig. Gen. Edward C. Pike.

Price left destroyed bridges in his wake and eventually made a demon-stration before Jefferson City. He concluded, however, that its seizure was beyond his grasp. Rosecrans, meanwhile, sent Maj. Gen. Alfred M. Pleasonton, a formidable Union cavalry commander, to assume com-mand of all Union forces at Jefferson City. Arriving in town on October 8, Pleasonton formed what he called the Provisional Cavalry Division, composed of brigades commanded by Gens. John McNeil, John. B. Sanborn, Egbert B. Brown, and Col. Edward F. Winslow. Once he was organized, Pleasonton sent Sanborn in pursuit of Price with "all the available cavalry, 4,100 men," formed into four brigades. They were under the command of Brown, McNeil, and Sanborn, and Winslow's cavalry brigade from Major General Smith's command. A section of artillery was attached to each brigade.

Price's apparent numbers evidently awed the Federal generals, and they never seemed to suspicion that much of his army was *unarmed*. Price was aware of their blindness and sometimes cleverly positioned his men as if they were heavily armed troops, as during the crises at the Battle of Westport and the Battle of Mine Creek (referred to later).[15]

Sanborn finally overtook and attacked Price's rearguard at Versailles, sixty miles west of the capital, and reported to Pleasonton that the Confederates were headed for Boonville, Missouri. On October 10, Price marched into that town, where, according to a Confederate report, "all the people turned out to greet us." While at Boonville, Price met with the guerrilla chiefs, Bill Anderson and Quantrill. He ordered Anderson and his one hundred men to tear up the tracks of the North Missouri Railroad and Quantrill to destroy the Hannibal & St. Joseph line. Anderson took this opportunity to present Price, whom he much admired, with a brace of silver pistols. Quantrill, who had learned to dislike Price, received his orders but made no effort to carry them out, possibly because he lacked enough men, but perhaps because he simply disliked the commander. Obviously, though, the Missouri guerrillas were expected to work hand in hand with the Confederate army, and usually they did, from start to finish.[16]

***

As Price was beginning his march into Missouri, the guerrilla offensive continued in the border counties. Union brigadier general Clinton B. Fisk, commander of the District of Northwest Missouri, sent a message dated August 13, 1864, to one of his officers, Maj. H. Hilliard, commanding him: "Let all your fighting material be placed on a war footing to chase and kill their desperado-organized expedition, to follow him until he [Bill Anderson] is dead; and compel this party to be exclusively an Anderson extermination party. Bushwhack him with dismounted men, and compel citizens to cooperate in the chase after him. If he will not fight you, fight him."

On August 28, 1864, an ominous new development in the guerrilla war occurred. On that day, Union captain Parke crossed the Missouri River with forty-four men in pursuit of a guerrilla named Clifton Holtzclaw. Near Rocheport, Parke came upon two of Holtzclaw's men and fired on them, wounding one, he believed. These men, apparently, were a decoy, for after advancing a mile, Parke was struck in the rear by a force estimated at one hundred, commanded by Holtzclaw and Bill Anderson. After a fight of fifteen minutes, Parke lost seven men killed and two wounded. The army report of the encounter tersely announced scalping: "four [of the Union soldiers] being scalped, one hung and scalped; three had their throats cut." Union commanders were discovering that guerrillas, like tigers at bay, are dangerous animals, indeed. Since the guerrillas were being executed upon capture, they had nothing to lose by their brutal retaliations.

On September 14, Union major Austin A. King reported killing six guerrillas, five of them Anderson's men, "their bridles being decked with humans scalps." On September 22, Anderson and his men attacked a Union supply train in the Perche Hills, "killing twelve soldiers and three Negro teamsters." This time, six of Anderson's men were overtaken, killed, *and scalped.* Now it was U.S. soldiers doing the scalping. As American soldiers discovered during the Vietnam War, psychological pressures operate on the chaser as well as the chased. Whether the actions described are in Bosnia, Afghanistan, the Middle East, or the Middle West, violence engenders reciprocal violence, and the level of violence intensifies over time. History has demonstrated that partisan warfare is especially brutal. The war on the Missouri border was no exception.

On September 24, Anderson and his men attacked Fayette, but the "provost guard" of the town fought desperately from the local courthouse, a stockade north of town, and the Female Academy building, driving off the partisans and killing "11" of them while "capturing 12 horses." Quantrill had been invited to participate in the raid on Fayette but had refused. He complained that "the place was too heavily garrisoned, that nothing would be gained, and that a lot of lives would be lost." Some of the guerrillas laughed at their old leader and remarked about "his sand being gone." Quantrill, who had always tried to be careful with his men's lives, had become the unused, now abused, mastermind of the guerrillas.[17]

In late September, the guerrillas began concentrating in Boone and Audrain Counties, north of the Missouri River, near Centralia. The town, fifteen miles west of the city of Mexico and thirty-five miles east of Fayette, was along the North Missouri Railroad. The guerrilla leaders in the area were Anderson, George Todd, Silas "Si" Gordon, Dave Poole, Cole Younger, and John Thrailkill. Their number is not known but is suspected to have been around 350 to 428, although guerrilla Frank James said there were but 225.[18] Whatever their number, they would prove to be sufficient.

By the morning of September 27, Anderson and eighty of his men advanced toward Centralia, while the rest of the guerrillas, certainly over two hundred, remained three miles south of the town, along Young's Creek, on the farm of Colonel Singleton. Centralia, during this period, was a largely pro-Southern town composed of a dozen houses, only two of which had multiple stories. The businesses in Centralia carried general stocks and whiskey. Only one hotel graced the town, the Eldorado House, owned by Joe J. Collier. Another hotel, the Boone House, once owned by T. S. Sneed, had been burned down a year earlier by what the townsmen called the "Dutch" (German American) militia. The town was on a flat plain, where from the second story of the hotel, one could see for miles around.[19]

Anderson's men rode into Centralia dressed in blue Union uniforms, as was their habit. While his men were occupied robbing the town, Anderson rode to the Eldorado House and conversed with Valentine Collier, the brother of the hotel's owner. Collier sent someone for Dr. Sneed, who was a Southern sympathizer. When Sneed arrived, Anderson told him, "This is a fine location doctor—a pretty place for a fight. If those Feds over at Sturgeon will come down, I'll give them a twist. I don't want to go there, but if they will come down here—I'll fight them. I don't suppose they will want to come here."

William "Bloody Bill" Anderson, the violent leader of a large band of Missouri guerrillas. Anderson's father had been killed by abolitionists and his sisters maimed and killed through the actions of Union authorities. The traumatized Anderson became psychotic by the end of the war. *State Historical Society of Missouri, Columbia*

Meanwhile, the guerrillas found a barrel of whiskey, rolled it into the street, knocked in its head, and began drinking the liquor from tin cups they had discovered, downing the biting liquor in great gulps. Other men broke into some boxes of new boots, immersed the footgear in the whiskey, and strolled down the street offering the locals a drink. One of the guerrillas found a large bolt of cloth, mounted his horse, and dragged the bolt behind him, whooping as he unrolled it down the street. As they became drunk, the partisans became noisier, more boisterous, and extremely dangerous.

At 11:00 A.M., a stagecoach drawn by four horses, an old Concord with leather springs, arrived in town from the Jefferson Road. The guerrillas surrounded it and ordered its passengers to get out. The passengers included several notables: James S. Rollins; John M. Samuel, a former sheriff; Sheriff James H. Waugh; Lafayette Hume; Boyle Gordon; Columbus Hickman; and Henry Keene. The men were on their way to a Democratic political convention. Rollins was ordered to hand over his money, and the guerrillas questioned him sharply. He told them: "My name is Johnson, and I am a minister of the Methodist Church South." Rollins was not only a politician but also an adroit liar. Unimpressed, one of the guerrillas demanded, "Hand over your money!" Sheriff Waugh told the guerrillas his name was "Smith." Another politician said, "We are Southern men and Confederate sympathizers; you ought not to rob us." A partisan replied: "What do we care. Hell's full of such Southern men. Why ain't you in the army, or out fighting?" Since these men were not major targets, they survived the day's violence.[20]

A half-hour later, a North Missouri passenger train was heard approaching the town from St. Louis. The guerrillas dashed to the station as the train approached. It consisted of a locomotive, express and baggage car, and three coaches, holding some 125 passengers including 26 Union soldiers on furlough. The soldiers were all unarmed but in uniform.

James Clark, the train's engineer, had been traveling deliberately at top speed. He and the passengers had been told before they set out from St. Louis that the area was infested with guerrillas. As Clark approached within a mile of Centralia, he could see soldiers milling around the depot. He said later that he "did not like their actions." Then, he saw men piling wood on the tracks, and he "pulled the throttle wide open and dropped down on the deck," hoping to bull his way through town. "When in front of them [the guerrillas] they opened fire on us," he said, "and a shower of bullets swept engine and train." According to Clark, the brakemen could not see the guerrillas, did not know what was going on, and threw on the brakes. The train screeched to a stop in front of the depot, its wheels still spinning and grinding but unable to move forward. Clark pulled back on the throttle and ducked to the floor. The guerrillas swarmed aboard the locomotive, discovering an unscathed but frightened Clark; the fireman had suffered a slight flesh wound. Both men were ordered off the locomotive, and Clark was commanded to pull down two American flags, "20 X 30, one on each side my headlight." He said, "I did not expect to live long enough to take them down."

The guerrillas also charged into the coaches screaming, "Surrender! Surrender!" The unarmed soldiers were defenseless and did so. Clark said twenty-seven soldiers were lined up on the east side of Ball's store and told to take off their clothes, "save their underclothing." Several of the soldiers were pistol-whipped and some kicked to obtain lively responses.

Anderson, meanwhile, went to the express car with several of his men, demanded the keys to the express safe, and took three thousand dollars from it. Frank James (who after the Civil War put this train-robbing experience to practical use when he became an outlaw) found a valise with several thousand dollars' worth of greenbacks in it. Once the express car had been robbed, Anderson returned to the front of Ball's store, where the soldiers were lined up, and loudly asked for a volunteer, a sergeant. Anderson wished to hold one of the soldiers as a hostage to trade for one of his men, Cave Wyatt, who had been captured recently. Thomas M. Goodman stepped forward. Goodman said he saw "the man who had taken my coat [with sergeants' stripes on it] approach his chief [Anderson]," and that prompted him to "volunteer." Anderson placed Goodman under the guard of two guerrillas, Hiram Litton and Richard Ellington.[21]

Arch Clements then turned to Anderson and pointed at the soldiers: "What are you going to do with these fellows, Captain?" Anderson replied, "*Parole* them, of course," giving special emphasis to the word "parole." Clements laughed and replied, "I thought so." Anderson then ordered Clements to take charge of the firing party. When Anderson signaled, Clements was to have the men "pour hell into them." A long line of guerrillas now faced the prisoners. When Anderson signaled, Clements screamed "Fire!" and there was an explosion of pistol fire. Smoke billowed in the air, and the guerrillas continued firing sporadically at the soldiers. Some of the attacked men dropped to their knees and begged for mercy. One of the soldiers, Sgt. Valentine Peters, however, attacked the guerrillas, knocking several of them down. He was shot five times and sunk to the ground and rolled under the station platform for protection. The station was torched, and he soon emerged and was shot and killed in a torrent of gunfire. Meanwhile, a number of soldiers ran for their lives and were shot in flight. One soldier was chased on horseback by a guerrilla and ran into an outbuilding. When the guerrilla dismounted and entered the front door of the shed, the soldier ran out the back door, raced to the front of the building, mounted the guerrilla's horse, and raced off wildly, perhaps the only soldier other than the hostage, Sergeant Goodman, to escape.

After the murder of the Union soldiers, the coaches and express car were lit, and the engineer was ordered to start the train, set it on its course westward, and leap off. Within minutes, the train, all its cars ablaze and its whistle blaring, rattled and chugged forward, a roll of gray smoke unfurling in a long roll behind it. It raced out of sight, coming to rest some two and one-half miles to the west, where it ran out of steam. Its cars were burned to cinders.

The guerrillas finally rode out of town. Sergeant Goodman, mounted on a mule with a guard on each side of him, rode with them. The guerrillas' destination was the Singleton farm, three miles to the south. One of the townsmen said later that the raid on Centralia had been "more like a nightmare than a reality." So numb were the people that they left the soldiers' bodies strung along the street like bloody, twisted manikins.[22]

As Anderson and his men concluded their assault of Centralia, Maj. A. V. E. Johnston and Companies A, G, and H, Thirty-ninth Regiment Missouri Volunteers, some 147 men, rapidly approached the town. The Union detachment was searching for guerrillas, and they had found them. Johnston's men were armed with Enfield rifles, muzzle-loading weapons that fired a one-ounce Minié ball of .577 caliber. The rifles were equipped with bayonets. Although infantrymen, the soldiers were mounted on "farm horses," and like much of the cavalry of the time, they used their horses for maneuvering but fought dismounted.

Johnston was appalled at the scene he found in Centralia and was intent on revenging himself on the guerrillas. After talking with Dr. Sneed and other locals, he learned that Anderson had entered the town with eighty men. The same citizens warned him, however, that a larger force, perhaps as many as four hundred men, was stationed south of town. Sneed took Johnston to the attic of the hotel, where they looked out a window. "There they are now," Sneed cried, noting about twenty mounted men riding south of town. When cautioned again by Sneed that the guerrillas likely outnumbered his force, Johnston answered: "They may have the advantage of me in numbers, but I will have the advantage of them in arms. My guns are of long range and I can fight them from a distance." Johnston had no inkling of what it was like to meet a guerrilla cavalry charge with pistols blazing at close range.

Johnston left 35 of his men in Centralia under Captain Thiess and Lieutenant Stafford to defend the town. With the remaining 115 men, he rode southward. Twenty-five men loped ahead of the main detachment to scout the advance; the remainder followed at a slower gait. The scouts soon noted enemy pickets to their front, who "galloped rapidly away," as if in surprise. The soldiers were not aware, however, that they were being "tolled"—decoyed—into a trap. The guerrilla pickets were Dave and John Poole, Frank and Jesse James, Ben Morrow, E. P. DeHart, Tuck Hill, Peyton Long, Harrison Trow, and Ed Greenwood. Meanwhile, the guerrillas who were at their camp three miles south of Centralia learned of Johnston's presence from two of their scouts. The partisans prepared to meet him, and Sergeant Goodman said they "formed into squads of ten or twenty." Arriving from the west, the Union troops were expected to trail the guerrilla decoy right up to the partisans' main position.

As the Union troops rode east across the Fullenweider farm, they saw Anderson's men a half-mile away at the edge of a thicket of plum trees. But many of the guerrillas were concealed from view. Out of Johnston's vision, hidden in branches on both sides of him, were Thrailkill on the left, Si Gordon and George Todd on the right. Dead ahead, behind Anderson and partially overlapping his line, were Dave Poole and his men.[23]

On seeing the guerrillas, Johnston, in typical cavalry fashion, had his men dismount. Every fourth man was designated to hold the horses while his three comrades fought. The men were told to fix bayonets (no one lived to remember why). The guerrillas dismounted but only to check and tighten their saddle girths, and then they quickly remounted. Anderson rode over to some of his men and said, "Boys, when we charge, break thru the line and keep straight for their horses. Keep straight on for their horses." Anderson intended for no Union troops to escape the battlefield; it was to be a killing ground for all. Anderson then rode to the end of the line, raised his hat over his head, and waved it in a grand flourish—the signal for the Battle of Centralia.

The guerrillas, ascending a moderately steep incline, rode slowly at first, then accelerated to a gallop, leaning over their horses' necks, an "old Comanche trick," to provide a smaller target. Their eerie, rebel yells rose and fell in guttural yips and yowls, rising finally to a screaming, roaring crescendo that carried across the valley to Johnston's tense men. When they were within "150 yards" of Johnston, the Union commander ordered a volley fired, and there was a deafening boom and a great cloud of smoke. A number of guerrillas slid from their saddles, some dead. But as was typical of gunfire directed downhill, too many shots strayed or overshot their targets to stop the charge. This was a critical development in the battle; the guerrillas, once they approached an enemy closely, could rain a deadly hail of continuous revolver fire into them as the soldiers attempted to reload, a relatively slow and tedious process. With the charge of their comrades, Todd and Thrailkill's men poured out of two hollows to the left and right of Johnston's Union force, flanking, enveloping, and infiltrating the Union soldiers. Sergeant Goodman said, "The guerrillas were riding around and in their ranks [the Union soldiers], firing, and shouting, 'Surrender! Surrender!' "[24]

Frank James, describing the action years later, said the soldiers "nearly all fired over our heads. . . . Shepherd and Kinney rode next to me on either side. The blood and brains from Shepherd splashed on my pants leg as he fell from his horse. Kinney was my closest friend. We had ridden together from Texas, fought side by side, slept together, and it hurt me when I heard him [say] 'Frank, I'm shot.' "

James continued: "In a twinkling we were on the Yankee line. They seemed terrorized. Hypnotized might be a better word. . . . Some of the Yankees were at 'fix bayonets,' some were biting off their cartridges, preparing to reload. Yelling, shooting our pistols, upon them we went. Not a single man of the line escaped. . . . The few who attempted to escape we followed into Centralia and on to Sturgeon." Only two men made it to Sturgeon, Louis Marquette, who died later of his wounds, and the sole survivor, Enoch Hunt.[25]

In a message to Brigadier General Fisk, Lt. Col. Daniel M. Draper, who went to the scene of the battle, reported the grisly aftermath:

> After the volley, they [the guerrillas] came on, and when within 100 yards the men [Union soldiers] began to break, many of them not firing the second shot, and none of them more than that. It then became a scene of murder and outrage at which the heart sickens. Most of them [the soldiers] were beaten over the head, seventeen of them were scalped, and one man had his privates cut off and placed in his mouth. Every man was shot in the head. One man had his nose cut off. One hundred and fifty dead bodies have been found, including the twenty-four taken from the train.

Other messages reinforced Draper's news. W. T. Clarke reported to Fisk that some of the soldiers' "ears were cut off and all commissioned officers were scalped." Sergeant Goodman said, "Men's heads were severed from their lifeless bodies, exchanged as to bodies, labeled with rough and obscene epitaphs and inscriptions, stuck upon their carbine points, tied to their saddle bows, or sat grinning at each other from the tops of fence stakes and stumps around the scene."[26]

When Frank James visited Centralia thirty-three years later, he visited the unmarked graves of two of his fallen guerrilla comrades, "Hank" Williams and Frank Shepherd. He reminisced to a newspaper reporter:

> To this complexion we must come at last. Our boys are scattered everywhere. You will find their graves in the hollows and on the hills, by the gulf and on these prairies. Many have no monument. They don't need any. They made their monuments while they lived. They left a record for daring courage that the world has not surpassed. . . . Their sleep is just as sweet here as it would be in a beautiful city cemetery.[27]

On October 26, 1864, Bill Anderson would join those men who died a month earlier at Centralia. The infamous guerrilla was killed finally by S. P. Cox, who commanded the Thirty-third Enrolled Missouri Militia, near Albany, Missouri, in Gentry County, around forty miles northeast of St.

Joseph, Missouri, in the northwest corner of the state. Cox, after learning the location of Anderson, dismounted his 150-man unit at Albany and had them take up positions in the woods adjoining the town. Then, he sent out a party of pickets to lure the guerrillas into a chase, to decoy them into an ambush that he had set for them. Cox was using guerrilla tactics. When the guerrillas charged, Cox said, his line "held their position without a break." Anderson led the advance and crossed though the Union lines, firing at point-blank range at the soldiers, possibly hitting and killing several of them. As he exited the lines, "some fifty steps" to the rear, he "received two balls in the head."[28]

Later, Anderson's body was searched. Cox said he carried "private papers and orders from General Price that identify him." In a message to Lt. Col. W. H. Stark, acting assistant adjutant general Maj. James Rainsford passed on the two orders from General Price found on Anderson's body. They were from the Confederate assistant adjutant general Maclean. One message, dated October 11, 1864, ordered Anderson and his command to be carried by "ferry-boat" to the north side of the Missouri River. The other message, with the same date, ordered Anderson to "destroy the North Missouri Railroad, going as far east as possible." Rainsford said he also found on Anderson's body his wife's "likeness" and "a small Confederate flag with these words inscribed on it: 'Presented to W. L. Anderson by his friend, F. M. R. Let it not be contaminated by Fed. hands.' " Present also were "letters from his wife in Texas, and a lock of her hair, about $600 in gold and green-backs," in addition to Anderson's splendid mare and "four revolvers, two watches" (one gold, the other silver).

Anderson's body was taken to the Richmond, Missouri, courthouse, where at least two pictures were taken of him. They show that his ring finger had been cut off, probably to remove his gold wedding band. Later, Anderson's head was cut off and "stuck . . . atop a telegraph pole," apparently as a warning to other rebels. According to contemporary newspaper accounts, militiamen visited his burial site later that evening and "spat and urinated on the grave."

A black man, "Uncle Charlie" Baker, who acted as Anderson's servant and hostler when he was fighting, said of him: "I want to say that Mr. Bill was a good master. He treated me very well, and I looked after his horses and family after his tragic death." Baker spent the next year after the guerrilla's death with Anderson's wife in Texas.

Sergeant Goodman, while he was a captive of Anderson, studied his "face" and described it:

> It looks not like one to be feared, for the sad expression of those
> eyes indicates a different character than is generally attributed to this

notorious guerrilla chief. Mercy may dwell within his heart; and cir-
cumstance, whose cruel hand often warps and destroys the best of
natures, may have had much to do in making this one man a living
exemplification of the couplet—

Man's inhumanity to man
Makes countless thousands mourn.[29]

***

At 10:00 P.M. on October 12, Price's army pulled out of Boonville,
Missouri, heading west. Price had recruited some twelve hundred to fifteen
hundred men in the town, most of them unarmed. As the army proceeded, it captured Glasgow (October 12), Sedalia (October 17), and Lexington
(October 19). Shelby and Marmaduke, rotating as the advance division, had
thrown the enemy back easily. But when Price's advance ran into Union
major general Blunt's men, about five miles from Lexington on the Salt
Pond Road, the resistance stiffened and the Confederate advance was
retarded somewhat.

Nonetheless, Price's army rolled on, and on October 21, Marmaduke
made contact with the defending Union pickets to the east of the Little
Blue River. Col. Thomas Moonlight with his artillery and supporting units
had been placed west of the river to delay the Southern attack. To further
their chances, Moonlight's men were armed with state-of-the-art repeating
rifles. Shelby was called to Marmaduke's support, and the Federals continued to fight fiercely from behind stone walls and earth and log works.
Marmaduke, however, finally discovered a ford a half-mile below a
destroyed bridge and crossed there in force and under fire. So fierce was
the fighting in the Battle of the Little Blue that Marmaduke had two horses shot out from under him. Nonetheless, the Federals were driven from
the position, and a running fight commenced on the road toward
Independence. The fight was led by Shelby and his men, who pushed the
Federals through the town and beyond. That night, Price's army
bivouacked in Independence.[30]

On that same day, Lt. George Todd, who had supplanted Quantrill as
the principal leader of the guerrilla movement in western Missouri, led a
band of scouts in the Confederate advance near the "old Staples place,"
two and one-half miles northeast of Independence. As Todd rode to the
crest of a hill, a sniper's rifle rang out, and a bullet struck the guerrilla in
the throat, shattering his neck. Todd fell from his horse and was carried
from the battlefield, bleeding profusely. He died a few hours later and was
buried in an Independence cemetery. One of his men, John McCorkle,
described the aftermath of Todd's death. "I stayed in Independence about

an hour," he related, "spending most of my time at the newly made grave of George Todd, whom I loved better than a brother."[31]

On the morning of October 22, Price's army marched from Independence on the Santa Fé Road, moving in the direction of the Big Blue River. Along the river, Maj. Gen. Samuel Curtis had constructed elaborate fortifications, trenches, and barricades. Maj. Gen. James Blunt had joined Curtis at that point, and their combined Union force consisted of some six thousand to eight thousand men. As Price advanced toward the Blue, his engineers pulled felled trees from his path, placed there by the enemy. Meanwhile, Shelby detached Sydney D. Jackman's brigade along the Kansas City Road, while he advanced his own men to Byram's Ford. Shelby crossed the Big Blue at the ford in the face of Brig. Gen. Charles Jennison's brigade. Driving Jennison from the field in the Battle of the Big Blue, Shelby took up a defensive position, allowing the Confederate supply train to pass.

During this time Confederate brigadier general Thompson pushed forward to the edge of Westport to determine the strength of the Union forces but then dropped back to the Big Blue again. Meanwhile, Confederate colonels Alexander Gordon and Sydney Jackman captured a twenty-four-pound howitzer and two flags from Curtis's men. This resulted in a frantic Union effort to regain them that continued until nightfall, when the appearance of General Thompson's men ended the clash. Maj. Gen. Alfred Pleasonton's army, by now, had made contact with Price's rearguard, commanded by Marmaduke, and by nightfall had pushed it westward to the brink of the Big Blue.

By this time, Price was looking for a way out of a serious situation. With Pleasonton's army to his rear, a huge Kansas army to his front, his train threatened, and the encirclement of his army a possibility, a means of escape had to be found. Compounding his problems, Pleasonton's army was beginning to overpower his rearguard. Indeed, on that very day, between two hundred and four hundred of Confederate brigadier general William L. Cabell's men had been cut off from his brigade, and he had lost two precious artillery pieces besides. Cabell's unit, nonetheless, continued to fight furiously after nightfall, and Marmaduke's division, at the rear of Price's army, soon joined in. But the Southerners were driven back throughout much of the night.[32]

To facilitate his inevitable move southward, Price had started his train down the Fort Scott Road (Military Road) on October 22. Marmaduke's division, which was on the same road as the train, but behind it, was assigned the task of protecting it. The next day, to give the train enough time to push southward to make way for the rest of the army's retreat, Shelby's small division and two of Fagan's brigades, at early light, on a cold, clear morning, attacked Jennison and Moonlight's position along the south side of Brush Creek. Soon, the Confederates had driven Curtis's "Army of the Border" a mile north to the edge of Westport in what has been called the Battle of Westport.

By now, Phillips and Winslow, of Pleasonton's command, had forced Brig. Gen. John B. Clark, leading a brigade of Marmaduke's division, to retreat from the Big Blue along the Harrisonville Road before a strong attack. Now, the Confederate train—and Price's whole army—was in jeopardy. Price, who was posted with the troops near Westport, ordered Shelby and Fagan to drop back to aid in the defense of the train. In the meantime, Price personally rushed back to the train with his escort to help set up defenses. Commanding only a few armed men at the time, Price lined up several thousand of his unarmed men in line of battle in an attempt to bluff Pleasonton concerning his true strength. In front of these men, in regular armed ranks, he formed the men of his escort and some of Tyler's brigade into a thin, gray line of some two hundred men. The ruse worked until General Cabell arrived with his men, and McCray's brigade, which had been at the front of the train, made its presence felt.[33]

Another serious problem for Price at this time was that Shelby and Fagan's rear and right flank, because of the retreat of Marmaduke and others, was now under attack by Pleasonton's men. Shelby and Fagan, however, fought their way valiantly and desperately to the rear, across an open prairie through the heart of Pleasonton's brigades, in a chaotic melee. As Shelby's men retreated, they turned on Sanborn's brigade, on Shelby's left flank, charged it, and shook it thoroughly. In response, Thurber's Union battery fired "double-shot grape" at them, and the Confederates retired. Fagan and Shelby regained contact with Price that evening beyond New Santa Fé.

On the morning of October 24, Price embarked southward on the Fort Scott Road (or Military Road), attempting to put space between his army and its pursuers. Paralleling his course, on his right flank, he discovered, were the troops of Moonlight's brigade, whose mission was to prevent Price's forces from desolating Kansas towns along the border. Price traveled a rigorous thirty-six miles that day in a driving rain, arriving at the Marais des Cygnes River that night, where his army camped at Trading Post.

The next day, Shelby led the Army of Missouri farther south, with Major Generals Marmaduke and Fagan's divisions manning the rear-guard. A large Union force followed them closely, firing at them continuously. Colonel Tyler's brigade was posted to the front and right-center of Price's train. Shelby's old brigade and Colonel Jackman's brigade were positioned to the right-front and in front of Price's army, respectively. As the Southern army reached the Little Osage River (Mine Creek), Price ordered Shelby to attack Fort Scott, a half score miles to the south-south-west. About this time, however, Price received an urgent dispatch from

Marmaduke and Fagan: an army estimated at "6,000 or 7,000" men was threatening them.

When Price's train had earlier reached a "deep ravine" leading to the ford over Mine Creek (a tributary of the Osage River), the bulk of his army, which trailed the train, had been forced to halt and wait for the train's passage. The onrushing Federals, who had been pursuing Price's army hotly for a number of miles, chose this propitious moment to attack the rear of the Southern army. At 2:00 P.M., some twenty-six hundred Federals made "a furious charge on the right and the left flank" of Price's rear as it halted before Mine Creek. Union lieutenant colonel Frederick Benteen (of Little Bighorn fame) and Phillips's brigades led the charge. As they were attacked, the Confederates, with no time to dismount and form into line of battle, fired from horseback. After firing a volley, and with no time to dismount to reload, panic overcame the Confederates, and the rear of Price's army collapsed in "hopeless confusion." General Clark described the rout as "an irresistible mass ungovernable," where "you scarcely knew who was friend or foe." Some of the men fought valiantly "in hand-to-hand conflict with the foe," while others "ignominiously [threw] away their arms." Among the captured were four or five hundred men, eight guns, Generals Marmaduke and Cabell, and Cols. William L. Jeffers and W. F. Slemmons. After losing their mounts, Marmaduke and Cabell had been apprehended by two enlisted men, an added disgrace. It was clearly the most disastrous episode in Price's raid.[34]

When Price learned of the attack on his rear, he ordered Shelby to take his old brigade in support of Fagan and Marmaduke. Price also rode to the rear, where he found Fagan and Marmaduke's divisions, in his words, "retreating in utter and indescribable confusion, many of them having thrown down their arms. They were deaf to all entreaties or commands, and in vain were all efforts to rally them." Fortunately, the reliable and formidable Shelby and his men manfully held off the Federals for two hours while Price regained a measure of order in his command. Price said he ordered his "immense lines of unarmed men . . . in line of battle on the prairie beyond the river." Once again, he hoped they could stave off an immediate assault by presenting the illusion of armed numbers and stability in his command. Shelby was placed in front of them, facing the enemy. Pleasonton and Curtis's men, exhausted by this time, turned away from the Battle of Mine Creek and proceeded into Fort Scott to refresh themselves. As Pleasonton described it, "The exhausted condition of my men and horses, having marched near 100 miles in two days and a night, and fighting the last thirty miles, required that I should proceed to the vicinity of Fort Scott for forage and subsistence." Price's army, equally exhausted and hungry, continued to plod south unmolested.[35]

On October 26, Price burned a number of his unusable wagons and continued his line of march southward for fifty-six miles, camping at Carthage, on the Spring River, where forage was obtainable. Encumbered by his Federal prisoners, Price paroled them. By October 28, the army reached Newtonia, with Shelby again in the advance. Shelby easily drove the Federal garrison from the town, which was commanded, Price said, by "Federal Captain Christian, a notorious bushwhacker, as it is termed—that is, robber and murderer—noted for his deeds of violence and blood." Price went into camp about four miles beyond Newtonia.

About 8:00 P.M. that day, three thousand cavalry led by General Blunt (some say one thousand) loomed into sight and made preparations for an audacious (but presumptuous) charge against the Confederates. Price said that Blunt "was repulsed and driven across the prairie for three miles with heavy loss." He added, "That was the last we saw of the enemy."

The Southern army passed into Arkansas on November 1. They had been suffering much deprivation but eventually reached an area of ample forage and subsistence. Price then reassigned some of his brigades and established a headquarters at Laynesport.

Price claimed that during his raid into Missouri, he had "marched 1,434 miles." In the event, he had failed to take St. Louis, failed to take Jefferson City, experienced a harrowing escape after the Battle of Westport, and suffered a humiliating defeat at Mine Creek, where he lost a number of precious artillery pieces, suffered many casualties, and surrendered officers, two of them general officers, and their men. However, he returned to Arkansas with an estimated "5,000 to 7,000 new recruits" and many rifles and muskets and other stores. In addition, he had diverted considerable Union manpower to the trans-Mississippi theater of operations, relieving pressure on the Confederate armies in the East and South.[36]

***

After Price exited Missouri and ended his 1864 raid, some of the western Missouri guerrillas returned home, others migrated south to Texas once more. The guerrilla command had been fractured by the turbulent events of 1864 and lost two of its principal captains, Anderson and Todd. Quantrill, who had remained in Missouri, now rallied a small group of guerrillas, thirty-three in number. One of Quantrill's men, Morgan Maddox, said Quantrill thought the war was coming to an end and wished to take some of the guerrillas east of the Mississippi River, where "they were not known" and would be "permitted to surrender." Another guerrilla, Sylvester Akers, said, "The object of Quantrill getting away from Missouri was to get to General Lee and surrender with him, being convinced that the Confederacy was near a collapse and that Lee would soon have to surrender." Quantrill, according to Akers, believed that neither "he

[Quantrill] nor his men would be permitted to surrender in Missouri or the West." Another story maintains that Quantrill went east to assassinate Lincoln, but no evidence supports this outrageous claim, which is but another transparent attempt to demonize him.

At this point, Quantrill apparently believed the South was finished and the next few months would expend its available options and resources. Sherman recently had driven a wedge through the heart of the South with his March to the Sea; the Union now controlled the Mississippi River, which divided the eastern and far western sections of the South; Tennessee and Georgia were in Union hands; Robert E. Lee and his bloodied army were bottled up in Virginia, exhausted from years of murderous warfare; and the South was being strangled by an effective maritime blockade. Clearly, the end of the war was near.

Quantrill rallied his men at several rendezvous points in western Missouri. Then, in mid-December 1864, he left the Kimmel farm, six miles from Independence, and headed toward southeast Missouri. His men wore Federal uniforms and pretended to be members of the Fourth Missouri Cavalry, the commander of which was "Captain Clarke," a name assumed by Quantrill. As they proceeded across the rolling hills, they intended to stop at the various Federal garrisons along the way for subsistence and forage.

In late December, they stopped at Tuscumbia, Missouri, a small town situated on the flood plain of the Osage River in Miller County, approximately 125 miles southeast of Independence. The guerrillas rode quietly into town. When challenged by a picket, Quantrill asked to speak with the local commander, who lived in a house overlooking the river; the rest of the garrison was lodged at the local hotel. During a discussion with that officer, Quantrill asked the commander about the various Federal garrisons in that part of Missouri—their locations and their strengths. Then, Quantrill drew his revolver and made the officer his prisoner. Quantrill led the commander to the local hotel at gunpoint and demanded that he surrender his men. Afterward, Quantrill paroled the men, save one, whom he took for a guide. Then, the partisans took the soldiers' weapons to the middle of the wide Osage River and dumped them unceremoniously into the muddy water.

Upon leaving Tuscumbia, the guerrillas traveled in a southeasterly direction, passing out of Missouri near Pocahontas, Arkansas (where Price, earlier that year, had passed into the state during his invasion). At this point, six of the guerrillas separated from Quantrill and departed for Texas. Quantrill and the rest of the men turned eastward and, employing a yawl, crossed the Mississippi River at Devil's Bend (or Devil's Elbow), fifteen miles north of Memphis, Tennessee. Shortly thereafter, they stopped at some of the small Federal posts for supplies, forage, and rations. Some of the Union soldiers doubtless admired their fine horseflesh.[37]

Once Quantrill arrived in Kentucky, he told the locals that he was leading a Union detachment to the Ohio River along the Hawesville Road.
Several Union soldiers asked if they could accompany him and Quantrill
agreed. One of the soldiers, a Lieutenant Barnett, had been acting as a
recruiter for the U.S. Twenty-fifth Colored Regiment. The other soldiers
were W. B. Lawton, a member of an Indiana regiment, and W. Townsley, a
soldier recently discharged from the Third Kentucky Cavalry. After traveling three miles, the guerrillas rode into the timber and hung Townsley; nine
miles down the road, they shot Lawton; and before they reached Hartford,
they had killed Barnett.

Thereafter, the guerrillas began a series of "robberies" in association
with some of the prominent local partisans, including Jerome Clarke
(a.k.a. "Sue Munday") and "One-armed" Berry's men. On February 28,
1865, with the help of these guerrillas, Quantrill raided Hickman,
Chaplintown, and Danville, Kentucky. After the last raid, a Union patrol
led by Capt. J. H. Bridgewater took up the chase and overtook the band
that evening near Harrodsburg, capturing twelve partisans.[38] A protract-
ed hunt for the rest of the guerrillas ensued, led by a Colonel Buckly
through Shelby County and a Captain Searcy on the road east of
Chaplintown. After the guerrillas burned the depot at Midway on
February 2, Captain Bridgewater resumed the trail and drove the partisans through Bradfordsville and Campbellsville.

On April 16, though still being pursued, Quantrill and his men stayed
at the home of Jonathan Davis, a judge of Spencer County, Kentucky. A
celebration was held that night to mark the death of Abraham Lincoln,
who had been assassinated the night before. Most of the guerrillas were
drunk at the party, and Quantrill apologized to the women. "Excuse us
ladies. We are a little in our cups today," he said. "The grand-daddy of all
the greenbacks, Abraham Lincoln, was shot in a theatre in Washington last
night." "One-Armed" Berry, who was also present, added: "Here's to the
death of Abraham Lincoln, hoping that his bones may serve in hell as a
gridiron to fry Yankees on." Guerrilla John McCorkle said that before the
party, when Quantrill read from a newspaper announcing Lincoln's death,
"we all began to cheer." Gen. Robert E. Lee, however, had surrendered at
the McLean house at Appomattox Court House on April 9, 1865. The
South's fate was sealed.[39]

Perhaps the guerrillas had gone to Kentucky partly to avoid being the
objects of the intense manhunts conducted against them in western
Missouri. What they discovered in Kentucky, however, was an even more
intense search for them by clever, knowledgeable huntsmen who knew
that country as well as the Missourians knew their own wooded countryside. Quantrill and his men were only able to stay alive in Kentucky with
the help of rebel sympathizers in the area. The local Federal authorities

became desperate to capture Quantrill and his band, dead or alive, and hired a Federal deserter and Kentucky Union guerrilla, Edwin Terrill, to accomplish the feat. Terrill, while only nineteen years old, was experienced in gunplay and fearless. Obviously, the Federal authorities believed that it would take a guerrilla to catch a guerrilla. Terrill and his men were placed on the Federal payroll and told to pose as Southern partisans, insinuate themselves into Quantrill's circle, and kill him.[40]

Terrill had been searching for the guerrillas for about a month, when on May 10, he found a trail of horsemen leading from Bloomfield to Taylorsville. He stopped at a blacksmith shop along the way to ask a workman if he had seen any horsemen pass. The man told him that riders had recently gone through a large gate onto the Wakefield farm and entered a lane leading to a barn atop the hill. Quantrill and fifteen of his men had taken up residence on the farm of James H. Wakefield, a covert Southern sympathizer who lived in the southern part of Spencer County near Taylorsville. The men had been using their time on the Wakefield farm to rest and Quantrill, who had recently lost his favorite horse, Charley, was currently breaking in a new mount.

Without warning, Terrill and his men descended on the barn at a full gallop. At the time, Wakefield was standing under an eave of the barn talking with guerrillas Dick Glasscock and Clark Hockensmith. When they saw mounted gunmen racing toward them, Hockensmith screamed, "Here they come!"

A driving rainstorm was in progress, and the guerrillas had been lounging in the barn, talking and playfully tossing corncobs at one another. While they did so, their horses had been eating from mangers inside the barn. When the guerrillas heard Hockensmith's warning, many of them ran out of the barn and toward the woods, not attempting to mount their horses so pressed were they for time. Quantrill, who had been asleep in the hayloft, roused himself, rushed for his horse, and grabbed at its reins. But the horse, unaccustomed to gunfire and excited, reared and yanked itself from his grasp. Quantrill ran outside and saw Hockensmith and Dick Glasscock riding off and yelled to them for help. Both men stopped and rode back to rescue their leader, firing at Terrill's men as they did so. Quantrill ran alongside Glasscock's mare and attempted to pull himself up into the saddle. At that moment, the horse was struck in the hip by a bullet and shimmied wildly. Quantrill and his comrades continued to fire at Terrill's men, and the guerrilla commander attempted to pull himself up behind Hockensmith. Just as he reached up to mount Hockensmith's horse, a bullet struck Quantrill in the shoulder blade, traveled downward into his spine, and paralyzed him from his shoulders down. He plummeted face down in the mud. As he fell, another bullet shot off his trigger finger.

Before Glasscock and Hockensmith had traveled four hundred yards, both were overtaken and killed. They had sacrificed their lives for their leader, demonstrating the solidarity and loyalty found in the guerrillas even this late in the war. Meanwhile, Quantrill lay face down in the mire, mortally wounded. Some of Terrill's men dismounted, walked up to the guerrilla chief, and rolled him over. They took his revolvers and yanked off his boots and some of his clothing.

Eventually, Quantrill was wrapped in a blanket and taken to Wakefield's house. Wakefield, who saw him at this time, said Quantrill could neither walk nor sit. When Terrill questioned him, Quantrill said only that he was Capt. William Clarke of the Fourth Missouri Cavalry. Apparently, he believed that he would be killed instantly if he told Terrill otherwise. Quantrill asked Terrill if he might remain at Wakefield's house to die, and Terrill agreed. In the meantime, Terrill's men began robbing Wakefield's house. Wakefield, concerned, drew Terrill and Taylor (Terrill's lieutenant) aside. He gave Terrill twenty dollars and a jug of whiskey and Taylor ten dollars to call off their men, which they did. Soon, a Dr. McClusky was summoned to the house to administer to Quantrill and dress his wounds. After examining the guerrilla chief, the doctor pronounced him mortally wounded.

Quantrill's men returned that night to learn the fate of their chief and sought to move him to safety, but Quantrill refused their help, telling them that he had promised Wakefield that he would stay and that Terrill was holding Wakefield accountable if he were moved. Terrill, in fact, had told Wakefield that his "property would be burned" if Quantrill was not there when he returned. The next day Terrill returned with a mule-drawn wagon filled with straw and carried Quantrill to a hospital in Louisville.

When Quantrill arrived at the hospital, some local women placed a bouquet of flowers in his room. The inscription read: "Compliments of Miss Maggie Frederick and Sallie Lovell to Mr. Quantrill." A number of people ministered to Quantrill while he was in the hospital, and one of them asked him if the stories about the Lawrence raid were true. He replied they were and added, "If he had captured Sen. James H. Lane he intended to burn him at the stake in Jackson County, Missouri." Twenty-seven days after he was wounded and after a lingering, painful stay at the military prison in Louisville, Quantrill died at 4:00 P.M., on June 6, 1865. The last vestige of the Confederacy, the Port of Galveston, Texas, had surrendered four days earlier. William Gregg, one of his lieutenants, who later became a deputy sheriff of Jackson County, Missouri, said of Quantrill, "I will ever hold his memory sacred."[41]

Sixteen of Quantrill's guerrillas surrendered at Samuel's Depot on July 26, 1865. Other guerrillas wangled exits from the war using other expedients, like John McCorkle, who was paroled as part of a Kentucky

Confederate unit. Before leaving Kentucky, McCorkle said he slept in a bed, and added, it was "the first time I had slept all night in a house in three years." For these former teen-aged boys from elite families, it had been a long, grisly war.[42]

Chapter 14

Reckoning

When the grass began greening and the trees budding in early 1865, some two hundred guerrillas trekked northward, leaving Texas about April 18 and arriving in Missouri around May 1. They discovered that Gen. Joseph E. Johnston had surrendered the remaining bulk of the Confederate army, and by this time, the guerrillas considered the war over. They found hiding places in western Missouri and waited to learn what surrender terms, if any, would be offered them. Col. Chester Harding Jr., at the headquarters of the Department of the Missouri, learned on May 9 from one of his officers, Maj. B. K. Davis, that "a large portion of them [the guerrillas] are anxious to give themselves up if they can be treated as prisoners of war. . . . Citizens think that if terms would be granted them a large portion of them would give themselves up."[1]

The two hundred guerrillas in Western Missouri were not peacefully occupied, however. On May 3, Lt. Ben F. Johnson, the commander at Pleasant Hill, reported that guerrillas Sy Porter, Bill Reynolds, and Dave Poole had killed a citizen, Richard Conner, and a discharged soldier, John G. Harper. Four days later, Archie Clements, now in command of one hundred of Bill Anderson's men, killed four railroad teamsters at Kingsville in a raid on that town. All of the guerrillas were reported to be wearing Federal uniforms. On the same day, forty guerrillas robbed the town of Holden. A day later, one of Colonel Harding's men sent a message saying, "I have sent troops to take care of the devils." Three guerrillas were killed in a subsequent pursuit. In response Clements sent a letter warning one of Harding's men, Maj. B. K. Davis, "of retaliation if his friends were hurt." Davis ignored him.

On the same day, Brig. Gen. Robert B. Mitchell told Col. C. W. Blair, the Union commander at Fort Scott, "As soon as you can learn the locality of the guerrillas on the border, strike them with all the available force at your disposal without further orders. Pay no attention to State or district lines." At about the same time, Gen. Grenville M. Dodge, commander of the Department of the Missouri, sent a message to Harding, saying, "Keep the cavalry on the move day and night." Within a week, Dodge had nine hundred cavalry on the way to Mitchell, to be used in "Bates, Cass, and Jackson

Counties, or wherever guerrillas may be in this neighborhood." It was getting hot for the guerrillas.[2]

Meanwhile, Federal authorities were determining what policy to adopt toward the remaining guerrillas: to continue to exterminate them or to offer them terms. On May 12, Dodge sent a message to his assistant adjutant general, Captain Clarke, outlining the Union plan: "Any of these bands that you describe that propose to lay down their arms can do so, and the military authorities will take no further action in the case. If they persist in resisting no terms will be granted them. They are nothing but outlaws. It is too late to surrender after our troops catch them in arms."[3]

In mid-May, Maj. B. K. Davis informed Harding that guerrilla chief Dave Poole was "collecting his men in order to give them up. Poole's first lieutenant is south of here doing the same thing, and I have every assurance that he will give himself up as soon as he gets his men together." On May 21, 1865, Dave Poole and "forty men" surrendered at Lexington, Missouri. According to Harding, Poole promised "that he will help us to bring in the rest of the bushwhackers, and is willing to go out for that purpose to-morrow morning."

On May 14, Archie Clements sent a letter to Maj. B. K. Davis proposing "with five men to meet an equal party [of Federals] at the Mound, on Warrensburg road, on the 17th instant, to learn particulars of terms, &c." It appears that the Federals were not enthusiastic about giving Archie relief, however. Davis told Harding, "If you move after him, I can assist you." After parleying with another Federal commander in Glasgow, Clements decided to go to Texas until things cooled off. On December 13, 1866, a year and a half later, he was gunned down on the streets of Lexington, Missouri, by an ambush set up by the Federal commander of the town.[4]

By May 31, 1865, Colonel Harding reported, "Over 200 bushwhackers have accepted the terms offered them at Lexington." According to Harding, not all of the local citizens were happy about this. He said, "The citizens who do not help us are vexed at the course pursued. They think we should meet these fellows in the brush and kill them. Or else violate our plighted faith when they are in our power." But Harding said it was not easy even for Poole, a guerrilla chief, to find his comrades in the dense bush. "It took Dave Poole nearly a week to collect his small band of forty. The men were lying by twos and threes in the brush from the Sni Hills to the mouth of the La Mine [River]. It is the same with other gangs; they live with their friends in the country, and are plowing or planting as we pass by." Harding had it broadcast "that the mercy extended to them [the guerrillas] is unparalleled and that we expect them to keep the same good faith which we show them. If they step over the line of their obligations they will be arrested and shot without trial." By this time, conditions in the area had vastly improved. Harding reported, "Farmers are returning to their farms.

No one need be afraid to travel alone north of this point."[5]

There was only one catch in General Dodge's seemingly merciful plan toward the guerrillas. As Dodge said in a report of July 18, 1865, "I simply stipulated that they [the guerrillas] should not be molested by the U.S. military authorities, thus leaving the civil authorities unrestrained to deal with them for the crimes they had committed in violation of the laws of the State

The guerrilla "Surrender Oath." Note that failure to comply with the oath called for the penalty of "death or other punishment by the military commission." *Courtesy of Claiborne Scholl Nappier* and of the United States and contrary to usages of war." As the guerrillas of the 1860s might have remarked, "That was a horse of a different color."[6]

After the war closed, some of the guerrillas claimed, like Cole Younger, a guerrilla lieutenant, that they were being harassed and bedeviled by local pro-Union farmers and law enforcement officers. In Younger's case, a warrant was sworn out for his arrest for the wartime "murder" of a man named Judy. Judy's father had been appointed sheriff of Cass County and was pursuing the matter aggressively. Warned by his friends and legal advisers that he was likely to be shot or hung before a trial could be conducted, Younger eventually took to the bush. Later, he and his brothers, along with Frank James and his brother, Jesse James, organized the most notorious outlaw gang in American history, the James-Younger gang. The former guerrillas pioneered bank and train robberies, and some of them defied capture for over fifteen years. A number of former guerrillas joined the James-Younger gang and applied the skills they had learned during the war to more profitable pursuits—in the railroad and banking businesses.

But the vast number of guerrillas returned to normal, relatively humdrum lives. William Gregg, one of Quantrill's lieutenants, became the deputy sheriff of Jackson County under a Republican administration. Cole Younger, in his autobiography, listed other regenerate guerrillas:

> John C. Hope was for two terms sheriff of Jackson county, Mo., in which is Kansas City, and Capt. J. M. Tucker was sheriff at Los Angeles, California. Henry Porter represented one of the Jackson county districts in the state legislature, removed to Texas, where he was made judge of the county court, and is now, I understand, a judge of probate in the state of Washington. "Pink" Gibson was for several years county judge in Johnson county; Harry Ogden served the state of Louisiana as lieutenant-governor and as one of its congressmen. Capt. J. C. Lea was for many years instructor in the military department of the University of New Mexico. . . . Jesse Hamblett was marshal at Lexington . . . Jim Hendricks, deputy sheriff of Lewis and Clark county, Montana.[7]

When the Civil War ended, the people in Lawrence, Kansas, gathered to celebrate. Star Spangled Banners festooned stores, fireworks erupted, and great bonfires blazed. But across the border in western Missouri, conditions were miserable. The slave economy had been destroyed, and nearly all of the black workers had been removed or had fled to Kansas. Rank grass grew in the main streets of many of the former towns. There were almost no schools, no churches, no stores, no jobs—and little hope. The situation was dismal. Nearly all of the homes in the border counties had been burned and outbuildings were ashes. The countryside abutting rutted paths and roadways was barren except for charred chimneys that pointed to the sky. Many of the sheep, cattle, horses, and mules, as well as stores of corn, oats, barley, and milo, now graced Kansans' farms. A former farming paradise was now a battered, bleak landscape called the "Burnt District." A generation of its young men lay beneath the sod, or their bones lay strewn in remote woods and brambles. Those guerrillas fortunate enough to have

Not all of the guerrillas returned to peaceful pursuits after the war. Jesse James used his skill and daring with revolvers to become a world-renowned bandit. *The Kansas State Historical Society, Topeka*

survived the war showed the scars of multiple bullet wounds, the effects of which also scarred their minds and souls. Young men, like Fletcher Taylor, had lost arms; some guerrillas had no legs; others had various traumatic physical and psychological injuries. An entire way of life had been destroyed in Western Missouri forever. Soon, emigrants from the East, northeast, and north-central United States began settling the area. Today, few people who dwell in western Missouri have family stories reaching to that period, and those that do tell tales whose accuracy has been dimmed by the passage of many years.

Quantrill's former guerrillas attending their annual reunion in the early 1900s. Not coincidentally, the reunions were often scheduled on August 21, the anniversary of the raid on Lawrence. *The Kansas State Historical Society, Topeka*

Afterword

Histories, like those of the Border War, have never been dispassionate exercises. People care about the past, and they invariably take sides on issues pertaining to it. History is much like politics. In that field, people usually orient themselves according to a particular political persuasion and that determines the way they view national and world events. Most political pundits, no matter how august, when asked a political question, give answers that are readily predictable. If they are Democrats, they issue a Democratic response, nearly always the party line. If they are Republicans, the process will be identical. Ordinary people respond in much the same way although they believe they are impartial. Few people, however, can achieve a very great degree of political objectivity. Historians are no exception—especially when they are dealing with a controversial subject.

But because historians seek to leave an accurate record of the past, they attempt to keep the facts as straight as possible and avoid letting their historical/political interpretations twist their data to create false perceptions. Nevertheless, bias invariably creeps into histories, even the best intentioned. For that reason, history should remain alive and active, and a variety of interpretations should be allowed to surface and compete for ascendancy. Then, through a process of honest synthesis, history may eventually acquire greater accuracy and credibility

Why do these differences in opinion and perspectives exist in histories? Don't all historians use the same data? No, they do not. A historian has the power to pick and choose among the vast materials he or she believes are relevant to a historical period. The historian may choose to talk or write about some things and ignore others; thus, in a sense, that individual may be distorting the truth through the omission of some data. Or he or she may choose biased accounts to support his or her thesis and ignore those that disagree. A historian also may make value judgments about the political and historical figures, and therefore, historical characters can be placed in a good light or in a bad one, depending on the historian's subjective assessments. In the process, the reader of histories may be shortchanged. The reader may be provided only data, opinions, and interpretations that conform to a particular historian's or group of historians' preconceived, perhaps biased, notions. A reader may become swayed by these pronouncements without being aware that there are other, dramatically different interpretations explaining the same historical phenomena. That is why it is important to hear all sides of the Border War question—not just the traditional one.

So what about my argument has provided the reader with a wider, more comprehensive perspective on the Border War? First, I systematically brought into the discussion the various events, both ideological and physical, that affected the Border War. For instance, I examined the divisions and animosities that developed between the South and North as early as the Continental Congress and which became even more accentuated during the Compromises of 1820, 1850, and the Kansas-Nebraska Act. This book also offered a close look at the power structure in Kansas and Missouri during the period 1854 to 1861 to give the reader a foundation and insight into the nature of the political situation in these two states so that he or she might better understand the period that followed. A study of the Massachusetts Emigrant Aid Society was also undertaken to showcase the impact of its leaders and agents on political developments in Kansas and Missouri. Moreover, the abolitionist societies operating underground railroads out of Illinois, Kansas, and Iowa were described in order to reveal the threat they posed to Missouri slave owners and their property as well as the agitation and consternation these societies caused to proslavery Southerners by their aggressive, criminal, and sometimes violent practices. The belligerent and, at times, violent actions of Missourians in Kansas from 1856 through 1860 were depicted, as well as the lawless behavior of Kansans in their rebellion against Federal authority, which leaned heavily toward treason. All of these various events and currents of thought and action fomented a virulent struggle between Missourians and their Southern allies and Kansans and their Northern allies. A mini-Civil War took place between Kansas and Missouri between 1854 and 1861 that eventually ignited and enflamed the entire nation in a horrendous conflict, the American Civil War.

I have cited, moreover, the *invariably ignored,* aggressive actions of Jayhawkers in southeast Kansas from 1858 to the beginning of the Civil War. In addition, I chronicled the subsequent desolation the Jayhawkers produced in western Missouri in the months after the Civil War broke out, when many of the same men who marauded into Missouri in 1858-61 were given Union commands and turned loose in Missouri to finish their grim work. The direct connection between the Jayhawker raids and the emergence of the guerrilla movement in Missouri should appear obvious to most students of history. And the attack on Lawrence, Kansas, on August 21, 1863, appears explainable as a culminating act of violence by Missourians in response to years of Kansas aggressions, not as an isolated act of senseless brutality, as it is sometimes portrayed.

The current characterization of the guerrillas as bandits and desperadoes perpetrating promiscuous and random robberies and murders was challenged through an examination of their background, motives, and connection to the Confederate army. The guerrillas, it was clearly demonstrated, were members of an elite class of Missourians who rose up in defense of their homeland against the incursions of Kansans and joined with the Confederate army in operations in Missouri against the Union army. No other Border War history has emphasized these facts, and few have even mentioned them! The degeneration of the behavior of these men was as much the result of their violent suppression as their willful violence. The sort of behavior the partisans exhibited is precisely the behavior one might have expected once the Federal extermination policy was implemented and pursued aggressively, relentlessly, and ruthlessly. While some of the guerrillas retained reasonably high standards of conduct, many, under the pressures exerted on them by the extermination policy and brutal search and destroy operations, were reduced to savages. Union generals, local commanders, and soldiers treated the guerrillas cruelly from the outset of the conflict, making their behavior virtually a natural and expected result of this brutality. Border War histories traditionally have treated the Missouri guerrillas' behavior in an unrealistic manner, never discussing the effects of this barbarous Federal extermination policy on the subsequent conduct of these young men. Hopefully, this book has provided an antidote for the simplistic treatment of the guerrillas and opened up a more thorough discussion of this subject, which many historians have either ignored or suppressed.

A close examination has also been made of William Clarke Quantrill. At the start of the war, Quantrill attempted to exchange prisoners and to contain the virulence of the conflict. But Union commanders spurned his overtures, and General Halleck's extermination policy was enforced. When the guerrillas became more and more difficult to handle in the winter of 1863-64, Quantrill was forced to the sidelines, and his more extreme and desperate lieutenants, Anderson, Todd, Taylor, and others, came to the fore. The guerrilla captains and their guerrilla charges did not remove Quantrill from his command because he was some sort of monster—as he has been so often portrayed—but rather because he was too principled and too moderate for the guerrilla rank and file. Despite Quantrill's demonstrated leadership abilities and tactical skills, his men ultimately rejected him because he sought, to a degree, to control and limit their brutal actions.

However, Quantrill has been demonized in most Border War histories beyond recognition. It is Quantrill who most historians vilify, using him for a convenient, although unfair target. They have characterized him as a demon, devil, and psychopathic killer in their histories and dredged up his early, checkered past in Kansas to attack his later character and actions. In addition, Quantrill has been a favorite villain in dozens of books and a half score of movies; thus the average reader has been bamboozled into thinking he was something he certainly was not. The demonization of a single man certainly serves as a convenient means of making a scapegoat of one combatant for the evils committed by others on both sides. If Quantrill was a "devil," then one does not have to answer embarrassing questions regarding why he acted/reacted so violently. "Demon" Quantrill provides a convenient excuse to avoid admitting the atrocities committed by Kansans and Federal forces. The real Quantrill was only too clearly an ordinary guerrilla leader in a no-holds-barred, brutal total war not of his own making or even his own liking. When you survey the globe, you will find guerrilla leaders like Quantrill everywhere, many of them considerably more violent than he ever was, but none quite so carefully and systematically vilified.[1]

Aside from Quantrill, great care has been employed in this book to outline the extent of the depredations and intrigues of John Brown, James Montgomery, Daniel Reed Anthony, James Henry Lane, Charles Rainsford Jennison, the various men called "Red Legs," and sundry other marauding Kansans. Many of their actions conformed to the definition of war crimes. Indeed, even more moderate Federal commanders like Ewing, Schofield, and Halleck perpetrated or condoned actions that could have landed them in the docks had the Union lost the war.

Ultimately, history is open-ended; one interpretation leads to another, and controversies are perpetuated through time. I compiled this history in

George Scholl and Gabe Parr, the only survivors of an eight-man squad of Missouri guerrillas decimated in an encounter with a large Federal patrol in 1864 in Boone County. Scholl, shown years after the war, proudly wears a badge showing the image of his demonized leader, William Clarke Quantrill, who Scholl described as "the man we followed and loved." *Courtesy of Claiborne Scholl Nappier*

the belief that the present histories of the Border War were incomplete. They seemed often to embody a pervasive, sometimes veiled, but always real Northern perspective that ignored the plight of slave owners, Southerners, and pro-Southern Missourians during the Civil War while minimizing their sufferings and exaggerating their offenses. In many respects, this modern trend has intensified because of the "political correctness movement." In addition, most studies of the Border War have been too limited in scope and failed to place the conflict in a meaningful political, psychological, and ideological context. This writer earnestly sought to remedy that deficiency.[2]

Notes

Chapter 1

1. Ronald C. Woolsey, "The West Becomes a Problem: The Missouri Controversy and Slavery Expansion as the Southern Dilemma," *Missouri Historical Review* 77, no. 3 (1983): 410-11; *Annals of Congress,* VI, U.S. 15th Cong., 2d Sess. (1858), 174, 185; John C. Rives, ed., *Abridgment of the Debates of Congress, 1789-1856* (New York, 1858), 341.

2. Thomas Jefferson to John Adams, January 22, 1821, in Samuel Flagg Bemis, *John Quincy Adams and the Union* (New York, 1956), 570.

3. *Annals of Congress,* VI, U.S. 16th Cong., 1st Sess. (1858), 355.

4. Barbour to James Madison, February 10, 1820, *Monroe Papers,* Library of Congress.

5. *Annals of Congress,* VI, U.S. 16th Cong., 1st Sess. (1858), 1204.

6. A. Theodore Andreas, *History of the State of Kansas* (Chicago: A. T. Andreas, 1883), 78. For an account of the Thirty-first Congress in relation to the Compromise of 1850, see Allan Nevins, *Ordeal of the Union* (New York: Scribner, 1947); Holman Hamilton, *Prologue to Conflict: The Crisis and Compromise of 1850* (Lexington: University of Kentucky Press, 1964); and Elbert B. Smith, *The Presidencies of Zachary Taylor and Millard Fillmore* (Lawrence: University Press of Kansas, 1988).

7. Woolsey, "The West Becomes a Problem," 3; Hamilton, *Prologue to Conflict*, 114, 135, 141 (for the importance of Douglas).

8. Thomas H. O'Connor, "Cotton Whigs in Kansas," *The Kansas Historical Quarterly* (Spring 1960): 42; Andreas, *History of the State of Kansas,* 80.

9. *Boston Daily Advertiser,* February 23, 1850; Boston *Times,* February 23, 1854; Amos A. Lawrence to George S. Park, January 23, 1857, *Amos A. Lawrence Letterbook,* vol. 2; Edward Everett Hale, M.H.S., May 27, 1854;

Amos A. Lawrence to Mr. Andrews, May 26, 1854, *Amos A. Lawrence Letterbook,* vol. 2.

10. O'Connor, "Cotton Whigs in Kansas," 43.

11. Ibid.

12. James C. Malin, ed., "F. H. Hodder's 'Stephen A. Douglas,'" *The Kansas Historical Quarterly* (August 1939): 227-28.

13. James C. Malin, "The Motives of Stephen A. Douglas in the Organization of Nebraska Territory: A Letter Dated December 17, 1853," *The Kansas Historical Quarterly* 19 (November 1951): 339 (hereafter referred to as "The Motives of Stephen A. Douglas").

14. Malin, "F. H. Hodder's 'Stephen A. Douglas,'" 233.

15. Malin, "The Motives of Stephen A. Douglas," 342.

16. Papers of the Emigrant Aid Society, Manuscript Division, Kansas State Historical Society; Edgar Langsdorf, "S. C. Pomeroy and the New England Emigrant Aid Company, 1854-1858," *The Kansas Historical Quarterly* 7, no. 3 (1938): 227.

17. Samuel A. Johnson, "The Emigrant Aid Company in Kansas," *The Kansas Historical Quarterly* 1, no. 5 (1932): 429-30.

18. Russell K. Hickman, "Speculative Activities of the Emigrant Aid Company," *The Kansas Historical Quarterly* 4, no. 3 (1935): 237.

19. Eli Thayer, *A History of the Kansas Crusade* (New York, 1889), 60.

20. Letters of Amos A. Lawrence about Kansas Affairs (typewritten copy), Archives of the Kansas State Historical Society, 148.

21. Johnson, "The Emigrant Aid Company in Kansas," 430-31.

22. Ibid., 239-41.

23. Charles Robinson, *The Kansas Conflict* (New York: Journal Publishing Co., 1892), in Louise Barry, "Charles Robinson—Yankee

'49er: His Journey to California," *The Kansas Historical Quarterly* 34, no. 2 (1968): 179. In reading Border War histories, it is quite impossible for the author to cringe when it is mentioned that the so-called Border Ruffians of Missouri carried the fearsome bowie knife, when we realize that the refined Dr. Robinson and his colleagues are described as wearing the selfsame tool.

24. Barry, "Charles Robinson—Yankee '49er: His Journey to California," 180.

25. Ibid., 187-88.

26. Langsdorf, "S. C. Pomeroy and the New England Emigrant Aid Company, 1854-1858," 228.

Chapter 2

1. R. Douglas Hurt, "Planters and Slavery in Dixie," *Missouri Historical Review* 88, no. 4 (1994): 398, 407, 413; Floyd C. Shoemaker, "Missouri—Heir of Southern Tradition and Individuality," *Missouri Historical Review* 36, no. 4 (1942): 435.

2. Sceva Bright Laughlin, "Missouri Politics during the Civil War," *Missouri Historical Review* 23, no. 3 (1929): 401.

3. Hurt, "Planters and Slavery in Dixie," 413; George Winston Smith, "New England Business Interests in Missouri during the Civil War," *Missouri Historical Review* 41, no. 1 (1946): 2. Of course, one has to convert the pre-Civil War dollar into modern currency to give it meaning, adjusting the inflationary effects on the money since that time. One dollar in 1860 would be equivalent to a conservatively estimated fourteen dollars to twenty dollars today.

4. Dick Steward, *Duels and the Roots of Violence in Missouri* (Columbia: University of Missouri Press, 2000), 7, 36, 46, 49, 58-74, 78, 112, 124.

5. Laughlin, "Missouri Politics during the Civil War," 404-5.

6. Benjamin C. Merkel, "The Slavery Issue and the Political Decline of Thomas Hart Benton, 1846-1856," *Missouri Historical Review* 38, no. 4 (1944): 388; Laughlin, "Missouri Politics during the Civil War," 406.

7. *Congressional Globe,* 30th Cong., 1st sess., 1078; Appendix, 685-86.

8. *Daily Missouri Republican,* April 13, 1848.

9. *Missouri House Journal,* 15th General Assembly, 1st Sess., 483.

10. William N. Chambers, *Old Bullion Benton; Senator from the New West* (Boston: Little, Brown & Company, 1956), 345.

11. Laughlin, "Missouri Politics during the Civil War," 407-8; William F. Switzler, *William F. Switzler's History of Missouri from 1541 to 1878* (1879; reprint, New York: Arno Press, 1975), 269.

12. Merkel, "The Slavery Issue," 395; *Address of John C. Calhoun to the People of the Southern States June 5, 1849,* 1-18.

13. John D. Morton, " 'A High Wall and a Deep Ditch': Thomas Hart Benton and the Compromise of 1850," *Missouri Historical Review* 94, no. 1 (1999): 8.

14. *North East Reporter,* August 17, 1854.

15. John W. Townsend, "David Rice Atchison," *Register of the Kentucky Historical Society* 8 (May 1910): 39; William E. Parrish, "David Rice Atchison, Frontier Politician," *Missouri Historical Review* 50, no. 4 (1956): 339-40.

16. *Columbia (Missouri) Intelligencer,* March 8, 1834; Parrish, "David Rice Atchison, Frontier Politician," 341.

17. William M. Paxton, *Annals of Platte County, Missouri* (Kansas City, Mo, 1897), 14.

18. *History of Clinton County,* Part I, (St. Joseph, Mo.: National Historical Company), 441-42.

19. William R. Jackson, *Missouri Democracy: A History of the Party and Its Representative—Past and Present,* 3 vols., vol. 1 (Chicago, 1935), 131; William E. Parrish, "David Rice Atchison: Faithful Champion of the South," *Missouri Historical Review* 51, no. 2 (1957): 113-25.

20. Parrish, "David Rice Atchison: Faithful Champion of the South," 122.

21. Laughlin, "Missouri Politics during the Civil War," 401a; Hurt, "Planters and Slavery in Dixie," 397-98.

22. Hurt, "Planters and Slavery in Dixie," 398; *Franklin, Missouri Intelligencer,* July 23, 1819; *Fayette, Missouri Intelligencer,* July 25, 1829; David Manchester to Lydia Manchester, April 19, 1819, Manchester Letters.

23. *Franklin, Missouri Intelligencer,* January 21, November 4, December 18, 1820; January 29, July 2, May 28, November 13, 1821; Hurt, "Planters and Slavery in Dixie," 398-99.

24. Hurt, "Planters and Slavery in Dixie," 401-2; Manuscript Census Schedules, Slaves, 1850 and 1860, Lafayette County and Saline County, Missouri; *Agriculture in the United States in 1860* (Washington, D.C., 1864), 233-34.

25. Letter, Nathaniel Leonard to Abiel Leonard, February 22, 1841; Virginia C. Bay to Abiel Leonard, April 29, 1856, in Abiel Leonard Collection.

26. Hurt, "Planters and Slavery in Dixie," 403.

27. Ibid., 404-6; Lewis Atherton, *Frontier Merchant in Mid-America* (Columbia: University of Missouri Press, 1971), 138-39; Eugene Genovese, *The Political Economy of Slavery: Studies in the Economy of the Slave South* (Middletown, Conn.: Wesleyan University Press, 1989), 56-57.

28. Letter, Walter R. Lenoir to William Lenoir, May 1, 1835, Lenoir Family Papers; Letter, Leland Wright to Abiel Leonard, 21 August 1859, and J. Bull to Abiel Leonard, 25 October 1845, in Abiel Leonard Collection.

29. Ibid. Slaves occupied various categories, such as field hands, house servants, and skilled laborers. The values and relationships differed with each classification.

30. Harrison A. Trexler, "The Value and the Sale of the Missouri Slave," *Missouri Historical Review* 8, no. 2 (1914): 79-80, 84.

31. Hurt, "Planters and Slavery in Dixie," 410; *Investing and Appraisement Record,* Saline County, vol. 1, 1855-61; Trexler, "The Value and the Sale of the Missouri Slave," 69-72.

32. Harrison A. Trexler, "Slavery in Missouri Territory," *Missouri Historical Review* 3, no. 3 (1909): 192. Floyd C. Shoemaker, *Missouri's Struggle for Statehood* (Jefferson City, Mo.: Stephens, 1916), 130-31. In 1860, there

were in the United States 3,953,760 slaves and 488,070 free blacks. Thus, 12 percent of all blacks at that time were free men, some of them long before the Emancipation Proclamation. Andreas, *History of the State of Kansas,* 75.

33. *St. Louis Gazette,* April 26, 1820.

34. *St. Louis Gazette,* May 3, 1820.

35. John M. Peck, *Father Clark; on the Pioneer Preacher* (New York: Sheldon, Lamport, and Blakeman, 1855), 259; Robert S. Douglass, *History of the Missouri Baptists* (Kansas City, Mo.: Western Baptist, 1934), 49.

36. American Antislavery Society, *First Annual Report,* 135-36.

37. Benjamin G. Merkel, "The Abolitionist Aspects of Missouri's Antislavery Controversy 1819-1865," *Missouri Historical Review* 49, no. 3 (1950): 241-47; Wilbur H. Siebert, *Underground Railroad from Slavery to Freedom* (New York: Macmillan, 1898), 156-57.

38. Letter, Jno. O. Roberts to Zebina Eastman, n.d., *Eastman Papers,* manuscript collection in the Chicago Historical Society.

39. Benjamin G. Merkel, "The Underground Railroad and the Missouri Borders," *Missouri Historical Review* 37, no. 3 (1943): 272.

40. Siebert, *Underground Railroad from Slavery to Freedom,* 56-57.

41. *Certificate of Pardon,* June 24, 1846.

42. *Quincy (Ill.) Whig,* August 27, 1842, June 19, 1844; Merkel, "The Underground Railroad," 274.

43. *Revised Statutes of the State of Illinois,* 1845, 180, 387-89.

44. *St. Louis Daily New Era,* September 22, 1847; Merkel, "The Underground Railroad," 276.

45. Jacob Van Ek, "The Underground Railroad in Iowa," *Palimpsest,* vol. 2, 130; Louis Pelzer, "The Negro and Slavery in Early Iowa," *Iowa Journal of History and Politics,* vol. 2, 480.

46. *Whig Messenger,* December 15, 1853.

47. Siebert, *Underground Railroad from Slavery to Freedom*, 112.

48. Sanborn, *Life and Letters of John Brown*, 483.

49. Harrison A. Trexler, *Slavery in Missouri, 1804-1865, Johns Hopkins University Studies in History and Political Science,* series 32, no. 2, (1914): 204.

50. Laughlin, "Missouri Politics during the Civil War," *Johns Hopkins University Studies in History and Political Science,* series 32, no. 2, (1914): 400.

Chapter 3

1. Floyd C. Shoemaker, "Missouri's Proslavery Fight for Kansas, 1854-55," *Missouri Historical Review* 48, no. 3 (1954): 222.

2. Ibid., 225.

3. Ibid., 227.

4. Robinson, *The Kansas Conflict*, 75; Andreas, *History of the State of Kansas*, 83.

5. Shoemaker, "Missouri's Proslavery Fight for Kansas, 1854-55," 232-33.

6. Russell K. Hickman, "The Reeder Administration Inaugurated," *Kansas Historical Quarterly* 36, no. 3 (1970): 318. Andreas, *History of the State of Kansas*, 83.

7. *Lawrence Journal,* January 12, 1891 (Blood's account); Robinson, *The Kansas Conflict,* 69-71.

8. Robinson, *The Kansas Conflict,* 69-71; "More Letters of Edward and Sarah Fitch, 1855-1863," ed. John M. Peterson, part 1, *Kansas History: A Journal of the Plains* 20, no. 1 (1997): 4; Leverett Wilson Spring, *Kansas: The Prelude to the War for the Union* (Boston: Houghton Mifflin Company, 1896), 35.

9. Andreas, *History of the State of Kansas,* 314-15.

10. Robinson, *The Kansas Conflict,* 79-80; Andreas, *History of the State of Kansas,* 314-15; Spring, *Kansas,* 35.

11. Andreas, *History of the State of Kansas,* 314-15; Robinson, *The Kansas Conflict,* 81.

12. Ibid.

13. Robinson, *The Kansas Conflict,* 88.

14. Ibid., 88-89.

15. Hickman, "The Reeder Administration Inaugurated," 305.

16. Message by Pres. Franklin Pierce to Congress, January 24, 1856, in James D. Richardson, *A Compilation of the Messages and Papers of the Presidents,* vol. 7 (New York, 1897), 2886.

17. Ibid.

18. Andreas, *History of the State of Kansas,* 92.

19. Floyd C. Shoemaker, "Missouri's Proslavery Fight for Kansas, 1854-1858," Missouri Historical Review 48, no. 4 (1948): 327-28; Robinson, *The Kansas Conflict,* 92-93, a Congressional committee report; Andreas, *History of the State of Kansas,* 95; Lloyd Lewis, "Propaganda and the Kansas-Missouri War," *Missouri Historical Review* 34, no. 1 (1939): 8, 14. Ironically, Horace Greeley finally became the victim of his own sort of unprincipled journalism when he ran for president against U. S. Grant in 1872. Greeley said of the campaign that he wasn't sure whether he was "running for the presidency or the penitentiary."

20. Andreas, *History of the State of Kansas,* 93, quoting from the *Platte Argus.*

21. Ibid., 87-89.

22. Robinson, *The Kansas Conflict,* 97.

23. Ibid., 97-98.

24. Ibid., 98.

25. Ibid., 102.

26. Ibid., 104-6, a majority Congressional committee report.

27. Ibid, 109; Marvin Ewy, "The United States in the Kansas Border Troubles, 1855-1856," *The Kansas Historical Quarterly* 32, no. 4 (1966): 385.

28. Andreas, *History of the State of Kansas*, 99, 104-5; "More Letters of Edward and Sarah Fitch, 1855-1856," 7; William Stanley Houle, ed., "A Southerner's Viewpoint of the Kansas Situation, 1856-1857," *The Kansas Historical Quarterly* 3, no. 1 (1934): 54; Ewy, "The United States in the Kansas Border Troubles, 1855-1856," 111.

Chapter 4

1. Robinson, *The Kansas Conflict*, 121.

2. Spring, *Kansas*, 85.

3. Robinson, *The Kansas Conflict*, 122.

4. Ibid., 123-25.

5. Ibid., 127-29.

6. David Edwin Harrell Jr., "Pardee Butler: Kansas Crusader," *Kansas Historical Quarterly* 34, no. 4 (1968): 388-92.

7. Robinson, *The Kansas Conflict*, 142-45.

8. Ibid., 146.

9. Ibid., 154-55; Spring, *Kansas*, 54-55.

10. Robinson, *The Kansas Conflict*, 167.

11. Ibid., 169.

12. Stephen Z. Starr, *Jennison's Jayhawkers: A Civil War Cavalry Regiment and Its Commander* (Baton Rouge: Louisiana State University Press, 1973), 13; Andreas, *History of the State of Kansas*, 106, 112-13; A. J. Chipman to S. N. Wood, August 20, 1861, Samuel Newitt Wood Papers, Kansas State Historical Society; "Lane of Kansas," *Kansas City Journal*, September 14, 1879.

13. Robinson, *The Kansas Conflict*, 172-73; Spring, *Kansas*, 68.

14. Spring, *Kansas*, 74, 76.

15. Ibid., 86, 89; Andreas, *History of the State of Kansas*, 115-17. Someone less charitable might call Samuel N. Wood a "thug"; Dale E. Watts, "How

Bloody Was Bleeding Kansas? Political Killings in Kansas Territory, 1854-1861," *Kansas History: A Journal of the Central Plains* 18, no. 2 (1995): 120.

16. Letters of Edward and Sarah Fitch, 1855-1863, 16; William E. Connelley, ed., *Collections of the Kansas State Historical Society,* vol. 13 (Topeka, Kans.: W. R. Smith, Kansas State Printing, 1915), 293-94, 296; *Herald of Freedom,* December 15, 1855; Andreas, *History of the State of Kansas,* 115-16.

17. Ewy, "The United States Army in the Kansas Border Troubles, 1855-1856," 386.

18. Martha B. Caldwell, "The Eldridge House," *Kansas Historical Quarterly* 9, no. 4 (1940): 350-51.

19. Ewy, "The United States Army in the Kansas Border Troubles, 1855-1856," 386-88; Spring, *Kansas,* 92; Andreas, *History of the State of Kansas,* 117; William E. Connelley, *History of Kansas: State and People,* 5 vols., vol. 1 (Chicago: The American Historical Society, Inc., 1928), 441.

20. Andreas, *History of the State of Kansas,* 120-24, quoting, John Brown, letter to his wife, Osawatomie, K.T., December 16, 1855; Connelley, *History of Kansas,* 447, 449.

21. James D. Richardson, ed., *A Compilation of the Messages and Papers of the Presidents,* 1789-1897, 10 vols., vol. 5 (Washington, D.C.: Government Printing Office, 1896-99), 340-55; Ewy, "The United States Army in the Kansas Border Troubles, 1855-1856," 388.

22. Robinson, *The Kansas Conflict,* 232; Andreas, *History of the State of Kansas,* 126, 423; Ewy, "The United States Army in the Kansas Border Troubles, 1855-1856," 389-90; Connelley, *History of Kansas,* 463; Houle, "A Southerner's Viewpoint of the Kansas Situation, 1856-1857," 47-48.

23. Robinson, *The Kansas Conflict,* 234-35. Sam Wood, notorious for his pugnacious, confrontational personality, was an ardent political agitator throughout his life. He was said to have a weakness for the political bribe and was found guilty of profiting from a school-bond swindle in the 1870s. He was murdered in 1885 in Hugoton, Kansas, for unknown reasons, but it was suspected to be for violent political squabbling. Sr. Jeanne McKenna, "With the Help of God and Lucy Stone," *Kansas Historical Quarterly* 36, no. 1 (1970): 13-14.

24. Shalor Winchell Eldridge, *Publications of the Kansas State Historical*

Society Embracing Recollections of Early Days in Kansas, vol. 2 (Topeka, Kans.: Imri Zumwalt, Kansas State Printing Plant, 1920), 41-42; Andreas, *History of the State of Kansas,* 467.

25. Caldwell, "The Eldridge House," 354-55; Robinson, *The Kansas Conflict,* 247, 254.

26. Robinson, *The Kansas Conflict,* 240, 261. Robinson understood, as most people who understand the dynamics of power do, that laws cannot be enforced without the acquiescence of the electorate.

27. Ewy, "The United States Army in the Kansas Border Troubles, 1855-1856," 391-92; Andreas, *History of the State of Kansas,* 131.

28. Jay Monaghan, *Civil War on the Western Border, 1854-1865* (Lincoln: Bison Press, 1948; reprint, Lincoln: University of Nebraska Press, 1955), 63; Robinson, *The Kansas Conflict,* 294-95.

29. Ewy, "The United States Army in the Kansas Border Troubles, 1855-1856," 392-93; Connelley, *History of Kansas,* 520.

30. Ewy, "The United States Army in the Kansas Border Troubles, 1855-1856," 395; Eldridge, *Publications of the Kansas State Historical Society,* 85-86; Connelley, *History of Kansas,* 520; O. E. Richards, "Kansas Experiences of Oscar G. Richards, of Eudora, in 1856," in *Transactions of the Kansas State Historical Society, 1905-06,* vol. 9, 547.

31. Letter, Cooke to Deas, September 5, 1856, *Kansas Historical Collections,* vol. 4, 485-87.

32. Ewy, "The United States Army in the Kansas Border Troubles, 1855-1856," 397.

33. *Transactions of the Kansas State Historical Society, 1905-06,* vol. 9, ed. George W. Martin (Topeka, Kans.: State Printing Office, 1906), 545-46; P. J. Staudenhaus, "Immigrants or Invaders? A Document," *Kansas Historical Quarterly* (Winter 1958): 394-98; "Executive Minutes of Governor John W. Geary, September 11, 1856," *Kansas Historical Collections,* 526, 583-86, 607-12; *New York Daily Tribune,* October 25, 21-25, 28, 29, 31, 1856; Robert Morrow, "Emigration to Kansas in 1856," *Kansas Historical Collections,* vol. 5, 305-6; Eldridge, *Publications of the Kansas State Historical Society,* 73, 77, 80-82, 110-11; Spring, *Kansas,* 169; Robinson, *The Kansas Conflict,* 299.

34. Houle, "A Southerner's Viewpoint of the Kansas Situation, 1856-1857," 151.

35. Samuel A. Johnson, "The Emigrant Aid Company in the Kansas Conflict," *Kansas Historical Quarterly* 6, no. 1 (1937): 32.

36. Floyd C. Shoemaker, "Missouri's Proslavery Fight for Kansas, 1854-1855," *Missouri Historical Review* 48, no. 4 (1948): 325.

Chapter 5

1. Connelley, *History of Kansas,* 483-84 ; W. O. Atkeson, *History of Bates County, Missouri* (Topeka, Kans.: Historical Publishing Company, 1918), 181-82.

2. James C. Malin, "The Hoogland Examination: The United States v. John Brown Jr., et al.," *Kansas Historical Quarterly* 7, no. 2 (May 1938): 133; Connelley, *History of Kansas,* 485.

3. Robinson, *The Kansas Conflict,* 265-66; Connelley, *History of Kansas,* 485-87.

4. Connelley, *History of Kansas,* 487-88; Robinson, *The Kansas Conflict,* 266.

5. Robinson, *The Kansas Conflict,* 266; Connelley, *History of Kansas,* 289-90.

6. Connelley, *History of Kansas,* 491; Robert W. Johannsen, ed., "A Footnote to the Pottawatomie Massacre, 1856," *Kansas Historical Quarterly* 22, no. 3 (1956): 236-41.

7. Robinson, *The Kansas Conflict,* 265-69; Connelley, *History of Kansas,* 492-93; James C. Malin, "Identification of the Stranger at the Pottawatomie Massacre," *Kansas Historical Quarterly* 9, no. 1 (1940): 3-11.

8. Malin, "Identification of the Stranger at the Pottawatomie Massacre," 3-11.

9. Robinson, *The Kansas Conflict,* 269.

10. Ibid., 274.

11. Ibid., 275.

12. Ibid., 276.

13. Ibid., 281-82.

14. Malin, "Identification of the Stranger at Pottawatomie Creek," 10-11.

15. Hildegarde Rose Herklotz, "Jayhawkers in Missouri, 1858-1863," First article, *Missouri Historical Review* 17, no. 3 (1923): 270.

16. Ibid., 267; *Council Grove Press,* November 30, 1863.

17. Hildegarde Rose Herklotz, "Jayhawkers in Missouri, 1858-1863," First article, 268.

18. Jonas Viles, "Documents Illustrating the Troubles on the Border, 1858," *Missouri Historical Review* 1, no. 4 (1907): 198-203; Herklotz, "Jayhawkers in Missouri, 1858-1863," First article, 271-72. Herklotz and Viles have done the most thorough studies of the incursions of Montgomery and Jennison into western Missouri during this period.

19. Herklotz, "Jayhawkers in Missouri, 1858-1863," First article, 271-73; Viles, "Documents Illustrating the Troubles on the Border, 1858," 208-9.

20. Stewart to Senate and House, January 6, 1859, Missouri, *House Journal,* 20th Assembly, 1st Session, App., 68; Viles, "Documents Illustrating the Troubles on the Border, 1858," 206-9.

21. Edward R. Smith, "Marais des Cygnes Tragedy," *Transactions of the Kansas State Historical Society, 1899-1900,* ed. George W. Martin, vol. 6 (Topeka, Kans.: W. Y. Morgan State Printer, 1900), 366-67; "The Marais des Cygnes Massacre," and A. H. Tannar, "Early Days in Kansas," *Collections of the Kansas State Historical Society, 1915-1918,* ed. William E. Connelley, vol. 14 (Topeka, Kans.: Kansas State Printing Plant, 1918), 213-15, 224-34; Atkeson, *History of Bates County, Missouri,* 186, quoting letter, William E. Connelley to W. O. Atkeson. Atkeson lists the site of the Marais des Cygnes Massacre as near what is today Stateline Road, due west of Amoret and then one and one-half miles north and approximately three-eighths of a mile southwest of that point on the state line. Brown's fort in Kansas was later built immediately east and adjacent to the massacre site, a location which provided, with the addition of other nearby mounds, "an unobstructed view to the eastward and all angles for forty or fifty miles with his [Brown's] trusty telescope." Apparently, Brown could not get too close to Missouri.

22. Viles, "Documents Illustrating the Troubles on the Border, 1858," 211; Connelley, *Collections of the Kansas State Historical Society, 1915-1918,* vol. 14, 224-34.

23. Floyd to Stewart, September 9, 1858, Missouri, *House Journal,* 20th Assembly, 1st Sess., App., 78.

24. Holcombe, *History of Vernon County,* 224-26; Oswald Garrison Villard, *John Brown—A Biography Fifty Years After* (Boston: Houghton Mifflin Company, 1911), 368.

25. Missouri, *House Journal,* 20th Assembly, 1st Session, App., 79; *Jefferson City Enquirer* in *Daily Missouri Democrat,* December 30, 1858.

26. Atkeson, *History of Bates County, Missouri,* 184-85.

27. Herklotz, "Jayhawkers in Missouri, 1858-1863," First article, 184-85.

28. Viles, "Documents Illustrating the Troubles on the Border, 1859," 296.

29. Herklotz, "Jayhawkers in Missouri, 1858-1863," First article, 283-84; William Elsey Connelley, *Quantrill and the Border Wars* (Cedar Rapids, Iowa: The Torch Press, Publishers, 1910), 106-9. Doy and Connelley claimed the blacks captured outside Lawrence were "free men," in the legal sense, but no evidence that this is true, except for their profession that it is true, appeared in either account.

30. O. E. Morse, "An Attempted Rescue of John Brown from Charleston, Va. Jail," *Transactions of the Kansas State Historical Society, 1903-1904,* ed. George W. Martin, vol. 8 (Topeka, Kans.: George A. Clark, State Printer, 1904), 214.

31. Ibid., 213-26.

32. Ibid., 213-26, 217; Smith, "New England Business Interests in Missouri during the Civil, War," 2; Redpath was an incendiary type of journalist and agitator. Lloyd Lewis said of him: "This Redpath went across Missouri into Kansas at the start of the troubles, determined to help produce a slave insurrection and national revolution, as he later admitted, a convulsion that would liberate the slave even if it wrecked the Union. A Britisher, he cared nothing for the stability of American institutions." According to Lewis, "The average age of the most important of these correspondents at the time Kansas was bleeding was 23—boys of 23 giving the world its news about one of the most delicate situations in our history!" Lewis also maintained, "What the record shows is that the Free-Soil states had more skill with words to bring to this propaganda battle than had the Cotton Kingdom." Lloyd Lewis, "Propaganda and the Kansas-Missouri War," *Missouri Historical Review* 92, no. 1 (1998): 147.

33. Morse, "An Attempted Rescue of John Brown," 219.

34. Ibid., 225; Richard O. Boyer, *The Legend of John Brown: A Biography* (New York: Alfred A. Knopf, 1973), 4; Odell Shepard, ed., *The Journal of Bronson Alcott,* (Boston, 1938), 316; Otho J. Scott, *The Secret Six: John Brown and the Abolitionist Movement* (New York: Times Books, 1979), 228-29; Frank Preston Stearns, *The Life and Public Services of George Luther Stearns* (Philadelphia: J. B. Lipincott, 1907), 188-89; Harold Schwartz, *Samuel Gridley Howe* (Cambridge, Mass.: Harvard University Press, 1956), 238-39; Richard J. Hinton, *John Brown and His Men* (1894; reprint, New York: Arno Press, 1968), in the appendix by Mary E. Stearns, "George Luther Stearns and John Brown," 226-27; Sen. Charles Sumner, Letters from Boston, Nov. 23, 1859, and from Senate Chamber, Dec. 8, 1859.

35. Stephen Z. Starr, *Jennison's Jayhawkers,* 30-31; Otto J. Scott, *The Secret Six: John Brown and the Abolitionist Movement,* 228-29.

36. Holcombe, *History of Vernon County, Missouri,* 245; Affidavits of George and Charity Hindes in, Missouri, *House Journal,* 21st Assembly, 1st Sess., App., 14-22; William Hutchinson, "Sketches of Kansas Pioneer Experience," *Transactions of the Kansas State Historical Society, 1901-1902,* vol. 7, 401-2; Unidentified clipping, Jennison Scrapbook, Kansas State Historical Society, Topeka, Kansas.

37. Williams to Stewart, November 20, 1860, Missouri, *House Journal,* 21st Assembly, 1st Sess., App., 6; Holcombe, *History of Vernon County, Missouri,* 245; *Osage Valley Star,* November 29, 1860; *Daily Missouri Republican,* November 23, 1860; *Liberty Weekly Tribune,* November 30, 1860; Jonas Viles, "Documents Illustrating the Troubles on the Border, 1860," *Missouri Historical Review* 2, no. 1 (1907): 74; Albert Castel, *A Frontier State at War, Kansas 1861-1865* (Ithaca, N.Y.: Cornell University Press, 1958), 6-7, 13-15, 24.

38. *Daily Missouri Republican,* December 3, 1860; Viles, "Documents Illustrating the Troubles on the Border, 1860," 61-67, 75; Hildegard Rose Herklotz, "Jayhawkers in Missouri, 1858-1863," Second article, *Missouri Historical Review* 17, no. 4 (1923): 505-13; "Convention of Linn and Bourbon Counties, December 1860," in Missouri, *House Journal,* 21st Assembly, 1st Sess., App., 23-24.

39. Viles, "Documents Illustrating the Troubles on the Border, 1860," 68-70; "Governor Medary's Administration," *Transactions of the Kansas State*

Historical Society, 1889-96, ed. F. G. Adams, vol. 5 (Topeka, Kans.: The Kansas State Printing Company, 1896), 631-32.

40. Frost to Stewart, December 8, 10, 1860; *Daily Missouri Republican,* December 11, 12, 1860; Hopewell, *History of the Missouri Volunteer Militia of St. Louis,* 28; "Report of the Committee on Militia, in Missouri," *State Journal,* 21st Assembly, 1st Sess., app., 565; Herklotz, "Jayhawkers in Missouri, 1858-1863," Second article, 511.

41. Jackson to House of Representatives, March 7, 1861, Missouri, *House Journal,* 21st Assembly, 1st Sess., App., 755-56.

Chapter 6

1. Raymond D. Thomas, "A Study in Missouri Politics, 1840-1870," Chapter 1, *Missouri Historical Review* 21, no. 2 (1927): 167; William H. Lyon, "Claiborne Fox Jackson and the Secession Crisis in Missouri," *Missouri Historical Review* 58, no. 4 (1964): 431. Lyon gave the election percentages as 35.2 for John C. Bell, 18.9 for Breckinridge, and 10.2 for Lincoln. Almost two-thirds of Lincoln's support came from St. Louis County. Historian Lyon said, "In the counties with the largest numbers of slaveholders, not one gave Breckinridge a plurality."

2. Missouri, *House Journal,* 21st General Assembly, 1860-1861, 18-43.

3. *New York Tribune Almanac,* 1861, 55.

4. Thomas, "A Study in Missouri Politics, 1840-1870," Chapter 1, 172. The Central Clique was a group of prominent politicians who operated in the central part of Missouri and controlled the Democratic Party.

5. Sceva Bright Laughlin, "Missouri Politics during the Civil War," Chapter 1, *Missouri Historical Review* 23, no. 3 (1929): 404, 408.

6. Ibid., 409, 420, 425.

7. *St. Louis Missouri Republican,* December 25, 1861.

8. Laughlin, "Missouri Politics during the Civil War," Chapter 1, 412.

9. Ibid., 413

10. Ibid.

11. Ibid., 416.

12. Ibid., 415.

13. Doris Davis Wallace, "The Political Campaign of 1860 in Missouri," *Missouri Historical Review* 70, no. 2 (1976): 171.

14. Laughlin, "Missouri Politics during the Civil War," Chapter 1, 415.

15. Lyon, "Claiborne Fox Jackson and the Secession Crisis in Missouri," 427.

16. Laughlin, "Missouri Politics during the Civil War," Chapter 1, 424.

17. Christopher Phillips, "Calculated Confederate: Claiborne Fox Jackson and the Strategy for Secession in Missouri," *Missouri Historical Review* 94, no. 4 (2000): 391-92.

18. William Roed, "Secessionist Strength in Missouri," *Missouri Historical Review* 72, no. 4 (1978): 419-21; *Journal of the Missouri State Convention,* February 1861, 5-7.

19. James O. Broadhead, in Howard Conard, ed., *Encyclopedia of the History of Missouri* (St. Louis, Mo.: Southern History Company, 1901), vol. 6, 331.

20. David Y. Thomas, "Missouri in the Confederacy," *Missouri Historical Review* 18, no. 3 (1924): 383.

21. *Confederate Military History,* vol. 9, 17-18.

22. Phillips, "Calculated Confederate" 398-99.

23. Raymond D. Thomas, "A Study in Missouri Politics, 1840-1870," Chapter 2, *Missouri Historical Review* 21, no. 3 (1927): 441; Gen. Daniel M. Frost, letter to Gov. Claiborne F. Jackson, January 24, 1861; Phillips, "Calculated Confederate," 399.

24. Leonard B. Wurthman Jr., "Frank Blair: Lincoln's Congressional Spokesman," *Missouri Historical Review* 64, no. 3 (1970): 266-67; Dick Steward, *Duels and the Roots of Violence in Missouri,* 131-32; Walter B. Stevens, "Lincoln and Missouri," *Missouri Historical Review* 10, no. 2 (1916): 64.

25. Wurthman, "Frank Blair: Lincoln's Congressional Spokesman," 263-69;

Walter B. Stevens, "Lincoln and Missouri," 64, 116 (for references to Blair's family connections).

26. *St. Joseph Weekly Free Democrat,* June 23, 1860.

27. Wallace, "The Political Campaign of 1860 in Missouri," 179.

28. Stevens, "Lincoln and Missouri," 74, 80.

29. Arthur Roy Kirkpatrick, "Missouri in the Early Months of the Civil War," *Missouri Historical Review* 55, no. 4 (1961): 249, 252.

30. Virgil C. Blum, "The Political and Military Activities of the German Element in St. Louis, 1859-1861," *Missouri Historical Review* 42, no. 2 (1948): 117; Phillips, "Calculated Confederate," 402.

31. Sceva Bright Laughlin, "Missouri Politics during the Civil War," Chapter 3, *Missouri Historical Review* 23, no. 4 (1929): 603; *The War of the Rebellion: A Compilation of the Official Records of the Union and Confederate Armies,* ser. 1, vol. 1 (Washington, D.C.: GPO, 1880), 656; hereafter referred to as *War of the Rebellion.*

32. Kirkpatrick, "Missouri in the Early Months of the Civil War," 252, 255.

33. Phillips, "Calculated Confederate," 407.

34. William Riley Brooksher, *Bloody Hill: the Civil War Battle of Wilson's Creek* (Washington, D.C.: Brassey's, 1995), 54; Walter B. Stevens, "Lincoln and Missouri," 74.

35. Claiborne F. Jackson, letter to David Walker, April 19, 1861.

36. Brooksher, *Bloody Hill,* 55. Greely and Gale was a Unionist business and had been deliberately marked as the addressee to alleviate any suspicion about the boxes although they were naturally not meant to receive the shipment; *War of the Rebellion,* ser. 1, vol. 3, 4. Some said the boxes were also marked "Ale." Edward Conrad Smith, *The Borderland in the Civil War* (New York: The Macmillan Co., 1927), 234.

37. Henry Boernstein (Heinrich Börnstein), *Memoirs of a Nobody: The Missouri Years of an Austrian Radical, 1849-1866* (St. Louis: Missouri Historical Society Press, 1997), 284, 295; Kirkpatrick, "Missouri in the Early Months of the Civil War," 252-53.

38. Boernstein, *Memoirs of a Nobody,* 287.

39. Laughlin, "Missouri Politics during the Civil War," Chapter 3, 603-4; Henry Boernstein, *Memoirs of a Nobody,* 281.

40. Boernstein, *Memoirs of a Nobody,* 288, 294; see Brooksher, *Bloody Hill,* 56-57, for an example of one of the more sensational Lyon-in-dress accounts. See also Jay Monagahan, *Civil War on the Western Border, 1854-1865,* where Lyon is portrayed carrying a "pistol under a basket of eggs" on his lap, for an extra fillip. The archetypal story seems to come from Col. Thomas L. Snead, Jackson's aide, in *Battles and Leaders of the Civil War . . . ,* vol. 1, ed. Robert Underwood Johnson and Clarence Clough Buel, vol. 1 (Seacaucus, N.J.: Castle, 1887). Snead liked the egg basket "filled . . . with loaded revolvers." There is also a similar story concerning the hulking guerrilla chief Cole Younger in Younger's auto-biography that tells of him spying on the defenses at Independence in 1861 dressed as an "apple woman." The author likes Boernstein's first-person account; Smith, *The Borderland in the Civil War,* 198-99.

41. *War of the Rebellion,"* ser. 1, vol. 3, 5-7.

42. Boernstein, *Memoirs of a Nobody,* 296.

43. *War of the Rebellion,* ser. 1, vol. 1, 688.

44. *War of the Rebellion,* ser. 1, vol. 3, 7; Boernstein, *Memoirs of a Nobody,* 296-98.

45. Phillips, "Calculated Confederate," 407; *War of the Rebellion,* ser. 1, vol. 3, 5, 7.

46. Brooksher, *Bloody Hill,* 55-63; Boernstein, *Memoirs of a Nobody,* 296-300; *War of the Rebellion,* ser. 1, vol. 1, 373 and ser. 1, vol. 3, 7; Smith, *The Borderland in the Civil War,* 239-40.

47. *La Grange National American,* May 18, 1861.

48. T. L. Snead, *The Fight for Missouri* (New York: Charles Scribner's Sons, 1886), 186-88; *St. Louis Missouri Republican,* May 25, 1861.

49. Snead, *The Fight for Missouri,* 196-97.

50. Kirkpatrick, "Missouri in the Early Months of the Civil War,"

245-46; *War of the Rebellion,* ser. 1, vol. 3, 11-14; Arthur Roy Kirkpatrick, "Missouri's Secessionist Government, 1861-1865," *Missouri Historical Review* 45, no. 2 (1951): 124; *War of the Rebellion,* ser. 1, vol. 3, 12-13.

51. Thomas C. Reynolds, "General Sterling Price and the Confederacy," unpublished memoir, Reynolds Papers, Missouri Historical Society Library, St. Louis, 42-43; Letters, Thomas C. Reynolds to Jefferson Davis, January 20, 1880, Reynolds Papers, Missouri Historical Society Library, St. Louis; Kirkpatrick, "Missouri in the Early Months of the Civil War," 262-63.

52. *War of the Rebellion,* ser. 1, vol. 3, 17-39, 94-95.

53. Ibid., 16-39, 94; Arthur Roy Kirkpatrick, "The Admission of Missouri to the Confederacy," *Missouri Historical Review* 55, no. 4 (1961): 368; Kirkpatrick, "Missouri's Secessionist Government, 1861-1865," 124.

54. George E. Knapp, *The Wilson's Creek Staff Ride and Battlefield Tour,* Special Study (Fort Leavenworth, Kans.: Combat Studies Institute, U.S. Army Command and General Staff College, 1993), Appendix D, 85-87; *War of the Rebellion,* ser. 1, vol. 3, 57. Lyon appears to have discovered how a large cavalry, like that wielded by the Southerners, can threaten an otherwise powerful army, especially in its effort to forage; *War of the Rebellion,* ser. 1, vol. 3, 395-98.

55. *War of the Rebellion,* ser. 1, vol. 3, 57-61.

56. Ibid., 115-16.

57. Ibid., 61-62, 67; Brian Dirck, " 'We Have Whipped Them Beautifully': The Arkansas Press and Wilson's Creek," *Missouri Historical Review* 84, no. 3 (1990): 282.

58. Dirck, "We Have Whipped them Beautifully," 69.

59. Ibid., 55, 106; *Battles and Leaders of the Civil War . . . ,* vol. 1, 297, 302.

60. Ibid., 95.

61. Ibid., 174, 188; Kirkpatrick, "The Admission of Missouri to the Confederacy," 375.

62. *War of the Rebellion,* ser. 1, vol. 3, 191.

63. Ibid., 171-93. See page 183 for likely inflated casualty figure; Brig.

Gen. B. M. Prentiss, message to Maj. Gen. John C. Frémont, September 22, 1861, in *War of the Rebellion*, ser. 1, vol. 3, 183. The same casualty information was sent by Frémont to Secretary of War Simon Cameron; *Battles and Leaders of the Civil War . . .* , vol. 1, 312-13. In a council of War, Mulligan's officers voted four to two to surrender. *War of the Rebellion*, ser. 1, vol. 3, 183; Wiley Britton, *The Civil War on the Border* (New York: G. P. Putnam's Sons, 1891), 141-43.

64. Kirkpatrick, "Missouri in the Early Months of the Civil War," 247-48.

65. Hildegarde Herklotz, "Jayhawkers in Missouri, 1858-1863," *Missouri Historical Review* 18, no. 1 (October 1923): 67.

Chapter 7

1. "Letters of George Caleb Bingham to James S. Rollins," ed. C. B. Rollins, February 12, 1862, *Missouri Historical Review* 33 (1938): 49-50; James Montgomery to George L. Stearns, June 26, July 5, 1861, George L. Stearns Papers, State Historical Society, Topeka, Kansas; Starr, *Jennison's Jayhawkers*, 39-40.

2. Robinson, *Kansas Conflict*, 434; Fox, "The Early History of the Seventh Cavalry," *Collections of the Kansas State Historical Society, 1909-1910*, ed. George W. Martin, vol. 11 (Topeka, Kans.: State Printing Office, 1910), footnote, 243; Starr, *Jennison's Jayhawkers*, 40; *War of the Rebellion*, ser. 1, vol. 3, 482.

3. Capt. W. E. Prince to Jennison, August 5, 1861, in Seventh Kansas Regimental Letter and Order Book; Fox, "The Early History of the Seventh Kansas Cavalry," 243; Charles Jennison Scrapbook, vol. 1, Kansas State Historical Society, 11.

4. Unsigned letter, Camp Prince, July 23, 1861, in *Leavenworth Daily Conservative*, July 27, 30, August 20, 1861; Starr, *Jennison's Jayhawkers*, 20-21, 41-42; Richard S. Brownlee, *Gray Ghosts of the Confederacy: Guerrilla Warfare in the West, 1861-1865* (Baton Rouge: Louisiana State University Press, 1958), 43.

5. *Leavenworth Daily Conservative*, September 20, 1861; *White Cloud Kansas Chief*, January 2, 1862.

6. Jay Monaghan, *Civil War on the Western Border, 1854-1865*, 81; Unidentified clipping, Jennison's Scrapbook; Unsigned letter, Camp

Prince, July 23, 1861, in *Leavenworth Daily Conservative,* July 11, 17, 27, 30; August 20, 1861; *White Cloud, Kansas Chief,* September 5, 1861; *Olathe Mirror,* June 25, 27, 1861; *Lawrence Republican,* July 17, 1861; *Elwood Free Press,* August 10, 1861; *Lawrence, Kansas State Journal,* August 8, 15, 1861; James Montgomery to George L. Stearns, June 26, George L. Stearns Papers, State Historical Society, Topeka, Kansas; Simeon M. Fox, "The Story of the Seventh Kansas," *Transactions of the Kansas State Historical Society,* 1903-1904, ed. George W. Martin, vol. 8 (Topeka, Kans: George A. Clark, 1904), 23.

7. Edgar Langsdorf, "Jim Lane and the Frontier Guard," *Kansas Historical Quarterly* 9 (1940): 13-25; Starr, *Jennison's Jayhawkers,* 43-45; Albert Castel, *A Frontier State at War,* 34-36; Monaghan, *Civil War on the Western Border,* 128; *War of the Rebellion,* ser. 3, vol. 1, 280-81; Fox, "The Story of the Seventh Cavalry," 14.

8. Starr, *Jennison's Jayhawkers,* 44.

9. Fox, "The Story of the Seventh Cavalry," 23-26; Fox, "The Early History of the Seventh Kansas Cavalry," 244-45; Herklotz, "Jayhawkers in Missouri, 1858-1863," 87.

10. "Letters of Daniel R. Anthony, 1857-1862," ed. Edgar Langsdorf and R. W. Richmond, Part 1, 1857, *Kansas Historical Quarterly* (Spring 1958): 22-23 (letters from Daniel Read Anthony to his father, Daniel Anthony, and sister, Susan B. Anthony, et al.); Starr, *Jennison's Jayhawkers,* 52-54, 57.

11. *War of the Rebellion,* ser. 1, vol. 3, 162, 185; ser. 1, vol. 53, 435-36; *Elwood Free Press,* September 24, 1861; Castel, *A Frontier State at War,* 52.

12. *War of the Rebellion,* ser. 1, vol. 3, 454-55; Langsdorf, "Jim Lane and the Frontier Guard," 22.

13. *War of the Rebellion,* ser. 1, vol. 3, 482.

14. Lane to Prince, August 25, 1861, *War of the Rebellion,* ser. 3, vol. 1, 454-55, 469. Langsdorf, "Jim Lane and the Frontier Guard," 22; Wendell H. Stephenson, "The Political Career of General James H. Lane," *Publications of the Kansas State Historical Society,* vol. 3 (Topeka, Kans.: State Printing Plant, 1930), 105, 114; "Lane," *Kansas Free State Press,* April 30, 1855, *Collections of the Kansas State Historical Society, 1923-25,* ed. William Elsey Connelley, vol. 16 (Topeka, Kans: B. P. Walker State Printer, 1925), 33; *Weston, Platte Argus,* in *Leavenworth Daily Conservative,* August 17, 1861.

15. William F. Zornow, *Kansas: A History of the Jayhawk State* (Norman: University of Oklahoma Press, 1957), 109.

16. John Speer, "The Burning of Osceola, Mo., by Lane and the Quantrill Massacre Contrasted," *Transactions of the Kansas State Historical Society, 1899-1901,* ed. George W. Martin, vol. 6 (Topeka, Kans.: W. Y. Morgan, State Printer, 1900), 305-12; H. E. Palmer, "The Black-Flag Character of War on the Border," *Transactions of the Kansas State Historical Society, 1905-06,* ed. George W. Martin, vol. 9 (Topeka, Kans.: State Printing Office, 1906), 457; Monaghan, *Civil War on the Western Border,* 195-97; Castel, *A Frontier State at War,* 53-55; *Dictionary of National Biography,* vol. 5, 577; *War of the Rebellion,* ser. 1, vol. 3, 196.

17. Monaghan, *Civil War on the Western Border,* 207; Herklotz, "Jayhawkers in Missouri, 1858-1863," 69; *Daily Missouri Republican,* October 16, 1861; Wiley Britton, *The Civil War on the Border,* 2 vols. vol. 1 (New York: G. P. Putnam's Sons, 1899), 147.

18. Fox, "The Early History of the Seventh Volunteer Cavalry," 250; Palmer, "The Black-Flag Character of War on the Border," 455-56.

19. David McCullough, *Truman* (New York: Simon & Schuster, 1992), 30-31.

20. Stephenson, "The Political Career of General James H. Lane," 116, quoting the *Leavenworth Daily Conservative,* September 21, October 10, 1861.

21. *War of the Rebellion,* ser. 1, vol. 35, 505-6; 515-16; 520-22; Castel, *A Frontier State at War,* 56, 62.

22. Sceva Bright Laughlin, "Missouri Politics during the Civil War," *Missouri Historical Review* 24, no. 1 (1929): 88-89; Leonard Wurthman, "Frank Blair: Lincoln's Congressional Spokesman," *Missouri Historical Review* 64, no. 3 (April 1970): 268-69, 273.

23. *War of the Rebellion,* ser. 1, vol. 3, 469.

24. Ibid., 553; Robert L. Turkoly-Joczik, "Frémont and the Western Department," *Missouri Historical Review* 82, no. 4 (1988): 379-80.

25. Britton, *The Civil War on the Border,* 175-79; "Letters of George Caleb Bingham to C. B. Rollins," February 12, 1862, 53-54; Palmer, "The Black-Flag Character of War on the Border," 46. A soldier who refers to himself

as a "Jayhawker," writing for the *Mishawaka Indiana Enterprise* refers to a raid by Jennison on approximately November 14, 1861, as one of many. See "This Regiment Will Make a Mark," ed. Jeffrey L. Patrick, *Kansas History a Journal of the West* 20, no. 1 (1997): 54.

26. Fox, "The Story of the Seventh Kansas," 28; "Letters of Daniel Anthony, 1857-1862," ed. Edgar Langsdorf and R. W. Richmond, Part 3, October 1, 1861-June 7, 1862, 362.

27. Fox, "The Story of the Seventh Kansas," 29; "Letters of Daniel Anthony, 1857-1862," Part 3, 355.

28. "Letters of Daniel Anthony, 1857-1862," Part 3, 355; George Miller, *Missouri's Memorable Decade, 1860-1870* (Columbia, Mo.: 1898), 73.

29. "Letters of Daniel R. Anthony, 1857-1862," Part 3, 356-57; Daniel Wilder, in *The Annals of Kansas* (Topeka, Kans., 1886), 274, said that the loot acquired by the slaves taken by Anthony allowed them to make a "gay procession" into Leavenworth some time later; *War of the Rebellion,* ser. 1, vol. 8, 46-47, 53, 507; Robert Allison Brown III, comp., "Wayside Rest in War and Peace," unpublished manuscript, 1966, foreword, 65, 138-47, 154. Most of the data, as shown, is taken from the letters of Elizabeth Brown Daniel. The author of this work received a copy of Robert A. Brown III's unpublished book manuscript from Mrs. Carol Unnewehr, Harrisonville, Missouri, also a descendant of Robert Allison Brown Sr. She lives in the historic Brown home.

30. *War of the Rebellion,* ser. 1, vol. 8, 507-8.

31. Pomeroy, War Diary, typescript, Kansas State Historical Society, Topeka, Kansas, 15.

32. Webster Moses to Mary Mowry, February 9, 1862, in Webster W. Moses Letters, Kansas State Historical Society, Topeka, Kansas.

33. "Letters of George Caleb Bingham to C. B. Rollins," February 12, 1862, 45-78; *Daily Missouri Democrat,* December 21, 1861; William Voran Powell, personal communication with the author.

34. Castel, *A Frontier State at War,* 55-56: Richard B. Sheridan, "From Slavery in Missouri to Freedom in Kansas: The Influx of Black Fugitives and Contrabands into Kansas, 1854-1865," *Kansas History: A Journal of the Central Plains* 12, no. 1: (1989): 37.

35. *War of the Rebellion,* ser. 1, vol. 8, 449.

36. Ibid., 546-47.

37. *Leavenworth Conservative,* April 18, 1862; Starr, *Jennison's Jayhawkers,* 133-44.

38. "Letters of Daniel Anthony, 1857-1862," Part 3, 366.

39. *Cincinatti Gazette,* August 4, 1862.

40. "The Civil War Letters of Bazel F. Lazear," ed. Vivian Kirkpatrick McLarty, *Missouri Historical Review* 92, no. 4 (1998): 394.

41. " 'Life Is Uncertain . . .': Willard Hall Mendenhall's 1862 Civil War Diary," Part 1, *Missouri Historical Review* 78, no. 4 (1984): 439-50.

42. " 'Life Is Uncertain . . .': Willard Hall Mendenhall's 1862 Civil War Diary," Part 2, *Missouri Historical Review* 79, no. 1 (1984): 66-83.

43. "The Quantrill Raid," *Collections of the Kansas State Historical Society, 1913-1914,* vol. 13 (Topeka, Kans.: Kansas State Printing Plant, 1915), 447.

44. Wiliam Elsey Connelley, *Quantrill and the Border Wars* (Cedar Rapids, Iowa: The Torch Press, Publishers, 1910), 411-13; Starr, *Jennison's Jayhawkers,* 214.

45. *War of the Rebellion,* ser. 1, vol. 23, 223.

46. George W. Martin, "Memorial Monuments and Tablets in Kansas," *Collections of the Kansas State Historical Society, 1909-1910,* ed. George W. Martin, vol. 11 (Topeka, Kans.: State Printing Office, 1910), 279; Castel, *A Frontier State at War,* 137; Lucien Carr, *Missouri: A Bone of Contention* (Boston and New York, 1888), 334.

47. Martin, "Memorial Monuments and Tablets in Kansas," 279-81.

48. Connelley, *Quantrill and the Border Wars,* 411-12; *War of the Rebellion,* ser. 1, vol. 23, 390. Starr, *Jennison's Jayhawkers,* 253.

49. Connelley, *Quantrill and the Border War,* 412-15. Other Red Legs for the public record were James Flood, Jerry Malcom, ____Hawkins, Jack Hays, John Blachley, Harry Lee, Newt Morrison, ____Gladhart, John Salathiel, Joseph Guilliford, Al Saviers, and ____ Alsup.

50. John Burke, *Buffalo Bill: The Noblest Whiteskin* (New York: G. P. Putnam's Sons, 1972), 42. "Julia Cody Goodman's Memoirs of Buffalo Bill," ed. Don Russell, *The Kansas Historical Quarterly* (Winter 1962): 488-89, 491; *Jennison's Jayhawkers,* 216, 384-85.

51. *Leavenworth Conservative,* September 20, 1861; Spring, *Kansas,* 285-86.

Chapter 8

1. Connelley, *Quantrill and the Border Wars,* 17, 42-44, 54-60. Much of Connelley's data on Quantrill's life was obtained from W. W. Scott, Quantrill's boyhood friend, who compiled information on Quantrill with the intention of writing his biography. Before he was able to do so, however, he died. Scott had contacts with Quantrill's mother, Caroline Quantrill, as well as most of his Canal Dover associates and gathered a large amount of varied information that was ultimately purchased by Connelley at Scott's death. Connelley, in addition, interviewed and corresponded with many other interested parties in his own right, and although highly biased against Quantrill, he is one of the foremost authorities on him. Connelley, who became the secretary of the Kansas State Historical Society, was a man with the instincts of a historian—a passion to record events accurately and completely. But he lacked the capacity to see any moral value or justification in the Southern cause, and his unmitigated Union bias marred his histories to a considerable extent, as even Union-leaning historians admit.

2. Ibid., 79, 84-85; *Quantrill Letters,* transcribed by Joanne Chiles Eakins, n.p., n.d., 21.

3. Connelley, *Quantrill and the Border Wars,* 75.

4. Quantrill Papers, Kansas State Historical Society, Topeka, Kansas; Connelley, *Quantrill and the Border Wars,* 75, 81-82. Quantrill's letters also appear in Connelley's book.

5. Connelley, *Quantrill and the Border Wars,* 91.

6. Quantrill Papers, Kansas State Historical Society, Topeka, Kansas; Connelley, *Quantrill and the Border Wars,* 89.

7. Quantrill Papers, Kansas State Historical Society, Topeka, Kansas.

8. Ibid.

9. Connelley, *Quantrill and the Border Wars,* 88.

10. Holland Wheeler, "Early Life of Quantrill in Kansas," *Transactions of the Kansas State Historical Society, 1901-1902,* ed. George W. Martin, vol. 7 (Topeka, Kans.: W. Y. Morgan Printer, 1902), 224-26.

11. Connelley, *Quantrill and the Border Wars,* 117-19.

12. Ibid., 106-9, 117-20.

13. Ibid., 134; John M. Lutz, "Quantrill and the Morgan Walker Tragedy," *Transactions of the Kansas State Historical Society,* ed. George W. Martin, vol. 8 (Topeka, Kans.: George A. Clark, 1904), 327.

14. Connelley, *Quantrill and the Border Wars,* 150.

15. Ibid., 118-20, 134-36, 138.

16. Ibid., 129, 141-44.

17. Lutz, "Quantrill and the Morgan Walker Tragedy," 324; Connelley, *Quantrill and the Border Wars,* 146-49.

18. Connelley, *Quantrill and the Border Wars,* 146-53.

19. Lutz, "Quantrill and the Morgan Walker Tragedy," 325; Connelley, *Quantrill and the Border Wars,* 152-56.

20. Connelley, *Quantrill and the Border Wars,* 152-65; Lutz, "Quantrill and the Morgan Walker Tragedy," 324.

21. Lutz, "Quantrill and the Morgan Walker Tragedy," 326; Albert Castel, *William Clarke Quantrill: His Life and Times* (Norman: University of Oklahoma Press, 1962, 1999), 39; Connelley, *Quantrill and the Border Wars,* 160-65, 174-77; Edward Leslie, *The Devil Knows How to Ride* (New York: De Capo Press, 1998), 76. Leslie has Morrison fall with "nineteen buckshot in his hide," a curiously detailed "fact" and supplies a quite detailed scene attending the killing: "The wounded man was flat on his back, delirious with pain, but Quantrill could not take the chance that he might recover enough to tell what he knew. He thrust his pistol barrel into Lipsey's mouth and pulled the trigger." Leslie also says, "There are no disagreements about what happened to the corpses. They were dumped into a hole and covered with dirt." Actually, there are other stories about the skeletons being used as medical specimens (see Connelley, page 177).

22. Connelley, *Quantrill and the Border Wars*, 178-80.

23. Brian Burnes, "Historical Marker Denotes Quantrill Residence in KC," *The Kansas City Star*, November 28, 1996; Laura R. Hockaday, "Unmarking History," *The Kansas City Star*, September 23, 1998. The first article refers to Quantrill staying with the Gills in 1859, which is impossible and probably a natural lapse in a family's memory of events over a century later; in the second article, Shutz said that the Gill plantation was between 114th Street Terrace and 121st Street, between Wornall Road on the east and State Line Road on the west in modern Kansas City; W. L. Webb, *Battles and Biographies of Missourians: or the Civil War Period of Our State* (Kansas City, Mo.: Hudson-Kimberly Publishing Co., 1900), 267.

24. Connelley, *Quantrill and the Border Wars*, 179-83.

25. Ibid., 173-95. Kansans used the word "ruffians" as a loaded catchword for their enemies in Missouri and Kansas, as in Connelley's example, without any respect for the denotation of the term. Modern historians, in my view, should be more wary of the term if they wish to pretend objectivity.

26. Ibid., 198-222; Robinson, *The Kansas Conflict*, 68-69; Connelley, *Quantrill and the Border Wars*, 222.

27. *War of the Rebellion*, ser. 1, vol. 8, 57.

28. Ibid., 336.

29. Connelley, *Quantrill and the Border Wars*, 225-28.

30. *War of the Rebellion*, ser. 2, vol. 3, 468; Connelley, *Quantrill and the Border Wars*, 237. While the author has chosen to use the term "Civil War" in deference to common custom, Southerners prefer the term "War Between the States" as being more accurate, citing the *Congressional Record* of March 2, 1928. In Senate Joint Resolution 41, Congress recognized the title "War Between the States" as proper because (1) the war was waged against two organized governments: the United States of America and the Confederate States of America (civil wars are fought usually between two parties within the same government); (2) it was not a "war of secession" because the Southern states seceded without much thought of war, unless it was forced on them to remain part of the Union, and the right of a state to secede had not been heretofore questioned; and (3) it was a "War Between the States" because it was a case of twenty-two non-seceding

states making war upon eleven seceding states to force them back into the Union. The source of these distinctions is Lt. Col. Edwin Kennedy.

31. *War of the Rebellion,* ser.1, vol. 8, 346-47; Connelley, *Quantrill and the Border Wars,* 238-47. For the proceedings of the military commission that had Hoy executed, see National Archives, Washington, D.C., Old Military Reference Branch; *Leavenworth Conservative,* July 29, 1862; *Leavenworth Times,* July 29, 1862; Declaration by Brig. Gen. James G. Blunt, Headquarters, Department of Kansas, July 26, 1862; *Tri-Weekly Missouri Republican,* August 1, 1862, 213. Samuel W. Carpenter, referred to as a "Government detective" during the tribunal trying Perry Hoy, appears to have been likely a spy since he lived but a short way from the bridge. He testified against Jeremiah "Perry" Hoy in his trial before the military commission, saying that Hoy was present at the murder of a "soldier" (name unknown at the trial) and that of a civilian named "Allison" (no first name known at the trial). Carpenter testified that the alleged killings occurred on 20 March 1862. Actually, they would have occurred on 22 March, if they occurred at all. Carpenter provided information as to the exact, inflammatory words, spoken by Quantrill to the bridge guard, even though he testified that he was hidden "thirty-five rods [577 feet] from them [the guerrillas] in the edge of the brush." Carpenter claimed that Quantrill said to Allison's son, "Boy! Go back to Kansas City and tell the sons of bitches you saw Quantrell's Band kill your father!"

Carpenter said that after the burning of the bridge, he led the soldiers of Col. Robert B. Mitchell's Second Cavalry to David Tate's house where Quantrill was hiding. When he got to the house, he knocked on the door and someone came to the door who told him that Quantrill and twenty-six guerrillas were inside. As recorded in the *War of the Rebellion* (see above citation), however, Colonel Mitchell told an entirely different story. In Mitchell's account, he sent one of his officers, a Major Pomeroy, with 120 men to the Tate house to arrest Tate for being "connected with Quantrill." Mitchell said, "When Major Pomeroy reached the house, he demanded entrance." It was Pomeroy who knocked on Tate's door, not Carpenter. No one told Pomeroy at the door how many men were inside; that was done by the two guerrillas who fled the house later. They informed Pomeroy that "Quantrill was in the house with 26 men."

Another fact of which Carpenter was not aware and which indicates that he was not even at the scene was that Quantrill shot through the door at the person rapping on Tate's door. Carpenter, had he been there, would have remembered that most clearly. Carpenter said that he was "positive [he saw Quantrill] on the night we set fire to the house" despite the fact that the Quantrill was always behind a closed door, it was pitch black, and the guerrillas broke out through the weather boarding at the back of the house in complete darkness.

Carpenter has every appearance of being a liar and trumped-up witness. The fact that the son of "Allison" failed to appear at the trial is also suspicious. Neither of the men Hoy was an accessory to killing, moreover, are named precisely, which is suspect since the detective had four months to learn their names and said that he already "knew them both" and was, after all, a supposed detective. Hoy was found guilty of being an accessory in the killings at the bridge and of violating "the laws and usages of war." He also was found guilty of "acts of a treasonable character."

Before Hoy was executed, Brigadier General Blunt, commander of the Department of Kansas, discovered that it was illegal to carry out the execution because of Army General Orders No. 71, which stipulated that the president of the United States must sign such an order for execution. Blunt sidestepped this technicality neatly, stating that "the case is of such a character and in view of the fact that this class of assassins are becoming so numerous and bold of late, I consider the public safety demands his execution without delay . . . trusting my action in this matter will meet the approval of the President." He sent the president an account of the execution, after the fact, and Lincoln made no complaint about having his orders disobeyed. However, the execution heightened the animosity felt by the guerrillas against those hunting them.

Although historian Albert Castel said, "Perry Hoy had been hanged at Fort Leavenworth," "at the end of August," both the *Tri-Weekly Missouri Republican,* 1 August 1862, and a hand-written letter to Abraham Lincoln from Capt. Thomas Moonlight, assistant adjutant general, from headquarters, Department of Kansas, dated July 28, 1862 said he was shot, and a month earlier than Castel infers. (A photocopy of the letter is in my possession.) I give special thanks to Susan Hejka for her investigations into Perry Hoy's trial and death and for photocopies of all the pertinent documents associated therewith. Castel, *William Clarke Quantrill: His Life and Times,* 95. See also W. L. Webb, 270-71, for another mention of Hoy's execution by firing squad.

Chapter 9

1. *War of the Rebellion,* ser. 1, vol. 8, 358-59; William H. Gregg, "A Little Dab of History Without Embellishment [sic]," Western Historical Manuscript Collection, Columbia, Missouri. Gregg's manuscript was recorded by Connelley years after the events described. While much of what Gregg said is generally true, some details are likely inaccurate. Like all "war stories," Gregg's account should be taken with some allowances. The same is true with John McCorkle's book, *Three Years with Quantrill,* which was dictated fifty years after the events described. McCorkle was one of

Quantrill's guerrillas, but his account is filled with inaccuracies. I use nothing from the "Memoirs of Frank Smith," a former guerrilla, an account held privately by historian Albert Castel, because only excerpts are obtainable, and the context of the remarks appears not to be part of the public record. In my view, most accounts recorded decades after the events described are correct in spirit only, the absolute veracity of the details having deteriorated in varying degrees over the years despite the earnest recollections of the tellers. Some recollections, naturally, are more accurate than others, depending on the quality of memory retention of the tellers. Much history, however, is made up of these kind of accounts, when better information is unavailable.

2. Gregg, "A Little Dab of History Without Embelishment [sic]," 360-61.

3. Connelley, *Quantrill and the Border Wars,* 317-18. For images of the distinctive hats, see pages 424, 440, 463-64, 473, 478. See photos of a guerrilla shirt in Donald L. Gilmore, "Revenge in Kansas, 1863," *History Today* 43 (March 1993): 52; for the best views, see, Carl W. Breihan, *The Killer Legions of Quantrill* (Seattle, Wash., 1971), 38, 45, 53.

4. *War of the Rebellion,* ser. 1, vol. 13, 57-58.

5. Ibid., 120-22. A message by Lt. Col. James T. Buel reported that the mail was going to Harrisonville and that the escort was composed of fifteen men. I use Cochran's figures, which said the destination was Pleasant Hill and the escort was twenty-four men; Buel ordered the escort, but Cochran conducted it. Connelley, *Quantrill and the Border Wars,* 254.

6. Ibid., 130.

7. Ibid., 131-32.

8. Ibid., 140.

9. William H. Gregg, "A Little Dab of History Without Embelishment [sic]"; *War of the Rebellion,* ser. 1, vol. 13, 154-60; Connelley, *Quantrill and the Border Wars,* 255-58, 262. *The American Heritage Dictionary of the English Language,* ed. William Morris (Boston: Houghton Mifflin Company, 1976), 446. Erysipelas is "an acute disease of the skin and subcutaneous tissue caused by a streptococcus and marked by spreading inflammation, also called "St. Anthony's Fire."

10. *War of the Rebellion,* ser. 1, vol. 13, 173.

11. Britton, *Civil War on the Border,* 313-25; Connelley, *Quantrill and the Border Wars,* 259-68; *War of the Rebellion,* ser. 1, vol. 13, 226-30; Castel, *William Clarke Quantrill: His Life and Times,* 93. Buel, in his official report of the battle, claimed that there were two axes of advance into the town, one a column traveling along the Big Spring Road and the other column moving along the Harrisonville Road. All the Union pickets were killed or later found to be missing. Buel also claimed the camp was around four hundred yards from the headquarters, not a half-mile. According to Buel, during the attack on the camp, Captain Breckinridge attempted a number of times to raise a "piece of his shirt . . . as a token of surrender," but "it was immediately pulled down by the men of his command." Buel said the negotiations for surrender were conducted between he and Colonel Thompson; whereas, historian Wiley Britton insisted Hays performed this function. At the end of hostilities, half of Buel's men were either missing, had fled, or were dead, the force paroled being only 150 men of Buel's original force of 312 men. Axline, in his report, described the camp as being three-quarters of a mile from headquarters. He said he heard firing at daybreak from the direction of headquarters, and three minutes later firing in the north part of his camp. The often-cited notion that Buel surrendered a still-potent force is not credible.

12. Britton, *The Civil War on the Border,* 326-35; Barry A. Crouch, "A 'Fiend in Human Shape'? William Clarke Quantrill and his Biographers," *Kansas History: A Journal of the Central Plains* 22, no. 2 (1999): 152.

13. Gregg, "A Little Dab of History Without Embelishment [sic]."

14. *War of the Rebellion,* ser. 1, vol. 8, 231, 253-56. In a report on August 12-14, Burris referred to "_____Toughs, my guide," likely the infamous Captain Tough of Red Leg notoriety. At one moment, it appears, the ubiquitous Tough was a thug and Red Leg, the next minute, a member of Blunt's or some other Union commander's staff.

15. Connelley, *Quantrill and the Border Wars,* 269-72; *War of the Rebellion,* ser. 1, vol. 13, 803; Gregg, "A Little Dab of History Without Embelishment [sic]."

16. *War of the Rebellion,* ser. 1, vol. 13, 267; Connelley, *Quantrill and the Border Wars,* 273.

17. Gregg, "A Little Dab of History Without Embelishment [sic]; *War of the Rebellion,* ser. 1, vol. 13, 313-14; Emancipation Proclamation: January 1, 1863, found at the Avalon Project at the Yale Law School, http://www.yale.edu/lawweb/avalon/emancipa.htm. Lincoln freed slaves

held in "Arkansas, Texas, Louisiana (except the parishes of St. Bernard, Plaquemines, Jefferson, St. John, St. Charles, St. James, Ascension, Assumption, Terrebone, Lafourche, St. Mary, St. Martin, and Orleans, including the city of New Orleans), Mississippi, Alabama, Florida, Georgia, South Carolina, North Carolina, and Virginia (except the forty-eight counties designated as West Virginia, and also the counties of Berkeley, Accomac, Northhampton, Elizabeth City, York, Princess Anne, and Norfolk, including the cities of Norfolk and Portsmouth."

18. *War of the Rebellion,* ser. 1, vol. 13, 347-48, 791; Connelley, *Quantrill and the Border Wars,* 274; William H. Gregg, "A Little Dab of History Without Embelishment [sic]. Gregg called the raid on Shawneetown and the assault on the wagon train in mid-October a "Waterhall" (a small disaster) because the guerrillas were not able to find much serviceable clothing, which they needed desperately. Gregg mentions nothing of Catherwood's assault on the rear of Quantrill's column on November 3.

19. Connelley, *Quantrill and the Border Wars,* 279-81; *War of the Rebellion,* ser. I, vol. 22, chap. 34, 907, letters dated November 2, 1863. In his letter to Reynolds, Price extolled Quantrill, saying, "Colonel Quantrill now has with him some 350 men of that daring and dashing character which has made the name of Quantrill so feared by our enemies, and have aided so much to keep Missouri, though overrun by Federals, identified with the Confederacy." Price does not appear to be distancing himself from Quantrill a whit. Historian William Connelley described Quantrill at this time from a rabid, Unionist perspective, saying, "If he was not blood-mad, insane, he was a monster, the most gory, blood-thirsty and horrible character in American history. And the actions of his whole life would indicate that he was degenerate and depraved rather than insane—that he loved to kill—delighted in murder and rapine." Clearly, as the reader will observe in future chapters, Quantrill was more humane than his chiefs or his men. You have to wonder whether Connelley, a Kentuckian, was ingratiating himself into the good graces of the New England abolitionists who were his Kansas friends.

20. *War of the Rebellion,* ser. 1, vol. 13, 618-19.

21. Castel, *A Frontier State at War,* 111-12.

Chapter 10

1. Don R. Bowen, "Guerrilla War in Western Missouri, 1862-1865: Historical Extensions of the Relative Deprivation Hypothesis," *Comparative Studies in Society and History* 19 (January 1977): 32.

2. Don R. Bowen, "Guerrilla War in Western Missouri, 1862-1865," 49-50 (excerpt from William Elsey Connelley).

3. Connelley, *Quantrill and the Border War*, 41.

4. Ibid., 123, 173. Thomas Goodrich, *Black Flag: Guerrilla Warfare on the Western Border, 1861-1865* (Bloomington and Indianapolis: Indiana University Press, 1995), 28. Goodrich's reference to the alleged eerie quality of Quantrill's name is not new. Robert G. Elliott referred to Quantrill's name as one of "barbaric strangeness" (see Eliot in references to "The Quantrill Raid"). Because the name is a traditional English one, this impression by Elliott seems somewhat odd. But in Elliott's case, because he was a victim of the Lawrence raid, Quantrill's name might have produced a traumatic, emotional response independent of the sound of the name. Moderns should not experience the same effect, it seems to the author.

5. Monaghan, *Civil War on the Western Border, 1861-1865*, 168, 198, 281-82.

6. Castel, *A Frontier State at War*, 138.

7. Goodrich, *Black Flag*, 35-36; Gregg, "A Little Dab of History Without Embelishment [sic]"; Connelley, *Quantrill and the Border War*, 283, originally obtained by W. W. Scott from Taylor, later obtained by Connelley for his collection of Border War data.

8. Don R. Bowen, "Quantrill, James, Younger, *et al.*: Leadership in a Guerrilla Movement, Missouri, 1861-1865," *Military Affairs* 41, no. 1 (1977): 42.

9. Ibid., 43-48; Bowen, "Guerrilla War in Western Missouri," 49. In investigating a person who lived in Cass County in 1862, the author, in a three-page-long list of names from the Cass County, Missouri, Census, found no property owners who held slaves, which appears to suggest the rarity of slave ownership. Only 2 percent of Missourians owned slaves. Of course, the percentage of slave ownership was larger in the areas along the Missouri and Mississippi Rivers. Western Missouri had fewer slaves than these areas.

10. Bowen, "Guerrilla War in Western Missouri, 1861-1865," 47, footnote 27.

11. In revolutions fought not by a middle class but by an underclass of

peasants, like in Mexico in the nineteenth century, the question of "bandit-ry" was even more difficult to define, explain, and justify. Emiliano Zapata, the guerrilla leader, learned that "the ending of banditry in general would prove to be impossible. It was one thing to make pious proclamations against theft, but Zapata understood that his forces had to eat, and eating meant that they had little recourse but banditry in places where the *pacíficos* [friendly population] would no longer cooperate." Zapata defended his poor fighters, saying, "One cannot call a person a bandit who, weak and helpless, was despoiled of his property by someone strong and powerful, and now that he cannot tolerate more, makes a superhuman effort to regain control over that which used to pertain to him. The despoiler is the bandit not the despoiled!" So the issue of "banditry" has many sides, depending on the nature of the guerrilla struggle and its economic and social setting. Both the Communists and the Nazis have referred to irregular opponents as "bandits" to give credibility to their eradication. But, as in the case of the Border War, to term large military units composed of middle- to upper-class young men "bandits" is unrealistic. Samuel Brunk, " 'The Sad Situation of Civilians and Soldiers': The Banditry of Zapatismo in the Mexican Revolution," *The American Historical Review* 101, no. 2 (1996): 337, 345; Zapata's manifesto, "A Todas la Pueblos en General," December 31, 1911, in Isidro Fabela and Josefina E. de Fabela, eds., *Documentos históricos de la revolución mexicana*, vol. 21: *Emiliano Zapata, el Plan de Ayala, y su política agraria* (Mexico City, 1970), 58-59; U.S. War Department, General Orders No. 100, Washington, D.C., April 24, 1863, found at the Avalon Project at the Yale Law School, http://www.yale.edu/lawweb/avalon/lieber.htm; John Newman Edwards, *Noted Guerrillas, or the Warfare on the Border* (Shawnee, Kans.: Two Trails Publishing, 1996), 19-20. Bowen, "Quantrill, James, Younger, et al.," footnote 12. Bowen says that Edwards "knew many of the guerrillas personally, and the staff of that command [Shelby's] seems, at times, to have been virtually inter-changeable with the guerrilla movement."

12. *War of the Rebellion*, ser. 2, vol. 3, 468; *Kansas City Weekly Journal of Commerce*, May 30, June 27, 1863. Not all nations abide by these "Rules of War," said Col. James Speicher (U.S. Army, retired), and countries "like North Vietnam never signed the accords and did not treat prisoners humanely, and that included execution." According to Dr. Jerold E. Brown, professor at the U.S. Army Command and General Staff College, another reason for the ban on executions is that "we treat captured guer-rillas more humanely today, not because we respect them more, but because we see them as sources of information. . . . They talk about themselves and their organizations, and they change sides without hesita-tion." All agreed that the public relations issue is important. Dr. Brown said, "You can't shoot captured guerrillas [today] without consequence."

Jerold E. Brown, interview by author, Fort Leavenworth, Kans., 15 October 2002.

13. Robert B. Asprey, *War in the Shadows: The Guerrilla in History,* vol. 1 (Garden City, N.Y.: Doubleday & Company, Inc., 1975), 140-41. Maj. Richard O. Hatch said, "Lieber's Code had an almost immediate international impact . . . [and] was adopted virtually in toto by Germany, Great Britain, and France. It was also the inspiration for the Brussels Congress of 1874, presided over by Baron Jomini, and served as the model for many of the substantive provisions of the Hague Conventions of 1899 and 1907." After World War I, there was an attempt to bring to trial 895 Germans for "war crimes," of which only forty-five were ultimately brought to trial, with only six convicted. The severest penalty was "imprisonment for four years." Richard O. Hatch, "Expansion of the Law of Personal Responsibility for War Crimes: The Demise of 'Acts of State' Immunity," student seminar paper, C600, *The Evolution of Modern Warfare,* U.S. Army Command and General Staff College, Fort Leavenworth, Kansas, 1995, in author's collection, available upon request. Halleck's book, *International Law; or, Rules Regulating the Intercourse of States in Peace and War* (San Francisco: H. H. Bancroft & Company, 1861), was largely a compilation of other people's views on international law and concepts related to war. His interest in the subject seems to demonstrate, however, the abstract, philosophical, legalistic approach Halleck took to moral issues.

14. Edwards, *Noted Guerrillas, or the Warfare on the Border,* 20; Connelley, *Quantrill and the Border Wars,* 382. C. M. Chase, a newspaperman, when he arrived in Lawrence after the raid, saw "a negro rushing through the streets on horseback, dragging the dead body of a dead rebel, with a rope around his neck hitched to his saddle. A crowd was following pelting the rebel with stones. . . . [Later,] the bones lay naked all winter in a ravine in the town, and negroes and boys sawed finger rings from some of them. No part of the body was ever given burial." It appears that the people of Lawrence were learning the lessons of reciprocal violence—if they had not already learned them. Milton Skaggs, a former minister, was the dragged person.

15. Paul Fussell, *Wartime: Understanding and Behavior in the Second World War* (New York: Oxford University Press, 1989), 268ff.

16. Jonathan Shay, *Achilles in Vietnam: Combat Trauma and the Undoing of Character* (New York: Simon & Schuster, 1994), 30, 33, 52. Dr. Shay worked with numerous patients suffering from posttraumatic stress disorders.

17. Ibid., 96, 178.

18. Personal e-mail communication between Donald L. Gilmore and Tony Swindell, July 31, August 29, 2001; Herbert Hendin and Ann Pollinger Haas, *Wounds of War: The Psychological Aftermath of Combat in Vietnam* (New York: Basic Books, Inc., Publishers, 1984), 15. It is interesting to note that Missouri guerrillas performed nearly identical mutilations during the last stages of the Civil War as those committed later by the Vietcong. W. T. Clarke wrote to Brig. Gen. Clinton P. Fisk on September 29, 1864, concerning the massacre of Union soldiers at Centralia: "Ears were cut off and all commissioned officers were scalped. One wounded man reports the privates cut from one wounded soldier while living and thrust in his mouth." He continued, "Most of them were shot through the head, then scalped, bayonets thrust through them, ears and noses cut off, and privates torn off." *War of the Rebellion,* ser. 1, vol. 41, 488-89. In the various reports, the guerrillas are referred to as "demons," "fiends," "villains," "inhuman," "savages," "devils," and "murderous assassins." *War of the Rebellion,* ser. 1, vol. 41, 49, 421, 453, 455, 457. One might ask, to what degree was this brutalizing of the guerrillas the product of Halleck's extermination policy? There is a saying, "As you sow, so shall you reap." The young men, most from fine families, were brought to such a low estate through the Federal army's savage, ruthless treatment toward them and their families. Though an unpopular and difficult argument for Unionist-leaning historians to accept, it, like the fact that the so-called Border Ruffians were not ruffians at all, must be recognized.

19. *War of the Rebellion,* ser. 1, vol. 13, 807-11. See the order of battle and troop numbers in the official records. The manpower in the Army of the Frontier, Central District of Missouri, and District of Kansas in relation to "aggregate present" was 19,092 men. If the Southwestern District of Missouri is added, there are 23,277 men. The above figures are for November 20, 1862; however, manpower changed continuously. Colorado units, as well as Iowa units, also were used frequently in western Missouri, which makes it harder to define aggregate total manpower. Obviously, though, the guerrillas were overwhelmingly outnumbered but still quite effective through 1863. Except for the rare instance of the sacking of Lawrence, when young conscripts under the command of Col. John D. Holt, in a chance encounter with the guerrillas, attached themselves to their force, the guerrillas seldom fielded 300 men when all were assembled.

War fighting takes place across a wide continuum of possibilities. At one end of the "spectrum," large-scale battles between armies and corps take place. When the combatants on one side are no longer able to field viable large-scale units, or in cases where they were never able to field such units, they may initiate guerrilla warfare, characterized by hit-and-run engagements. When guerrilla actions are no longer feasible, the weaker combatants, if they still have the will to resist and are not affected by moral qualms, will begin terrorist operations, attacking not only enemy forces in "bee-sting" attacks, but more importantly, assaulting enemy noncombatants in an attempt to enervate the weaker will of ordinary citizens in their powerful opponents' countries. In the last form of warfare, while relatively few people are killed, the killing inspires greater disgust and fear and causes dissidents in the population of the powerful country to wish to sue for peace.

Chapter 11

1. Gregg, "A Little Dab of History Without Embelishment [sic]," 17. William Gregg, one of Quantrill's lieutenants, said, "Quantrill and his men went to Lawrence with 'hell in their neck' and raised 'hell' after they got there."

2. Connelley, *Quantrill and the Border Wars*, 310. After the war, Noland refused to talk to historian William Connelley about his spying, fearing retribution by Kansans. Several men who had lived in Lawrence before the sacking of the town were driven out of the town and state after the raid or were killed because of suspicions they had acted as spies. There is a black guerrilla present in many pictures of the guerrilla reunions after the war. He is likely Noland, although there was at least one other black guerrilla, Bill Anderson's hostler. The reunions aroused considerable animosity in Kansans because they were often deliberately held on the anniversary of the sacking of Lawrence. There was nothing incongruent in blacks, like Noland, functioning as freemen and riding with the guerillas. There were hundreds of thousands of black free men in the North and the South before the Civil War erupted, many of them living in Virginia, some as middle-class businessmen. A prominent wagon maker in Independence, Missouri, during this period was black, and he employed whites as well as slaves in his business.

3. *War of the Rebellion,* ser. 1, vol. 23, 223-24.

4. Ibid., 320.

5. D. Hubbard, "Reminiscences of the Yeager Raid, on the Santa Fé Trail, in 1863," *Transactions of the Kansas State Historical Society, 1903-1904,* vol. 8, (Topeka, Kans.: The Kansas State Printing Plant, 1904), 168-71; *Council Grove Press,* May 11, 1863; *Kansas City Weekly Western Journal of Commerce,* May 10, 1863; *Kansas City Daily Journal of Commerce,* May 16, 1863; Ethylene B. Thruston, "Captain Dick Yeager—Quantrill Man," *Westport Historical Quarterly* 4 (June 1968): 3-4; Leslie, *The Devil Knows How to Ride,*

164-66. Dick Yeager's father, Judge James Yeager, "was the presiding judge of the Jackson County court in 1840 . . . a freighter . . . and was a state legislator for a term of two years." Dick Yeager, before the war, worked as a freighter for his father. Returning from a freighting run, he found his family's farm stripped bare by Jennison and joined Quantrill. *Branded as Rebels,* comp., Joanne Chiles Eakins and Donald R. Hale. (Independence, Mo.: Print America, 1993), 482-83.

6. *Kansas City Weekly Journal of Commerce,* June 20, 1863.

7. *Kansas City Post,* May 2, 1912; O. S. Barton, *Three Years with Quantrill: A True Story by His Scout John McCorkle* (Norman: University of Oklahoma Press, 1992), 120-23; Connelley, *Quantrill and the Border Wars,* 298-307. Connelley says that the Anderson sisters imprisoned in the building were "Josephine, Mary, and Jenny"; Castel, *William Clarke Quantrill,* 119-20.

8. *War of the Rebellion,* ser. 1, vol. 23, 460-61.

9. *War of the Rebellion,* ser. 1, vol. 22, pt. 2, 428.

10. Gregg, "A Little Dab of History Without Embelishment [sic]"; Webb, *Battles and Biographies of Missourians,* 275.

11. Brig. Gen. Thomas Ewing Jr., in his formal report of the Lawrence raid, said his information was that the guerrillas had gathered at the Pardee farm on August 17 and 18 in the "southwest part of Saline County." Other accounts place the site in Johnson County. The site of old Harrelson, the guerrillas' bivouac area on the night of August 19 (according to John Newman Edwards) is about one mile south of 58 Highway, along 71 Highway, just south of modern Belton, Missouri, along the Grand River. A few years ago, a Frisco railroad sign heralded the location. Brigadier General Ewing, in his report of the Lawrence raid, fixed the bivouac area eight miles northwest of Harrisonville. Harrelson, one and one-half miles from that location may have been the nearest identifiable site from that place if it was not the actual bivouac area. The railroad is now defunct. Edwards, *Noted Guerrillas,* 191; Connelley, *Quantrill and the Border Wars,* 311-15.
    As the guerrillas proceeded across western Missouri, Federal units were moving in pursuit. Lt. Col. Bazel F. Lazear heard on August 20 of Quantrill's passage twelve miles north of Warrensburg and pursued him with two companies of the First Missouri. Lazear also ordered Maj. A. W. Mullins at Pleasant Hill to move on the partisans from that point. *War of the Rebellion,* ser. 1, vol. 22, pt. 2, 579-85 (Ewing's official report of the sacking of Lawrence).

12. Gregg, "A Little Dab of History Without Embelishment [sic]";
Connelley, *Quantrill and the Border Wars,* 308-15.

13. J. A. Pike, "Statement of Capt. J. A. Pike Concerning the Quantrill
Raid," *Collections of the Kansas State Historical Society, 1915-1918,* vol. 14
(Topeka, Kans.: The Kansas State Printing Plant, 1918), 313-14; Connelley,
Quantrill and the Border Wars, 314-16. Pike's statement was made in 1917,
fifty-four years after the event. When Capt. Charles F. Coleman joined up
with Pike's small force at Aubry and took up Quantrill's trail, it was so dark,
Pike said, that they "had to strike matches to find the trail." Connelley, in
his account says that Pike should have "hung upon the flanks of the guerrillas column; he could have annoyed and retarded it. He could have
delayed it a few hours." Connelley, never a man to mince words, talks of
Pike's "inefficiency, stupidity, diffidence." The question remains, did Pike
have one undermanned company or two companies. Either way, it probably would have been suicidal to approach Quantrill outnumbered more
than $4^1/_2$ to 1 or more. However, Pike could have received support since
there were other cavalry posts south of Aubry at Trading Post and
Rockville, and Ewing insisted in his formal report of the Lawrence raid
that Pike had nearly 100 men. He likely did and lied about it later or mis-
remembered. *War of the Rebellion,* ser. 1, vol. 22, pt. 2, 579-85.

Several attempts were made to warn Lawrence, one by a Shawnee
Indian, Pelathe, who rode a thoroughbred mare to the exhaustion level,
then gashed her shoulder with a knife and rubbed gunpowder into the
wound to enliven her. Finally, when even this failed, he ran on foot. As he
reached Lawrence, the sound of gunfire indicated to him that he was too
late. Three men from Eudora also made the attempt, David Kraus, Casper
Marfelius, and Jerry Reel. One of the men, Kraus, was injured, another,
Reel, was killed when he fell from his horse. The third man, detained in aiding the mortally wounded Reel, gave up the effort.

14. Gregg, "A Little Dab of History without Embelishment [sic]";
Connelley, *Quantrill and the Border Wars,* 323-27.

15. Historian Albert Castel said the man dragging the Star Spangled
Banner was Larkin Skaggs, which is extremely doubtful. No Kansan who
witnessed the scene could have accurately identified Skaggs. The guerrillas
wore broad-brimmed hats and were covered with road dust. The continual mention of Skaggs in Kansas histories gives him mythical overtones.
While Skaggs was a real person, he was and has become a Kansas bogey-
man, as in this example and some others. Castel, *William Clarke Quantrill,*
127. The ubiquitous Skaggs is also accounted for as the killer of John Speer
Jr., which may or may not be accurate.

16. Shalor Winchell Eldridge, "The Quantrill Raid as Seen from the Eldridge House," as described by R. G. [Robert Gaston] Elliott, *Publications of the Kansas State Historical Society Embracing Recollections of Early Days in Kansas.* vol. 2. (Topeka, Kans.: Kansas State Printing Plant, 1920), 184; Connelley, *Quantrill and the Border Wars,* 285-397; Amos Lawrence's copy of a letter of Mrs. G. W. Collamore sent in 1863, Amos Lawrence Papers, Kansas State Historical Society, Topeka, Kansas.

17. Eldridge, "The Quantrill Raid as Seen from the Eldridge House," 185, 188.

18. Ibid., 184-85, 194; "Erastus D. Ladd's Description of the Lawrence Massacre," with an introduction by Russell E. Bidlack, *The Kansas Historical Quarterly* 29, no. 2 (1963): 117. Ewing, in his official report of the Lawrence raid, said that the people of Lawrence "had an abundance of arms in their city arsenal, and could have met Quantrill, on half an hour's notice, with 500 men." They were not to be given the luxury of a half hour's notice. *War of the Rebellion,* ser. 1., vol. 22, pt. 2, 579-85.

19. Robert S. Stevens in a letter addressed to "Friends" dated August 23, 1863. The author received a copy of this letter (in the author's file) and other information and data through the courtesy of Robert C. Stevens, the great-grandson of Robert S. Stevens, on October 15, 1996; Elliott, "The Quantrill Raid," 185.

20. Further data contained in letters and other data sent from Robert C. Stevens to the author; Robert Gaston Elliot, "A Look at Early Lawrence: Letters from Robert Gaston Elliott," ed. Carolyn Berneking, *The Kansas Historical Quarterly* 43, no. 3 (1977): 291; Sara Robinson, "The Governor's Wife Recalls the Raid," in Richard B. Sheridan, *Quantrill and the Lawrence Massacre: A Reader* (Lawrence, Kans.: n.p., 1997), 208; Elliott, "The Quantrill Raid," 190; Connelley, *Quantrill and the Border Wars,* 341-45.

21. Eldridge, "The Quantrill Raid," 193-94.

22. Gregg, "A Little Dab of History Without Embelishment [sic]"; Lucien Carr, *Missouri: A Bone of Contention,* 334.

23. Eldridge, "The Quantrill Raid," 188; Connelley, *Quantrill and the Border Wars,* 352-53, 398.

24. Connelley, *Quantrill and the Border Wars,* 362-66.

25. Robert S. Stevens letter to "Friends," dated August 23, 1863; R. G. Elliott, in "The Quantrill Raid," said that only two men returned to the Whitney House. He claimed that Skaggs rode a magnificent white thoroughbred. Information from Robert C. Stevens.

26. Connelley, *Quantrill and the Border War*, 380-82. A number of soldiers had been on the north bank of the Kansas River when Quantrill entered town and cut the ferry cable. There were so few of them, however, that they made no effort to cross the river. They did snipe at guerrillas who approached the river and hit one named Bledsoe. The scalping in Lawrence and the scalping at the border of Missouri guerrillas is probably the first scalping of the Border War. In this case, it was fully sanctioned by Union troops and by authorities in Lawrence. A quid pro quo was the response.

27. Burton J. Williams, "Quantrill's Raid on Lawrence: A Question of Complicity," *Kansas Historical Quarterly* 34, no. 2 (1968): 143, 145; Castel, *A Frontier State at War*, 140. Today, some people in Lawrence say 200 men may have been killed in the attack. They also emphasize that the raid left 85 widows and 250 fatherless children. George F. McCleary Jr. and Karen S. Cook, "Self Guided Tour, Quantrill's Raid: The Lawrence Massacre," (Lawrence, Kans.: published by the Convention and Visitor's Bureau, n.d.).

28. Gregg, "A Little Dab of History Without Embelishment [sic]"; Connelley, *Quantrill and the Border Wars*, 396-405.

29. Gregg, "A Little Dab of History Without Embelishment [sic]." The place where Quantrill crossed Bull Creek consists of a level rock ledge that crosses the river at a point usually without any appreciable water depth. One could drive a tractor-trailer across this point today with ease. Crossing the river at this place was not an accident. Paola was near Quantrill's old home area, and he likely knew of this crossing point. It was necessary for Quantrill to cross the river with ambulances and wagons filled with ammunition as well as the remaining plunder from Lawrence. The crossing point was not just suitable; it was ideal. The author has been to this remote, shady spot. When the Union troops approached Bull Creek, their horses were so desperate for water that they became uncontrollable and charged the river. This nearly panicked the defenders on the other side of the river into firing on them; Connelley, *Quantrill and the Border Wars*, 405-10; *War of the Rebellion*, ser. 1, vol. 22, pt. 2, 579-85. Ewing said that "four men of the Eleventh Ohio were sun-stricken, among them Lieutenant Dick, who accompanied me and who fell dead on dismounting to rest." The day, apparently, was a steaming Kansas one.

30. Connelley, *Quantrill and the Border Wars,* 396-412.

31. A sniper had wounded Bledsoe by shooting across the Kaw (Kansas) River early in the raid. O. S. Barton, *Three Years with Quantrill,* 127-28.

32. *War of the Rebellion,* ser. 1, vol. 22, pt. 2, 579-85; Connelley, *Quantrill and the Border Wars,* 396-412.

Chapter 12

1. *War of the Rebellion,* ser. 1, vol. 23, 471-73; Castel, *William Clarke Quantrill,* 144; Connelley, *Quantrill and the Border Wars,* 417-18. Connelley said that Lane went to a cabin with Ewing and "drew up Orders No. 11." This scenario seems unlikely to have occurred; but if Ewing drew it up for Lane, it was exactly what Ewing wished to draw up for Schofield and himself, so it is doubtful that it was done under duress.

2. *War of the Rebellion,* ser. 1, vol. 23, 473.

3. Ann Davis Niepman, "General Orders No. 11 and Border Warfare during the Civil War," *Missouri Historical Review* 66, no. 2 (1966): 185-86.

4. *Leavenworth Daily Times,* August 22, 1863; *Leavenworth Daily Conservative,* August 22, 1863.

5. *War of the Rebellion,* ser. 1, vol. 22, pt. 2, 572-75.

6. Lew Larkin, *Bingham, Fighting Artist* (Kansas City, Mo.: State Publishing Co., 1955), 222. Bingham saw Ewing as both disreputable and an instrument of tyranny. As he said, "A little blue cloth and a few brass buttons neither make a soldier nor unmake a thief." Bingham was probably referring to Ewing's elaborate business manipulations as one of the members of the "Executive Committee" of the Leavenworth, Pawnee & Western Railroad Company, in which he participated in the bribing of "[James H.] Lane [U.S. senator], [Samuel C.] Pomeroy [U.S. senator], [Martin] Conway, [Mark W.] Delahay [a U.S. judge]," almost a who's who in Kansas, and others in obtaining Delaware Indian lands for his railroad's right of way at what has been charitably described as "less than their actual market value." Whether a "higher law" was invoked in this transaction is unknown. Another Kansas worthy, D. W. Wilder, was also involved in these corrupt proceedings. Castel, *A Frontier State at War,* 220-21; *Report of the Pacific Railway Commission,* 1595-98, 1622, 1674-76; *Congressional Globe,* 37th Cong., 2d Sess., pt. 4, Appendix, 383; Roy P. Basler, ed., *The Complete Works of Lincoln,* 8 vols., vol. 4 (New

Brunswick, N.J., 1953), 400-402; "Proposition for Sale," document in *Treaties Between the United States and Indian Tribes,* 350-62; Ewing to James C. Stone, December 31, 1861, in Ewing Papers, Kansas State Historical Society; *Leavenworth Daily Conservative,* March 4, 1862; *White Cloud Kansas Chief,* June 23, 1864; Robinson, *Kansas Conflict,* 418. Dorothy Penn, "George Caleb Bingham," *Missouri Historical Review* 40, no. 3 (1946): 352-54. Bingham, a famous artist, painted the famous *Order No. 11,* which depicts Ewing and Jennison engaged in atrocities against the people of western Missouri during the enforcement of the order. Bingham had warned Ewing if he instituted General Orders No. 11, then "I will make you infamous with pen and brush as far as I am able." Later, when Ewing ran for governor of Ohio, Bingham, a man of his word, campaigned against him vigorously, and Ewing lost by a small margin, the loss probably attributable to Bingham; Niepman, "General Orders No. 11 and Border Warfare," 197.

7. W. L. Webb, *Battles and Biographies of Missourians,* 258-59.

8. Niepman, "General Orders No. 11 and Border Warfare," 209-10; Albert Castel, "Orders No. 11 and the Civil War on the Border," *Missouri Historical Review* 57, no. 4 (1963): 359.

9. *Kansas City Star,* March 6, 1939.

10. Niepman, "General Orders No. 11 and Border Warfare," 201, 203, 205; "The Civil War Letters of Colonel Bazel F. Lazear," ed. Vivian Kirkpatrick McLarty, *Missouri Historical Review* 44, no. 4 (1950): 390.

11. *War of the Rebellion,* ser. 1, vol. 22, 688-89, 691-701; Connelley, *Quantrill and the Border Wars,* 421-34; Gregg, "A Little Dab of History Without Embelisment [sic]." General Blunt said 87 men were killed in the attack during which Quantrill led a force of 650 guerrillas. Blunt said that in his first encounter with the partisans, "I approached their [the guerrillas'] line, alone, to ascertain their true character." James G. Blunt, "General Blunt's Account of His Civil War Experiences," *Kansas Historical Quarterly* 1, no. 3 (1932): 247-48. Even historian William Connelley admitted that Quantrill was likely made a full colonel, though many of his critics have refused to admit him this honor in their writing.

12. *War of the Rebellion,* ser. 1, vol. 53, 908-9.

13. Connelley, *Quantrill and the Border Wars,* 441.

14. Ibid., 439, 442-43.

15. Ibid., W. L. Potter, letter to W. W. Scott, quoted in Connelley, 442-43.

16. Ibid., 441-45. W. L. Potter, who passed on much of this information about what happened in Sherman and Bonham, Texas, to W. W. Scott and thence to Connelley, called General McCulloch, a "featherbed general." It was Fletch Taylor, Quantrill's enemy, who started the vicious rumor, probably totally unfounded, that Sarah Catherine King (a.k.a Kate Clarke), Quantrill's beloved, managed a bawdy house in St. Louis after the war. Unionist-leaning historians have pounced on this unproved, perhaps sexist, claim to further demonize Quantrill. Of course, many upright, unattached women in those days, losing a mate or parents and in desperation, resorted to prostitution. But this does not establish that Kate participated in such activity, nor is it a legitimate complaint by Unionist-leaning historians against Quantrill.

17. Ibid., 444-47. Corroborative evidence concerning some of the above events can be found also in Gregg, "A Little Dab of History Without Embelisment [sic]."

Chapter 13

1. Connelley, *Quantrill and the Border Wars,* 448-50, 455. Quantrill was the type of leader who thrives in an ordinary military setting, where a relatively fixed, hierarchical rank structure exists that bases ascendancy on established criteria. But in a guerrilla setting, where group dynamics and personalities reign, military talent can be overshadowed and a leader ousted through personal intrigue, as Quantrill was. The western Missouri guerrillas were always a loosely knit, democratic organization, with all the weaknesses and strengths that implies.

2. Gregg, "A Little Bit of History Without Embelisment [sic]"; *War of the Rebellion,* ser. 1, vol. 41, pt. 2, 49-50.

3. *War of the Rebellion,* ser. 1, vol. 41, pt. 2, 66-67.

4. Howard V. Canan, "The Missouri Paw Paw Militia of 1863-1864," *Missouri Historical Review* 62, no. 4 (1968): 431-36; *War of the Rebellion,* ser. 1, vol. 41, pt. 1, 56-57. Paw Paws are trees growing in western Missouri that bear an elongated fruit, cucumber in size and shape, that tastes like an over-sweet, vile-tasting banana to some people. Colonel Canan, in his generally excellent article, said that "Abraham Lincoln . . . did not understand conditions in Missouri and failed to assign sufficient troop strength to control the guerrillas." It appears to the author that Lincoln understood completely the situation in Missouri. His failure to send sufficient troops to the state for

almost the entire duration of the war was because he considered it the least critical theater in the war. The modern U.S. Army refers to such a strategy as employing "economy of force," where you weaken certain theaters or areas to further strengthen more critical areas. This appears to be what Lincoln and his advisers were doing in Missouri. Whether the strategy was wise is another matter. Lincoln seemed always to focus on a strategy that gave primacy to actions in the East. So did the South, perhaps ill-advisedly.

5. Canan, "The Missouri Paw Paw Militia of 1863-1864," 437-47; *War of the Rebellion,* ser. 1, vol. 41, pt. 1, 57-59.

6. *War of the Rebellion,* ser. 1, vol. 41, pt. 1, 49, 53; *History of Clay and Platte Counties, Missouri* (St. Louis, Mo.: National Historical Company, 1885), 722-26. Jennison's wife, the history said, left him after learning that he kept "a house of ill-fame [bawdy house] at Fort Leavenworth, ostensibly a restaurant or eating house, with a doggery and gambling dive annex. Another shining light of the loyal patriots set to rule over and murder and plunder decent people! [said the author of the history]" (page 724).

7. *History of Clay and Platte Counties, Missouri,* 623-25, 728-29. Smith's instructions to Price lacked a decisive, unequivocal call to battle, a blueprint for victory; rather, they were mincing pronouncements, couched in implicit and explicit suggestions concerning retreat, on when and how to fly. W. R. Boggs, Smiths' chief of staff, told Price, "Rally the loyal men of Missouri, and remember that our great want is men, and that your object should be, if you cannot maintain yourself in that country, to bring as large an accession [recruits] as possible to our force." Then, after telling Price to "make St. Louis the objective point of your movement, which, if rapidly made, will put you in possession of that place, its supplies, and military stores . . ." etc., Boggs added, "Should you be compelled to withdraw from the State, make your retreat through Kansas and the Indian Territory, sweeping that country of its mules, horses, cattle, and military supplies of all kinds." So Price's move into Missouri was not so much a military one, directed toward great battles, as a marauding run to gain men and supplies for the South and to attract Northern troops west of the Mississippi River. Because he was outnumbered 2 to 1 or more in the last phases of his campaign, including Westport, any military defeats Price suffered were to be expected, and any victories over him ought to be considered anticipated. The seizure of St. Louis, a city critical to the North and easily reinforced by Federal troops, was never a viable objective. Bloated with a host of unarmed recruits and other poorly trained and unintegrated ones, Price's army was a stumbling, unwieldy force, susceptible and vulnerable to defeat, which luckily vacated the state

relatively intact through the gallant efforts of its veteran generals, other officers, and valiant cavalrymen.

8. Ibid., 702-3.

9. Ibid., 623, 718-26, 729.

10. Ibid., 628-29; Edgar Langsdorf, "Price's Raid and the Battle of Mine Creek," *The Kansas Historical Quarterly* 30, no. 3 (1964): 282-83.

11. War of the Rebellion, ser. 1, vol. 41, pt. 1, 652-53.

12. Ibid., 446, 714. Ewing made no mention of this ruthless use of non-combatants in his formal report of the Battle of Pilot Knob, but it appeared in the *War of the Rebellion* records in Price's court of inquiry, conducted after the Missouri raid. Unionist-leaning historians invariably fail to cite this cynical, one might say reprehensible, use of noncombatants. Historian Albert Castel remarked on the "gallant" Ewing and quoted an unnamed writer who refers to Pilot Knob as the "Thermopylae of the West." Historian William Connelley's assessment of the battle and Price's raid is far more accurate. He said, "There was never the remotest possibility that anything could be accomplished by it [Price's raid], and that the army did finally escape from the trap it made for itself [at Westport] was due solely to the iron command of Shelby." Albert Castel, "War and Politics: The Price Raid of 1864," *The Kansas Historical Quarterly* 24, no. 2 (1958): 131; Connelley, *Quantrill and the Border Wars*, 454.

13. *War of the Rebellion,* ser. 1, vol. 41, pt. 1, 458-59, 707. The first account is from the battle report of Union captain W. C. F. Montgomery, Battery H, Second Missouri Light Artillery.

14. Ibid., 325-26, 450-51, 458-59.

15. Langsdorf, "Price's Raid," 285-86; *War of the Rebellion,* ser. 1, vol. 41, pt. 1, 309-11, 340, (Rosecrans' and Pleasonton's reports).

16. *War of the Rebellion,* ser. 1, vol. 41, pt. 1, 632, 645; Langsdorf, "Price's Raid," 287.

17. *War of the Rebellion,* ser. 1, vol. 41, pt. 3, 217; *War of the Rebellion,* ser. 1, vol. 41, pt. 1, 194, 217, 299-300, 329-30, 440. Lt. Col. Dan. M. Draper, Ninth Missouri State Militia Cavalry, said there were only "five dead on the ground" in Fayette when he arrived. Connelley claims eighteen were killed,

forty-two wounded. Connelley, *Quantrill and the Border Wars,* 452-53. Castel used the number "thirteen bushwhackers dead" and "thirty" wounded. It is, however, unsafe to predict more deaths than a U.S. Army report, which during that period were usually inflated. Castel, *William Clarke Quantrill: His Life and Times,* 184-85. *War of the Rebellion,* ser. 1, vol. 41, pt. 3, 217, reports that the attack on Fayette occurred on September 11, 1864.

18. Edgar T. Rodemyre, *History of Centralia, Missouri.* (Centralia, Mo.: Press of the Fireside Guard, 1936), 24, 64.

19. Ibid., 15-16, 24-25. At one time during the war, the citizens of Centralia hoisted a one-hundred-foot flagstaff with the Confederate Stars and Bars. When Union forces occupied the town, it was hauled down, torn into small strips by Mrs. T. S. Sneed, and burned carefully in her fireplace. Mrs. Sneed even stirred the ashes so that the Federals would find no evidence of it. When the St. Charles Home Guards, a "Dutch militia," continually ate at Sneed's hotel "free of charge," Mrs. Sneed demanded payment. They responded by burning down the hotel and stationing men with "bayonets fixed on their muskets" to shoot any person "who attempted to go near the building" to put out the fire. So when Anderson entered the town, there was only one hotel, though some accounts mention two. The so-called "Dutch" militia were German Americans. The word "Dutch," as used by the guerrillas, was a corruption of "Deutsch," the word for Germans in the German language. The Germans in Missouri were among the guerrillas' worst enemies, and the partisans chose every opportunity to strike at them.

20. Ibid., 25-27.

21. Thos. M. Goodman, *A Thrilling Record: Founded on Facts and Observations Obtained during the Day's Experience with Colonel William T. Anderson, (the Notorious Guerrilla Chieftain)* (Des Moines, Iowa: Mills & Co., Steam Book & Job Printing House, 1868), 7, 21-23; Rodemyre, *History of Centralia, Missouri,* 23-32, 56-61. Frank James denied that he was in Centralia during the raid, saying, "Anderson captured a train, carried off a lot of stuff about which I know nothing save from hearsay"—a typical, well-practiced Frank James alibi.

22. *War of the Rebellion,* ser. 1, vol. 41, pt. 3, 423, 454, 456-57, 488-89; Rodemyre, *History of Centralia, Missouri,* 30-32. Sergeant Goodman eventually escaped days later by merely walking away from his captors while they were preoccupied with crossing the Missouri River. He was well treated by the guerrillas generally, but he might have been killed had he not escaped. Goodman, *A Thrilling Record,* 28, 58-60.

23. Rodemyre, *History of Centralia, Missouri*, 33-41. Frank James said the guerrilla pickets included Wood, Bill Stuart, and Zach Sunderland. *War of the Rebellion*, ser. 1, vol. 41, pt. 1, 443; Goodman, *A Thrilling Record*, 32.

24. Rodemyre, *History of Centralia, Missouri*, 33-41; *War of the Rebellion*, ser. 1, vol. 41, pt. 3, 488. Sergeant Goodman said that Anderson started the charge by crying "Charge!" Goodman, *A Thrilling Record*, 34.

25. Rodemyre, *History of Centralia, Missouri*, 65. Maj. Gen. W. S. Rosecrans said, "116 were murdered at Centralia." *War of the Rebellion*, ser. 1, vol. 41, pt. 1, 317. Dodie Maurer provided the author with the names of the soldiers successfully fleeing to Sturgeon, obtained from files at the *Fireside Guard* office in Centralia by Dodie Maurer and her husband, newspaperman Joseph J. Maurer. Rodemyre was editor and publisher of that newspaper.

26. *War of the Rebellion*, ser. 1, vol. 41, pt. 1, 440-41; *War of the Rebellion*, ser. 1, vol. 41, pt. 4, 489; Goodman, *A Thrilling Record*, 35.

27. Rodemyre, *History of Centralia, Missouri*, 66.

28. *War of the Rebellion*, ser. 1, vol. 41, pt. 1, 442. Brig. Gen. James Craig, Enrolled Missouri Militia, commented in a message to Major General Rosecrans on November 30, 1864, that Cox "was in command at my request without a commission, because I believed he would find and whip Anderson. The Government issued him a commission to-day as a lieutenant-colonel, which I will carry to him." *War of the Rebellion*, ser. 1, vol. 41, pt. 4, 727. Some accounts say Anderson was killed on October 27, which is incorrect. See *War of the Rebellion*, ser. 1, vol. 41, pt. 1, 443, for Cox's account, who was the man who did the killing.

29. *War of the Rebellion*, ser. 1, vol. 41, pt. 4, 354, 727; Albert Castel and Thomas Goodrich, *Bloody Bill Anderson, the Short, Savage Life of a Civil War Guerrilla* (Mechanicsburg, Pa.: Stackpole Books), 130; *Liberty Tribune*, November 4, 11, 1864; *Kansas City Weekly Journal*, November 5, 1864; *Kingston (Mo.) Caldwell Banner of Liberty*, November 18, 1864; *The Richmond Missourian*, July 4, July 27, 1938; Rodemyre, *History of Centralia, Missouri*, 75; Castel, *William Clarke Quantrill*, 199; Goodman, *A Thrilling Record*, 29-30.

30. *War of the Rebellion*, ser. 1, vol. 41, pt. 1, 633-34, 645-46, 656-57.

31. Connelley, *Quantrill and the Border Wars*, 455; Castel, *William Clarke Quantrill*, 198; O. S. Barton, *Three Years with Quantrill*, 176.

32. *War of the Rebellion*, ser. 1, vol. 41, pt. 1, 533, 635. Curtis and Blunt's

men at Westport were not the best troops, many of them being hastily assembled militiamen with poor arms and equipment and red patches attached to their clothing to denote their status. But there were many of them, they were well led, and had a number of veterans in their ranks to firm up the units. Paul B. Jenkins, in *The Battle of Westport* (Kansas City, Mo.: Franklin Hudson Publishing Company, 1906), 154, said, "The truth was that Price had close to 9,000 armed men with him at the time of the Battle of Westport. Opposed to him were somewhere near 15,000 under General Curtis [the general's own statement, dated two days before Westport], and 6,500 more under Pleasonton."

33. *War of the Rebellion,* ser. 1, vol. 41, pt. 1, 635-36; "McLain's Battery and Price's 1864 Invasion: A Letter from Lt. Caleb S. Burdsal, Jr.," ed. Bryce A. Suderow, *Kansas History: A Journal of the Plains* 6, no. 1 (1983): 31. Pleasonton's initial attack at the Big Blue was to have been made by Gen. Egbert B. Brown. When Pleasonton reached the Blue River on October 23 to determine why his attack had not been initiated promptly, he found General Brown and his men dawdling aimlessly. Pleasonton fired General Brown on the spot and ordered Sanborn and McNeil to begin the attack, which was done successfully.

34. Langsdorf, "Price's Raid," 295, 297; *War of the Rebellion,* ser. 1, vol. 41, pt. 1, 340-42, 636-37. General Pleasonton said, "1,000 men were taken prisoners." General Pleasonton, exhibiting his splendid character as a cavalryman, ordered Benteen and Phillips to attack immediately. He said later, "I did not hesitate to attack at once."

35. *War of the Rebellion,* ser. 1, vol. 41, pt. 1, 533, 636-37, 684-85. Despite the fact that several hundred Confederate soldiers died and are buried at or near the battle site at Mine Creek, the Kansas State Historical Society and the State of Kansas have refused to acknowledge their existence or place a memorial at the site. This is a concrete example of the continuing bias exhibited by some historians and others espousing and acting upon Unionist sentiment concerning the subject of the Border War. Nonetheless, the Kansas Division, Sons of Confederate Veterans, through the intercession of Dr. John Spencer, director, Mine Creek Battlefield Foundation (a private organization), recently placed a memorial to these men just outside the state-owned part of the battle site.

36. Ibid., 638-39, 721 (Price's court of inquiry). Some say Sanford came to Blunt's rescue at Newtonia and drove Price southward. This is not Price's story, however; nor is it mentioned in Col. S. D. Jackman's report or any of the other Southern reports. Another interesting development was that Pleasonton refused to let Curtis have control of the

Southern prisoners captured at Mine Creek. Whether he feared for their safety is unknown, but it is possible.

37. Connelley, *Quantrill and the Border Wars,* 451-59; *War of the Rebellion,* ser. 1, vol. 49, pt. 1, 657.

38. *War of the Rebellion,* ser.1, vol. 49, pt.1, 18, 626, 657.

39. O. S. Barton, *Three Years With Quantrill,* 204-5; *War of the Rebellion,* ser.1, vol. 49, pt.1, 635; Connelley, *Quantrill and the Border Wars,* 460-65.

40. Connelley, *Quantrill and the Border Wars,* 467-69.

41. Ibid., 471-83; Gregg, "A Little Dab of History Without Embelishment [sic]."

42. O. S. Barton, *Three Years With Quantrill,* 210.

Chapter 14

1. *War of the Rebellion Record,* ser. 1, vol. 48, pt. 2, 370-71.

2. Ibid., 342, 356, 370, 455.

3. Ibid., 423.

4. Ibid., 470, 528.

5. Ibid., 470, 705-6.

6. *War of the Rebellion Record,* ser. 1, vol. 48, pt. 1, 334.

7. Ibid.

Afterword

1. John C. Tibbetts, "Riding With the Devil: The Movie Adventures of William Clarke Quantrill." *Kansas History: A Journal of the Plains* (Autumn 1999): 182-99. In an article about Quantrill's life as it has been portrayed in motion pictures, Tibbetts remarked about "the demonic associations" linked with Quantrill's guerrillas. He cites, for instance, the myth that the guerrillas swore to a " 'Black Oath,' in the names of God and the Devil." In the movie *Kansas Raiders,* Quantrill is referred to as "a fiend with 'two horns, two hoofs,

and a long tail.' " In the motion picture *Dark Command*, he is portrayed as a "ruthless sociopath" referred to by the local citizenry as "Old Nick." Finally, Marjorie Main, who plays his mother, attempts to exterminate him, saying, "I borned a dirty murderin' snake that's broke my heart to see it crawlin' along. I curse the day I had you." American icon, John Wayne, then, steps forward like a deus ex machina and kills the evil Quantrill. In contrast, in real life, Quantrill's mother never ceased defending him to the end of her life.

In the movie *Jayhawkers*, Quantrill is viewed as the "Napoleon of the Plains." In *Red Mountain*, another motion picture, the guerrilla chief conspires to form a "Confederacy of Plains Indians." Tibbetts said accurately, "Hollywood's image of Quantrill as fascist demagogue and/or grasping imperialist . . . finds little support in the historical record." In the latest movie on Quantrill, *Ride With the Devil*, directed by Ang Lee, Quantrill is described by the protagonist, Jake Roedel, a guerrilla, as "a girlish man in appearance, with fine features and heavy lidded eyes [who] killed in bulk and at every opportunity." These are "Yankee words," placed in the mouth of an 1860s Missourian, as interpreted by a modern Missourian with socialized Northern sentiments, writer Daniel Woodrell. No nineteenth-century Missourian of Southern sentiment would have described Quantrill the way Roedel does. Therefore, Roedel serves as a "Yankee" foil whose "refined" Northern perspective is meant to be contrasted against that of the crass, insensitive Southern boys. Although this movie was not particularly successful, purveying Yankee ideology ordinarily has sold well. The author of this book acted as a consultant for the latter motion picture and believes Lee's representation of the guerrillas, as depicted through the words of Roedel, does present a more realistic portrayal of the guerrillas than any other movie on the subject, even with its faults.

2. Confederate major general Patrick Cleburne, before his death in late 1864 at the Battle of Franklin, Tennessee, stated, with extraordinary prescience, that if the South lost the Civil War, subsequent histories would be written in a distorted manner. His warning to his fellow officers ought to be contemplated.

January 2, 1864

COMMANDING GENERAL, THE CORPS, DIVISION, BRIGADE, AND REGIMENTAL COMMANDER OF THE ARMY OF THE TENNESSEE:

. . . Every man should endeavor to understand the meaning of subjugation before it is too late. . . . It means the history of the heroic struggle will be written by the enemy; that our youth will be trained by Northern schoolteachers; will learn from Northern school books their version of the war; will be impressed by the influences of history and education to regard our gallant dead as traitors, our maimed veterans as fit objects for derision. . . .

It is said slavery is all we are fighting for, and if we give it up we give up all. Even if this were true, which we deny, slavery is not all our enemies are fighting for. It is merely the pretense to establish sectional superiority and a more centralized form of government, and to deprive us of our rights and liberties.

Robert F. Durden, *The Gray and the Black: The Confederate Debate on Emancipation* (Baton Rouge: Louisiana State University Press, 1972), 55, 62.

In the same message cited above (written in early 1864), Cleburne, with great insight into Southern military affairs, formally suggested to the Confederate military hierarchy that Southern blacks should be freed and recruited to fight the Northern foe, allowing them to join the other blacks already fighting for the Confederacy. Otherwise, Cleburne saw the weakening, outnumbered South faced with inevitable defeat in the war. A large number of other Southern officers signed their names at the bottom of his message. Cleburne's views were suppressed, however, because the Southern leadership was not yet ready to make such a drastic move—ideologically, philosophically, and politically. They also feared the dissemination of Cleburne's proposal would undermine Southern morale, acknowledge that the South was losing the war.

Select Bibliography

Newspapers

Boston Daily Advertiser, February 23, 1850.

Boston Times, February 23, 1854.

Council Grove Press, May 11, November 30, 1863.

Daily Missouri Democrat, December 21, 1861.

Daily Missouri Republican, April 13, 1848; November 23, December 3, 11-12, 1860; October 16, 1861.

Elwood (Kans.) Free Press, August 10, September 24, 1861.

Fayette Missouri Intelligencer, July 25, 1829.

Franklin Missouri Intelligencer, July 23, 1819; January 21, November 4, December 18, 1820; January 29, July 2, May 28, November 13, 1821.

Herald of Freedom, December 15, 1855.

Jefferson City Enquirer in *Daily Missouri Democrat,* December 30, 1858.

Kansas City Daily Journal of Commerce, May 16, 1863.

Kansas City Journal, September 14, 1879.

Kansas City Post, May 2, 1912.

Kansas City Star, March 6, 1939; November 28, 1996; September 23, 1998.

Kansas City Weekly Journal of Commerce, May 10, 30, June 20, 27, 1863.

La Grange (Mo.) National American, May 18, 1861.

Lawrence Journal, January 12, 1891.

Lawrence Kansas State Journal, August 8, 15, 1861.

Lawrence Republican, July 17, 1861.

Leavenworth (Kans.) Daily Conservative, July 11, 17, 23, 27, 30, August 20, September 20-21, October 10, 1861; April 18, July 29, 1862; August 22, 1863.

Leavenworth (Kans.) Daily Times, August 22, 1863.

Leavenworth (Kans.) Times, July 29, 1862.

Liberty Weekly Tribune, November 30, 1860.

New York Daily Tribune, October 21-25, 28, 29, 31, 1856.

New York Tribune Almanac, 1861.

North East Reporter, August 17, 1854.

Olathe (Kans.) Mirror, June 27, July 25, 1861.

Osage Valley Star, November 29, 1860.

Quincy Whig, August 27, 1842; June 19, 1844.

St. Joseph Weekly Free Democrat, June 23, 1860.

St. Louis Daily New Era, September 22, 1847.

St. Louis Gazette, April 26, May 3, 1820.

St. Louis Missouri Republican, May 25, December 25, 1861.

Tri-Weekly Missouri Republican, August 1, 1862.

Whig Messenger, December 15, 1853.

White Cloud Kansas Chief, September 5, 1861; January 2, 1862.

Books and Articles

Agriculture in the United States in 1860. Washington, D.C., 1864.

American Antislavery Society. *First Annual Report*.

Andreas, A. Theodore. *History of the State of Kansas*. Chicago: A. T. Andreas, 1883.

Annals of Congress. Vol. 7 U.S. 16th Cong., 1st Sess. (1858), 355, 1204.

Annals of Congress. Vol. 6 U.S. 15th Cong., 2d Sess. (1858), 174, 185.

The Annals of Kansas. Topeka, Kans., 1886.

Anthony, Daniel R. "Letters of Daniel R. Anthony, 1857-1862," Edited by Edgar Langsdorf and R. W. Richmond. *The Kansas Historical Quarterly* 24, no. 1 (1958).

———. "Letters of Daniel R. Anthony, 1857-1862," Edited by Edgar Langsdorf and R. W. Richmond. *The Kansas Historical Quarterly* 24, no. 3 (1958).

Asprey, Robert B. *War in the Shadows: The Guerrilla in History*. Vol. 1. Garden City, N.Y.: Doubleday & Company, Inc., 1975.

Atherton, Lewis. *Frontier Merchant in Mid-America*. Columbia: University of Missouri Press, 1971.

Atkeson, W. O. *History of Bates County, Missouri*. Topeka, Kans.: Historical Publishing Company, 1918.

Barry, Louise. "Charles Robinson—Yankee '49er: His Journey to California." *The Kansas Historical Quarterly* 34, no. 2 (1968).

Barton, O. S. *Three Years with Quantrill: A True Story by His Scout John McCorkle*. Norman: University of Oklahoma Press, 1992.

Bemis, Samuel Flagg. *John Quincy Adams and the Union*. New York: Knopf, 1956.

Bingham, George Caleb. "Letters of George Caleb Bingham to James S. Rollins." Edited by C. B. Rollins. *Missouri Historical Review* 33 (1938).

Blum, Virgil C. "The Political and Military Activities of the German Element in St. Louis, 1859-1861." *Missouri Historical Review* 42, no. 2 (1948).

Blunt, James G. "General Blunt's Account of His Civil War Experiences." *The Kansas Historical Quarterly* 1, no. 3 (1932).

Boernstein, Henry [Heinrich Börnstein]. *Memoirs of a Nobody: The Missouri Years of an Austrian Radical, 1849-1866.* St. Louis: Missouri Historical Society Press, 1997.

Bowen, Don R. "Guerrilla War in Western Missouri, 1862-1865: Historical Extensions of the Relative Deprivation Hypothesis." *Comparative Studies in Society and History* 19 (January 1977).

——————."Quantrill, James, Younger, *et al.*: Leadership in a Guerrilla Movement, Missouri, 1861-1865," *Military Affairs* 41, no. 1 (1977).

Britton, Wiley. *The Civil War on the Border.* Vol. 1. New York: G. P. Putnam's Sons, 1899.

Brooksher, William Riley. *Bloody Hill: the Civil War Battle of Wilson's Creek.* Washington, D.C.: Brassey's, 1995.

Brown, Robert Allison III, comp. "Wayside Rest in War and Peace." Manuscript, personal collection of Carol Unnewehr. 1966.

Brownlee, Richard S. *Gray Ghosts of the Confederacy: Guerrilla Warfare in the West, 1861-1865.* Baton Rouge: Louisiana State University Press, 1958.

Brunk, Samuel. " 'The Sad Situation of Civilians and Soldiers': The Banditry of Zapatismo in the Mexican Revolution." *The American Historical Review* 101, no. 2 (1996).

Burke, John. *Buffalo Bill: The Noblest Whiteskin.* New York: G. P. Putnam's Sons, 1972.

Bursdal, Caleb S. Jr. "McLain's Battery and Price's 1864 Invasion: A Letter from Lt. Caleb S. Burdsal, Jr.," Edited by Bryce A. Suderow. *Kansas History: A Journal of the Central Plains* 6, no. 1 (1983).

Caldwell, Martha B. "The Eldridge House," *The Kansas Historical Quarterly* 9, no. 4 (1940).

Calhoun, John C. *Address of John C. Calhoun to the People of the Southern States June 5, 1849.*

Canan, Howard V. "The Missouri Paw Paw Militia of 1863-1864." *Missouri Historical Review* 62, no. 4 (1968).

Carr, Lucien. *Missouri: A Bone of Contention.* Boston and New York, 1888.

Castel, Albert. *A Frontier State at War: Kansas 1861-1865.* Ithaca, N.Y.: Cornell University Press, 1958.

———. "Orders No. 11 and the Civil War on the Border." *Missouri Historical Review* 57, no. 4 (1963).

———. "War and Politics: The Price Raid of 1864." *The Kansas Historical Quarterly* 24, no. 2 (1958).

———. *William Clarke Quantrill: His Life and Times.* Norman: University of Oklahoma Press, 1962, 1999.

Chambers, William N. *Old Bullion Benton; Senator from the New West.* Boston: Little, Brown & Company, 1956.

Collections of the Kansas State Historical Society. Edited by William E. Connelley. Vol. 13. Topeka, Kans.: W. R. Smith, Kansas State Printing, 1915.

Conard, Howard L., ed. *Encyclopedia of the History of Missouri.* Vol. 6. St. Louis, Mo.: Southern History Company, 1901.

Congressional Globe, 30th Cong., 1st Sess., 1078; Appendix 685-86.

Connelley, William Elsey. *History of Kansas: State and People.* Vol. 1. Chicago: The American Historical Society, Inc., 1928.

———. *Quantrill and the Border Wars.* Cedar Rapids, Iowa: The Torch Press, Publishers, 1910.

Crouch, Barry M. " 'A Fiend in Human Shape'? William Clarke Quantrill and His Biographers." *Kansas History: A Journal of the Central Plains* 22 (Summer 1999).

Dirck, Brian. " 'We Have Whipped Them Beautifully': The Arkansas Press and Wilson's Creek." *Missouri Historical Review* 84, no. 3 (1990).

Douglass, Robert S. *History of the Missouri Baptists.* Kansas City, Mo.: Western Baptist, 1934.

Durden, Robert F. *The Gray and the Black: The Confederate Debate on Emancipation.* Baton Rouge: Louisiana State University Press, 1972.

Eakins, Joanne Chiles, and Donald R. Hale, comp. *Branded as Rebels,* Independence, Mo.: Print America, 1993.

Edwards, John Newman. *Noted Guerrillas, or the Warfare on the Border.* Shawnee, Kans.: Two Trails Publishing, 1996.

Eldridge, Shalor Winchell. *Publications of the Kansas State Historical Society Embracing Recollections of Early Days in Kansas.* Vol. 2. Topeka, Kans.: Imri Zumwalt, Kansas State Printing Plant, 1920.

————. "The Quantrill Raid as Seen from the Eldridge House" as described by R. G. [Robert Gaston] Elliott. *Publications of the Kansas State Historical Society Embracing Recollections of Early Days in Kansas.* Vol. 2. Topeka, Kans.: Kansas State Printing Plant, 1920.

Elliott, Robert Gaston. "A Look at Early Lawrence: Letters from Robert Gaston Elliott." Edited by Carolyn Berneking. *The Kansas Historical Quarterly* 43, no. 3 (1977).

Ewy, Marvin. "The United States in the Kansas Border Troubles, 1855-1856." *The Kansas Historical Quarterly* 32, no. 4 (1966).

"Executive Minutes of Governor John W. Geary, September 11, 1856." *Kansas Historical Collections.*

Fitch, Edward, and Sarah Fitch. "Letters of Edward and Sarah Fitch, 1855-1863." Edited by John M. Peterson. *Kansas History: A Journal of the Central Plains* 20, no. 1 (1957).

————. "More Letters of Edward and Sarah Fitch, 1855-1856." Edited by John M. Peterson. *Kansas History: A Journal of the Central Plains* 20, no. 1 (1997).

Fox, Simeon. "The Early History of the Seventh Cavalry." *Collections of the Kansas State Historical Society, 1909-1910.* Edited by George W. Martin. Vol. 11. Topeka, Kans.: State Printing Office, 1910.

———. "The Story of the Seventh Kansas." *Transactions of the Kansas State Historical Society, 1903-1904*. Edited by George W. Martin. Vol. 8. Topeka, Kans.: George A. Clark, 1904.

Fussell, Paul. *Wartime: Understanding and Behavior in the Second World War.* New York: Oxford University Press, 1989.

Genovese, Eugene. *The Political Economy of Slavery: Studies in the Economy of the Slave South.* Middletown, Conn.: Wesleyan University Press, 1989.

Gilmore, Donald L. "Revenge in Kansas, 1863." *History Today* 43 (March 1993).

———. "Total War on the Missouri Border." *Journal of the West* 35, no. 3 (1996).

Goodman, Julia Cody. "Julia Cody Goodman's Memoirs of Buffalo Bill." Edited by Don Russell. *The Kansas Historical Quarterly* 28, no. 4 (1962).

Goodman, Thomas M. *Sergeant Thomas M. Goodman's Thrilling Record.* Maryville, Mo.: Rush Printing Company, 1960 [facsimile copy of 1868 book].

Goodrich, Thomas. *Black Flag: Guerrilla Warfare on the Western Border, 1861-1865.* Bloomington and Indianapolis: Indiana University Press, 1995.

Gregg, William H. "A Little Dab of History Without Embelishment [sic]." Western Historical Manuscript Collection, Columbia, Missouri.

Hale, Everett Edward. Missouri Historical Society, May 27, 1854.

Halleck, Henry. *International Law; or, Rules Regulating the Intercourse of States in Peace and War.* San Francisco: H. H. Bancroft & Company, 1861.

Hamilton, Holman. *Prologue to Conflict: The Crisis and Compromise of 1850.* Lexington: University of Kentucky Press, 1964.

Harrell, David Edwin Jr. "Pardee Butler: Kansas Crusader." *The Kansas Historical Quarterly* 34, no. 4 (1968).

Hendin, Herbert, and Ann Pollinger Haas. *Wounds of War: The Psychological Aftermath of Combat in Vietnam.* New York: Basic Books, Inc., Publishers, 1984.

Herklotz, Hildegarde. "Jayhawkers in Missouri 1858-1863," First Article, *Missouri Historical Review* 17, no. 3 (1923).

———. "Jayhawkers in Missouri, 1858-1863." Second Article. *Missouri Historical Review* 17, no. 4 (1923).

———. "Jayhawkers in Missouri, 1858-1863." Third Article. *Missouri Historical Review* 18, no. 1 (1923).

Hickman, Russell K. "Speculative Activities of the Emigrant Aid Company." *The Kansas Historical Quarterly* 4, no. 3 (1935).

———. "The Reeder Administration Inaugurated." *Kansas Historical Quarterly* 36, no. 3 (1970).

Hopewell, Menta. *History of the Missouri Volunteer Militia of St. Louis.* N.p., 1861.

Hoole, William Stanley, ed. "A Southerner's Viewpoint of the Kansas Situation, 1856-1857." *The Kansas Historical Quarterly* 3, no. 1 (1934).

Hubbard, D. "Reminiscences of the Yeager Raid, on the Santa Fé Trail, in 1863." *Transactions of the Kansas State Historical Society, 1903-1904.* Vol. 8. Topeka, Kans.: The Kansas State Printing Plant, 1904.

Hurd, Harvey B. *Revised Statutes of the State of Illinois.* Chicago: Chicago Legal News Co., 1897.

Hurt, R. Douglas. "Planters and Slavery in Dixie." *Missouri Historical Review* 88, no. 4 (1994).

Hutchinson, William. "Sketches of Kansas Pioneer Experience." *Transactions of the Kansas State Historical Society, 1901-1902.* Vol. 7.

Investing and Appraisement Record, Saline County. Vol. 1. 1856-61.

Jackson, William R. *Missouri Democracy: A History of the Party and Its Representatives—Past and Present.* Vol. 1. Chicago, 1935.

Jenkins, Paul B. *The Battle of Westport.* Kansas City, Mo.: Franklin Hudson Publishing Company, 1906.

Johannsen, Robert W. ed. "A Footnote to the Pottawatomie Massacre, 1856." *The Kansas Historical Quarterly* (Autumn 1956).

Johnson, Robert Underwood, and Clarence Clough Buel, eds. *Battles and Leaders of the Civil War* . . . Vol. 1. Seacaucus, N.J.: Castle, 1887.

Johnson, Samuel A. "The Emigrant Aid Company in the Kansas Conflict." *The Kansas Historical Quarterly* (February 1937).

———. "The Emigrant Aid Company in Kansas." *The Kansas Historical Quarterly* 1, no. 5 (1932).

Journal of the Missouri State Convention, February 1861.

Kirkpatrick, Arthur Roy. "The Admission of Missouri to the Confederacy." *Missouri Historical Review* 55, no. 4 (1961).

———. "Missouri in the Early Months of the Civil War." *Missouri Historical Review* 55, no. 4 (1961).

———. "Missouri's Secessionist Government, 1861-1865." *Missouri Historical Review* 45, no. 2 (1951).

Knapp, George E. *The Wilson's Creek Staff Ride and Battlefield Tour.* Special Study. Fort Leavenworth, Kans.: Combat Studies Institute, U.S. Army Command and General Staff College, 1993.

Ladd, Erastus D. "Erastus D. Ladd's Description of the Lawrence Massacre." Edited and with an introduction by Russell E. Bidlack. *The Kansas Historical Quarterly* 29, no. 2 (1963).

"Lane." *Kansas Free State Press,* April 30, 1855, *Collections of the Kansas State Historical Society, 1923-25.* Edited by William Elsey Connelley. Vol. 16. Topeka, Kans.: B. P. Walker State Printer, 1925.

Langsdorf, Edgar. "Jim Lane and the Frontier Guard." *The Kansas Historical Quarterly* 9, no. 1 (1940).

———. "Price's Raid and the Battle of Mine Creek." *The Kansas Historical Quarterly* 30, no. 3 (1964).

———. "S. C. Pomeroy and the New England Emigrant Aid Company, 1854-1858." *The Kansas Historical Quarterly* 7, no. 3 (1938).

Larkin, Lew. *Bingham: Fighting Artist.* St. Louis, Mo.: State Publishing Co., 1955.

Laughlin, Sceva Bright. "Missouri Politics during the Civil War." Chap. 1. *Missouri Historical Review* 23, no. 3 (1929).

———. "Missouri Politics during the Civil War." Chap. 3. *Missouri Historical Review* 23, no. 4 (1929).

———. "Missouri Politics during the Civil War." *Missouri Historical Review* 24, no. 1 (1929).

———. "Missouri Politics during the Civil War." *Missouri Historical Review* 23, no. 3 (1929).

Lazear, Bazel F. "The Civil War Letters of Bazel F. Lazear." Edited by Vivian Kirkpatrick McLarty. *Missouri Historical Review* 92, no. 4 (1998).

———. "The Civil War Letters of Colonel Bazel F. Lazear." Edited by Vivian Kirkpatrick McLarty. *Missouri Historical Review* 44, no. 4 (1950).

Leslie, Edward. *The Devil Knows How to Ride.* New York: De Capo Press, 1998.

Lewis, Lloyd. "Propaganda and the Kansas-Missouri War." *Missouri Historical Review* 92, no. 1 (1998).

Lutz, John M. "Quantrill and the Morgan Walker Tragedy." *Transactions of the Kansas State Historical Society.* Edited by George W. Martin. Vol. 8. Topeka, Kans.: George A. Clark, 1904.

Lyon, William H. "Claiborne Fox Jackson and the Secession Crisis in Missouri." *Missouri Historical Review* 58, no. 4 (1964).

McCullough, David. *Truman.* New York: Simon & Schuster, 1992.

McKenna, Sr. Jeanne. "With the Help of God and Lucy Stone." *The Kansas Historical Quarterly* 36, no. 1 (1970).

Malin, James C. ed. "F. H. Hodder's 'Stephen A. Douglas.' " *The Kansas Historical Quarterly* 8, no. 3 (1939).

———. "The Hoogland Examination: The United States v. John Brown, Jr., et al." *The Kansas Historical Quarterly* 7, no. 2 (1938).

———. "Identification of the Stranger at the Pottawatomie Massacre." *The Kansas Historical Quarterly* 9, no. 1 (1940).

————. "The Motives of Stephen A. Douglas in the Organization of Nebraska Territory: A Letter Dated December 17, 1853." *The Kansas Historical Quarterly* 19 (November 1951).

Manuscript Census Schedules, Slaves, 1850 and 1860, Lafayette County and Saline County, Missouri.

"The Marais des Cygnes Massacre," and A. H. Tannar, "Early Days in Kansas," in *Collections of the Kansas State Historical Society, 1915-1918*. Edited by William E. Connelley. Vol. 14. Topeka, Kans: Kansas State Printing Plant, 1918.

Martin, George W. "Memorial Monuments and Tablets in Kansas." *Collections of the Kansas State Historical Society, 1909-1910*. Edited by George W. Martin. Vol. 11. Topeka, Kans.: State Printing Office, 1910.

Mendenhall, Willard Hall. " 'Life Is Uncertain . . .': Willard Hall Mendenhall's 1862 Civil War Diary." Edited by Margaret Mendenhall Frazier and James W. Goodrich. Part 1. *Missouri Historical Review* 78, no. 4 (1984).

————. " 'Life Is Uncertain . . . ': Willard Hall Mendenhall's 1862 Civil War Diary." Edited by Margaret Mendenhall Frazier and James W. Goodrich. Part 2. *Missouri Historical Review* 79, no. 1 (1984).

Merkel, Benjamin C. "The Abolitionist Aspects of Missouri's Antislavery Controversy 1819-1865." *Missouri Historical Review* 49, no. 3 (1950).

————. "The Slavery Issue and the Political Decline of Thomas Hart Benton, 1846-1856." *Missouri Historical Review* 38, no. 4 (1944).

————. "The Underground Railroad and the Missouri Borders." *Missouri Historical Review* 37, no. 3 (1943).

Miller, George. *Missouri's Memorable Decade, 1860-1870*. Columbia, Mo., 1898.

Missouri House Journal. 15th General Assembly, 1st Sess.

Missouri House Journal. 21st General Assembly, 1860-61.

Monaghan, Jay. *Civil War on the Western Border, 1854-1865*. Lincoln: Bison Press, 1948. Reprint. Lincoln: University of Nebraska Press, 1955.

Monroe Papers. Library of Congress.

Morrow, Robert. "Emigration to Kansas in 1856." *Kansas Historical Collections*. Vol. 5. State Historical Society of Kansas.

Morse, O. E. "An Attempted Rescue of John Brown from Charleston, Va. Jail." *Transactions of the Kansas State Historical Society, 1903-1904*. Edited by George W. Martin. Vol. 8. Topeka, Kans.: George A. Clark, State Printer, 1904.

Morton, John D. " 'A High Wall and a Deep Ditch': Thomas Hart Benton and the Compromise of 1850." *Missouri Historical Review* 94, no. 1 (1999).

Niepman, Ann Davis. "General Orders No. 11 and Border Warfare during the Civil War." *Missouri Historical Review* 66, no. 2 (1966).

Nevins, Allan. *Ordeal of the Union.* New York: Scribner, 1947.

O'Connor, Thomas H. "Cotton Whigs in Kansas." *The Kansas Historical Quarterly* (Spring 1960).

Palmer, H. E. "The Black-Flag Character of War on the Border." *Transactions of the Kansas State Historical Society, 1905-06*. Edited by George W. Martin. Vol. 9. Topeka, Kans.: State Printing Office, 1906.

Papers of the Emigrant Aid Society. Manuscript Division. Kansas State Historical Society.

Parrish, William E. "David Rice Atchison: Faithful Champion of the South." *Missouri Historical Review* 51, no. 2 (1957).

———. "David Rice Atchison, Frontier Politician." *Missouri Historical Review* 50, no. 4 (1956).

Paxton, William M. *Annals of Platte County, Missouri.* Kansas City, Mo., 1897.

Peck, John M. *Father Clark; or the Pioneer Preacher.* New York: Sheldon, Lamport, and Blakeman, 1855.

Pelzer, Louis. "The Negro and Slavery in Early Iowa." *Iowa Journal of History and Politics* 2, no. 4 (1904).

Phillips, Christopher. "Calculated Confederate: Claiborne Fox Jackson and the Strategy for Secession in Missouri." *Missouri Historical Review* 94, no. 4 (2000).

Pike, J. A. "Statement of Capt. J. A. Pike Concerning the Quantrill Raid." *Collections of the Kansas State Historical Society, 1915-1918.* Vol. 14. Topeka, Kans.: The Kansas State Printing Plant, 1918.

"The Quantrill Raid." *Collections of the Kansas State Historical Society, 1913-1914.* Vol. 13. Topeka, Kans.: Kansas State Printing Plant, 1915.

Reynolds, Thomas C. "General Sterling Price and the Confederacy." Unpublished memoir. Reynolds Papers, Missouri Historical Society Library, St. Louis.

Richards, O. E. "Kansas Experiences of Oscar G. Richards, of Eudora, in 1856." *Transactions of the Kansas State Historical Society, 1905-06.* Edited by George W. Martin. Vol. 9. Topeka, Kans.: State Printing Office, 1906.

Richardson, James D., ed. *A Compilation of the Messages and Papers of the Presidents, 1789-1897.* Vol. 5. Washington, D.C.: Government Printing Office, 1896-99.

Rives, John C., ed. *Abridgment of the Debates of Congress, 1789-1856.* New York, 1858.

Robinson, Charles. *The Kansas Conflict.* Lawrence, Kans.: Journal Publishing Co., 1898.

Robinson, Sara. "The Governor's Wife Recalls the Raid." In Richard B. Sheridan, *Quantrill and the Lawrence Massacre—a Reader.* Edited by Richard B. Sheridan, Lawrence, Kans.: n.p., 1997.

Rodemyre, Edgar T. *History of Centralia, Missouri.* Centralia, Mo.: Press of the Fireside Guard, 1936.

Roed, William. "Secessionist Strength in Missouri." *Missouri Historical Review* 72, no. 4 (1978).

Shay, Jonathan. *Achilles in Vietnam: Combat Trauma and the Undoing of Character.* New York: Simon & Schuster, 1994.

Sheridan, Richard B. "From Slavery in Missouri to Freedom in Kansas: The Influx of Black Fugitives and Contrabands into Kansas, 1854-1865." *Kansas History: A Journal of the Central Plains* 12, no. 1 (1989).

Shoemaker, Floyd C. "Missouri—Heir of Southern Tradition and

Individuality." *Missouri Historical Review* 36, no. 4 (1942).

———. "Missouri's Proslavery Fight for Kansas, 1854-55." *Missouri Historical Review* 48, no. 3 (1954).

———. "Missouri's Proslavery Fight for Kansas, 1854-1858." *Missouri Historical Review* 48, no. 4 (1948).

———. *Missouri's Struggle for Statehood.* Jefferson City, Mo.: Stephens, 1916.

Siebert, Wilbur H. *Underground Railroad from Slavery to Freedom.* New York: Macmillan, 1898.

Smith, Edward R. "Marais des Cygnes Tragedy." *Transactions of the Kansas State Historical Society, 1899-1900.* Edited by George W. Martin. Vol. 6. Topeka, Kans.: W. Y. Morgan State Printer, 1900.

Smith, Elbert B. *The Presidencies of Zachary Taylor and Millard Fillmore.* Lawrence: University Press of Kansas, 1988.

Smith, George Winston. "New England Business Interests in Missouri during the Civil War." *Missouri Historical Review* 41, no. 1 (1946).

Snead, Thomas L. *The Fight for Missouri.* New York: Charles Scribner's Sons, 1886.

Speer, John. "The Burning of Osceola, Mo., by Lane and the Quantrill Massacre Contrasted." *Transactions of the Kansas State Historical Society, 1899-1901.* Edited by George W. Martin. Vol. 6. Topeka, Kans.: W. Y. Morgan, State Printer, 1900.

Spring, Leverett Wilson. *Kansas: The Prelude to the War for the Union.* Boston: Houghton Mifflin Company, 1896.

Starr, Stephen Z. *Jennison's Jayhawkers: A Civil War Cavalry Regiment and Its Commander.* Baton Rouge: Louisiana State University Press, 1973.

Staudenhaus, P. J. "Immigrants or Invaders? A Document." *The Kansas Historical Quarterly* 24, no. 4 (1958): 394-98.

Stephenson, Wendell H. "The Political Career of General James H. Lane." *Publications of the Kansas State Historical Society.* Vol. 3. Topeka, Kans.: Kansas Printing Office, 1930.

Stevens, Robert S. Letter addressed to "Friends." August 23, 1863. Collection of Robert C. Stevens.

Stevens, Walter B. "Lincoln and Missouri." *Missouri Historical Review* 10, no. 2 (1916).

Steward, Dick. *Duels and the Roots of Violence in Missouri*. Columbia: University of Missouri Press, 2000.

Switzler, William F. *Switzler's Illustrated History of Missouri from 1541 to 1878*. 1879. Reprint, New York: Arno Press, 1975.

Thayer, Eli. *A History of the Kansas Crusade*. New York: Harper & Brothers, 1889.

"This Regiment Will Make a Mark." Edited by Jeffrey L. Patrick. *Kansas History: A Journal of the Central Plains* 20, no. 1 (1997): 54.

Thomas, David Y. "Missouri in the Confederacy." *Missouri Historical Review* 18, no. 3 (1924).

Thomas, Raymond D. "A Study in Missouri Politics, 1840-1870." Chap. 1. *Missouri Historical Review* 21, no. 2 (1927).

———. "A Study in Missouri Politics, 1840-1870." Chap, 2. *Missouri Historical Review* 21, no. 3 (1927).

Thruston, Ethylene B. "Captain Dick Yeager—Quantrill Man." *Westport Historical Quarterly* 4 (June 1968).

Tibbetts, John C. "Riding With the Devil: The Movie Adventures of William Clarke Quantrill." *Kansas History: A Journal of the Central Plains* 22, no. 3 (1999).

Townsend, John W. "David Rice Atchison." *Register of the Kentucky Historical Society* 8 (May 1910).

Trexler, Harrison A. *Slavery in Missouri, 1804-1865,* Johns Hopkins University Studies in History and Political Science, ser. 32, no. 2.

———. "Slavery in Missouri Territory." *Missouri Historical Review* 3, no. 3 (1909).

———. "The Value and the Sale of the Missouri Slave." *Missouri Historical*

Review 8 no. 2 (1914).

Turkoly-Joczik, Robert L. "Frémont and the Western Department." *Missouri Historical Review* 82, no. 4 (1988).

Viles, Jonas. "Documents Illustrating the Troubles on the Border, 1858." *Missouri Historical Review* 1, no. 4 (1907).

———. "Documents Illustrating the Troubles on the Border, 1860." *Missouri Historical Review* 2, no. 1 (1907).

Villard, Oswald Garrison. *John Brown—A Biography Fifty Years After.* Boston: Houghton Mifflin Company, 1911.

Wallace, Doris Davis. "The Political Campaign of 1860 in Missouri." *Missouri Historical Review* 70, no. 2 (1976).

Watts, Dale E. "How Bloody Was Bleeding Kansas? Political Killings in Kansas Territory, 1854-1861." *Kansas History: A Journal of the Central Plains* 18, no. 2 (1995).

Webb, W. L. *Battles and Biographies of Missourians: or the Civil War Period of Our State.* Kansas City, Mo.: Hudson-Kimberly Publishing Co., 1900.

Wheeler, Holland. "Early Life of Quantrill in Kansas." *Transactions of the Kansas State Historical Society, 1901-1902.* Edited by George W. Martin. Vol. 7. Topeka, Kans.: W. Y. Morgan Printer, 1902.

Williams, Burton J. "Quantrill's Raid on Lawrence: A Question of Complicity." *The Kansas Historical Quarterly* 34, no. 2 (1968).

Woolsey, Ronald C. "The West Becomes a Problem: The Missouri Controversy and Slavery Expansion as the Southern Dilemma." *Missouri Historical Review* 77, no. 3 (1983).

Wurthman, Leonard B. Jr. "Frank Blair: Lincoln's Congressional Spokesman." *Missouri Historical Review* 64, no. 3 (1970).

Younger, Coleman. *The Story of Cole Younger by Himself.* 1903. Reprint, Houston, Tex.: The Frontier Press of Texas, 1955.

Zapata. "A Todas la Pueblos en General." Documentos históricos de la revolución mexicana. Vol. 21. Edited by Isidro Fabela and Josefina E. de Fabela.

Mexico City: Emiliano Zapata, el Plan de Ayala, y su política agraria, 1970.

Zornow, William F. *Kansas: A History of the Jayhawk State*. Norman: University of Oklahoma Press, 1957.

Manuscripts

Western Historical Manuscript Collection (Columbia, Missouri.)

    Wiliam H. Gregg Manuscript

Western Historical Manuscript Collection (University of Missouri-Kansas City)

    Abiel Leonard Collection

Collections of the Kansas State Historical Society

    Amos A. Lawrence Papers

    C.M. Chase Letters

    George Luther Stearns Papers

    James Henry Lane Papers

    James Montgomery Papers

    Jennison Scrapbook

    Letters of Amos A. Lawrence

    Pomeroy, War Diary

    Quantrill Papers

    Samuel Newitt Wood Papers

    Simon M. Fox Papers

    Thomas Ewing, Jr. Papers

    Webster W. Moses Letters

Collection in the Chicago Historical Society

The Southern Historical Collections (University of North Carolina, Chapel Hill)

National Archives (Washington, D.C.)

Old Military Reference Branch

Federal Documents

U.S. War Department. General Orders No. 100. *Instructions for the Government of Armies in the Field.* Washington, D.C., April 24, 1863.

The War of the Rebellion: A Compilation of the Official Records of the Union and Confederate Armies. 128 vols. and atlas. Washington, D.C.: Government Printing Office, 1881-1901.

Index

377

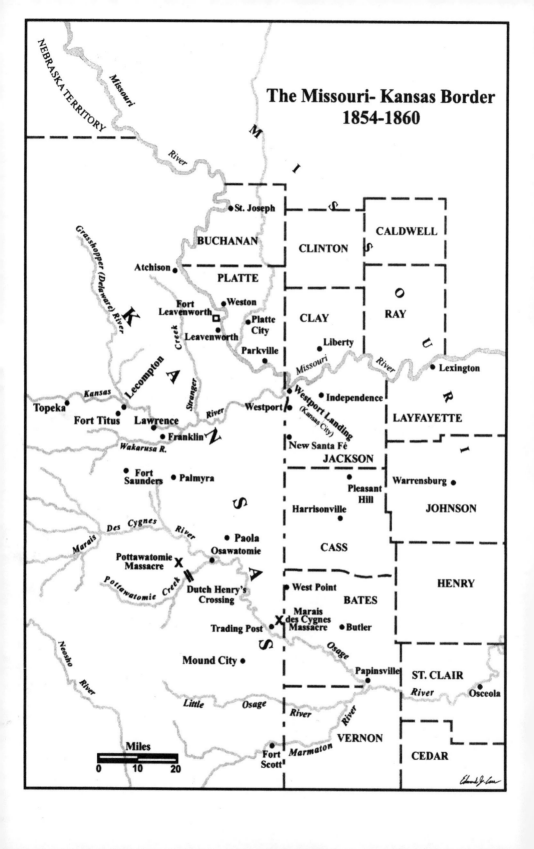

The Missouri- Kansas Border
1854-1860

NEBRASKA TERRITORY

Missouri River

M I S S O U R I

St. Joseph

BUCHANAN

CLINTON

CALDWELL

Atchison

PLATTE

Grasshopper (Delaware) River

Weston
Fort
Leavenworth

Platte
City

CLAY

RAY

Creek

Leavenworth

Parkville

Liberty

K

Lexington

Stranger

Missouri River

Lecompton

A

Kansas

River

Topeka

Fort Titus

Lawrence

Westport

Westport Landing
(Kansas City)

Independence

LAYFAYETTE

Franklin

N

New Santa Fé

Wakarusa R.

JACKSON

Fort
Saunders

Palmyra

Warrensburg

Pleasant
Hill

JOHNSON

S

Harrisonville

Des Cygnes River

Paola

Osawatomie

CASS

Marais

Pottawatomie
Massacre

X

A

West Point

Pottawatomie Creek

Dutch Henry's
Crossing

BATES

HENRY

Marais
des Cygnes
Massacre

Trading Post

X

Butler

S

Neosho River

Mound City

Osage

Papinsville

ST. CLAIR

River

Osceola

Little Osage River

River

River

Marmaton

VERNON

CEDAR

Miles

0   10   20

Fort
Scott